Tenth Edition

W9-CXK-308

The Manager's Bookshelf

A MOSAIC OF CONTEMPORARY VIEWS

Jon L. Pierce
University of Minnesota Duluth

John W. Newstrom
University of Minnesota Duluth

PEARSON

Boston   Columbus   Indianapolis   New York   San Francisco   Upper Saddle River
Amsterdam   Cape Town   Dubai   London   Madrid   Milan   Munich   Paris   Montréal   Toronto
Delhi   Mexico City   São Paulo   Sydney   Hong Kong   Seoul   Singapore   Taipei   Tokyo

Editor in Chief: Stephanie Wall
Senior Acquisitions Editor: April Cole
Director of Editorial Services: Ashley Santora
Editorial Assistant: Bernie Ollila
Director of Marketing: Maggie Moylan
Senior Marketing Manager: Nikki Ayana Jones
Marketing Assistant: Gianna Sandri
Production Manager: Tom Benfatti
Creative Director: Jayne Conte

Cover Designer: Suzanne Behnke
Cover Art: Fotolia
Full-Service Project Management: Sudha Balasundaram/ S4Carlisle Publishing Services
Composition: S4Carlisle Publishing Services
Printer/Binder: STP Courier
Cover Printer: STP Courier
Text Font: Minion Pro

Library of Congress Cataloging-in-Publication Data
The manager's bookshelf : a mosaic of contemporary views / Jon L. Pierce, John W. Newstrom. —10th ed.
   p. cm.
Includes bibliographical references and index.
ISBN-13: 978-0-13-304359-4
ISBN-10: 0-13-304359-2
   1. Management literature—United States.   I. Pierce, Jon L. (Jon Lepley).   II. Newstrom, John W
HD70.U5M32 2014
658—dc23
                                                                                    2012030473

10 9 8 7 6 5 4 3 2 1

ISBN 10: 0-13-304359-2
ISBN 13: 978-0-13-304359-4

We dedicate this book to our beloved grandchildren—Madison, Peter, Eric, Sawyer, William, Graham, Ruth Emma, Ruth Lillian, Axel, and Pearl—who give us great pleasure, pride, and strong hope for the future.

BRIEF CONTENTS

CONTENTS

PREFACE

The last several decades were marked by a proliferation of books published on topics in management, leadership, and various organizational issues. This explosion of products apparently reflects an intense and continuing fascination by managers, future managers, and the general public with the inner workings of organizations and their managers, work teams and their leaders, and employees. Bookstores around the country and distribution sources on the Internet continue to offer a large number of management books, and many of these books have appeared on various "business best-seller" lists—some remaining there for months and years at a time. Clearly, managers and others (including business school students at both graduate and undergraduate levels, as well as liberal arts students who are headed for a career in business or public organizations) remain intrigued by, and are searching for insights, perspectives, and answers in, the popular business literature.

We prepared *The Manager's Bookshelf: A Mosaic of Contemporary Views* to serve the needs of both managers and management students. Significant numbers of individuals in both of these groups do not have sufficient time to read widely, yet many people find themselves involved in conversations where someone else refers to ideas such as evidence-based management, vision, self-directed work teams, Mojo, ethics, fun at work, or organizational politics. We believe that a laudable and critical goal for managers, as well as all students of management, is to remain current in their understanding of the wide range of views being expressed about organizational and management practices. To help you become a better-informed organizational citizen, we prepared *The Manager's Bookshelf*, which introduces you to a broad array of popular management books—both recent and "classic."

NEW TO THIS EDITION

The 10th edition of *The Manager's Bookshelf* introduces a fresh new set of readings into the book. A dozen new best sellers are included, replacing numerous other books that had become somewhat dated. The goal of these (and previous) revisions was to make *The Manager's Bookshelf* an undeniably comprehensive and up-to-date compendium of highly readable book summaries. Here are the major changes we designed and built into the new edition:

- In response to user feedback, we abbreviated and streamlined Part 1, so that it now contains two key readings: (1) our Introduction (exploring the popularity of best sellers, the rationale for the book, the typical contents of the best sellers, a structured format for critiquing them, our selection strategy, and commentary on the authors of the best sellers) and (2) some cautionary observations provided by four reflective scholars.
- We have gradually expanded the size of Part 2, "Best-Seller 'Classics,'" as additional books prove themselves to be enduring across time in their popularity.
- We inserted a new section, Part 5, that provides solid perspectives on the important topic of organizational culture.
- At the urging of reviewers, we created a brief section on teams and teamwork.
- We changed the thrust of Part 11 so as to capture both the rational and intuitive perspectives on managerial decision making.
- We developed a new Part 13 on social technologies at work.

- Part 16, "Contemporary Thinking About Management," was expanded to include Henry Mintzberg's unique perspectives on managing, as well as Thomas Friedman's thoughts on how the world is changing.
- Other new inclusions in this edition accent themes of leadership transparency, Mojo, collaborative intelligence, "Super Crunchers," and irrationality.

A COLLAGE AND A MOSAIC

The Manager's Bookshelf, as a book of concise *summaries*, does not express the views of just one individual on the management of organizations, nor does it attempt to integrate the views of several dozen authors. Instead, *this book is a collage*—a composite portrait constructed from a variety of classic and contemporary sources (approximately 80 percent of the books summarized here were published in the twenty-first century). *The Manager's Bookshelf* provides you with insights into many aspects of organizational management from the perspectives of a diverse and sometimes provocative group of management writers, including some highly regarded authors such as Peter Drucker, Jim Collins, Barbara Kellerman, Thomas Friedman, Jeffrey Pfeffer, Stephen Covey, John Kotter, Spencer Johnson, and Michael Porter. Through this collection we will introduce you to the thoughts, philosophies, views, and experiences of a number of authors whose works have caught the attention of today's management community—and often captivated them in the process.

This book contains a rich array of pieces—a veritable *mosaic* that provides a fascinating overall portrait of management. From a topical perspective, its inclusions focus on motivation, ethics, social technologies, corporate strategy, leadership styles, and other key concerns of managers. This collection includes the views from a variety of individuals—some practitioners (e.g., Bill George), some philosophers (e.g., Peter Drucker and Warren Bennis), some management consultants (e.g., Jim Collins and Marshall Goldsmith), and some organizational scholars (e.g., Jeff Pfeffer and John Kotter). The selections reflect a wide variety in terms of their tone and tenor, as well as the diverse bases for their conclusions. Indeed, critics have praised some of the authors' works as passionate, invaluable, stimulating, and insightful, whereas other business books have been attacked as being overly academic, superficial, redundant, glib, or unrealistic.

NATURE OF THE INCLUSIONS

The nature and source of the ideas expressed in this collection are diverse. Some inclusions are prescriptive in nature, whereas others are more dispassionately descriptive; some are thoughtful and philosophical, whereas others limit themselves to reporting directly on their personal or organizational experiences; some of these works represent armchair speculation, whereas others are based on empirical study. Finally, the selections take a variety of forms, but the majority of the inclusions are concise and objective summaries of popular books that have been specially prepared for inclusion in *The Manager's Bookshelf*.

This mosaic of readings can provide you with useful insights, provoke your own reflective thinking, and spark stimulating dialogue with your colleagues about the management of today's organizations. We expect that these readings will prompt you to raise questions of yourself and your peers about the viability of many of the ideas expressed by these authors regarding the practice of organizational management. We hope and predict that these readings will prompt you to read the full text of many of the authors' works; these books often contain rich anecdotes, compelling stories, provocative assertions, and detailed data that are not possible to include in our summaries. Finally, we hope that these summaries will encourage you to continue your managerial self-development through a variety of avenues, including ongoing reading of both the popular and scientific (research-based) literature. If these goals are met, our purpose for assembling this collection will be realized.

INSTRUCTOR'S MANUAL

This book offers, to adopters, an Instructor's Manual that includes suggestions for using best sellers in the classroom, a sample classroom assignment, and provocative questions for each reading to guide instructors in classroom discussion.

The Instructor's Manual is available to adopting instructors for download at www.pearsonhighered.com/irc. Registration is simple and gives the instructor immediate access to other titles and new editions. Instructors should visit http://247.pearsoned.com/ for answers to frequently asked questions and for toll-free user-support phone numbers.

COURSESMART

CourseSmart eTextbooks were developed for students looking to save on required or recommended textbooks. Students simply select their eText by title or author and purchase immediate access to the content for the duration of the course using any major credit card. With a CourseSmart eText, students can search for specific keywords or page numbers, take notes online, print out reading assignments that incorporate lecture notes, and bookmark important passages for later review. For more information or to purchase a CourseSmart eTextbook, visit www.coursesmart.com.

Jon L. Pierce
John W. Newstrom

ACKNOWLEDGMENTS

We express our sincere and very warm appreciation to several colleagues who played key roles in the preparation of this edition of *The Manager's Bookshelf: A Mosaic of Contemporary Views*. Their commitment and dedication to students of organizations and management, coupled with their varied contributions, made this improved and updated edition possible.

We would also like to single out our late friend and colleague, Larry L. Cummings (Carlson School of Management at the University of Minnesota and "The Institute"), for his "Reflections on the Best Sellers" contained in Part 1 of our book. We also value the additional comments provided on managerial best sellers offered by Brad Jackson, Anne Cummings, and John Newstrom, which greatly enrich the discussion in that section.

CONTRIBUTORS TO THIS EDITION

We extend our thanks to a number of individuals who provided us with a great deal of assistance and support for the preparation of this book. Many of our management colleagues, former students, and professional managerial associates took the time and effort—always under tight time pressures—to contribute to this book by carefully reading and preparing a summary of one of the selected books. Many of these individuals wanted to offer their personal opinion, add their endorsements or criticisms, and surface elements of their own management philosophies, but at our urging they stuck to their assigned task. To them we express our thanks for their time, energy, and commitment to furthering management education.

The following individuals prepared book summaries for this edition of *The Manager's Bookshelf*:

Best-Seller "Classics"

John D. Stavig and Shaker A. Zahra, University of Minnesota—Drucker's *The Practice of Management*

Charles C. Manz, University of Massachusetts, Amherst—Blanchard and Johnson's *The One Minute Manager*

William B. Gartner, Georgetown University, and M. James Naughton, Expert-Knowledge Systems, Inc.—Deming's *Out of the Crisis*

Gayle Porter, Rutgers University—McGregor's *The Human Side of Enterprise*

John W. Newstrom, University of Minnesota Duluth—Maslow's *Maslow on Management*

John W. Newstrom, University of Minnesota Duluth—Covey's *The Seven Habits of Highly Effective People*

Dorothy Marcic, Vanderbilt University—Senge's *The Fifth Discipline*

Sara A. Morris, Old Dominion University—Porter's *Competitive Advantage*

High- and Low-Performing Organizations

Mary Kate Gross, U.S. Department of Veteran's Affairs—Collins's *Good to Great*

Allen Harmon, University of Minnesota Duluth and WDSE-TV—Marcus's *Big Winners and Big Losers*

Tanya Pietz, Riverwood Healthcare Center—Collins's *How the Mighty Fall*

Organizational Strategy and Execution

Cathy A. Hanson, City of Manhattan Beach—Beer and Associates *Higher Ambition*

Stephen Rubenfeld, University of Minnesota Duluth—Cascio's *Responsible Restructuring*

Organizational Culture

Patrick Heraty, Hilbert College—Bennis, Goleman, and O'Toole's *Transparency*

Motivation

Shelley Ovrom, City of Azusa—Sirota, Mischkind, and Meltzer's *The Enthusiastic Employee*

Cathy A. Hanson, City of Manhattan Beach—Luthans, Youssef, and Avolio's *Psychological Capital*

AnneMarie Kaul, Fiduciary Counseling, Inc.—Katzenbach's *Why Pride Matters More Than Money*

Meghan Brown, Target Corporation—Goldsmith's *MOJO*

Leadership and Power

Jodi Nelson, SISU Medical Solutions—Cameron's *Positive Leadership*

Warren Candy, Allete/Minnesota Power—Kellerman's *Bad Leadership*

Kristie J. Loescher, University of Texas at Austin—Pfeffer's *Power*

Teams and Teamwork

David L. Beal, formerly of Consolidated Papers, Inc.—Beyerlein, Freedman, McGee, and Moran's *Beyond Teams*

Organizational Change

Peter Stark, University of Minnesota Duluth—Quinn's *Building the Bridge as You Walk on It*

David L. Beal, formerly of Consolidated Papers, Inc.—Kotter's *A Sense of Urgency*

"Undiscussable" Issues at Work

Kelly L. Nelson, AK Steel—Van Fleet and Van Fleet's *Workplace Survival*

Stephen Rubenfeld, University of Minnesota Duluth—Sutton's *The No-Asshole Rule*

AnneMarie Kaul, Fiduciary Counseling, Inc.—Reardon's *It's All Politics*

Managerial Decision Making

Amber Christian, Phoenix Endeavors—Kahneman's *Thinking, Fast and Slow*

Brian Russell, University of Kansas—Ayres's *Super Crunchers*

Rebecca M. C. Boll, Central Minnesota Federal Credit Union—Gigerenzer's *Gut Feelings*

Ethics and Authenticity in the Workplace

Linda Hefferin, Elgin Community College—Bazerman and Tenbrunsel's *Blind Spots*

Randy Skalberg, University of Minnesota Duluth—George's *Authentic Leadership*

Emotions: Positive, Negative, and Irrational

Gary P. Olson, Center for Alcohol and Drug Treatment—Pattakos's *Prisoners of Our Thoughts*

Gary J. Colpaert, Milwaukee's Eye Institute—Frost's *Toxic Emotions at Work*

Fred J. Dorn, Career Management Resources—Ariely's *The Upside of Irrationality*, and *Predictably Irrational*

Social Technologies at Work

Amber Christian, Phoenix Endeavors, LLC—Li and Bernoff's *Groundswell*

Richard Kimbrough, University of Nebraska–Lincoln—Handley and Chapman's *Content Rules*

Management Fables: Lessons for Success

Gary Stark, Northern Michigan University—Johnson's *Who Moved My Cheese?*

John W. Newstrom, University of Minnesota Duluth—Lundin, Paul, and Christensen's *Fish!*

John W. Newstrom, University of Minnesota Duluth—Pike, Ford, and Newstrom's *The Fun Minute Manager*

Contemporary Thinking About Management

Adam Surma, Target Corporation—Pfeffer's *What Were They Thinking?*

Bob Stine, University of Minnesota College of Continuing Education—Mintzberg's *Managing*

Jannifer David, University of Minnesota Duluth—Pfeffer and Sutton's *Hard Facts, Dangerous Half-Truths, and Total Nonsense*

Bob Stine, University of Minnesota College of Continuing Education—Friedman's *Hot, Flat, and Crowded*

Several persons provided gracious and constructive feedback on the previous edition and offered useful suggestions for improvement; the reviewers include Barry Brock, Casey G. Cegielski, Christopher Clott, Fred J. Dorn, Patrick Heraty, Richard Kimbrough, Jerry Kinard, Kristie Loescher, Belinda A. Raines, and Brian Russell. We also appreciate the recommendations for inclusions in this 10th edition made by several reviewers, adopters, and friends. To our spouses, who provided always-patient emotional support and encouragement, we want to say a very enthusiastic "Thank you" for helping us complete this project—and many others over the past several years—in a timely fashion. We appreciate the supportive environment provided by Dean Kjell Knudsen of the Labovitz School of Business and Economics, and our colleagues in the Department of Management Studies here at the University of Minnesota Duluth. We gratefully acknowledge the continued project commitment from Stephanie Wall and the editorial support and assistance that we have received from April Cole, Lynn Savino Wendel, and Claudia Fernandes, all at Prentice Hall.

Jon L. Pierce
John W. Newstrom

ABOUT THE EDITORS

Jon L. Pierce is a Morse-Alumni Distinguished Teaching Professor of Management and Organization in the Department of Management Studies, Labovitz School of Business and Economics at the University of Minnesota Duluth (UMD). He received his Ph.D. in Management and Organizational Studies at the University of Wisconsin–Madison. He is the author of more than 70 papers that have been published in academic journals and various professional conference proceedings. His publications have appeared in the *Academy of Management Journal, Academy of Management Review, Educational and Psychological Measurement, Journal of Management, Journal of Managerial Psychology, Journal of Organizational Behavior, Journal of Applied Behavioral Science, Journal of Social Psychology, Journal of Occupational and Organizational Psychology, Organizational Dynamics, Organizational Behavior and Human Performance, Personnel Psychology,* and *Review of General Psychology.*

His research interests are focused on the psychology of work and organizations, with particular focus on organization-based self-esteem, psychological ownership, and collective psychological ownership. He has served on the editorial review board for the *Academy of Management Journal, Personnel Psychology, Journal of Management,* and the *Scandinavian Management Journal,* and serves as an ad hoc reviewer for several other management and organizational behavior journals. He is the coauthor of seven other books: *Management, Managing, Management and Organizational Behavior: An Integrated Perspective, Psychological Ownership in the Organizational Context: Theory, Research Evidence, and Application* and, along with John W. Newstrom, *Alternative Work Schedules, Windows into Management,* and *Leaders and the Leadership Process* (now in its sixth edition). Along with Randall B. Dunham, he is the recipient of the Yoder-Heneman Personnel Research Award; in 2000, he was inducted into the *Academy of Management Journal*'s Hall of Fame; in 2005, he received UMD's prestigious Chancellor's Award for Distinguished Research. Dr. Pierce may be contacted at jpierce@d.umn.edu.

John W. Newstrom is a Morse-Alumni Distinguished Teaching Professor Emeritus of Management in the Labovitz School of Business and Economics at the University of Minnesota Duluth. Prior to that, he completed his doctoral degree in Management and Industrial Relations at the University of Minnesota and then taught at Arizona State University for several years. His work has appeared in publications such as *Academy of Management Executive, Personnel Psychology, California Management Review, Journal of Management, Academy of Management Journal, Human Resource Planning, Supervision, Business Horizons,* and the *Journal of Management Development.* He has served as an editorial reviewer for the *Academy of Management Review, Academy of Management Journal, Academy of Management Executive, Human Resource Development Quarterly, Advanced Management Journal,* and the *Journal of Management Development.*

He is the author or coauthor of over 45 books in various editions, including *The Fun Minute Manager* (with Bob Pike and Robert C. Ford), *Organizational Behavior: Human Behavior at Work* (13th edition), *Supervision* (10th edition), *Transfer of Training* (with Mary Broad), *Leading with a Laugh* (with Robert C. Ford), and *The Big Book of Teambuilding Games* (with Ed Scannell). He is a member of the University of Minnesota's Academy of Distinguished Teachers and has served on the boards of directors for several nonprofit organizations. He has also actively served as a seminar leader for leadership development programs around the country and as a consultant to many other organizations. One of his current interests lies in helping managers create and sustain a fun and productive work environment for their employees. Dr. Newstrom may be contacted at jnewstro@d.umn.edu.

PART ONE

Introduction

Part 1 contains two readings. The first, *Understanding and Using the Best Sellers*, prepared by us (Pierce and Newstrom), the editors of *The Manager's Bookshelf*, provides insight into why such large numbers of management-oriented books have found themselves in bookstores, on coffee tables in homes, on Internet bookselling sites, and on the bookshelves of those who manage today's organizations. Four elements stand out in Reading 1:

1. We discuss the rationale for this mosaic of contemporary views on organizations and management and provide you with insight into the nature and character of (and authors in) *The Manager's Bookshelf.*
2. We challenge you to read and critically reflect upon this collection of thoughts and experiences.
3. We invite you to debate the ideas and philosophies that are presented here.
4. We encourage you to let these contemporary management books stimulate your thinking, to motivate you to look more systematically into the science of organizations and management, and to provide you with the fun of learning something new.

We also share a substantial concern that these contemporary books will be seen as "quick-and-dirty" cures for organizational woes. Therefore, we encourage you to read books such as Ralph H. Kilmann's *Beyond the Quick Fix: Managing Five Tracks to Organizational Success.* In it, the author provides a valuable message that should serve as the backdrop to your consumption and assessment of all of the purported "one-minute" cures for organizational problems and for the management of today's complex organizations. Kilmann encourages managers to *stop perpetuating the myth of organizational and management simplicity* and to develop a more complete and integrated approach to the management of today's complex organizations.

Many other writers have echoed these thoughts and cautions. For example:

- Marcus Alexander and Harry Korine (*Harvard Business Review*, December 2008, p. 74) contended that the unquestioned assumptions underlying management trends/fads "often lead to sloppy thinking" and "preclude careful examination of the pros and cons of the specific choices made by a single company in a particular context."
- John Hollon (*Worforce Management*, June 9, 2008, p. 42) concluded that "Everyone is looking for the magic formula that will help make them a great manager who can drive workers (and the organization) to the next level."
- Jeffrey Pfeffer and Robert I. Sutton (*Harvard Business Review*, January 2006, p. 63) asserted that "Executives routinely dose their organizations with strategic snake oil: discredited nostrums, partial remedies, or untested management miracle cures."
- Chris Argyris (*Flawed Advice and the Managerial Trap*) contends that popular management advice, while published as valid and actionable and widely adopted, leads to unintended consequences and an inability to systematically correct the identified deficiencies.
- Eric W. Ford and colleagues (*Academy of Management Executive*, 2005, 19:4, p. 24) contended that "rather than being interested in systematic and long-term solutions, managers are generally infatuated with the latest fads and fashions in their search for quick fixes."
- Geoffrey Colvin (*Fortune*, June 28, 2004, p. 166), in "A Concise History of Management Hooey," suggested that "Idea-starved managers … were so hungry they created an entirely new phenomenon in publishing, the business bestseller."
- Danny Miller and associates (*Business Horizons*, July–August 2004, p. 7) begin their condemnation of management fads by getting right to the point: "Many popular administrative ideas are epitomized by a search for the quick fix—a simple solution that all organizations can embrace to make employees more productive, customers happier, or profits greater."
- Charles S. Jacobs (*Management Rewired,* 2009) asserts that "Many of the management practices we've taken for granted are not only ineffective, (but) they actually produce the opposite of what we contend."
- Shari Caudron (*TD*, June 2002, p. 40) noted that the fads presented in management best sellers are taken up with great enthusiasm for a short while and then quickly discarded. This, she suggests, is done because "the tools were sold into companies by charlatans who didn't understand the concepts but knew the right buzzwords."
- Kristine Ellis (*Training*, April 2001, p. 41) concluded that the worst of the best sellers are promoted as "magic bullets" to solve organizational problems but often become little more than the prevailing "flavor of the month."
- Business columnist Dale Dauten (*The Arizona Republic*, February 19, 2004, p. D3) suggested that there are three types of business books on the market to avoid: the Obvious (compilations of clichéd truths), the Envious (stories of successful businesspeople), and the Obnoxious (books that insult your intelligence).
- Danny Miller and Jon Hartwick (*Harvard Business Review*, October 2002, p. 26) noted that management fads usually have short life cycles and are quickly replaced by new ones. Typical fads, according to Miller and Hartwick, are simple, prescriptive, falsely encouraging, broadly generic, overly simplistic, closely matched to contemporary business problems, and novel and fresh appearing, and achieve their legitimacy through the status and prestige of gurus (as opposed to the merits of empirical evidence).

- Jeffrey Pfeffer (*Harvard Business Review*, February 2005, p. 54) surveyed the 30,000-plus business books in print and concluded that "Much of this advice is, at best, a waste of time. At worst, it can—if followed—create more problems than it solves."
- Another cautionary perspective is provided in *The Witch Doctors.* After systematically and objectively reviewing a wide array of popular management books, authors John Micklethwait and Adrian Wooldridge concluded that managers must become critical consumers of these products. Being critical means being suspicious of the faddish contentions, remaining unconvinced by simplistic argumentation by the authors, being selective about which theory might work for you, and becoming broadly informed about the merits and deficiencies of each proposal.
- Going back in history several centuries, English philosopher and empiricist Sir Francis Bacon (*Of Studies*, 1625) stated that we should "read not ... to believe and take for granted, but to weigh and consider. Some books are to be tasted, others to be swallowed, and some few to be chewed and digested."

Readers interested in more comprehensive and critical portraits of the management best-seller literature are encouraged to read "Management Fads: Emergence, Evolution, and Implications for Managers" by Jane Whitney Gibson and Dana V. Tesone (*Academy of Management Executive*, 2001, 15:4, pp. 122–133) or "Separating Fads from Facts: Lessons from *The Good, the Fad, and the Ugly*" by David J. Ketchen, Jr. and Jeremy C. Short (*Business Horizons*, 2011, 54, pp. 17–22). Another useful source lies in the reviews of four books on management fads in "Resource Reviews" (*Academy of Management Learning and Education*, 2003, 2:3, pp. 313–321).

You will discover, from your reading of the best-seller summaries in this book, that there are currently several types of author "voices" that provide messages relevant to management education. One is the *organizational scholar* (e.g., Wayne Cascio), who by training and a lifetime of careful work has a strong foundation of rich theories of management and organization and rigorous empirical observations of organizations in action to draw upon. Another source includes *management consultants and management practitioners* (e.g., Bill George), who offer us perspectives from their lives on or near the "organizational firing line." A third source of ideas lies in the *professional writers* (e.g., Tom Friedman), who identify an interesting idea, trend, or concept and proceed to develop and expand it into a book appropriate for a managerial audience.

Traditional academics—students of tight theory and rigorous empirical study of organizational behavior—often find a large disparity among these three perspectives on management and organization. Confronted with the increasing popularity of the "best sellers," the editors of *The Manager's Bookshelf* have raised a number of questions about this nontraditional management literature. For example:

- Is this material "intellectual pornography," as some have claimed?
- Should college and university students be required to consume this material as a central part of their management education?
- Should managers of today's organizations be encouraged to take this material seriously?
- What contributions to management education and development come from this array of management books?
- What are the major deficiencies or limitations of these books?

For answers to these questions, we turned to three colleagues (Professors Larry L. Cummings, Brad Jackson, and Anne Cummings). We asked each of them to reflect upon the current and continued popularity of this "best-seller" literature. The questions we asked them (and their responses) are intended to help you frame, reflect back upon, and critically and cautiously consume this literature. Their reflections on the role of the popular books in management education are included in Reading 2 in this part. New to this edition are the observations that John Newstrom, one of the editors of this and the previous nine editions of The Manager's Bookshelf, has made regarding changes, trends, and phenomena in the field of management best sellers across the past 30 years.

1 Understanding and Using the Best Sellers

Jon L. Pierce and John W. Newstrom

For several decades now, large numbers of newly published books have focused on various aspects of management. These books have been in high demand at local bookstores and on the Internet. Several individuals have authored books that have sold millions of copies, among them Peter Drucker (*The Practice of Management*), Tom Peters and Bob Waterman (*In Search of Excellence*), Spencer Johnson (*Who Moved My Cheese?*), Jim Collins (*Good to Great*), Stephen Covey (*The Seven Habits of Highly Effective People*), Kenneth Blanchard and Spencer Johnson (*The One Minute Manager*), and Thomas Friedman (*The World Is Flat*).

Some of these books have stayed on "best-seller" lists for many weeks, months, and even years. What are the reasons for their popularity? Why have business books continued to catch the public's attention through both good economic times and bad?

We have all read newspaper stories about (and many have felt the shock waves and personal impact of) downsizing, pension fund losses, restructuring, corporate ethical scandals, outsourcing of jobs, globalization, and excessive executive compensation and benefits. We have all read stories about the sometimes-remarkable success of foreign organizations. We have continued to watch bigger and bigger portions of our markets being dominated by foreign-owned and foreign-controlled organizations. We have witnessed foreign interests purchase certain segments of America, while more and more jobs have been moved offshore. Perhaps in response to these trends, a tremendous thirst for *American* success stories and a desire to learn what would prevent some of these negative phenomena have arisen. In essence, the public is receptive and the timing is right for the writing, publication, and sale of popular management books.

A second reason for the upsurge in management books stems from another form of competition. Many management consultants, fighting for visibility and a way to differentiate their services, have written books they hope will become best sellers. Through the printed word they hope to provide a unique take-home product for their clients, communicate their management philosophies, gain wide exposure for themselves or their firms, and profit handsomely.

Third, the best sellers also provide an optimistic message to a receptive market. In difficult economic times or under conditions of extreme pressure to produce short-term results, managers may be as eager to swallow easy formulas for business success as sick patients are to consume their prescribed medicines. Sensing this propensity, the authors of the best sellers (and of many other books with lesser records) often claim, at least implicitly, to present managers with an easy cure for their organizational woes, or with an easy path to personal success. In a world characterized by chaos, environmental turbulence, and intense global competition, managers are driven to search for the ideas provided by others that might be turned into a competitive advantage.

Fourth, we are witnessing an increased belief in and commitment to proactive organizational change and a search for differentiating one's approach. Increasing numbers of managers are rejecting the notion that "if it ain't broke, don't fix it," and instead are adopting a more constructive bias toward action. These managers are seriously looking for and experimenting with different approaches toward organizational management. Many of the popular books provide managers with insights into new and different ways of managing. At a minimum, readers are engaging in the process of benchmarking their competition and adopting "best practices" that have worked for others; hopefully, they are using the established practices of others as a springboard to developing even better ideas themselves.

In their search for the "quick fix," generations of risk-taking American managers have adopted a series of organizational management concepts, such as management by objectives, job enlargement, job enrichment, sensitivity training, flextime, matrix organizational structures, and a variety of labor–management participative schemes, such as quality circles, total quality management, and quality of work–life programs. Each has experienced its own life cycle, often going through the stages of market discovery, wild acceptance by passionate believers, careful questioning of it by serious critics, broad disillusionment with its shortcomings, and sometimes later being abandoned and replaced by another emerging management technique (while a few advocates remain staunchly supportive of the fad).[1]

As a consequence of this managerial tendency to embrace ideas and then soon discard them, many viable managerial techniques have received a tarnished image. For example, many of the Japanese participative management systems that were copied by American managers found their way into the garbage cans of an earlier generation of American managers. The continuing demand for quick fixes stimulates a ready market for new, reborn, and revitalized management ideas. We encourage you to read and seriously reflect on the questionable probability of finding a legitimate quick fix. The search for solutions to major organizational problems in terms of "one-minute" answers reflects a Band-Aid® approach to management—one that is destined to ultimately fail and one that we condemn as a poor way to enrich the body of management knowledge and practice.

We alert you to this managerial tendency to look for "new" solutions to current organizational problems. The rush to resolve problems and take advantage of opportunities frequently leads to the search for simple remedies for complex organizational problems. Yet few of today's organizational problems can be solved with any single approach. The high-involvement management, the learning organization, and the compassionate corporate culture advocated in today's generation of popular management books may also join the list of tried-and-abandoned solutions to organizational woes if implemented without a broader context and deeper understanding. We especially hope that the quick-fix approach to organizational problem solving that characterizes the management style of many will not be promoted as a result of this mosaic (i.e., *The Manager's Bookshelf*) of today's popular business books.

RATIONALE FOR THIS BOOK

The business world has been buzzing with terms like *vision, alignment, flow, pride, authenticity, innovation, credibility, narcissism, paradigms, stewardship, the learning organization, the spirit of work, the soul of business, transformational and charismatic leaders, knowledge management, high-involvement management and organizations,* and *corporate cultures.* On the negative side, these terms feed the management world's preoccupation with quick fixes and the perpetuation of management fads. On the positive side, many of these concepts serve as catalysts to the further development of sound management philosophies and practices.

In the mid-twentieth century, a few books occasionally entered the limelight (e.g., *Parkinson's Law, The Peter Principle, The Effective Executive,* and *My Years with General Motors*), but for the most part they did not generate the widespread and prolonged popularity of the current generation of business books. Then, too, many were not written in the readable style that makes most contemporary books so easy to consume.

Managers find the current wave of books not only interesting but also enjoyable and entertaining to read. A small survey conducted by the Center for Creative Leadership found that a significant number of managers who participated in a study of their all-around reading selections chose one or more management books as their favorite.[2] In essence, many of the popular management books are being read by managers—probably because the books are often supportive of their present management philosophies! Many managers report that these books are insightful, easily readable, interestingly presented, and seemingly practical. Whether the prescriptions in these books have had (or ever will have) a real and lasting impact on the effective management of organizations remains to be determined.

Despite the overall popularity of many business best sellers, some managers do not read *any* current management books, and many others have read only a limited number or small parts of a few.* Similarly, many university students studying management have heard about some of these books, but not read them. *The Manager's Bookshelf* presents perspectives from (but not a criticism of) a number of those popular management books. *The Manager's Bookshelf* is designed for managers who are interested in the best sellers but do not have time to read all of them in their entirety and for students of management who want to be well informed as they prepare to enter the work world. Reading about the views expressed in many of the best sellers will expand the knowledge and business vocabulary of both groups and enable them to engage in more meaningful conversations with their managerial colleagues.

Although reading the book summaries provided here can serve as a useful introduction to this literature, they should not be viewed as a substitute for immersion in the original material, nor do they remove the need for further reading of the more substantive management books and professional journals. The good news is that the popularity of these books suggests that millions of managers are reading them and are exhibiting an interest in learning about what has worked for other managers and firms. This is an important step toward the development of an open-system paradigm for themselves and for their organizations.

We strongly advocate that both managers and students be informed organizational citizens. Therefore, we believe it is important for you to know and understand what is being written about organizations and management. We also believe that it is important for you to know what is being read by the managers who surround you, some of which is contained in best sellers, and much of which is contained in more traditional management books, as well as in professional and scientific journals.[3]

CONTENTS OF THE BEST SELLERS

What topics do these best-selling books cover, what is their form, and what is their merit? Although many authors cover a wide range of topics and others do not have a clear focus, most of these books fall into one of several categories. Some attempt to describe the more effective

---

*For a discussion on incorporating these types of management books into management training programs, see John W. Newstrom and Jon L. Pierce, "The Potential Role of Popular Business Books in Management Development Programs," *Journal of Management Development*, 1989, 8:2, 13–24.

and ineffective companies and identify what made them successes or failures. Others focus on "micro" issues in leadership, motivation, or ethics. One group of authors focuses their attention on broad questions of corporate strategy and competitive tactics for implementing strategy. Some focus on pressing issues facing the contemporary organization, such as social responsibility, globalism, the natural environment, workforce diversity, and the virtual workplace.

In terms of form, many contain apparently simple answers and trite prescriptions. Others are built around literally hundreds of spellbinding anecdotes and stories. Some have used interviews of executives as their source of information; others have adopted the parable format for getting their point across. As a group, their presentation style is rich in diversity. As editors of this mosaic, we have necessarily had to exclude thousands of books while attempting to provide you with a rich exposure to an array of perspectives. For the most part, we have not included books that focus on a single executive's career success (e.g., Steve Jobs at Apple), a single successful firm (e.g., Zappos or Southwest Airlines) or failed organization (e.g., Enron), or a historical reinterpretation of a key person's practices (e.g., *Leadership Secrets of Sitting Bull*) or highly specialized context (e.g., *Mob Rules*).

Judging the merits of individual best sellers is a difficult task (and one that we will leave for readers and management critics to engage in). Some critics have taken the extreme position of calling these books "intellectual wallpaper" and "business pornography." Certainly labels like these, justified or not, should caution readers. A better perspective is provided by an assessment of the sources, often anecdotal, of many of the books. In other words, much of the information in business best sellers stems from the experiences and observations of a single individual and is often infused with the subjective opinions of that writer. Unlike the more traditional academic literature, these books do not all share a sound scientific foundation. Requirements pertaining to objectivity, reproducibility of observations, and tests for reliability and validity have not guided the creation of much of the material. As a consequence, the authors are at liberty to say whatever they want (and often with as much passion as they desire).

Unlike authors who publish research-based knowledge, authors of management best sellers do not need to submit their work to a panel of reviewers who then critically evaluate the ideas, logic, and data. The authors of these popular management books are able to proclaim as sound management principles virtually anything that is intuitively acceptable to their publishers and readers. Therefore, readers need to be cautious consumers who are vigilant about being misled. The ideas presented in these books need to be critically compared with the well-established thoughts from more traditional sources of managerial wisdom.

CRITIQUING THESE POPULAR BOOKS

Although the notion of one-minute management is seductive, we may safely conclude that there are no fast-acting cures to deep and complex business problems. Recognizing that simple solutions are not likely to be found in 200 pages of anecdotal stories and that the best sellers frequently present (or appear to present) quick fixes and simple solutions, we strongly encourage you to read these popular books, looking less for simple solutions and more toward using them to stimulate your thinking and challenge the way you go about doing your business. We encourage you not only to achieve comprehension and understanding but ultimately to arrive at the level of critique and synthesis—far more useful long-term skills.

To help you approach these works more critically, we encourage you to use the following questions to guide your evaluation:[4]

- **Author Credentials:** How do the authors' backgrounds and personal characteristics uniquely qualify them to write this book? What relevant experience do they have? What unique access or perspective do they have? What prior writing experience do they have, and how was it accepted in the marketplace? What is their research background (capacity to design, conduct, and interpret the results of their observations)?
- **Rationale:** Why did the authors write the book? Is their self-proclaimed reason legitimate?
- **Face Validity:** On initial examination of the book's major characteristics and themes (but before reading the entire book and actually examining the evidence provided), do you react positively or negatively? Are you inclined to accept or reject the authors' conclusions? Are the major contentions believable? Does the book fit with your prior experience and expectations, or does it rock them to the core?
- **Target Audience:** For whom is this book uniquely written? What level of manager in the organizational hierarchy would most benefit from reading the book and why? Is it for *you*?
- **Integration of Existing Knowledge:** A field of inquiry can best move forward only if it draws upon and then extends existing knowledge. Was this book (inappropriately) written in isolation of existing knowledge? Do the authors demonstrate an awareness of and build upon existing knowledge, while giving appropriate credit to other sources of ideas?
- **Readability/Interest:** Do the authors engage your mind? Are relevant, practical illustrations provided that indicate how the ideas have been or could be applied? Are the language and format used appealing to you?
- **Internal Validity:** To what degree do the authors provide substantive evidence that the phenomenon, practice, or ideas presented actually and directly produce a valued result? Does an internally consistent presentation of ideas demonstrate the processes through which the causes for their observations are understood?
- **Reliability/Consistency:** To what degree do the authors' conclusions converge with other sources of information available to you, or with the product of other methods of data collection? Do the authors stay internally consistent in their "pitch" from beginning to end of the book?
- **Distinctiveness:** Is the material presented new, creative, and distinctive (providing a unique "value-added" dimension), or is it merely a presentation of "old wine in new bottles"?
- **Objectivity:** To what extent do the authors have a self-serving or political agenda, or have the authors presented information that was systematically gathered and objectively evaluated? Have the authors offered both the pros and cons of their views?
- **External Validity:** Are the ideas likely to work in your unique situation, or are they bound to the narrow context within which the authors operated? What are the similarities that give you confidence that the recommendations made can be safely and effectively applied to your context?
- **Practicality:** Are the ideas adaptable? Do the authors provide concrete suggestions for application? Are the ideas readily transferable to the workplace in such a way that the typical reader could be expected to know what to do with them a few days later at work? Is it possible to produce an action plan directly from the material that you have read?

These are only some of the questions that should be asked as you read and evaluate any popular management book.

NATURE OF THIS BOOK

This is the 10th edition of *The Manager's Bookshelf*, providing strong evidence regarding the public's interest in business best sellers. Recent language editions have also appeared in Italian, Spanish, and Chinese, pointing to the international popularity of these books. The current edition includes many books that were not previously summarized, representing a substantial revision. *The Manager's Bookshelf* provides a comprehensive introduction to many of the major best sellers in the management field during recent years.

The selections contained in this book are of two types: excerpts of original material and summaries prepared by a panel of reviewers. In one case (e.g., Edgar H. Schein), the author's original thoughts and words were captured by selecting an article (representing part of the book) that the author had written for publication in a professional journal. Here the reader will see the author's ideas directly, though only sampled or much condensed from the original source.

The major format chosen for inclusion is a comprehensive, but brief and readable, summary of the best seller prepared by persons selected for their relevant expertise, interest, and familiarity. These summaries are primarily descriptive, designed to provide readers with an overall understanding of the book. These summaries are not judgmental in nature, nor are they necessarily a complete or precise reflection of the book author's management philosophy.

Determining what constituted a management best seller worthy of inclusion was easy in some cases and more difficult in others. From the thousands of books available for selection, the ones included here rated highly on one or more of these criteria:

1. *Market Acceptance:* Several books have achieved national notoriety by selling hundreds of thousands, and, occasionally, millions, of copies.
2. *Provocativeness:* Some books present thought-provoking viewpoints that run counter to "traditional" management thought.
3. *Distinctiveness:* A wide variety of topical themes of interest to organizational managers and students of management is presented.
4. *Representativeness:* In an attempt to avoid duplication from books with similar content within a topical area, many popular books were necessarily excluded.
5. *Author Reputation:* Some authors (e.g., John Kotter or Jim Collins) have a strong reputation for the quality of their thinking and the insights they have generated; therefore, some of their newer products were included.

AUTHORS OF THE BEST SELLERS

It is appropriate for a reader to examine a management best seller and inquire, "Who is the author of this book?" Certainly the authors come from varied backgrounds, which can be both a strength and weakness for the best sellers as a whole. Their diversity of experience and perspective is rich, yet it is possible that some authors are ill-qualified to speak and portray themselves as experts.

Some of the authors have been critically described as self-serving egotists who have little to say constructively about management, but who say it with a flair and passion such that reading their books may appear to be very exciting. Some books are seemingly the product of armchair humorists who set out to entertain their readers with tongue in cheek. Other books on the best-seller lists have been written with the aid of a ghostwriter (i.e., by someone who takes information that has been provided by another and then converts it into the lead author's story) or a professional writer who helps a busy executive organize and present his or her thoughts. Other books are the product of a CEO's reflection on his or her career or heartfelt positions on contemporary issues in organizations (e.g., author Bill George). A rather new and refreshing change has been the emergence in the best-seller literature of books prepared by respected academic professionals who have capably applied the best of their substantive research to pressing management problems and subsequently integrated their thoughts into book form. (Examples in this edition of such academics include Wayne Cascio, Alfred Marcus, Kim Cameron, Jeffrey Pfeffer, Henry Mintzberg, and Richard Hackman.) In summary, it may be fascinating to read the "inside story" or delve into a series of exciting anecdotes and "war stories," but the reader still has the opportunity and obligation to challenge the author's credentials for making broad generalizations from that experience base.

Conclusions

We encourage you to read and reflect on this collection of thoughts from the authors of today's generation of management books. We invite you to expand and enrich your insights into management as a result of learning from this set of popular books. We challenge you to question and debate the pros and cons of the ideas and philosophies that are presented by these authors. We hope you will ask when, where, how, and why these ideas are applicable. Examine the set of readings provided here, let them stimulate your thinking, and, in the process, learn something new. You'll find that learning—and especially critical thinking—can be both fun and addictive!

Notes

1. See, for example, Barbara Ettore, "What's the Next Business Buzzword?" *Management Review*, 1997, 86:8, 33–35; "Business Fads: What's In—and Out," *Business Week*, January 20, 1986; W. W. Armstrong, "The Boss Has Read Another New Book!" *Management Review*, June 1994, 83:6, 61–64.
2. Frank Freeman, "Books That Mean Business: The Management Best Sellers," *Academy of Management Review*, 1985, 10, 345–350.
3. See, for example, a report on executive reading preferences by Marilyn Wellemeyer in "Books Bosses Read," *Fortune*, April 27, 1987.
4. See John W. Newstrom and Jon L. Pierce, "An Analytic Framework for Assessing Popular Business Books," *Journal of Management Development*, 1993, 12:4, 20–28.

2 Reflections on the Best Sellers and a Cautionary Note

Jon L. Pierce and John W. Newstrom, with
Larry L. Cummings, Brad Jackson, and Anne Cummings

Dr. Larry L. Cummings was the Carlson Professor of Management in the Carlson School of Management at the University of Minnesota. He previously taught at Columbia University, Indiana University, the University of British Columbia, the University of Wisconsin in Madison, and Northwestern University. Dr. Cummings published more than 80 journal articles and 16 books. He served as the editor of the *Academy of Management Journal*, as a member of the Academy's Board of Governors, and as president of the same association. Dr. Cummings was a consultant for many corporations, including Dow Chemical, Cummins Engine, Eli Lilly, Prudential, Samsonite, Touche-Ross, and Moore Business Forms.

Professor Brad Jackson is the Fletcher Building Education Trust Chair and Codirector of the New Zealand Leadership Institute at The University of Auckland Business School. Brad has spoken to academic and business audiences throughout the world and has published five books—*Management Gurus and Management Fashions, The Hero Manager, Organisational Behaviour in New Zealand, A Very Short, Fairly Interesting and Reasonably Cheap Book About Studying Leadership*, and *Demystifying Business Celebrity*. He has edited the Sage Handbook of Leadership, and Major Works in Leadership. He is Vice-Chair of the International Leadership Association.

Dr. Anne Cummings taught General Management, Organizational Behavior, Teams, Negotiations, and Leadership for undergraduate, M.B.A., Ph.D., and Executive Education audiences at the University of Pennsylvania's Wharton School, and subsequently served on the Management Studies faculty at the University of Minnesota Duluth. Dr. Cummings won the David W. Hauck teaching award at Wharton in recognition of her outstanding ability to lead, stimulate, and challenge students. She holds a Ph.D. in Organizational Behavior from the University of Illinois at Urbana-Champaign, and her research has appeared in the *Academy of Management Journal, Journal of Applied Psychology, California Management Review*, and *Leadership Quarterly*.

This closing section provides our reflections upon management (both the body of knowledge and its practice), as well as upon the wave of management books that has almost become an institutionalized part of the popular press. We hope it will provide some helpful perspectives and point you in some new directions.

One of the world's premier management gurus, the late Peter F. Drucker, suggested that managing is a "liberal art." It is "liberal" because it deals not only with fundamental knowledge but also self-knowledge, wisdom, and leadership; it is an "art" because it is also concerned with practice and application. According to Drucker, "managers draw on all the knowledge and insights of the humanities and the social sciences—on psychology and philosophy, on economics and history, on ethics—as well as on the physical sciences."* Building on this, we note that management can be defined as the skillful application of a body of knowledge to a particular organizational situation. This definition suggests that management is an art form as well as a science. That is, there is a body of knowledge that has to be applied with the fine touch and instinctive sense of the master artist. Peter Drucker reminds us that the fundamental task of management is to "make people capable of joint performance through common goals, common values, the right structure, and the training and development they need to perform and to respond to change" (p. 4). Consequently, execution of the management role and performance of the managerial functions are more complex than the simple application of a few management concepts. The development of effective management, therefore, requires the development of an in-depth understanding of organizational and management concepts, careful sensitivity to individuals and groups, and the capacity to grasp when and how to apply this knowledge.

The organizational arena presents today's manager with a number of challenges. The past few decades have been marked by a rapid growth of knowledge about organizations and management systems. As a consequence of this growth in management information, we strongly believe that it is important for today's manager to engage in lifelong learning by continually remaining a student of management. It is also clear to us that our understanding of organizations and management systems is still in the early stages of development. That is, there remain many unanswered questions that pertain to the effective management of organizations.

Many observers of the perils facing today's organizations have charged that the crises facing American organizations today are largely a function of "bad management"—the failure, in large part, to recognize that management is about human beings. It is the ability, according to Drucker, "to make people capable of joint performance, [and] to make their strengths effective and their weaknesses irrelevant. This is what organization is all about, and it is the reason that management is the critical, determining force" (p. 10). Similarly, Tom Peters and Bob Waterman have observed that the growth of our society during the twentieth century was so rapid that almost any management approach appeared to work and work well. The real test of effective management systems did not appear until recent decades, when competitive, economic, political, and social pressures created a form of environmental turbulence that pushed existing managerial tactics beyond their limits. Not only are students of management challenged to learn about effective management principles, but are also confronted with the need to develop the skills and intuitive sense to apply that management knowledge. This approach is totally consistent with the concept of evidence-based management, as introduced by Pfeffer and Sutton in Part 16, Reading 3.

Fortunately, there are many organizations in our society from which they can learn, and there is a wealth of knowledge that has been created that focuses on effective organizational management. There are at least two literatures that provide rich opportunities for regular reading. First, there is the traditional management literature found in management and organization textbooks and academic journals (e.g., *Academy of Management Journal, Administrative Science Quarterly, Journal of Organizational Behavior, Harvard Business Review, Organizational Dynamics, Managerial Psychology, Research in Organizational Behavior,* and *California Management Review*). Second, the past few decades have seen the emergence of a nontraditional management

---

*Page references are to Peter F. Drucker, "Management as a Social Function and Liberal Art," *The Essential Drucker: The Best of Sixty Years of Peter Drucker's Essential Writings on Management.* Harper Business, 2003.

literature written by management gurus, management practitioners, and management consul-tants who describe their organizational experiences and provide a number of other management themes. Knowledge about effective and ineffective management systems can be gleaned by listening to the management scholar, philosopher, and practitioner.

Because not all that is published in the academic journals or in the popular press meets combined tests of scientific rigor and practicality, it is important that motivated readers immerse themselves in both of these literatures. Yet, neither source should be approached and subsequently consumed without engaging in critical thinking.

CRITICAL THINKING AND CAUTIOUS CONSUMPTION

We believe that the ideas promoted in these best sellers should not be integrated blindly into any organization. Each should be subjected to careful scrutiny in order to identify its inherent strengths and weaknesses; each should be examined within the context of the unique organiza-tional setting in which it may be implemented; and modifications and fine-tuning of the tech-nique may be required in order to tailor it to a specific organizational setting and management philosophy. In addition, we strongly encourage juxtaposing the concepts, ideas, and management practices presented in these books with the scientific management literature. To what extent have these "popular press" ideas been subjected to investigation following the canons of the scientific method? Have they been supported? Are they endorsed by other respected management philoso-phers and practitioners? If these ideas or similar ones have not been rigorously examined scientifi-cally, it would be prudent to ask the important question "Why not?" If these ideas have not been endorsed by others, we should once again raise the question "Why not?" before blindly entering them into our storehouse of knowledge and "bag of management practices." Finally, the process that is used to implement the management technique may be as important to its success as the technique itself, as good ideas (techniques, programs) may still fail if the processes employed to implement them are seriously flawed.

This is an era of an information—knowledge explosion. We would like to remind consum-ers of information of the relevance of the saying *caveat emptor* (let the buyer beware) from the product domain, because there are both good and questionable informational products on the best-seller market. Fortunately, advisory services such as Consumer Reports exist to advise us on the consumption of consumer goods. There is, however, no similar guide for our consumption of information in the popular management press. Just because a book has been published or even become a best seller does not mean that the information contained therein is worthy of direct consumption. It may be a best seller because it presents an optimistic message, it is enjoyable reading, it contains simple solutions that appeal to those searching for easy answers, the author is a recognized figure, or it has been successfully marketed to the public.

The information in all management literature should be approached with caution; it should be examined and questioned. We suggest that a more appropriate guide for readers might be *caveat lector, sapeat lector* (which loosely translates to "Let the reader beware, but first let the reader be informed"). The pop-management literature should not be substituted for more scientific-based knowledge about effective management. In addition, this knowledge should be compared and contrasted with what we know about organizations and management systems from other sources—the opinions of other experts, the academic management literature, and our own prior organizational experiences.

We invite you to question this best-seller literature. In the process, there are many ques-tions that should be asked. For example, What are the author's credentials, and are they relevant to the book? Has the author remained an objective observer of the reported events? Why did the author write this book? What kind of information is being presented (e.g., opinion, values, facts)? Does this information make sense when it is placed into previously developed theories? Could I take this information and apply it to another situation at a different point in time and in a different place, or was it unique to the author's experience? These and similar questions should be part of the information screening process.

INTERVIEWS WITH THREE ORGANIZATIONAL SCHOLARS

As we became increasingly familiar with the best sellers through our roles as editors, we began asking a number of questions about this type of literature. We then sought and talked with three distinguished management scholars—Professors L. L. Cummings, Brad Jackson, and Anne Cummings. Following are excerpts from those interviews.

Exploring the Contributions of Best Sellers

We have witnessed an explosion in the number and type of books that have been written on management and organizations for the trade market. Many of these books have found themselves on various "best-seller" lists. What, in your opinion, has been the impact of these publications? What is the nature of their contribution?

LARRY CUMMINGS'S PERSPECTIVE   Quite frankly, I think these books have made a number of subtle contributions, most of which have not been labeled or identified by either the business press or the academic press. In addition, many of their contributions have been inappropriately or inaccurately labeled.

Permit me to elaborate. I think it is generally true that a number of these very popular "best-seller list" books, as you put it, have been thought to be reasonably accurate translations or interpretations of successful organizational practice. Although this is not the way that these books have been reviewed in the academic press, my interactions with managers, business practitioners, and M.B.A. students reveal that many of these books are viewed as describing organizational structure, practices, and cultures that are thought to contribute to excellence.

On the other hand, when I evaluate the books myself and when I pay careful attention to the reviews by respected, well-trained, balanced academicians, it is my opinion that these books offer very little, if anything, in the way of generalizable knowledge about successful organizational practice. As organizational case studies, they are the most dangerous of the lot, in that the data (information) presented has not been systematically, carefully, and cautiously collected and interpreted. Of course, that criticism is common for case studies. Cases were never meant to be contributions to scientific knowledge. Even the best ones are primarily pedagogical aids, or the basis for subsequent theory construction.

The reason I describe the cases presented in books like *In Search of Excellence* as frequently among the most dangerous is because they are so well done (i.e., in a marketing and journalistic sense), and therefore, they are easily read and so believable. They are likely to influence the naive, those who consume them without critically evaluating their content. They epitomize the glamour and the action orientation, and even the machoism of American management practice; that is, they represent the epitome of competition, control, and order as dominant interpersonal and organizational values.

Rather, I think the contributions of these books, in general, have been to provide an apology, a rationale, or a positioning, if you like, of American management as something that is not just on the defensive with regard to other world competitors. Instead, they have highlighted American management as having many good things to offer: a sense of spirit, a sense of identification, and a sense of clear caricature. This has served to fill a very important need. In American management thought there has emerged a lack of self-confidence and a lack of belief that what we are doing is proactive, effective, and correct. From this perspective, these books have served a useful role in trying to present an upbeat, optimistic characterization.

BRAD JACKSON'S PERSPECTIVE   It is very difficult to assess the true nature of the impact that the best sellers have on management practice. We might infer from the huge number of books that are sold each year that their impact might be quite substantial. Corporations and consulting firms purchase many business best sellers on a bulk basis. It is difficult to ascertain how many of these are actually distributed and received. The next question to consider, of course, is the extent to which these books are actually read. Anecdotal evidence (as well as personal experience!) suggests that, even with the best intentions, most readers manage to peruse the book jacket, the testimonials, the preface, and, at best, the introductory chapter. Few find the time to read the book's entire contents.

Most crucially, however, we should try to understand the nature of the impact that the reading of a best seller, even if it is very partial, has on how the individual manager perceives the world and how he or she acts on that world as a result of being exposed to the ideas expressed in this genre of books. This is a task that is fraught with difficulty, as managers are exposed to so many different influences and are shaped and constrained by a wide range of organizational environments. In my book, *Management Gurus and Management Fashions* (Jackson, 2001), I suggest that business best sellers not only make an intellectual contribution, but also provide quite important psychological and emotional support to managers. It is no accident that we can observe the swelling of the personal growth section of the business book section during times of widespread turbulence.

During the 1990s, organizations across all sectors embraced new management ideas (management fashions) that were promoted by management gurus in business best sellers. Organizational improvement programs such as total quality management, business process reengineering, the balanced scorecard, and knowledge management were seized upon as the panacea for organizations desperate to retain their competitive edge or merely survive. Vestiges of these and older programs can still be traced in the language, systems, and structures of these organizations, but their influence and attention are well past their peak. We have very little to go on in terms of understanding how these management fashions are adapted and institutionalized, but a few studies have shown that these ideas tend to be only selectively adopted or they are reworked or even actively resisted by managers and employees. The bottom line is that it is very difficult to accurately trace the impact of best sellers. However, we should be prepared to accept that the final impact is likely to be quite different than what the best-selling author originally intended!

ANNE CUMMINGS'S PERSPECTIVE   These best-selling business books have offered my teaching a variety of important contributions:

- They offer powerful corporate examples that I use for illustrating conceptual points in class. I often find the examples of what didn't work (and the ensuing discussion about why) as useful (if not more useful!) than the examples of what did work.
- They update me on the newest terminology and techniques that managers are reading about, which helps me to communicate efficiently and effectively with them, using their vocabulary.

- They stimulate interesting conversations with Executive Education participants, who often question the value of the latest fads and want to explore how these new ideas compare to their managerial experience and to the conceptual foundations about management that they learned a decade earlier.
- Some of the books offer basic frameworks for viewing problems and issues, and this encourages students to begin thinking conceptually. I can then nudge students toward thinking further about cause–effect relationships, contingencies, and the utility of academic research.
- Some of the books offer important insights into environmental trends, shifting managerial pressures, and even new ways of thinking about things—sometimes long before academics explore these areas.

Possible Concerns About Best Sellers

In addition to a large volume of sales, surveys reveal that many of these books have been purchased and presumably read by those who are managing today's organizations. Does this trouble you? More specifically, are there any concerns that you have, given the extreme popularity of these types of books?

LARRY CUMMINGS'S PERSPECTIVE   I am of two minds with regard to this question. First, I think that the sales of these books are not an accurate reflection of the degree, the extent, or the carefulness with which they have been read. Nor do I believe that the sales volumes tell us anything about the pervasiveness of their impact. Like many popular items (fads), many of these books have been purchased for desktop dressing. In many cases, the preface, the introduction, and the conclusion (maybe the summary on the dust jacket) have been read such that the essence of the book is picked up, and it can become a part of managerial and social conversation.

Obviously, this characterization does not accurately describe everyone in significant positions of management who has purchased these books. There are many managers who make sincere attempts to follow the management literature thoroughly and to evaluate it critically. I think that most of the people with whom I come in contact in management circles, both in training for management and in actual management positions, who have carefully read the books are not deceived by them. They are able to put them in the perspective of representations or characterizations of a fairly dramatic sort. As a consequence, I am not too concerned about the books being overly persuasive in some dangerous, Machiavellian, or subterranean sense.

On the other hand, I do have a concern of a different nature regarding these books. That concern focuses upon the possibility that the experiences they describe will be taken as legitimate bases or legitimate directions for the study of management processes. These books represent discourse by the method of emphasizing the extremes, in particular the extremes of success. I think a much more fruitful approach to studying and developing prescriptions for management thought and management action is to use the method of differences rather than the method of extremes.

The method of differences would require us to study the conditions that gave rise to success at Chrysler, or McDonald's, or which currently gives rise to success at Merck or any of the other best-managed companies. However, through this method we would also contrast these companies with firms in the same industries that are not as successful. The method of contrast (differences) is likely to lead to empirical results that are much less dramatic, much less exciting, much less subject to journalistic account (i.e., they're likely to be more boring to read), but it is much more likely to lead to observations that are more generalizable across managerial situations, as well as being generative in terms of ideas for further management research.

Thus, the issue is based on the fundamental method that underlies these characterizations. My concern is not only from a methodological perspective. It also centers on our ethical and professional obligations to make sure that the knowledge we transmit does not lead people to overgeneralize. Rather, it should provide them with information that is diagnostic rather than purely prescriptive.

The method of extremes does not lead to a diagnostic frame of mind. It does not lead to a frame of mind that questions why something happened, under what conditions it happened, or under what conditions it would not happen. The method of differences is much more likely to lead to the discovery of the conditional nature of knowledge and the conditional nature of prescriptions.

BRAD JACKSON'S PERSPECTIVE   I tend to be less concerned about the large volume of business best sellers than a lot of my academic colleagues. While I wish that there were bigger public appetites for more academically oriented management books, I am generally encouraged by the widespread interest in business and management. It's important for managers to take an interest in what is going on beyond their immediate work environment and to ask questions about why things are being done in a certain way and what could be done differently. Best sellers typically challenge the status quo in provocative and dramatic ways that readily engage managers' attentions. Subsequently, many managers wish to learn more and sign up for some form of formal management education. It is in this forum that they can become exposed to alternative and more rigorously researched accounts of management theory and practice that challenge some of the assumptions made in the best sellers. I have found that encouraging managers to take a more critical reading of the business best sellers can be highly instructive for both them and me, especially when they are presented alongside academically oriented texts, which they find to be slightly less accessible, but ultimately more rewarding.

ANNE CUMMINGS'S PERSPECTIVE   My greatest concern with these books is that many readers do not have the time, motivation, or managerial experience to appropriately apply the contents. Unfortunately, a few students seem to be mostly interested in "speaking the language" with bravado just to demonstrate how up-to-date they are. Others seem to want to simply imitate the successful examples that they have read about, as though these reports of alleged best practices represent a "cookbook" approach that can be easily applied elsewhere. Most managers consider their time an extremely valuable resource and consider this reading a "luxury"; they tell me they therefore approach these readings looking for "take-aways" from each one—short lists of guiding principles, practical procedures they can implement immediately, or a simple diagram or model to organize a project or change they are leading. All students of management can benefit from remembering that the process of building solid theories and best practices from isolated case examples (i.e., inductive learning) is a complex one; some discipline and patience are required to avoid premature generalizing before valid evidence is available and well understood. The challenge is for readers to expend some real effort and apply critical thinking to these products—to analyze when and why the practices might be successful. Demanding conversations with colleagues, mentors, and competitors; comparing apparent discrepancies; and asking tough "why" and "how" questions are all useful techniques to achieve this discipline.

Recent Changes in Best Sellers

The modern era of business best-seller popularity now spans several decades. Have you witnessed any changes or evolution in the nature of these best-seller books during this time?

BRAD JACKSON'S PERSPECTIVE   Looking back, I characterize the 1990s as the "guru decade." This was the era in which a few highly influential management gurus such as Michael Hammer, Tom Peters, Michael Porter, Peter Senge, and Stephen Covey reigned supreme among the best sellers. Their larger-than-life presences helped to spawn a few very powerful management ideas that drove a lot of conventional management thinking in North America and beyond. I do not see the same concentration of interest in either management gurus or management fashions in the current business book market. Instead I see a lot of niche-based ideas that are being promoted by specific consulting firms. None of these seem to have had the same pervasive influence that the gurus previously held. On the other hand, I see a lot of interest in biographical accounts of what I call "hero managers" such as Jack Welch, Richard Branson, and Lou Gerstner. Most of these are inspirational self-celebratory accounts, but, of course, there has also been a lot more interest in exposing some of the darker sides of corporate life in the wake of the Enron and other corporate scandals.

JOHN NEWSTROM'S PERSPECTIVE   I have closely monitored the field of business best sellers for over thirty years. I have read, analyzed, and discussed many books in considerable detail while also "keeping my finger on the pulse" by more casual observation of hundreds of other business and management books. Although it may be unfair to suggest that significant trends have occurred during this period, it is wholly reasonable to conclude that the field of best sellers has witnessed several interesting phenomena. I'll briefly proffer those here:

- There has been an unending publication of what I refer to as *"one-hour" books* in management. These are books that, because of their brevity (perhaps 100 pages), simplistic writing style (often presented in the form of fables), and page layout (large print, wide margins, and frequently double-spaced text) can usually be read from cover to cover in a very minimal length of time (perhaps the length of a typical airplane flight). This has made them highly appealing to a readership that is often reluctant to devote dozens of hours to immersing themselves in dense material while juggling many other responsibilities.
- There have been many *re*leases (no pun intended) of what I critically refer to as *"re-books."* At the risk of *re*iterating a previously expressed theme of "old wine in new bottles," I believe that considerable numbers of the books appearing over the years have little new to offer; they simply *re*iterate or *re*gurgitate (i.e., *re*state, *re*hash, *re*phrase, *re*tell, *re*confirm, *re*view) the same themes—and occasionally the same stories—as previous books have done. Note, however, that I am less critical of new books that legitimately seek to modify and extend previous knowledge. *Constructive* re-books, then, are often characterized by not only reminding and reinforcing the earlier conclusions of other authors but also refining, revising, or reimagining the material to push the state of the art forward a bit.
- Another trend I've witnessed is the existence of business books proclaiming to identify so-called "immutable" laws. I urge caution to any reader of these titles, challenging them to question whether it is truly likely that a series of 6, 10, or 21 new immutable (absolute, indisputable, unassailable) principles of management were recently discovered by these management evangelists.

- A closely related genre of business best sellers falls into the category of "Leadership Secrets of _____" (e.g., Sitting Bull, Abraham Lincoln, Billy Graham, Colin Powell, Hillary Clinton, Santa Claus, or the Mafia). Book authors and publishers seem to believe that if they attach almost any source reference to "Leadership Secrets" that people will truly believe it has instant credibility. These historical reconstructions attempt to identify golden nuggets of wisdom, much as prospectors did when sifting through the tailings from old gold mines—but rarely with rich results.

- One modest trend has been the shift from near-exclusive laudatory books about corporate executives (often autobiographical) to much more critical (and sometimes scathing) documentations of managerial and organizational weaknesses, failures, and downfalls. The former is best illustrated by the books *Iacocca, Jack Welch on Leadership,* and General Norman Schwartzkopf's *It Doesn't Take a Hero*; recent years have seen a broad array of exposés (e.g., *BPs Tony Hayward and the Failure of Leadership, Derailed: Five Lessons Learned from Catastrophic Failures of Leadership, Chainsaw: The Notorious Career of Al Dunlap*). The positive takeaway from this trend is that many books are now becoming much more honest and candid about both the strengths and weaknesses of our leaders and organizations.

- One of the more encouraging trends, on the other hand, has been the increasingly common appearance of books prepared by authors with substantive research credentials or well-established respect for their thought processes. These authors (such as Edward Lawler, Richard Hackman, and Fred Luthans) typically have conducted in-depth reviews of the extant literature as well as gathered original research information as the bases for solid conclusions.

- One thing that clearly has not changed substantially across thirty years is the widespread and seemingly insatiable hunger (or unquenchable thirst) on the part of consumers for guidance, insight, wisdom, handholding, and simplistic prescriptions for success. In that sense, the market hasn't seemed to change much since Shepherd Mead first published *How to Succeed in Business without Really Trying* in 1952.

Words of Advice

Do you have any insights or reflections or words of advice to offer readers of business best sellers?

BRAD JACKSON'S PERSPECTIVE   I like to share the advice that Micklethwait and Wooldridge (*The Witch Doctors,* 1996) give at the end of their excellent exposé on the management theory industry. They argue that because management theory is comparatively immature and underdeveloped, it is vital that managers become selective and critical consumers of the products and services offered by the management theory industry. In particular, they suggest that managers should bear in mind the following advice when making book purchase decisions:

1. Anything that you suspect is bunk almost certainly is.
2. Beware of authors who aggrandize themselves more than their work.
3. Beware of authors who argue almost exclusively by analogy.
4. Be selective. No one management theory will cure all ills.
5. Bear in mind that the cure can sometimes be worse than the disease.
6. Supplement these books with reactions from academic reviewers to get an informed and critical perspective on the value of new management theories and their proponents.

All I would add to this succinct list is to encourage managers to read more widely and to look to other disciplines such as philosophy, history, psychology, and art for supplemental insights into management practice and organizational life. I'm always surprised by how much I learn when I browse through books in the other sections of the library or bookstore.

Conclusion

We hope that you have enjoyed reading the views of these management scholars (Professors Larry Cummings, Brad Jackson, and Anne Cummings) on the role of popular management books. In addition, we hope that the readings contained in the 10th edition of *The Manager's Bookshelf* will stimulate your thinking about effective and ineffective practices of management. We reiterate that there is no single universally applicable practice of management, for management is the skillful application of a body of knowledge to a particular situation. We invite you to continue expanding your understanding of new and developing management concepts. In a friendly sort of way, we challenge you to develop the skills to know when and how to apply this knowledge in the practice of management.

PART TWO

Best-Seller "Classics"

Many of the books contained in earlier editions of *The Manager's Bookshelf* as a part of our mosaic of contemporary views continue to have a message that many managers reference frequently and still want to study. As a result, for the 10th edition of *The Manager's Bookshelf* we have included summaries of eight key books that continue to be popular "classic" references for managers today.

Peter F. Drucker—a writer, consultant, and teacher—was the Marie Rankin Clarke Professor of Social Sciences and Management at Claremont Graduate University and previously taught at New York University. He received his doctorate from University of Frankfurt, Germany, in 1931. Having awed the world with his writings across a half-century until his death at age 95 in 2005, Drucker was variously described as "the man who invented management," "the patron saint of socially aware executives," a "prolific and profound management thinker," "The Dr. Spock of American business," and "the world's foremost pioneer of management theory." He was the author of 40 books and an astounding 35 articles that appeared in the prestigious *Harvard Business Review* journal. In 2002, he was awarded the Presidential Medal of Freedom, the nation's highest civilian award.

In *The Practice of Management*, Drucker suggests that executives ask several penetrating questions, such as, What is our business? Who is our customer? What does our customer value most? He argues that management is a distinct (but previously underappreciated) function that is practice oriented and can be improved through education. He emphasizes the importance of the external environment, pursuing multiple goals, accenting innovation and knowledge workers, acting with integrity, following a systematic decision-making process, and viewing the firm as a social institution. He also pioneered the concept of management by objectives (MBO).

Kenneth Blanchard and Spencer Johnson, in the enormously popular book *The One Minute Manager*, build their prescriptions for effective human resource management on two basic principles. First, they suggest that quality time with the subordinate is of utmost importance. Second, they suggest that employees are basically capable of self-management. These two principles provide the basis for their prescriptions on goal setting, praising, and reprimanding as the cornerstones of effective management. *The One Minute Manager* was identified as one of the "seven essential popular business books" by M. L. Jenson (*eBook Crossroads*, December 5, 2005).

Kenneth Blanchard was a professor of management at the University of Massachusetts, and remains active as a writer, management consultant, and cofounder of the Blanchard Companies. Blanchard has also published *The Power of Ethical Management, Gung Ho, The One-Minute Apology, Servant Leader, Whale Done, The Heart of a Leader, The Leadership Pill, The Secret*, and *Raving Fans*; his books have collectively sold over 17 million copies. Spencer Johnson, the holder of a medical doctorate, is interested in stress and has written the popular books *Who Moved My Cheese?* and *The Present.*

Quality, customer service, total quality management, and continuous improvement have been organizational buzzwords for the past several years. One of the leaders in developing strategies for building quality into manufacturing processes was the late W. Edwards Deming. During the 1950s, Deming went to Japan to teach statistical control, where his ideas received a very warm reception. The Japanese built on Deming's ideas and moved the responsibility for quality from the ranks of middle management down to the shop-floor level. Deming's ideas on quality control soon became an integral feature in Japanese management. Deming has been hailed by his admirers both as the "prophet of quality" and the "man of the century." He certainly demonstrated a powerful force of personality and singular focus.

Total quality control (TQC) means that responsibility for quality is a part of every employee's job. Deming's *Out of the Crisis* calls for long-term organizational transformation through the implementation of a 14-step plan of action focusing on leadership, constant innovation, and removal of barriers to performance. Interested readers may also wish to examine other works about Deming and his influence in *The World of W. Edwards Deming, The Deming Dimension, Thinking About Quality*, and *Deming's Road to Continual Improvement.*

A true classic in the management literature is Douglas McGregor's *The Human Side of Enterprise*, first published in 1960. Because of the book's popularity, its timeless theme, and genuine relevance for organizations in the twenty-first century, McGregor's seminal work continues to be valuable reading.

McGregor explores alternative assumptions that managers might hold and that drive different approaches to the management of organizations and their employees. Through the presentation of two sets of assumptions—labeled Theory X and Theory Y—McGregor urges managers to see employees as capable of innovation, creativity, commitment, high levels of sustained effort, and the exercise of self-direction and self-control.

Douglas McGregor received his doctorate at Harvard University. Before his death in 1964, he served on the faculties of Harvard University and the Massachusetts Institute of Technology and was president of Antioch College. McGregor is also the author of *The Professional Manager.*

A contemporary of McGregor, Abraham Maslow has sometimes been called the "greatest psychologist since Freud," and a "significant contributor to the humanistic psychology movement." He is well known to psychology students for his books *Toward a Psychology of Being* and *The Psychology of Science.* However, he is equally well known to most business students for his highly popularized and defining work on postulating a hierarchy of human needs, beginning at the physiological level and proceeding up through safety, social, esteem, and self-actualizing levels and suggesting that any need level, when fully satisfied, can no longer be a powerful motivator. Maslow also published *Eupsychian Management*, which received little acclaim in the 1960s but has been republished (with additional material from a variety of his admirers) as *Maslow on Management.* In this book, Maslow lays out the underlying assumptions for a eupsychian (humanistic) organization. Maslow taught at Brooklyn College and Brandeis University and, while writing his final book, was an in-depth observer of worker behaviors at the Non-Linear Systems plant in Del Mar, California. For an illustration of Maslow's enduring impact on management, see Chip Conley's recent book, *Peak: How Great Companies Get Their Mojo from Maslow.*

Stephen R. Covey was a well-known speaker, author of several books, and chief executive officer (CEO) of the Franklin Covey Company prior to his death in 2012. His first book, *The Seven Habits of Highly Effective People*, remains on best-seller lists and has sold over 20 million copies across the world. In it, he offers a series of prescriptions to guide managers as they chart their courses in turbulent times. Drawn from his extensive review of the "success literature," Covey urges people to develop a character ethic based on seven key habits: people being proactive, identifying their values, disciplining themselves to work on high-priority items, seeking win–win solutions, listening with empathy, synergizing with others, and engaging in extensive reading and studying for self-development.

Covey has also published *The Seven Habits of Highly Effective Families*, which adapts the basic effectiveness principles and applies them to families. *First Things First* urges people to manage their time and life well so as to achieve goals consistent with their values. His book *Principle-Centered Leadership* identifies seven human attributes—self-awareness, imagination, willpower, an abundance mentality, courage, creativity, and self-renewal—that, when combined with eight key behaviors (e.g., priority on service, radiating positive energy), help produce effective and principled leaders. His other books include *Living the Seven Habits, The 8th Habit, Reflections for Highly Effective People, Everyday Greatness, Predictable Results in Unpredictable Times*, and *Great Work, Great Career.* Covey's son and colleague, Stephen M. R. Covey, has followed in his father's footsteps by publishing *The Speed of Trust.*

Peter M. Senge is the director of the Systems Thinking and Organizational Learning Program at MIT's Sloan School of Management. His book *The Fifth Discipline* emphasizes the importance of organizations developing the capacity to engage in effective learning. Senge identifies and discusses a set of disabilities that are fatal to organizations, especially those operating in rapidly changing environments. The fifth discipline—systems thinking—is presented as the cornerstone for the learning organization. Personal mastery, mental models, shared vision, and team learning are presented as the core disciplines and the focus for building the learning organization. Senge has also published *The Fifth Discipline Fieldbook* and *The Dance of Change.*

Michael E. Porter, a Harvard Business School faculty member and holder of the Bishop Lawrence University Professorship, continues to make contributions to our understanding of organizations and their competitive strategies. He received the 1986 George R. Terry book award for his book *Competitive Advantage*, which was published in 1985. *Competitive Advantage* was a follow-up to his earlier book *Competitive*

Strategy. Porter is also the author of *Competitive Advantage of Nations.* He has argued that firms can achieve above-average profits by synthesizing and applying their unique strengths effectively within their industry. They can do this either through creating a cost advantage or by differentiating a product or service from that of their competitors. The key, which some firms seemingly ignore, is to link strategy formulation successfully with strategy implementation. Porter encouraged managers to study their industry in depth, select a course of competitive advantage, develop a set of strategies that adapt the firm to its external environment, and draw on their executive leadership talents.

In *Competitive Advantage,* Porter provides insight into the complexity of industry competition by identifying five underlying forces. Low cost, differentiation, and focus are presented as generic strategies for the strategic positioning of a firm within its industry. The popularity of this book is revealed by its widespread adoption by managers and academics, as it has undergone its 16th printing in English and translation into 17 languages. Interested readers might wish to explore "An Interview with Michael Porter" by Nicholas Argyres and Anita M. McGahan in the *Academy of Management Executive,* 2002, 16:2, pp. 43–52, or Joan Magretta's book, *Understanding Michael Porter: The Essential Guide to Competition and Strategy* (2011).

1

The Practice of Management

Peter F. Drucker

Summary Prepared by John D. Stavig and Shaker A. Zahra

John D. Stavig is the Professional Director of the Center for Entrepreneurial Studies at the Carlson School of Management, University of Minnesota. He holds a B.S.B. from the Carlson School and an M.B.A. from the Wharton School. John has over 15 years of experience in management consulting, private equity, and industry. As a founding principal of a $100 million private equity fund, he sourced and managed investments in numerous early-stage communications firms. John also served as CEO, CFO, and board member for several start-up and early-stage technology firms, and led numerous investments, acquisitions, and divestitures. As a principal at Gemini Consulting and Arthur Andersen, he provided strategic and financial consulting services to senior executives in Fortune 1000 firms throughout the world. John has also taught in the M.B.A. program at the University of St. Thomas.

Shaker A. Zahra is the Robert E. Buuck Chair of Entrepreneurship and Professor of Strategy at the Carlson School of Management at the University of Minnesota. He is also the Codirector of the Center for Entrepreneurial Studies and Codirector of the Integrative Leadership Center. His research has appeared in leading journals. He has also published or edited 10 books. His research has received several major awards. He is the Chair for the Entrepreneurship Division of the Academy of Management. His teaching, research, and service activities have received several awards.

Management is the brain of an enterprise and the primary source of long-term differentiation between firms. It is the disciplined and integrated practice of managing business, managers, workers, and work. It is also the creative process that drives **innovation** (the process of transforming discoveries into products, goods, and services) and entrepreneurship in a company. Management is entrusted with the responsibility for directing resources for the attainment of profits and the betterment of society.

Management is a practice, rather than an exact science or profession. As such, it requires judgment. *Management represents a systematic and fluid process of establishing and pursuing shared objectives for the enterprise, managers, and workers.* The role of management is to create a customer and organize the firm's resources toward the attainment of shared objectives. Managers must live in both the present and the future by balancing often-conflicting objectives.

Peter F. Drucker. *The Practice of Management.* New York: Harper & Row Publishers, Inc., 1954.

They need also to develop and maintain the logical linkages among strategy, objectives, and incentives throughout the enterprise.

The quality and performance of management are the only sustainable advantages for a business. A business is a social institution, created and managed by people. Rather than adapting to external conditions, management is creative and forward looking. It is the proactive creator of economic growth by deliberate action. Managing a business must always be entrepreneurial, focusing on creating customers through innovation and marketing. Management drives continued improvements and avoids inertia.

A CONCEPT OF THE FIRM

Organizations—and their managers—should be:

- Outward looking—both influenced by and shaping their external environment.
- A social institution—created by people; contributing to society.
- Pursuing multiple goals—both financial and nonfinancial.
- Innovative—emphasizing creativity, innovation, and entrepreneurship.
- Focused—answering and aligning resources to the question, *What is our primary business?*
- Spirited—creating self-controlled and motivated managers.

Management has important economic and social responsibilities. Though economic performance is the first priority and management must make a profit to cover its risk premium, it must also consider the impact of its policies and decisions on society.

Advances in technology and automation will challenge managerial capabilities. These advances will lead to a more highly skilled workforce and the growth of **knowledge workers** (employees with high levels of education, skills, and competencies) and create demand for managers with better capabilities to lead these employees. Rank-and-file jobs will become increasingly managerial, resulting in a displacement of jobs, rather than replacement. Properly executed, the application and management of automation will drive productivity and wealth creation.

THE JOBS OF MANAGEMENT

Determining the Business and Purpose

Management's first responsibility is to answer the question, *What is our business?* This is a challenging question that requires deliberate analysis based upon a thorough understanding of who the customers are, what they're actually buying, and what they value. Customers must be the foundation of the business, based upon the value they receive. Forward-looking companies seek to assess market potential and structure and introduce innovations that deliver value to customers, a process that determines what the business should be long term. Therefore, a company's entrepreneurial functions of innovation and marketing must cut across the entire business in order to satisfy customer needs. Customer satisfaction should be a company's primary goal. Profit is not the purpose of business, but rather a test of the validity of the business. *A firm's objective cannot simply be profit maximization.*

Setting and Measuring Progress Against the Objectives of a Business

Fundamental to the management of the business is the development of shared objectives. This must be derived from a creative and fluid process of deliberate goal setting. Objectives are required in every area of the business where performance impacts the survival and success of the business. Objectives determine what action to take today to obtain results tomorrow. Objectives must be forward looking, and management should anticipate the future and be prepared to respond. Deliberate emphasis on innovation in setting objectives can be most valuable in areas where it appears less obvious. Management must implement regular, systematic, and unbiased measurements against set objectives, ideally based on feedback from the customer. Objectives should include areas of manager performance and development, worker performance and attitudes, and social responsibility. **Social responsibility** is simply the contribution a firm makes to its society. To some, this means making a profit, whereas others expect the firm to do more than this by ameliorating social problems. Setting objectives to improve worker performance and attitudes is one of the greatest challenges for management.

Balancing objectives across the different parts of a business is a critical role of management and requires judgment. Objectives can be changing, conflicting, intangible, and of differing duration. Objectives must be balanced based on organizational priorities and timing. A balanced set of objectives can serve as the "instrument panel" for piloting business.

Managing Managers by Objectives

Managers are the basic resource of business. They depreciate the fastest and require the greatest nourishment. **Management by objectives (MBO)** is the process in which employees set goals, justify them, determine resources needed to accomplish them, and establish timetables for their completion. These goals reflect the overall objectives of the organization. MBO develops individual responsibility toward a common direction. For an enterprise to grow beyond a single leader, an organized and integrated team that focuses on shared objectives is needed. Also required is the regular, systematic, and unbiased measurement of performance and the results against established objectives.

Being a manager means sharing in the responsibility for the enterprise. Every manager should responsibly participate in the development of the objectives in the unit he or she works for. Objectives must be clear and specific. They should be balanced and incorporate short- and long-term, tangible and intangible objectives. Objectives must be measurable—clear, simple, rational, relevant, reliable, and understandable.

Using MBO, emphasis on teamwork and shared goals should occur at every level of management. To ensure cooperation, individual managers should be measured on the following: performance from the individual unit, contribution to help other units achieve their objectives, and contribution expected from other units. MBO fosters self-control and motivation. This requires managers to convert objectives into personal goals, enabling them to direct, measure, and motivate themselves. To be in control and motivated, a manager's job should have the following characteristics: clear and measurable contribution to the success of the enterprise; directed and controlled by objectives, rather than the boss; broad scope and authority—decisions pushed down as far as possible; and duty to assist subordinates and peer managers to attain their objectives.

Productively Utilizing All Resources

Management is responsible for the productive utilization of all resources to meet overall objectives. It should create a desired balance between all factors of production that will give the greatest output for the smallest effort. Productivity must incorporate both direct labor and managerial talent, because management is the scarcest and most expensive resource in the organization. Management should be the creative driver of increased productivity, rather than parasitical overhead. Companies should focus on increasing contributed value and the proportion of this value retained as profit.

Management should also understand company capabilities and consider outsourcing certain activities, even if potentially profitable. By evaluating this process mix, management will focus its resources on the activities that the company is best at performing, enabling it to create the most value for its customers.

Fostering a Positive Spirit

The spirit of the organization determines the motivation of its managers. It must be built on integrity and demonstrated by the actions of its leaders. Excellence and continuous improvement of the performance of the whole group must be encouraged, recognized, and rewarded. Managerial focus should underscore strengths, not weaknesses. Recognition, promotion, and financial incentives need to be tied to objectives and team performance. A positive spirit prepares a person for leadership, enabling the execution of objectives and the attainment of superior results.

Developing Managers

Managers are the firm's scarcest and most expensive resource. Management must challenge employees at all levels to pursue self-development to meet future managerial requirements. Although management should encourage and direct the development of employees, the responsibility for development must remain with the subordinate manager. This development should place a large number of individuals in positions with general management responsibility across the business, rather than in a rotational program that promotes functional specialization for a select few. It is imperative that management create the opportunities and test the ability of its future managers to run and lead a whole business long before they reach the top.

Management of the Worker and Work

A key role for management is to define the nature of work, create a stimulating work environment, set standards, and train employees to assume progressively higher and more challenging responsibilities. Work should be rewarding—both financially and psychologically—in order to improve productivity.

Structure of Management

The **management structure** of an organization—the way managers divide, share, coordinate, and evaluate the work they do in planning and organizing the firm's overall operations—must facilitate the achievement of its objectives. *Structure does not always create good performance, but it can certainly inhibit results.* The structure should be flat, simple, and focused on performance. In determining the appropriate structure, management should consider the following: What activities are needed to achieve objectives? What decisions, and at what level, are necessary to achieve objectives? To what degree are activities and decisions interdependent?

Management structure should focus on business performance and results, contain the least possible number of levels, and enable the training and testing of future managers. When possible, autonomous product businesses are superior in meeting these requirements. A functional organization, even when decentralized, encourages specialization at the expense of company-wide perspective, adds unnecessary levels of management, and limits the development of future general managers.

2

The One Minute Manager

Kenneth Blanchard and Spencer Johnson
Summary Prepared by Charles C. Manz

Charles C. Manz is a Professor of Management at the University of Massachusetts at Amherst. He holds a doctorate in Organizational Behavior from Pennsylvania State University. His professional publications and presentations concern topics such as self-leadership, vicarious learning, self-managed work groups, leadership, power and control, and group processes. He is the author of the book *The Art of Self-Leadership* and coauthor of *The Leadership Wisdom of Jesus*.

The most distinguishing characteristic of *The One Minute Manager* by Kenneth Blanchard and Spencer Johnson is its major philosophical theme: Good management does not take a lot of time. This dominant theme seems to be based on two underlying premises: (1) *Quality* of time spent with subordinates (as with one's children) is more important than quantity; and (2) in the end, people (subordinates) should really be managing themselves.

The book is built around a story that provides an occasion for learning about effective management. The story centers on the quest of "a young man" to find an effective manager. In his search he finds all kinds of managers, but very few that he considers effective. According to the story, the young man finds primarily two kinds of managers. One type is a hard-nosed manager who is concerned with the bottom line (profit) and tends to be directive in style. With this type of manager, the young man believes, the organization tends to win at the expense of the subordinates. The other type of manager is one who is concerned more about the employees than about performance. This "nice" kind of manager seems to allow the employees to win at the expense of the organization. In contrast to these two types of managers, the book suggests, an effective manager (as seen through the eyes of the young man) is one who manages so that both the organization and the people involved benefit (win).

The dilemma that the young man faces is that the few managers who do seem to be effective will not share their secrets. That is only true until he meets the "One Minute Manager." It turns out that this almost legendary manager is not only willing to share the secrets of his effectiveness but is so available that he is able to meet almost any time the young man wants to meet, except at the time of his weekly two-hour meeting with his subordinates. After an initial meeting with the one-minute manager, the young man is sent off to talk to his subordinates to learn, directly from those affected, the secrets of one-minute management. Thus the story

Kenneth Blanchard and Spencer Johnson. *The One Minute Manager*. La Jolla, CA: Blanchard-Johnson Publishers, 1981.

begins, and in the remaining pages, the wisdom, experience, and management strategies of the one-minute manager are revealed as the authors communicate, through him and his subordinates, their view on effective management practice.

In addition to general philosophical management advice (e.g., managers can reap good results from their subordinates without expending much time), the book suggests that effective management means that both the organization and its employees win, and that people will do better work when they feel good about themselves; it also offers some specific prescriptions. These prescriptions center around three primary management techniques that have been addressed in the management literature for years: goal setting, positive reinforcement in the form of praise, and verbal reprimand. The authors suggest that applications of each of the techniques can be accomplished in very little time, in fact in as little as one minute (hence the strategies are labeled "one-minute goals," "one-minute praisings," and "one-minute reprimands"). The suggestions made in the book for effective use of each of these strategies will be summarized in the following sections.

ONE-MINUTE GOALS

One-minute goals clarify responsibilities and the nature of performance standards. Without them, employees will not know what is expected of them, being left instead to grope in the dark for what they ought to be doing. A great deal of research and writing has been done on the importance of goals in reaching a level of performance (c.f., Locke, Shaw, Saari, and Latham, 1981). The advice offered in *The One Minute Manager* regarding effective use of performance goals is quite consistent with the findings of this previous work. Specifically, the authors point out through one of the one-minute manager's subordinates that effective use of one-minute goals includes the following:

- agreement between the manager and subordinate regarding what needs to be done;
- recording of each goal on a single page in no more than 250 words that can be read by almost anyone in less than a minute;
- communication of clear performance standards regarding what is expected of subordinates regarding each goal; and
- continuous review of each goal, current performance, and the difference between the two.

These components are presented with a heavy emphasis on having employees use them to manage themselves. This point is driven home as the employee who shares this part of one-minute management recalls how the one-minute manager taught him about one-minute goals. In the recounted story, the one-minute manager refuses to take credit for having solved a problem of the subordinate and is in fact irritated by the very idea of getting credit for it. He insists that the subordinate solved his own problem and orders him to go out and start solving his own future problems without taking up the one-minute manager's time.

ONE-MINUTE PRAISING

The next employee encountered by the young man shares with him the secrets of one-minute praising. Again, the ideas presented regarding this technique pretty well parallel research findings on the use of positive reinforcement (c.f., Luthans and Kreitner, 1986). One basic suggestion for this technique is that managers should spend their time trying to catch subordinates doing something *right* rather than doing something wrong. In order to facilitate this, the one-minute manager monitors new employees closely at first and has them keep detailed records of their progress (which he reviews). When the manager is able to discover something that the employee is doing right, the occasion is set for one-minute praising (positive reinforcement). The specific components suggested for applying this technique include the following:

- letting others know that you are going to let them know how they are doing;
- praising positive performance as soon as possible after it has occurred, letting employees know specifically what they did right and how good you feel about it;
- allowing the message that you really feel good about their performance to sink in for a moment, and encouraging them to do the same; and
- using a handshake or other form of touch when it is appropriate (more on this later).

Again, these steps are described with a significant self-management flavor. The employee points out that after working for a manager like this for a while you start catching yourself doing things right and using self-praise.

ONE-MINUTE REPRIMANDS

The final employee that the young man visits tells him about one-minute reprimands. This potentially more somber subject is presented in a quite positive tone. In fact, the employee begins by pointing out that she often praises herself and sometimes asks the one-minute manager for a praising when she has done something well. But she goes on to explain that when she has done something wrong, the one-minute manager is quick to respond, letting her know exactly what she has done wrong and how he feels about it. After the reprimand is over, he proceeds to tell her how competent he thinks she really is, essentially praising her as a *person* despite rejecting the undesired *behavior*. Specifically, the book points out that one-minute reprimands should include the following:

- let people know that you will, in a frank manner, communicate to them how they are doing;
- reprimand poor performance as soon as possible, telling people exactly what they did wrong and how you feel about it (followed by a pause allowing the message to sink in);
- reaffirm how valuable you feel the employees are, using touch if appropriate, while making it clear that it is their *performance* that is unacceptable in this situation; and
- make sure that when the reprimand episode is over it is over.

OTHER ISSUES AND RELATED MANAGEMENT TECHNIQUES

Good management does not take a lot of time; it just takes wise application of three proven management strategies—one-minute goals, one-minute praisings, and one-minute reprimands. Beyond this, the book deals with some other issues relevant to these strategies, such as "under what conditions is physical touch appropriate?" The authors suggest that the use of appropriate touch can be helpful when you know the person well and wish to help that person succeed. It should be done so that you are giving something to the person such as encouragement or support, not taking something away.

The authors also address the issue of manipulation, suggesting that employees should be informed about, and agree to, the manager's use of one-minute management. The key is to be honest and open in the use of this approach. They also deal briefly with several other issues. For example, Blanchard and Johnson suggest that it is important to move a subordinate gradually to perform a new desired behavior by reinforcing approximations to the behavior until it is finally successfully performed. The technical term for this is "shaping." A person's behavior is shaped by continuously praising improvements rather than waiting until a person completely performs correctly. If a manager waits until a new employee completely performs correctly, the employee may well give up long before successful performance is achieved because of the absence of reinforcement along the way.

The strategies can also be substituted for one another when appropriate. With new employees, for instance, dealing with low performance should focus on goal setting and then trying to catch them doing something right rather than using reprimand. Because a new employee's lack of experience likely produces an insufficient confidence level, this makes reprimand inappropriate, whereas goal setting and praise can be quite effective. The authors also suggest that if a manager is going to be tough on a person, the manager is better off being tough first and then being supportive, rather than the other way around.

Eventually, at the end of the story, the young man is hired by the one-minute manager and over time becomes a seasoned one-minute manager himself. As he looks back over his experiences, he recognizes numerous benefits of the one-minute management approach—more results in less time, time to think and plan, less stress and better health, similar benefits experienced by subordinates, and reduced absenteeism and turnover.

Conclusion

The bottom-line message is that effective management requires that you care sincerely about people but have definite expectations that are expressed openly about their behavior. Also, one thing that is even more valuable than learning to be a one-minute manager is having one for a boss, which in the end means you really work for yourself. And finally, these management techniques are not a competitive advantage to be hoarded but a gift to be shared with others. This is true because, in the end, the one who shares the gift will be at least as richly rewarded as the one who receives it.

Notes

1. Locke, E., K. Shaw, L. Saari, and G. Latham. "Goal Setting and Task Performance 1969–1980." *Psychological Bulletin,* 1981, 90, 125–152.
2. Luthans, F., and T. Davis. "Behavioral Self-management (BSM): The Missing Link in Managerial Effectiveness." *Organizational Dynamics,* 1979, 8, 42–60.
3. Luthans, F., and R. Kreitner. *Organizational Behavior Modification and Beyond.* Glenview, IL: Scott, Foresman and Co., 1986.
4. Manz, C. C. *The Art of Self-Leadership: Strategies for Personal Effectiveness in Your Life and Work.* Upper Saddle River, NJ: Prentice Hall, 1983.
5. Manz, C. C. "Self-Leadership: Toward an Expanded Theory of Self-influence Processes in Organizations." *Academy of Management Review,* 1986, 11, 585–600.
6. Manz, C. C., and H. P. Sims, Jr. "Self-Management as a Substitute for Leadership: A Social Learning Theory Perspective." *Academy of Management Review,* 1980, 5, 361–367.

3

Out of the Crisis

W. Edwards Deming

Summary Prepared by William B. Gartner and M. James Naughton

William B. Gartner is a professor at Georgetown University.

M. James Naughton is the owner of Expert-Knowledge Systems, Inc.

Deming provides an ambitious objective for his book when he begins by saying:

> The aim of this book is transformation of the style of American management. Transformation of American style of management is not a job of reconstruction, nor is it revision. It requires a whole new structure, from foundation upward. *Mutation* might be the word, except that *mutation* implies unordered spontaneity. Transformation must take place with directed effort.

Few individuals have had as much positive impact on the world economy as Dr. W. Edwards Deming. With the broadcast of the NBC white paper "If Japan Can, Why Can't We?" on June 24, 1980, Dr. Deming gained national exposure as the man responsible for the managerial theory that has governed Japan's transformation into a nation of world leaders in the production of high-quality goods. This transformation did not happen overnight. Since 1950, when Dr. Deming first spoke to Japan's top managers on the improvement of quality, Japanese organizations have pioneered in the adaptation of Dr. Deming's ideas.

As a result of his seminars, Japan has had an annual national competition for quality improvement (the Deming Prize) since 1951. Japan has numerous journals and books devoted to exploring and furthering the implications of Deming's theory. However, it has only been within the last few years that numerous books have been published in the United States on "the Deming Theory of Management." An overview of the ideas that underlie Deming's theory, which cut across all major topical areas in management, will be provided here.

DISEASES AND OBSTACLES

Deming's book is not merely about productivity and quality control; it is a broad vision of the nature of organizations and how organizations should be changed. Deming identifies a set of chronic ailments that can plague any organization and limit its success. These, which he calls

W. Edwards Deming. *Out of the Crisis.* Cambridge, MA: MIT Press, 1986.

"deadly diseases," include an overemphasis on short-term profits, human resource practices that encourage both managers and employees to be mobile and not organizationally loyal, merit ratings and review systems that are based on fear of one's supervisor, an absence of a single driving purpose, and management that is based on visible figures alone.

The reason that managers are not as effective as they could be is that they are the prisoners of some structural characteristics and personal assumptions that prevent their success. Among the obstacles that Deming discusses are the insulation of top management from the other employees in the organization, lack of adequate technical knowledge, a long history of total reliance on final inspection as a way of ensuring a quality product, the managerial belief that all problems originate within the workforce, a reliance on meeting specifications, and the failure to synthesize human operators with computer systems for control.

THE CONCEPT OF VARIABILITY

The basis for Deming's theory is the observation that variability exists everywhere in everything. *Only through the study and analysis of variability, using statistics, can a phenomenon be understood well enough to manipulate and change it.* In many respects, using statistics is not very radical. Statistics are fundamental to nearly all academic research. But Deming asks that the right kind of statistics (analytical) be applied to our everyday lives as well. And that is the rub. To recognize the pervasiveness of variability and to function so that the sources of this variability can be defined and measured are radical. In Deming's world, the use of statistical thinking is not an academic game; it is a way of life.

The concept of variability is to management theory and practice what the concept of the germ theory of disease was to the development of modern medicine. Medicine had been "successfully" practiced without the knowledge of germs. In a pregerm theory paradigm, some patients got better, some got worse, and some stayed the same; in each case, some rationale could be used to explain the outcome. With the emergence of germ theory, all medical phenomena took on new meanings. Medical procedures thought to be good practice, such as physicians attending women in birth, turned out to be causes of disease because of the septic condition of the physicians' hands. Instead of rendering improved health care, the physicians' germ-laden hands achieved the opposite result. One can imagine the first proponents of the germ theory telling their colleagues who were still ignorant of the theory to wash their hands between patients. The pioneers must have sounded crazy. In the same vein, managers and academics who do not have a thorough understanding of variability will fail to grasp the radical change in thought that Deming envisions. Deming's propositions may seem as simplistic as "wash your hands!" rather than an entirely new paradigm of profound challenges to present-day managerial thinking and behaviors.

An illustration of variability that is widely cited in the books on Deming's theory is the "red bead experiment." Dr. Deming, at his four-day seminar, asks for 10 volunteers from the attendees. Six of the students become workers, two become inspectors of the workers' production, one becomes the inspector of the inspectors' work, and one becomes the recorder. Dr. Deming mixes together 3,000 white beads and 750 red beads in a large box. He instructs the workers to scoop out beads from the box with a beveled paddle that scoops out 50 beads at a time. Each scoop of the paddle is treated as a day's production. Only white beads are acceptable. Red beads are defects. After each worker scoops a paddle of beads from the box, the two inspectors count the defects, the inspector of the inspectors inspects the inspectors' count, and the recorder writes down the inspectors' agreed-upon number of defects. Invariably, each worker's scoop contains some red beads. Deming plays the role of the manager by exhorting the workers to produce no defects. When a worker scoops few red beads, he may be praised. Scooping many red beads brings criticism and an exhortation to do better, otherwise "we will go out of business." The manager reacts to each scoop of beads as if it had meaning in itself rather than as part of a pattern.

Dr. Deming's statistical analysis of the workers' production indicates that the process of producing white beads is in statistical control; that is, the variability of this production system is stable. The near-term prediction about the *pattern,* but not the individual draws, of the system's performance can be made. Near-future draws will yield an average, over many experiments, of 9.4 red beads. Any one draw may range between 1 and 18 red beads. In other words, the actual number of red beads scooped by each worker is out of that worker's control. The worker, as Dr. Deming says, "is only delivering the defects." Management, which controls the system, has caused the defects through design of the system. There are a number of insights people draw from this experiment. Walton lists the following:

- Variation is part of any process.
- Planning requires prediction of how things and people will perform. Tests and experiments of past performance can be useful, but not definitive.
- Workers work within a system that—try as they might—is beyond their control. It is the system, not their individual skills, that determines how they perform.
- Only management can change the system.
- Some workers will always be above average, some below.[1]

The red bead experiment illustrates the behavior of systems of stable variability. In Deming's theory, a system is all of the aspects of the organization and environment—employees, managers, equipment, facilities, government, customers, suppliers, shareholders, and so forth—fitted together, with the aim of producing some type of output. Stability implies that the output has regularity to it, so that predictions regarding the output of the system can be made. But many of these systems are inherently unstable. Bringing a system into stability is one of the fundamental managerial activities in the Deming theory.

In Deming's theory, a stable system, that is, a system that shows signs of being in statistical control, behaves in a manner similar to the red bead experiment. In systems, a single datum point is of little use in understanding the causes that influenced the production of that point. It is necessary to withhold judgment about changes in the output of the system until sufficient evidence (additional data points) becomes available to suggest whether or not the system being examined is stable. Statistical theory provides tools to help evaluate the stability of systems. Once a system is stable, its productive capability can be determined; that is, the average output of the system and the spread of variability around that average can be described. This can be used to predict the near-term future behavior of the system.

The inefficiencies inherent in "not knowing what we are doing," that is, in working with systems not in statistical control, might not seem to be that great a competitive penalty if all organizations are similarly out of control. Yet we are beginning to realize that the quality of outputs from organizations that are managed using Deming's theory are many magnitudes beyond what non-Deming organizations have been producing. The differences in quality and productivity can be mind boggling.

For example, both Scherkenbach[2] and Walton[3] reported that when the Ford Motor Company began using transmissions produced by the Japanese automobile manufacturer Mazda, Ford found that customers overwhelmingly preferred cars with Mazda transmissions to cars with Ford-manufactured transmissions—because the warranty repairs were 10 times lower, and the cars were quieter and shifted more smoothly. When Ford engineers compared their transmissions to the Mazda transmissions, they found that the piece-to-piece variation in the Mazda transmissions was nearly three times less than in the Ford pieces. Both Ford and Mazda conformed to the engineering standards specified by Ford, but Mazda transmissions were far more uniform. More uniform products also cost less to manufacture. With less variability there is less rework and less need for inspection. Only systems in statistical control can begin to reduce variability and thereby improve the quality and quantity of their output. Both authors reported that after Ford began to implement Deming's theory over the next five years, warranty repair frequencies dropped by 45 percent and "things gone wrong" reports from customers dropped by 50 percent.

FOURTEEN STEPS MANAGEMENT MUST TAKE

The task of transformation of an entire organization to use the Deming theory becomes an enormous burden for management, and Deming frequently suggests that this process is likely to take a minimum of 10 years. The framework for transforming an organization is outlined in the 14 points (pp. 23–24):

1. Create constancy of purpose toward improvement of product and service, aiming to become competitive, to stay in business, and to provide jobs.
2. Adopt the new philosophy. We are in a new economic age. Western management must awaken to the challenge, must learn their responsibilities, and must take on leadership in order to bring about change.
3. Cease dependence on inspection to achieve quality. Eliminate the need for inspection on a mass basis by building quality into the product in the first place.
4. End the practice of awarding business on the basis of the price tag. Instead, minimize total cost. Move toward a single supplier for any one time and develop long-term relationships of loyalty and trust with that supplier.
5. Improve constantly and forever the systems of production and service in order to improve quality and productivity. Thus, one constantly decreases costs.
6. Institute training on the job.
7. Institute leadership. Supervisors should be able to help people to do a better job, and they should use machines and gadgets wisely. Supervision of management and supervision of production workers need to be overhauled.
8. Drive out fear, so that everyone may work effectively for the company.
9. Break down barriers between departments. People in research, design, sales, and production must work as a team. They should foresee production problems and problems that could be encountered when using the product or service.
10. Eliminate slogans, exhortations, and targets that demand zero defects and new levels of productivity. These only create adversarial relationships because frequently the cause of low quality and low productivity is the system, and not the workforce.
11. a. Eliminate work standards (quotas) on the factory floor. Substitute leadership.
    b. Eliminate **management by objectives**. Eliminate management by numbers or numerical goals. Substitute leadership.

12. **a.** Remove barriers that rob hourly workers of their right to pride of workmanship. The responsibility of supervisors must be changed from sheer numbers to quality.

    b. Remove barriers that rob people in management and in engineering of their right to pride of workmanship. This means, *inter alia,* abolishing the annual merit rating and management by objectives.

13. Institute a vigorous program of education and self-improvement.

14. Put everybody in the company to work to accomplish the transformation. The transformation is everybody's job.

As mentioned earlier, these 14 points should not be treated as a list of aphorisms, nor can each of them be treated separately without recognizing the interrelationships among them.

Conclusions

Out of the Crisis is full of examples and ideas, and Deming calls for a radical revision of American management practice. To his credit, Deming constantly recognizes ideas and examples from individuals practicing various aspects of his theory. This constant recognition of other individuals provides a subtle indication that a body of practitioners exists that has had successful experiences applying his 14 steps and other ideas.

A transformation in American management needs to occur; it can take place, and it has begun already in those firms applying Deming's theory. Deming offers a new paradigm for the practice of management that requires a dramatic rethinking and replacement of old methods by those trained in traditional management techniques. In conclusion, Deming recognizes that "it takes courage to admit that you have been doing something wrong, to admit that you have something to learn, that there is a better way."[4]

Notes

1. William B. Gartner and M. James Naughton, "The Deming Theory of Management," *Academy of Management Review,* January 1988, 138–142.

2. William W. Scherkenbach. *The Deming Route to Quality and Productivity: Roadmaps and Roadblocks.* Milwaukee, WI: ASQC, 1986.

3. Mary Walton. *The Deming Management Method.* New York: Dodd, Mead & Company, 1986.

4. Walton, *The Deming Management Method,* p. 223.

4   The Human Side of Enterprise

Douglas McGregor
Summary Prepared by Gayle Porter

Gayle Porter obtained her doctorate from the Ohio State University in Organizational Behavior and Human Resource Management and is now at Rutgers University—Camden. Articles and ongoing research interests include the effects of dispositional differences in the workplace; group perceptions of efficacy and esteem; and the comparison of influence on employees through reward systems, leadership, and employee development efforts. Her prior experience includes positions as Director of Curriculum Development for a human resource management degree program; consultant on training programs, financial operations, and computer applications; financial manager for an oil and gas production company; and financial specialist for NCR Corporation.

The Human Side of Enterprise was written during an ongoing comparative study of management development programs in several large companies. In McGregor's view, the making of managers has less to do with formal efforts in development than with how the task of management is understood within that organization. This fundamental understanding determines the policies and procedures within which managers operate and guide the selection of people identified as having the potential for management positions. During the late 1950s, McGregor believed that major industrial advances of the next half-century would occur on the human side of enterprise, and he was intrigued by the inconsistent assumptions about what makes managers behave as they do. His criticism of the conventional assumptions, which he labels Theory X, is that they limit options. Theory Y provides an alternative set of assumptions that are much needed due to the extent of unrealized human potential in most organizations.

THE THEORETICAL ASSUMPTIONS OF MANAGEMENT

Regardless of the economic success of a firm, few managers are satisfied with their ability to predict and control the behavior of members of the organization. Effective prediction and control are central to the task of management, and there can be no prediction without some underlying theory. Therefore, *all managerial decisions and actions rest on a personally held theory, a set of assumptions about behavior.* The assumptions management holds about controlling its human resources determine the whole character of the enterprise.

Douglas McGregor. *The Human Side of Enterprise.* New York: McGraw-Hill, 1960.

In application, problems occur related to these assumptions. First, managers may not realize that they hold and apply conflicting ideas and that one may cancel out the other. For example, a manager may delegate based on the assumption that employees should have responsibility, but then nullify that action by close monitoring, which indicates the belief that employees can't handle the responsibility. Another problem is failure to view control as **selective adaptation**, when dealing with human behavior. People adjust to certain natural laws in other fields; for example, engineers don't dig channels and expect water to run uphill! With humans, however, there is a tendency to try to control in direct violation of human nature. Then, when they fail to achieve the desired results, they look for every other possible cause rather than examine the inappropriate choice of a method to control behavior.

Any influence is based on dependence, so the nature and degree of dependence are critical factors in determining what methods of control will be effective. Conventional organization theory is based on authority as a key premise. It is the central and indispensable means of managerial control and recognizes only upward dependence. In recent decades, workers have become less dependent on a single employer, and society has provided certain safeguards related to unemployment. This limits the upward dependence and, correspondingly, the ability to control by authority alone. In addition, employees have the ability to engage in countermeasures such as slowdowns, lowered standards of performance, or even sabotage to defeat authority they resent.

Organizations are more accurately represented as systems of **interdependence**. Subordinates depend on managers to help them meet their needs, but managers also depend on subordinates to achieve their own and the organization's goals. Although there is nothing inherently bad or wrong in the use of authority to control, in certain circumstances it fails to bring the desired results. Circumstances change even from hour to hour, and the role of the manager is to select the appropriate means of influence based on the situation at a given point in time. If employees exhibit lazy, indifferent behavior, the causes lie in management methods of organization and control.

Theory X is a term used to represent a set of assumptions. Principles found in traditional management literature could only have derived from assumptions such as the following, which have had a major impact on managerial strategy in organizations:

1. The average human being has an inherent dislike of work and will avoid it if possible.
2. Because of this human characteristic of dislike of work, most people must be coerced, controlled, directed, and threatened with punishment to get them to put forth adequate effort toward the achievement of organizational objectives.
3. The average human being prefers to be directed, wishes to avoid responsibility, has relatively little ambition, and wants security above all.

These assumptions are not without basis, or they would never have persisted as they have. They do explain some observed human behavior, but other observations are not consistent with this view. Theory X assumptions also encourage us to categorize certain behaviors as human nature, when they may actually be symptoms of a condition in which workers have been deprived of an opportunity to satisfy higher-order needs (social and egoistic needs).

A strong tradition exists of viewing employment as an employee's agreement to accept control by others in exchange for rewards that are only of value outside the workplace. For example, wages (except for status differences), vacation, medical benefits, stock purchase plans, and profit sharing are of little value during the actual time on the job. Work is the necessary evil to endure for rewards away from the job. In this conception of human resources we can never discover, let alone utilize, the potentialities of the average human being.

Many efforts to provide more equitable and generous treatment to employees and to provide a safe and pleasant work environment have been designed without any real change in strategy. Very often what is proposed as a new management strategy is nothing more than a different tactic within the old Theory X assumptions. Organizations have progressively made available the means to satisfy lower-order needs for subsistence and safety. As the nature of the dependency relationship changes, management has gradually deprived itself of the opportunity to use control based solely on assumptions of Theory X. A new strategy is needed.

Theory Y assumptions are dynamic, indicate the possibility of human growth and development, and stress the necessity for selective adaptation:

1. The expenditure of physical and mental effort in work is as natural as play or rest.
2. External control and the threat of punishment are not the only means for bringing about effort toward organizational objectives. People will exercise self-direction and self-control in the service of objectives to which they are committed.
3. Commitment to objectives is a function of the rewards associated with their achievement (*satisfaction of ego and self-actualization needs can be products of effort directed toward organizational objectives*).
4. The average human being learns, under proper conditions, not only to accept but also to seek responsibility.
5. The capacity to exercise a relatively high degree of imagination, ingenuity, and creativity in the solution of organizational problems is widely, not narrowly, distributed in the population.
6. Under the conditions of modern industrial life, the intellectual potentialities of the average human being are only partially utilized.

The Theory Y assumptions challenge a number of deeply ingrained managerial habits of thought and action; they lead to a management philosophy of integration and self-control. Theory X assumes that the organization's requirements take precedence over the needs of the individual members, and that the worker must always adjust to the needs of the organization as management perceives them. In contrast, the principle of *integration* proposes that conditions can be created such that individuals can best achieve their own goals by directing their efforts toward the success of the enterprise. Based on the premise that the assumptions of Theory Y are valid, the next logical question is whether, and to what extent, such conditions can be created. How will employees be convinced that applying their skills, knowledge, and ingenuity in support of the organization is a more attractive alternative than other ways to utilize their capacities?

THEORY IN PRACTICE

The essence of applying Theory Y assumptions is guiding the subordinates to develop themselves rather than developing the subordinates by telling them what they need to do. An important consideration is that the subordinates' acceptance of responsibility for self-developing (i.e., self-direction and self-control) has been shown to relate to their commitment to objectives. But the overall aim is to further the growth of the individual, and it must be approached as a managerial strategy rather than simply as a personnel technique. Forms and procedures are of little value. Once the concept is provided, managers who welcome the assumptions of Theory Y will create their own processes for implementation; managers with underlying Theory X assumptions cannot create the conditions for integration and self-control no matter what tools are provided.

The development process becomes one of role clarification and mutual agreement regarding the subordinate's job responsibilities. This requires the manager's willingness to accept some risk and allow mistakes as part of the growth process. It also is time consuming in terms of discussions and allowing opportunity for self-discovery. However, it is not a new set of duties on top of the manager's existing load. It is a different way of fulfilling the existing responsibilities.

One procedure that violates Theory Y assumptions is the typical utilization of performance appraisals. Theory X leads quite naturally into this means of directing individual efforts toward organizational objectives. Through the performance appraisal process, management tells people what to do, monitors their activities, judges how well they have done, and rewards or punishes them accordingly. Because the appraisals are used for administrative purposes (e.g., pay, promotion, retention decisions), this is a demonstration of management's overall control strategy. Any consideration of personal goals is covered by the expectation that rewards of salary and position are enough. If the advancement available through this system is not a desired reward, the individuals are placed in a position of acting against their own objectives and advancing for the benefit of the organization only. The alternative (e.g., turning down a promotion) may bring negative outcomes such as lack of future options or being identified as employees with no potential.

The principle of integration requires active and responsible participation of employees in decisions affecting them. One plan that demonstrates Theory Y assumptions is *the Scanlon Plan*. A central feature in this plan is the cost-reduction sharing that provides a meaningful cause-and-effect connection between employee behavior and the reward received. The reward is directly related to the success of the organization, and it is distributed frequently. This provides a more effective learning reinforcement than the traditional performance appraisal methods. The second central feature of the Scanlon Plan is effective participation, a formal method through which members contribute brains and ingenuity as well as their physical efforts on the job. This provides a means for social and ego satisfaction, so employees have a stake in the success of the firm beyond the economic rewards. Implementation of the Scanlon Plan is not a program or set of procedures; it must be accepted as a way of life and can vary depending on the circumstances of the particular company. It is entirely consistent with Theory Y assumptions.

Theory X leads to emphasis on tactics of control, whereas Theory Y is more concerned with the nature of the relationship. Eliciting the desired response in a Theory Y context is a matter of creating an environment or set of conditions to enable self-direction. The day-to-day behavior of an immediate supervisor or manager is perhaps the most critical factor in such an environment. Through sometimes subtle behaviors superiors demonstrate their attitudes and create what is referred to as the psychological "climate" of the relationship.

Management style does not seem to be important. Within many different styles, subordinates may or may not develop confidence in the manager's deeper integrity, based on other behavioral cues. Lack of confidence in the relationship causes anxiety and undesirable reactions from the employees. No ready formula is available to relay integrity. Insincere attempts to apply a technique or style—such as using participation only to manipulate subordinates into believing they have some input to decisions—are usually recognized as a gimmick and soon destroy confidence.

In addition to manager–subordinate relationships, problems connected to Theory X assumptions can be observed in other organizational associations, such as staff–line relationships. Upper management may create working roles for staff groups to "police" line managers' activities, giving them an influence that equates psychologically to direct line authority. Top management with Theory X assumptions can delegate and still retain control. The staff function provides an opportunity to monitor indirectly, to set policy for limiting decisions and actions, and to obtain information on everything happening before a problem can occur.

Staff personnel often come from a very specialized education with little preparation for what their role should be in an organization. With full confidence in their objective methods and training to find "the best answer," they often are unprepared for the resistance of line managers who don't share this confidence and don't trust the derived solutions. The staff may conclude that line managers are stupid, are unconcerned with the general welfare of the organization, and care only about their own authority and independence. They essentially adopt the Theory X assumptions and readily accept the opportunity to create a system of measurements for control of the line operations.

To utilize staff groups within the context of Theory Y, managers must emphasize the principle of self-control. As a resource to all parts and levels of the organization, staff reports and data should be supplied to all members who can use such information to control their own job—not subordinates' jobs. If summary data indicate something wrong within the manager's unit of responsibility, the manager would turn to subordinates, not to the staff, for more information. If the subordinates are practicing similar self-control using staff-provided information, they have most likely discovered the same problem and taken action before this inquiry occurs. There is no solution to the problem of staff–line relationships in authoritative terms that can address organizational objectives adequately. However, a manager operating by Theory Y assumptions will apply them similarly to all relationships—upward, downward, and peer level—including the staff–line associations.

THE DEVELOPMENT OF MANAGERIAL TALENT

Leadership is a relationship with four major variables: the characteristics of the leader; the attitudes, needs, and other personal characteristics of the followers; the characteristics of the organization, such as its purpose, structure, and the nature of its task; and the social, economic, and political environment in which the organization operates. Specifying which leader characteristics will result in effective performance depends on the other factors, so it is a complex relationship. Even if researchers were able to determine the universal characteristics of a good relationship between the leader and the other situational factors, there are still many ways to achieve the same thing. For example, mutual confidence seems important in the relationship, but there are a number of ways that confidence can be developed and maintained. Different personal characteristics could achieve the same desired relationship.

Also, because it is so difficult to predict the situational conditions an organization will face, future management needs are unpredictable. The major task, then, is to provide a heterogeneous supply of human resources from which individuals can be selected as appropriate at a future time. This requires attracting recruits from a variety of sources and with a variety of backgrounds, which complicates setting criteria for selection. Also, the management development programs in an organization should involve many people rather than a few with similar qualities and abilities. Finally, management's goal must be to develop the unique capacities of each individual, rather than common objectives for all participants. We must place high value on people in general—seek to enable them to develop to their fullest potential in whatever role they best can fill. Not everyone must pursue the top jobs; outstanding leadership is needed at every level.

Individuals must develop themselves and will do so optimally only in terms of what each of them sees as meaningful and valuable. What might be called a "manufacturing approach" to management development involves designing programs to build managers; this end product becomes a supply of managerial talent to be used as needed. A preferred alternative approach is to "grow talent" under the assumption that people will grow into what they are capable of becoming, if they are provided the right conditions for that growth. There is little relationship (possibly even a negative one) between the formal structure for management development and actual achievement of the organization, because programs and procedures do not *cause* management development.

Learning is fairly straightforward when the individual desires new knowledge or skill. Unfortunately, many development offerings soon become a scheduled assignment for entire categories of people. Learning is limited in these conditions, because the motivation is low. Further, negative attitudes develop toward training in general, which interferes with creating an overall climate conducive to growth. In many cases, managers may have a purpose in sending subordinates to training that is not shared with or understood by that individual. This creates anxiety or confusion, which also interferes with learning. It is best if attendance in training and development programs is the result of joint target setting, wherein the individual expresses a need and it can be determined that a particular program will benefit both the individual and the organization.

Classroom learning can be valuable to satisfying needs of both parties. However, it can only be effective when there is an organizational climate conducive to growth. Learning is always an active process, whether related to motor skills or acquisition of knowledge; it cannot be injected into the learner, so motivation is critical. Practice and feedback are essential when behavior changes are involved. Classroom methods such as case analysis and role playing provide an opportunity to experiment with decisions and behaviors in a safe environment, to receive immediate feedback, and to go back and try other alternatives. Some applications of classroom learning may be observed directly on the job. In other cases, the application may be more subtle, in the form of increased understanding or challenging one's own preconceptions. Care must be taken so that pressures to evaluate the benefits of classroom learning don't result in application of inappropriate criteria for success while the true value of the experience is overlooked.

Separate attention is given to management groups or teams at various levels. Within Theory X assumptions, direction and control are jeopardized by effective group functioning. On the other hand, a manager who recognizes interdependencies in the organization—one who is less interested in personal power than in creating conditions so human resources will voluntarily achieve organization objectives—will seek to build strong management groups. Creating a managerial team requires unity of purpose among those individuals. If the group is nothing more than several individuals competing for power and recognition, it is not a team. Again, the climate of the relationships and the fundamental understanding of the role of managers in the organization will be critical. One day the hierarchical structure of reporting relationships will disappear from organizational charts and give way to a series of linked groups. This shift in patterns of relationships will be a slow transition, but will signify recognition of employee capacity to collaborate in joint efforts. Then we may begin to discover how seriously management has underestimated the true potential of the organization's human resources.

Conclusion

Theory X is not an evil set of assumptions, but rather a limiting one. Use of authority to influence has its place, even within the Theory Y assumptions, but it does not work in all circumstances. Certain societal changes suggest why Theory X increasingly may cause problems for organizations needing more innovation and flexibility in their operating philosophy. It is critically important for managers to honestly examine the assumptions that underlie their own behavior toward subordinates. To do so requires first accepting the two possibilities, Theory X and Theory Y, and then examining one's own actions in the context of that comparison. Fully understanding the implications on each side will help identify whether the observed choices of how to influence people are likely to bring about the desired results.

5 Maslow on Management

Abraham H. Maslow
Summary Prepared by John W. Newstrom

I t should be possible to implement an enlightened management policy in an organization, where employees can *self-actualize* (institute their own ideas, make decisions, learn from their mistakes, and grow in their capabilities) while creating *synergy* (attaining beneficial results simultaneously for the individual and the organization). Such a policy (and associated practices) would not necessarily apply to all people, because everyone is at a different level on the motivational hierarchy (from physiological to safety to love to esteem to self-actualization). Nevertheless, the assumptions that would need to be true in order to create an ideal (eupsychian) society can be identified and then explored. They include the following dimensions. People are

- psychologically healthy;
- not fixated at the safety-need level;
- capable of growth, which occurs through delight and through boredom;
- able to grow to a high level of personal maturity;
- courageous, with the ability to conquer their fears and endure anxiety.

They have

- the impulse to achieve;
- the capacity to be objective about themselves and about others;
- the capacity to be trusted to some degree;
- a strong will to grow, experiment, select their own friends, carry out their own ideas, and self-actualize;
- the ability to enjoy good teamwork, friendships, group spirit, group harmony, belongingness, and group love;
- the capacity to be improved to some degree;
- the ability to identify with a common objective and contribute to it;
- a conscience and feelings.

Everyone prefers

- to love and to respect his or her boss;
- to be a prime mover rather than a passive helper;

Abraham H. Maslow. *Maslow on Management*. New York: Wiley & Sons, Inc., 1998.

- to use all their capacities;
- to work rather than being idle;
- to have meaningful work;
- to be justly and fairly appreciated, preferably in public;
- to feel important, needed, useful, successful, proud, and respected;
- to have responsibility;
- to have personhood, identity, and uniqueness as a person;
- to create rather than destroy;
- to be interested rather than bored;
- to improve things, make things right, and do things better.

Given this portrait of a certain type of individual described by these assumptions, we can conclude the following:

- Authoritarian managers are dysfunctional for them;
- People can benefit by being stretched, strained, and challenged once in a while;
- Everyone should be informed as completely as possible;
- These types of persons will do best at what they have chosen, based on what they like most;
- Everybody needs to be absolutely clear about the organization's goals, directions, and purposes.

In conclusion, *enlightened management is the wave of the future.* It will be seen more and more for a very simple reason that can be stated as a fundamental principle of human behavior: "Treating people well spoils them for being treated badly." In other words, once employees have experienced any aspect of enlightened management, they will never wish to return to an authoritarian environment. Further, as other workers hear about enlightened work organizations, they will either seek to work there or demand that their own workplaces become more enlightened.

6 The Seven Habits of Highly Effective People

Stephen R. Covey

Summary Prepared by John W. Newstrom

There are two types of literature on how to succeed. The first type focuses on a *personality ethic*. It claims that you are what you appear to be; appearance is everything. It accents public image, social consciousness, and the ability to interact superficially with others. However, exclusive attention to these factors will eventually provide evidence of a lack of integrity, an absence of depth, a short-term personal success orientation, and basic deficiency in one's own humanness.

The second type of success literature revolves around a *character ethic*. It provides proven pathways to move from dependent relationships to independence, and ultimately to interdependent success with other people. It requires a willingness to subordinate one's short-term needs to more important long-term goals. It requires effort, perseverance, and patience with oneself. One's character is, after all, a composite of habits, which are unconscious patterns of actions.

Habits can be developed through rigorous practice until they become second nature. There are seven key habits that form the basis for character development and build a strong foundation for interpersonal success in life and at work:

1. ***Be Proactive:*** Make things happen. Take the initiative and be responsible for your life. Work on areas where you can have an impact and pay less attention to areas outside your area of concern. When you do respond to others, do so on the basis of your principles.
2. ***Begin With the End in Mind:*** Know where you're going; develop a personal mission statement; develop a sense of who you are and what you value. Maintain a long-term focus.
3. ***Put First Things First:*** Distinguish between tasks that are urgent and not so urgent and between activities that are important and not so important; then organize and execute around those priorities. Avoid being in a reactive mode, and pursue opportunities instead. Ask yourself, "What one thing could I do (today) that would make a tremendous difference in my work or personal life?"
4. ***Think "Win–Win:"*** Try to avoid competing, and search for ways to develop mutually beneficial relationships instead. Build an "emotional bank account" with others through frequent acts of courtesy, kindness, honesty, and commitment keeping. Develop the traits of integrity, maturity, and an abundance mentality (acting as if there is plenty of everything out there for everybody).

Stephen R. Covey. *The Seven Habits of Highly Effective People: Restoring the Character Ethic.* New York: Simon & Schuster, 1989.

5. ***Seek to Understand, and then to be Understood:*** Practice empathetic communications, in which you recognize feelings and emotions in others. Listen carefully to people. Try giving them "psychological air."

6. ***Synergize:*** Value and exploit the mental, emotional, and psychological differences among people to produce results that demonstrate creative energy superior to what a single person could have accomplished alone.

7. ***Sharpen the Saw:*** Do not allow yourself to get stale in any domain of your life, and don't waste time on activities that do not contribute to one of your goals and values. Seek ways to renew yourself periodically in all four elements of your nature—physical (via exercise, good nutrition, and stress control), mental (through reading, thought, and writing), social (through service to others), and spiritual (through study and meditation). In short, practice continuous learning and self-improvement, and your character will lead you to increased success.

7

The Fifth Discipline

Peter M. Senge
Summary Prepared by Dorothy Marcic

Dorothy Marcic is Adjunct Professor at Vanderbilt University's Owen Graduate School of Management. Previously, she served as Director of Graduate Programs in Human Resource Development at Peabody College and Fulbright Scholar at the University of Economics—Prague, and held academic appointments at Arizona State University and the University of Wisconsin— La Crosse. Dorothy's research and consulting interests include how to develop the kinds of structures, values, and systems that help create learning organizations that are uplifting to employees. Addressing that issue is one of the 10 books she has authored—*Managing with the Wisdom of Love: Uncovering Virtue in Organizations.*

Learning disabilities can be fatal to organizations, causing them to have an average life span of only 40 years—half a human being's life. *Organizations need to be learners, and often they are not.* Somehow some survive, but never live up to their potential. What happens if what we term *excellence* is really no more than mediocrity? Only those firms that become learners will succeed in the increasingly turbulent, competitive global market.

LEARNING DISABILITIES

There are seven learning disabilities common to organizations.

IDENTIFICATION WITH ONE'S POSITION[1] American workers are trained to see themselves as what they do, not who they are. Therefore, if laid off, they find it difficult, if not impossible, to find work doing something else. Worse for the organization, though, is the limited thinking this attitude creates. By claiming an identity related to the job, workers are cut off from seeing how their responsibility connects to other jobs. For example, one American car had three assembly bolts on one component. The similar Japanese make had only one bolt. Why? Because the Detroit manufacturer had three engineers for that component, while a similar Japanese manufacturer had only one.

Peter M. Senge. *The Fifth Discipline: The Art and Practice of the Learning Organization.* New York: Doubleday, 1990.

EXTERNAL ENEMIES   This belief is a result of the previously stated disability. *External enemies* refers to people focusing blame on anything but themselves or their unit. Fault is regularly blamed on factors such as the economy, the weather, or the government. Marketing blames manufacturing, and manufacturing blames engineering. Such external faultfinding keeps the organization from seeing what the real problems are and prevents them from tackling the real issues head-on.

THE ILLUSION OF TAKING CHARGE   Being proactive is seen as good management—doing something about "those problems." All too often, though, being proactive is a disguise for reactiveness against that awful enemy out there.

THE FIXATION ON EVENTS   Much attention in organizations is paid to events—last month's sales, the new product, who just got hired, and so on. Our society, too, is geared toward short-term thinking, which in turn stifles the type of generative learning that permits a look at the real threats—the slowly declining processes of quality, service, or design.

THE PARABLE OF THE BOILED FROG   An experiment was once conducted by placing a frog in boiling water. The frog, sensing danger in the extreme heat, immediately jumped out to safety. However, placing the frog in cool water and slowly turning up the heat resulted in the frog getting groggier and groggier and finally boiling to death. Why? Because the frog's survival mechanisms are programmed to look for sudden changes in the environment, not gradual changes. Similarly, during the 1960s, the U.S. auto industry saw no threat by Japan, which had only 4 percent of the market. Not until the 1980s when Japan had over 21 percent of the market did the Big Three begin to look at their core assumptions. Now with Japan holding about 30 percent share of the market, it is not certain if this frog (U.S. automakers) is capable of jumping out of the boiling water. Looking at gradual processes requires slowing down our frenetic pace and watching for the subtle cues.

THE DELUSION OF LEARNING FROM EXPERIENCE   Learning from experience is powerful. This is how we learn to walk and talk. However, we now live in a time when direct consequences of actions may take months or years to appear. Decisions in research and development (R&D) may take up to a decade to bear fruit, and their actual consequences may be influenced by manufacturing and marketing along the way. Organizations often choose to deal with these complexities by breaking themselves up into smaller and smaller components, further reducing their ability to see problems in their entirety.

THE MYTH OF THE MANAGEMENT TEAM   Most large organizations have a group of bright, experienced leaders who are supposed to know all the answers. They were trained to believe there are answers to all problems and they should find them. People are rarely rewarded for bringing up difficult issues or for looking at parts of a problem that make them harder to grasp. Most teams end up operating below the lowest IQ of any member. What results are "skilled incompetents"—people who know all too well how to keep *from* learning.

SYSTEMS THINKING

Five disciplines are required for a learning organization: personal mastery, mental models, shared vision, team learning, and systems thinking. The fifth one, systems thinking, is the most important. Without systems thinking, the other disciplines do not have the same effect.

The Laws of the Fifth Discipline

TODAY'S PROBLEMS RESULT FROM YESTERDAY'S SOLUTIONS A carpet merchant kept pushing down a bump in the rug, only to have it reappear elsewhere, until he lifted a corner and out slithered a snake. Sometimes fixing one part of the system only brings difficulties to other parts of the system. For example, solving an internal inventory problem may lead to angry customers who now get late shipments.

PUSH HARD AND THE SYSTEM PUSHES BACK EVEN HARDER Systems theory calls this compensating feedback, which is a common way of reducing the effects of an intervention. Some cities, for example, build low-cost housing and set up job programs, only to have more poor people than ever. Why? Because many moved to the cities from neighboring areas so that they, too, could take advantage of the low-cost housing and job opportunities.

BEHAVIOR GETS BETTER BEFORE IT GETS WORSE Some decisions actually look good in the short term, but produce *compensating feedback* and crisis in the end. The really effective decisions often produce difficulties in the short run but create more health in the long term. This is why behaviors such as building a power base or working hard just to please the boss come back to haunt you.

THE BEST WAY OUT IS TO GO BACK IN We often choose familiar solutions, ones that feel comfortable and not scary. But the effective ways often mean going straight into what we are afraid of facing. What does *not* work is pushing harder on the same old solutions (also called the "what we need here is a bigger hammer" syndrome).

THE CURE CAN BE WORSE THAN THE DISEASE The result of applying nonsystematic solutions to problems is the need for more and more of the same. It can become addictive. Someone begins mild drinking to alleviate work tension. The individual feels better and then takes on more work, creating more tension and a need for more alcohol, and the person finally becomes an alcoholic. Sometimes these types of solutions only result in shifting the burden. The government enters the scene by providing more welfare and leaves the host system weaker and less able to solve its own problems. This ultimately necessitates still more aid from the government. Companies can try to shift their burdens to consultants, but then become more and more dependent on them to solve their problems.

FASTER IS SLOWER Every system, whether ecological or organizational, has an optimal rate of growth. Faster and faster is not always better. (After all, the tortoise finally did win the race.) Complex human systems require new ways of thinking. Quickly jumping in and fixing what *looks* bad usually provides solutions for a problem's symptoms and not for the problem itself.

CAUSE AND EFFECT ARE NOT ALWAYS RELATED CLOSELY IN TIME AND SPACE *Effects* here mean the symptoms we see, such as drug abuse and unemployment, whereas *causes* mean the interactions of the underlying system that bring about these conditions. We often assume cause is near to effect. If there is a sales problem, then incentives for the sales force should fix it, or if there is inadequate housing, then build more houses. Unfortunately, this does not often work, for the real causes lie elsewhere.

TINY CHANGES MAY PRODUCE BIG RESULTS; AREAS OF GREATEST LEVERAGE ARE FREQUENTLY THE LEAST OBVIOUS System science teaches that the most obvious solutions usually do not work. Although simple solutions frequently make short-run improvements, they commonly contribute to long-term deteriorations. The *nonobvious* and *well-focused* solutions are more likely to provide leverage and bring positive change. For example, ships have a tiny trim tab on one edge of the rudder that has great influence on the movement of that ship, so small changes in the trim tab bring big shifts in the ship's course. However, there are no simple rules for applying leverage to organizations. It requires looking for the structure of what is going on rather than merely seeing the events.

YOU CAN HAVE YOUR CAKE AND EAT IT TOO—BUT NOT AT THE SAME TIME   Sometimes the most difficult problems come from "snapshot" rather than "process" thinking. For example, it was previously believed by American manufacturers that quality and low cost could not be achieved simultaneously. One had to be chosen over the other. What was missed, however, was the notion that improving quality may also mean eliminating waste and unnecessary time (both adding costs), which in the end would mean lower costs. Real leverage comes when it can be seen that seemingly opposing needs can be met over time.

CUTTING THE ELEPHANT IN HALF DOES NOT CREATE TWO ELEPHANTS   Some problems can be solved by looking at parts of the organization, whereas others require holistic thinking. What is needed is an understanding of the boundaries for each problem. Unfortunately, most organizations are designed to prevent people from seeing systemic problems, either by creating rigid structures or by leaving problems behind for others to clean up.

THERE IS NO BLAME   Systems thinking teaches that there are no outside causes to problems; instead, you and your "enemy" are part of the same system. Any cure requires understanding how that is seen.

THE OTHER DISCIPLINES

Personal Mastery

Organizations can learn only when the individuals involved learn. This requires personal mastery, which is the discipline of personal learning and growth, where people are continually expanding their ability to create the kind of life they want. From their quest comes the spirit of the learning organization.

Personal mastery involves seeing one's life as a creative work, being able to clarify what is really important, and learning to see current reality more clearly. The difference between what's important, what we want, and where we are now produces a "creative tension." Personal mastery means being able to generate and maintain creative tension.

Those who have high personal mastery have a vision, which is more like a calling, and they are in a continual learning mode. They never really "arrive." Filled with more commitment, they take initiative and greater responsibility in their work.

Previously, organizations supported an employee's development only if it would help the organization, which fits in with the traditional "contract" between employee and organization ("an honest day's pay in exchange for an honest day's work"). The new, and coming, way is to see it rather as a "covenant," which comes from a shared vision of goals, ideas, and management processes.

Working toward personal mastery requires living with emotional tension, not letting our goals get eroded. As Somerset Maugham said, "Only mediocre people are always at their best." One of the worst blocks to achieving personal mastery is the common belief that we cannot have what we want. Being committed to the truth is a powerful weapon against this, for it does not allow us to deceive ourselves. Another means of seeking personal mastery is to integrate our reason and intuition. We live in a society that values reason and devalues intuition. However, using both together is very powerful and may be one of the fundamental contributions to systems thinking.

Mental Models

Mental models are internal images of how the world works and can range from simple generalizations (people are lazy) to complex theories (assumptions about why my coworkers interact the way they do). For example, for decades the Detroit automakers believed people bought cars mainly for styling, not for quality or reliability. These beliefs, which were really unconscious assumptions, worked well for many years, but ran into trouble when competition from Japan began. It took a long time for Detroit even to begin to see the mistakes in their beliefs. One company that managed to change its mental model through incubating a business worldview was Shell.

Traditional hierarchical organizations have the dogma of organizing, managing, and controlling. In the new learning organization, though, the revised "dogma" will be values, vision, and mental models.

Hanover Insurance began changes in 1969 designed to overcome the "basic disease of the hierarchy." Three values espoused were

1. *Openness*—seen as an antidote to the dysfunctional interactions in face-to-face meetings.
2. *Merit,* or making decisions based on the good of the organization—seen as the antidote to decision making by organizational politics.
3. *Localness*—the antidote to doing the dirty stuff the boss does not want to do.

Chris Argyris and colleagues developed "action science" as a means for reflecting on the reasoning underlying our actions. This helps people change the defensive routines that lead them to skilled incompetence. Similarly, John Beckett created a course on the historical survey of main philosophies of thought, East and West, as a sort of "sandpaper on the brain." These ideas exposed managers to their own assumptions and mental models and provided other ways to view the world.

Shared Vision

A shared vision is not an idea. Rather it is a force in people's hearts, a sense of purpose that provides energy and focus for learning. Visions are often exhilarating. Shared vision is important because it may be the beginning step to get people who mistrusted each other to start working together. Abraham Maslow studied high-performing teams and found that they had a shared vision. Shared visions can mobilize courage so naturally that people don't even know the extent of their strength. When John Kennedy created the shared vision in 1961 of putting a man on the moon by the end of the decade, only 15 percent of the technology had been created. Yet it led to numerous acts of daring and courage.

Learning organizations are not achievable without shared vision. Without that incredible pull toward the deeply felt goal, the forces of *status quo* will overwhelm the pursuit. As Robert Fritz once said, "In the presence of greatness, pettiness disappears." Conversely, in the absence of a great vision, pettiness is supreme.

Strategic planning often does not involve building a shared vision, but rather announcing the vision of top management, asking people, at best, to enroll, and, at worst, to comply. The critical step is gaining commitment from people. This is done by taking a personal vision and building it into a shared vision. In the traditional hierarchical organization, compliance is one of the desired outcomes. For learning organizations, commitment must be the key goal. Shared vision, though, is not possible without personal mastery, which is needed to foster continued commitment to a lofty goal.

Team Learning

Bill Russell of the Boston Celtics wrote about being on a team of specialists whose performance depended on one another's individual excellence and how well they worked together. Sometimes that created a feeling of magic. He is talking about *alignment,* where a group functions as a whole unit, rather than as individuals working at cross purposes. When a team is aligned, its energies are focused and harmonized. They do not need to sacrifice their own interests. Instead, alignment occurs when the shared vision becomes an extension of the personal vision. Alignment is a necessary condition to empower others and ultimately empower the team.

Never before today has there been greater need for mastering team learning, which requires mastering both dialogue and discussion. *Dialogue* involves a creative and free search of complex and even subtle issues, whereas *discussion* implies different views being presented and defended. Both skills are useful, but most teams cannot tell the difference between the two. The purpose of dialogue is to increase individual understanding. Here, assumptions are suspended and participants regard one another as on the same level. Discussion, on the other hand, comes from the same root word as *percussion* and *concussion* and involves a sort of verbal ping-pong game whose object is winning. Although this is a useful technique, it must be balanced with dialogue. A continued emphasis on winning is not compatible with the search for truth and coherence.

One of the major blocks to healthy dialogue and discussion is what Chris Argyris calls *defensive routines.* These are habitual styles of interacting that protect us from threat or embarrassment. These include the avoidance of conflict (smoothing over) and the feeling that one has to appear competent and to know the answers at all times.

Team learning, like any other skill, requires practice. Musicians and athletes understand this principle. Work teams need to learn that lesson as well.

OTHER ISSUES

Organizational politics is a perversion of truth, yet most people are so accustomed to it, they do not even notice it anymore. A learning organization is not possible in such an environment. In order to move past the politics, one thing needed is openness—both speaking openly and honestly about the real and important issues and being willing to challenge one's own way of thinking.

Localness, too, is essential to the learning organization, for decisions need to be pushed down the organizational hierarchy in order to unleash people's commitment. This gives them the freedom to act.

One thing lacking in many organizations is time to reflect and think. If someone is sitting quietly, we assume he or she is not busy and feel free to interrupt. Many managers, however, are too busy to "just think." This should not be blamed on the tumultuous environment of many crises. Research suggests that, even when given ample time, managers still do not devote any of it to adequate reflection. Therefore, habits need to be changed, as well as how we structure our days.

Competitive Advantage

Michael E. Porter
Summary Prepared by Sara A. Morris

Sara A. Morris received her Ph.D. in Business Policy and Strategy from the University of Texas at Austin. Now on the faculty at Old Dominion University, she teaches capstone courses in strategic management and graduate seminars in competitive strategy. Her current research is in business ethics and social responsibility and concerns CEO misconduct and the use of unethical techniques for obtaining competitor information.

How can a firm obtain and maintain an advantage over its competitors? The answer lies in an understanding of industries, the five forces that drive competition in an industry, and three generic strategies that a firm can use to protect itself against these forces. An industry is a group of firms producing essentially the same products and/or services for the same customers. The profit potential of an industry is determined by the cumulative strength of five forces that affect competition in an industry:

1. Jockeying for position on the part of current competitors in the industry
2. Potential for new competitors to enter the industry
3. The threat of substitutes for the industry's products or services
4. The economic power of suppliers of raw materials to the industry
5. The bargaining power of the industry's customers

Three strategies that a firm can use to neutralize the power of these five forces are low costs, differentiation, and focus. Several specific action steps are required to execute each of these three generic strategies.

PRINCIPLES OF COMPETITIVE ADVANTAGE

A firm creates a competitive advantage for itself by providing more value for customers than competitors provide. Customers value either (1) equivalent benefits at a lower price than competitors charge or (2) greater benefits that more than compensate for a higher price than competitors

Michael E. Porter. *Competitive Advantage: Creating and Sustaining Superior Performance.* New York: Free Press, 1985.

charge. Thus, there are two possible competitive advantages, one based on costs and the other on differentiation (benefits). Each of these tactics will be discussed in detail, following an examination of the value chain.

THE VALUE CHAIN

The *value chain,* consisting of value-producing activities and margin, is a basic tool for analyzing the large number of discrete activities within a firm that are potential sources of competitive advantage. The inclusion of margin in the value chain is a reminder that, in order for a firm to profit from its competitive advantage, the value to customers must exceed the costs of generating it. Value-producing activities fall into nine categories—five categories of primary activities and four categories of support activities. Primary activities include inbound logistics, operations, outbound logistics, marketing/sales, and service. Support activities include procurement (of all of the inputs used everywhere in the value chain), technology development (for the myriad of technologies that are used in every primary and support activity), human resource management (of all types of personnel throughout the organization), and the firm infrastructure (general management, planning, finance, accounting, legal and government affairs, quality management, etc.).

Firms perform hundreds or thousands of discrete steps in transforming raw materials into finished products. The value chain decomposes the nine value-producing activities into numerous subactivities because each separate subactivity can contribute to the firm's relative cost position and create a basis for differentiation. In most subactivities, the firm is not significantly different from its rivals. The strategically relevant subactivities are those that currently or potentially distinguish the firm from competitors.

Value chain activities are not independent from one another, but interrelated. The cost or performance of one activity is linked to many other activities. For example, the amount of after-sale service needed depends on the quality of the raw materials procured, the degree of quality control in operations, the amount of training given to the sales force regarding matching customer sophistication and model attributes, and other factors. Competitive advantage can be created by linkages among activities as well as by individual activities. Two ways that firms can derive competitive advantage from linkages are through optimization of linkages and coordination of linkages.

The configuration and economics of the value chain are determined by the firm's *competitive scope.* By affecting the value chain, scope also affects competitive advantage. Four dimensions of scope are as follows:

1. *Segment Scope:* varieties of products made and buyers served
2. *Vertical Scope:* the extent of activities performed internally rather than purchased from outside
3. *Geographic Scope:* the range of locations served
4. *Industry Scope:* the number of industries in which the firm competes

Broad-scope firms operate multiple value chains and attempt to exploit interrelationships among activities across the chains to gain competitive advantages. Narrow-scope firms use focus strategies to pursue competitive advantages; by concentrating on single value chains, they attempt to perfect the linkages within the value chain.

COMPETITIVE ADVANTAGE THROUGH LOW COST

The starting point for achieving a cost advantage is a thorough analysis of costs in the value chain. The analyst must be able to assign operating costs and assets (fixed and working capital) to each separate value chain activity. There are 10 major factors that are generally under the firm's control and that drive costs:

1. Economies (or diseconomies) of scale
2. Learning, which the firm can control by managing with the learning curve and keeping learning proprietary
3. Capacity utilization, which the firm can control by leveling throughput and/or reducing the penalty for throughput fluctuations
4. Linkages within the value chain, which the firm can control by recognizing and exploiting
5. Interrelationships between business units (in multi-industry firms), which the firm can control by sharing appropriate activities and/or transferring management know-how
6. The extent of vertical integration
7. Timing, which the firm can control by exploiting first-mover or late-mover advantages, and/or timing purchases over the business cycle
8. Discretionary policies (regarding products made, buyers served, human resources used, etc.)
9. Location
10. Institutional factors imposed by government and unions, which the firm can influence if not control outright

Moreover, costs are dynamic; they will change over time due to changes in industry growth rate, differential scale sensitivity, differential learning rates, changes in technology, aging, and the like. Each individual value chain activity must be analyzed separately for its cost drivers and cost dynamics.

By definition, the firm has a cost-based competitive advantage if the total costs of all its value chain activities are lower than any competitor's. A firm's cost position relative to competitors depends on the composition of its value chain compared to competitors' chains, and the firm's position relative to its competitors vis-à-vis the cost drivers of each value chain activity. Two ways that a firm can achieve a cost advantage, therefore, are (1) by controlling cost drivers and (2) by reconfiguring the value chain through means such as changing the production process, the distribution channel, or the raw materials. A cost-based competitive advantage will be sustainable only if competitors cannot imitate it. The cost drivers that tend to be harder to imitate are economies of scale, interrelationships, linkages, proprietary learning, and new technologies that are brought about through discretionary policies.

COMPETITIVE ADVANTAGE THROUGH DIFFERENTIATION

Successful *differentiation* occurs when a firm creates something unique that is valuable to buyers and for which buyers are willing to pay a price premium in excess of the extra costs incurred by the producer. This statement begs two questions: (1) What makes something valuable to buyers, and (2) why does the producer incur extra costs? With regard to the first question, a firm can create value for buyers by raising buyer performance or by lowering buyer costs (in ways besides selling the product at a lower price). With regard to the second question, differentiation is usually inherently costly because uniqueness requires the producer to perform value chain activities better than competitors.

In order to achieve a differentiation advantage, strategists must be thoroughly familiar with the many discrete activities in their own value chain(s) and in the buyer's value chain and must have a passing knowledge of the value chains of competitors. Each discrete activity in the firm's value chain represents an opportunity for differentiating. The firm's impact on the buyer's value chain determines the value the firm can create through raising buyer performance or lowering buyer costs. Because competitive advantages are by definition relative, a firm's value chain must be compared to those of its competitors.

For each separate activity in the firm's value chain, there are *uniqueness drivers* analogous to the cost drivers described previously. The most important uniqueness driver is probably the set of policy choices managers make (regarding product features, services provided, technologies employed, quality of the raw materials, and so forth). Other uniqueness drivers, in approximate order of importance, are linkages within the value chain and with suppliers and distribution channels, timing, location, interrelationships, learning, vertical integration, scale, and institutional factors.

Buyers use two types of purchasing criteria: (1) *use criteria,* which reflect real value, and (2) *signaling criteria,* which reflect perceived value in advance of purchase and verification. Use criteria include product characteristics, delivery time, ready availability, and other factors that affect buyer value through raising buyer performance or lowering buyer costs. Signaling criteria include the producing firm's reputation and advertising, the product's packaging and advertising, and other factors through which the buyer can infer the probable value of the product before the real value can be known. Differentiators must identify buyer purchasing criteria; the buyer's value chain is the place to start.

Armed with an understanding of multiple value chains, uniqueness drivers, and buyer purchasing criteria, managers can pursue differentiation. There are four basic routes to a differentiation-based competitive advantage. One route is to enhance the sources of uniqueness, by proliferating the sources of differentiation in the value chain, for example. A second route is to make the cost of differentiation an advantage by exploiting sources of differentiation that are not costly, minimizing differentiation costs by controlling cost drivers, and/or reducing costs in activities that do not affect buyer value. Another route is to change the rules to create uniqueness, such as discovering unrecognized purchase criteria. The fourth route is to reconfigure the value chain to be unique in entirely new ways.

A differentiation-based competitive advantage will be sustainable only if buyers' needs and perceptions remain stable and competitors cannot imitate the uniqueness. The firm can strongly influence the buyer's perceptions by continuing to improve on use criteria and by reinforcing them with appropriate signals. The firm is, nevertheless, at risk that buyers' needs will shift, eliminating the value of a particular form of differentiation. The sustainability of differentiation against imitation by competitors depends on its sources, the drivers of uniqueness. The competitive advantage will be more sustainable if the uniqueness drivers involve barriers such as proprietary learning, linkages, interrelationships, and first-mover advantages; if the firm has low costs in differentiating; if there are multiple sources of differentiation; and/or if the firm can create switching costs for customers.

TECHNOLOGY AND COMPETITIVE ADVANTAGE

One of the most significant drivers of competition is technological change. Because technologies are embedded in every activity in the value chain as well as in the linkages among value chain activities, a firm can achieve and/or maintain low costs or differentiation through technology.

The first step in using technology wisely is to identify the multitude of technologies in the value chain. Then, the astute manager must become aware of relevant technological improvements coming from competitors, other industries, and scientific breakthroughs.

A firm's technology strategy involves choices among new technologies, and choices about timing and licensing. Rather than pursuing technological improvements involving all value chain activities and linkages indiscriminately, managers should restrict their attention to technological changes that make a difference. New technologies are important if they can affect (1) the firm's particular competitive advantage, either directly or through its drivers, or (2) any of the five forces that drive competition in the industry. A firm's timing matters in technological changes because the technology leader will experience first-mover advantages (e.g., reputation as a pioneer, opportunity to define industry standards) as well as disadvantages (e.g., costs of educating buyers, demand uncertainty). Thus, the choice of whether to be a technology leader or follower should be made according to the sustainability of the technological lead. When a firm's competitive advantage rests on technology, licensing the technology to other firms is risky. Although there are conditions under which licensing may be warranted (to tap an otherwise inaccessible market, for example), often the firm inadvertently creates strong rivals and/or gives away a competitive advantage for a small royalty fee.

COMPETITOR SELECTION

A firm must be ever vigilant in pursuing and protecting its competitive advantage; however, there are dangers in relentlessly attacking all rivals. It is prudent to distinguish desirable competitors from undesirable ones. Desirable competitors may enable a firm to increase its competitive advantage (e.g., by absorbing demand fluctuations, or by providing a standard against which buyers compare costs or differentiation) or may improve industry structure (i.e., may weaken one or more of the five forces that collectively determine the intensity of competition in an industry). Characteristics of desirable competitors include realistic assumptions; clear, self-perceived weaknesses; enough credibility to be acceptable to customers; enough viability to deter new entrants; and enough strength to motivate the firm to continue to improve its competitive advantage. A smart industry leader will encourage some competitors and discourage others through tactics such as technology licensing and selective retaliation.

SCOPE AND COMPETITIVE ADVANTAGE

An industry consists of heterogeneous parts, or segments, due to differences in buyer behavior and differences in the economics of producing different products or services for these buyers. Therefore, the intensity of competition (i.e., the collective strength of the five competitive forces) varies among segments of the same industry. Moreover, because segments of the same industry have different value chains, the requirements for competitive advantage differ widely among industry segments. The existence of multiple industry segments forces a firm to decide on competitive scope, or where in the industry to compete. The attractiveness of any particular industry segment depends on the collective strength of the five competitive forces, the segment's size and growth rate, and the fit between a firm's abilities and the segment's needs. The firm may broadly target many segments or may use the generic strategy of focus to serve one or a few segments.

The competitive scope decision requires the manager to analyze all the current and potential industry segments. To identify product segments, all the product varieties in an industry must be examined for differences they can create in the five competitive forces and the value chain. The industry's products may differ in terms of features, technology or design, packaging, performance, services, and in many other ways. To identify buyer segments, all the different types of buyers in an industry must be examined for differences they can create in the five competitive forces and the value chain. Buyers can differ by type (e.g., several types of industrial buyers, several types of consumer buyers), distribution channel, and geographic location (according to weather zone, country stage of development, etc.).

When the value chains of different segments in the same industry are related at multiple points, a firm can share value-producing activities among segments. Such segment interrelationships encourage firms to use a broad-target strategy, unless the costs of coordination, compromise, and inflexibility in jointly accomplishing value-producing activities outweigh the benefits of sharing. Broad-target strategies often involve too many segments, thereby pushing coordination, compromise, and inflexibility costs too high and making the broadly targeted firm vulnerable to firms with good focus strategies.

Whereas broad-target strategies are based on similarities in the value chains among segments, focus strategies are based on differences between segments' value chains. A focuser can optimize the value chain for one or a few segments and achieve lower costs or better differentiation than broad-target firms because the focuser can avoid the costs of coordination, compromise, and inflexibility required for serving multiple segments. The sustainability of a focus strategy is determined by its sustainability against (1) broad-target competitors, (2) imitators, and (3) substitutes, the next topic of interest.

Both the industry's product or service and its substitutes perform the same generic function for the buyer (i.e., fill the same role in the buyer's value chain). The threat of substitution depends on (1) the relative value/price of the substitute compared to the industry's product, (2) the cost of switching to the substitute, and (3) the buyer's propensity to switch. The relative value/price compares the substitute to the industry's product in terms of usage rate, delivery and installation, direct and indirect costs of use, buyer performance, complementary products, uncertainty, and so forth. Switching costs include redesign costs, retraining costs, and risk of failure. Buyer propensity to substitute depends on resources available, risk profile, technological orientation, and the like. The threat of substitution often changes over time because of changes in relative price, relative value, switching costs, or propensity to substitute. To defend against substitutes, the focuser can reduce costs, improve the product, raise switching costs, improve complementary goods, and so on.

CORPORATE STRATEGY AND COMPETITIVE ADVANTAGE

Whereas business-level strategy is concerned with the firm's course of actions within an individual industry, corporate-level strategy is generally concerned with the multi-industry firm's course of actions across industries. By exploiting interrelationships among its business units in distinct but related industries, the multi-industry corporation can increase its competitive advantage within one or more of those industries. Porter uses the term *horizontal strategy* to refer to a corporation's coordinated set of goals and policies that apply across its business units, and argues that horizontal strategy may be the most critical issue facing diversified firms today. It is through its horizontal strategy that a corporation achieves synergy.

There are three types of interrelationships among a multi-industry corporation's business units: tangible, intangible, and competitor induced. *Tangible interrelationships* occur when different business units have common elements in their value chains, such as the same buyers, technologies, or purchased inputs. These common elements create opportunities to share value chain activities among related business units. Sharing activities may lower costs or increase differentiation, thereby adding to competitive advantage. However, the benefits of sharing do not always exceed the costs of sharing. One cost of sharing is the need for more coordination in the shared value chain activities. Another cost is the need for compromise in the way shared value chain activities are performed; the compromise must be acceptable to both business units, but may be optimal for neither. A third cost of sharing is greater inflexibility in responding to changing environmental conditions.

A second type of interrelationship, *intangible interrelationships,* occurs when different business units can transfer general management know-how even though they have no common elements in their value chains. It is possible, though less likely, for intangible interrelationships to lead to competitive advantage. A third type of interrelationship, *competitor-induced interrelationships,* occurs when two diversified corporations compete against each other in more than one business unit. Such multipoint competition between two corporations means that any action in one line of business can affect the entire range of jointly contested industries. Therefore, for multipoint competitors, a competitive advantage in one line of business will have implications for all the linked industries.

Any diversified corporation will face impediments to exploiting interrelationships: The managers of business units that receive fewer benefits than they contribute will resist sharing; managers of all business units will tend to protect their turf; incentive systems may not appropriately measure and reward a business unit's contributions to other units; and so forth. Therefore, corporate-level executives must articulate an explicit horizontal strategy and organize to facilitate horizontal relations. Examples of organizational practices and mechanisms that are particularly helpful are horizontal structures (e.g., groupings of business units, interunit task forces), horizontal systems (e.g., interunit strategic planning systems and capital budgeting systems), horizontal human resource practices (e.g., cross-business job rotation and management forums), and horizontal conflict resolution processes.

A special case of interrelationships occurs when the industry's product is used or purchased with complementary products. Because the sale of one promotes the sale of the other, complementary products have the opposite effect of substitutes. Three types of decisions that a corporation must make regarding complementary products concern whether to control these products internally (as opposed to letting other firms supply them), whether to bundle them (i.e., sell complementary products together as a package), and whether to cross-subsidize them (i.e., price complementary products based on their interrelationships instead of their individual costs). All three types of decisions have repercussions for competitive advantage.

IMPLICATIONS FOR OFFENSIVE AND DEFENSIVE COMPETITIVE STRATEGY

The *industry scenario* is a planning tool that may be used to guide the formulation of competitive strategy in the face of major uncertainties about the future. Constructing industry scenarios involves identifying uncertainties that may affect the industry, determining the causal factors, making a range of plausible assumptions about each important causal factor, combining assumptions into internally consistent scenarios, analyzing the industry structure that would prevail under each scenario, identifying competitive advantages under each scenario, and predicting the behavior of competitors under each scenario. Managers may then design competitive strategies based on the most probable scenario, the most attractive scenario, hedging (protecting the firm against the worst-case scenario), or preserving flexibility.

Defensive strategy is intended to lower the probability of attack from a new entrant into the industry or an existing competitor seeking to reposition itself. The preferred defensive strategy is deterrence. The old saying about "the best offense is a good defense" holds here; a firm with a competitive advantage that continues to lower its costs or improve its differentiation is very difficult to beat. Nevertheless, when deterrence fails, the firm must respond to an attack under way. When a firm's position is being challenged, defensive tactics include raising structural barriers (e.g., blocking distribution channels, raising buyer switching costs) and increasing expected retaliation.

Sometimes attacking an industry leader makes sense. The most important rule in offensive strategy is never to attack a leader head-on with an imitation strategy. In order to attack an industry leader successfully, the challenger must have a sustainable competitive advantage, must be close to the leader in costs and differentiation, and must have some means to thwart leader retaliation. There are three primary avenues to attack a leader: (1) change the way individual value-producing activities are performed or reconfigure the entire value chain; (2) redefine the competitive scope compared to the leader; (3) pure spending on the part of the challenger. The leader is particularly vulnerable when the industry is undergoing significant changes, such as technological improvements, changes in the buyer's value chain, or the emergence of new distribution channels.

PART THREE

High- and Low-Performing Organizations

Most organizations don't want merely to survive; they want to be effective, or even excellent, at what they do. To do so requires a prior definition of success, and defining success often encourages the managers of an organization to examine the actions of their best competitors for comparative models (benchmarks). They assume that if they can identify the organizational characteristics that allow others to succeed, then these attributes can be transplanted (or adapted, or even improved upon) to facilitate their own success. Consequently, a wide variety of organizations and management groups have shown strong interest in discovering what high-performing organizations actually do and determining their guiding principles. (Interested readers are also encouraged to consult Part 8 for presentations on high-performance teams.)

Jim Collins is the author of three best-seller business books—*Built to Last, Good to Great,* and *How the Mighty Fall,* which have collectively sold more than 10 million copies worldwide. The first book was on *Business Week*'s best-seller list for more than six years. Collins has recently followed up his earlier successes with *Great by Choice* (co-written with Norman Hansen). *Good to Great* identifies five key factors common to sustained success, such as preserving core values, focusing on facts before making decisions, hiring the right people, and finding leaders who combine personal humility with strong professional intensity. The transition from good company to great company typically involves five stages—Disciplined People, Disciplined Thought, and Disciplined Action.

In *Big Winners and Big Losers*, Alfred A. Marcus reports on his findings from a detailed review of the performance of the 1,000 largest corporations in the United States. Marcus reports that there is a consistent pattern that distinguishes the big winners from the big losers. Marcus concluded that the more effective firms identify high-potential markets, develop products and services to satisfy consumer demand, and demonstrate the capacity to make continual adaptations to their strategies so that they do not experience decline.

Marcus received his Ph.D. from Harvard University and currently holds the Edson Spencer Chair of Strategic Management and Technological Leadership in the Carlson

School of Management at the Minneapolis campus of the University of Minnesota. He is the author or coeditor of 11 books (including *Strategic Foresight: A New Look at Scenarios*), and he has published numerous articles in such journals as the *Academy of Management Review, California Management Review*, and the *Strategic Management Journal.*

In *How the Mighty Fall*, Jim Collins examines organizations such as Bank of America, Motorola, Circuit City, A & P, and Zenith to identify what made them slip into major decline (and sometimes total failure). Collins makes a strong eye-opening assertion: that *every institution is vulnerable to decline.* He identifies five stages of decline: hubris born of success, undisciplined pursuit of more, denial of risk and peril, grasping for salvation, and capitulation to irrelevance or death. Fortunately, he concludes, the pattern of decline can be avoided, detected, and reversed as seen by examples at Hewlett-Packard, Merck, IBM, Delta, and Nucor, which all emerged from adversity stronger than ever.

1

Good to Great

Jim Collins
Summary Prepared by Mary Kate Gross

Mary Kate Gross is a Veterans Service Representative with the U.S. Department of Veterans Affairs, where she assists veterans in applying for benefits and/or services associated with injuries they sustained while in the military service. In addition, she enjoys sharing her passion for dance by teaching young girls the basics of tap and ballet. She obtained her bachelor's degree in Organizational Management from the University of Minnesota Duluth. She is now a member of the Labovitz School of Business Alumni Board, where she acts as the Student Body Liaison.

INTRODUCTION

There are good companies and there are great companies. However, most companies rarely achieve the status of greatness, as they remain content with just being good. Consequently, a key question emerges: *Can a good company make the leap to greatness, and if so, how?* The question is answered by shedding light on the similarities of companies that were able to go from good to great and what distinguished them from companies that didn't—the issue of "what's inside the black box?" The answers uncovered are timeless and universal. Therefore, they can be applied by any organization in order to improve performance and rank, regardless of a changing economy.

THE STUDY

Companies that had what it took to make good results into great results were selected from a list of companies on the Fortune 500 list from 1965 to 1996. They exhibited a pattern of 15 years of cumulative stock returns at or below the general stock market and then experienced a transition point that was followed by cumulative returns at least three times the market average for the next 15 years. In order to eliminate companies that had a lucky break, one-time success, or those that had a single great leader, the 15-year time span was chosen. The criterion of three times the market's rate of return was chosen as it exceeded the performance of already widely known great companies. Last, companies chosen had a pattern of good to great independent of how successful the industry was. Based on the criteria used, 11 companies were selected for in-depth study and analysis.

Jim Collins. *Good to Great: Why Some Companies Make the Leap . . . and Others Don't.* New York: HarperCollins, 2001.

In order to discover the key differences at play in going from good to great, the newly great companies were compared with similar companies that were either unsuccessful in making the leap or had challenges in maintaining great results. Comparison companies were grouped into two sets. First, direct comparison companies were companies in the same industry with similar resources and opportunities as the good to great companies during the time of transition, but that failed to make the leap to greatness. Eleven direct comparison companies were selected. The second set of comparison companies was considered unsustained, as they were companies that initially made the leap to greatness, but were unable to maintain results. The study revealed six comparison companies that failed to sustain their success.

THREE STAGES OF DEVELOPMENT

The *differences between the good-to-great companies and the comparison companies were developed into concepts of what makes a company achieve greatness.* Each of the concepts was required to show up in 100 percent of the successful companies and in less than 30 percent of the comparison companies or the concept was thrown out. The transformation from good to great starts with a buildup, followed by a breakthrough, and consists of three stages: Disciplined People, Disciplined Thought, and Disciplined Actions. Within these stages there are two key concepts. The entire process of going from good to great is represented by a **flywheel**—the continuous turning and momentum of effort in one direction leading to a point of breakthrough.

Stage One—Disciplined People

Every good-to-great company had a Level 5 Leader during its era of transition, whereas a contrasting pattern of lacking powerful leadership was found in the comparison companies. Therefore, the first key component of stage one (Disciplined People) is Level 5 Leadership, or leaders who have fulfilled all five layers of the hierarchy of executive capabilities. **Level 5** Leaders are individuals who channel their egos and ambitions away from themselves and instead toward the larger goal of the institution and building a great company by doing whatever must be done. It's important to note that a leader does not need to be brought in from the outside to shake things up within a company in order to achieve greatness. In addition, a Level 5 Leader wants to see the company be as or more successful in the future while knowing that he or she may never be credited for the roots of success he or she created. In the comparison companies, leaders failed to set up the future generation for success by either setting their successors up for failure and/or choosing weak successors. *Modesty is a key trait of a Level 5 Leader,* as it's important to talk about the contributions of others and give others credit. Leaders in good-to-great companies never sought credit as superheroes, whereas leaders in the unsustained and comparison companies tended to exhibit very large personal egos that eventually led to a failing or stagnant company. Last, Level 5 Leaders exhibit the **Window and the Mirror Pattern**, where they look out the window and apportion credit to factors other than themselves (such as other persons, events, or luck) when things go well. However, when things go poorly, they look into the mirror to accept responsibility rather than blaming bad luck.

Once the right leader is in place, the next step is getting the right people on board while eliminating the wrong people. This is the second concept of stage one, *First Who . . . Then What.* After having the right people on board one can decide which direction to go. Starting by asking "who" questions rather than "what" questions allows a company to be better able to adapt to change. It is easier to make a change in direction when the right people are on board, as they are present, not because of the direction the company was going, but rather because of the people they are with. Having the right people also generally eliminates the problem of how to motivate and manage people. The right people, independent of the compensation structure in place, are your most important asset because they tend to be self-motivated to achieve greatness. Therefore, a rigorous culture is created where standards are set at all levels and at all times when trying to find the right people. Rigorousness is created by not hiring those who don't fit in with the company, knowing and acting on when to make a change in people, and by putting your best people on your biggest opportunities, not your biggest problems. Last, having a great vision without great people still doesn't mean you will be great. When you ask first what, then ask who, you often find the *"genius with a thousand helpers"* model at play—or a situation where the "what" is based on the talents of an individual or genius who is driving the success, with people helping to implement the ideas. As long as the genius continues to stick around, success continues. However, once the genius disappears, the helpers left behind are unsuccessful in mimicking the genius.

Stage Two—Disciplined Thought

Knowing how the world is changing around a company is vital, but what companies *do* with that information is the key to becoming great. Therefore, the first key concept of the second stage, Disciplined Thought, is, *Confront the Brutal Facts—Yet Never Lose Faith.* By continuously looking at the facts of reality and following what the data portray, good and bad, companies are able to make good decisions. When a series of good decisions comes together, breakthrough is possible. Confronting the brutal facts fosters a workplace climate where the truth is heard and talked about. Having an honest climate eliminates false hope within the culture, which can be de-motivating. Asking questions to solely gain understanding rather than place blame or use manipulation fosters a climate where the truth will be told. In addition to asking questions, engaging in intense dialogue and debate allows for the best answers or the truth to surface. It's important to turn any piece of information into information that cannot be ignored. Evaluating information as it is occurring allows companies to see red flags and react immediately, rather than after something goes wrong.

The key to achieving greatness is to follow the **Stockdale Paradox**, which is having unwavering faith that you will prevail in the end despite the difficulties at hand (while also remaining realistic). Companies face challenges of all shapes and sizes, but those that achieved greatness looked at those experiences as defining moments that made them stronger.

With great information comes building a great company strategy. Companies that achieved greatness guided their strategy by using the **Hedgehog Concept**—a simple understanding of the intersection of three circles of thought—toguide their actions. The Hedgehog Concept is the second factor found within the Disciplined Thought stage and is the turning point in going from good to great. The three circles of thought are:

1. ***Determine What you Can Be the Best in the World at, and, Just as Important, What you cannot be the Best at:*** Then focus your strategy around things you can be the best at and if you cannot be the best at it, then it shouldn't be the basis of your Hedgehog Concept, even if you have been doing that business for years.
2. ***Determine What Drives Your Economic Engine:*** Understand your own economics and what economic denominator or profit per x (e.g., profit per employee or profit per customer visit) would increase over time that would give the greatest impact. Continuing to apply this principle is what creates greatness and will help one remain great.
3. ***Determine What you are Deeply Passionate About and only do Those Activities:*** Growth is not your Hedgehog Concept. If you have the right concept and make decisions that align with your concept, momentum will build. The intriguing question, then, is not how to grow, but rather how not to grow too fast. Defining your Hedgehog Concept takes time; it is a process rather than one specific event and does not rely on being in a good industry.

Stage Three—Disciplined Action

The third stage of the framework, Disciplined Action, works within the context of the Hedgehog Concept. The key is to build a Culture of Discipline, or a culture of people whose disciplined actions are found to be within the three circles of thought and are consistent with the Hedgehog Concept. However, freedom and responsibility are built into the culture where the people aren't managed, but the *system* is managed. The key is to get self-disciplined people on board from the start and have them take disciplined actions while being willing to do whatever it takes to become great. Leaders are responsible for building the framework for a culture of discipline, and great companies do not rely on personal disciplinarian actions of force to achieve it. A company needs to have the discipline to ignore opportunities that do not fit within its Hedgehog Concept. There is no such thing as a "once in a lifetime" opportunity if it doesn't fit within the three circles of thought. Companies that achieved greatness compiled a "stop doing" list used for budgeting instead of a "to do" list. Budgeting within the context of moving from good to great is determining what activities support one's Hedgehog Concept and strengthening those activities while eliminating activities that don't. *It's not always about being disciplined to do the right thing; it's also about having the discipline to stop doing the wrong things.*

The keys to achieving greatness are timeless, and as the economy is ever changing, so is technology. Therefore, the second key concept of the Disciplined Action stage is Technology Accelerators. Great companies look at technology differently. Rather than ask what the role of technology is, they ask, *"How do we apply technology so that it fits within the Hedgehog Concept?"* Greatness is found by being creative in how one uses technology, not the fear of being left behind. Companies then become so creative that they become pioneers in the application of a specific technology that fits within their Hedgehog Concept. Having the discipline to ignore technology that does not fit within the intersection of the three circles is important, as well as knowing that the transition process never starts with the pioneering of technology. The use of technology alone is not a factor in achieving greatness, as it is an accelerator of momentum, not a creator. Used incorrectly, it can be an accelerator in the demise of a company as well.

Conclusion

The transition from good to great doesn't happen with one event, moment, action, or program. It is an accumulation of actions, decisions, and processes in a common direction that come together to turn the flywheel of results. Although the buildup process varies in time and some pushes are bigger than others, the constant buildups eventually lead to a point of breakthrough. Power in the flywheel comes from continuous improvement and results. With results, people become more energized and willing to join the movement, causing momentum to build. The process continues, as more momentum to achieve greatness results in continuous improvement.

Achieving greatness is one thing and staying there is another. It is just as hard to build something into greatness as to build something that attains mediocrity. Companies that achieved greatness didn't have a name for the transition process, and in some cases, didn't even know they were experiencing a transformation until after the fact. **Coherence** is found within the flywheel, as each piece of the system integrated together is more powerful than the sum of its parts. Breakthrough is reached through the integration of disciplined actions that align with the Hedgehog Concept that are performed by disciplined people who have the ability to have disciplined thoughts. The consistent application of this model will build momentum that will eventually lead to a point of breakthrough and maximum results.

2 Big Winners and Big Losers

Alfred A. Marcus

Summary Prepared by Allen Harmon

Allen Harmon is President and General Manager of WDSE-TV, the community-licensed PBS member station serving northeastern Minnesota and northwestern Wisconsin. He also currently serves as an Adjunct Instructor in the Labovitz School of Business and Economics at the University of Minnesota Duluth, where he teaches Strategic Management. Before joining WDSE, Mr. Harmon held a series of senior management positions in a regional investor-owned electric utility. He earned an M.B.A. from Indiana University's Kelly School of Business and has completed the University of Minnesota Carlson School of Management Executive Development Program.

A natural parity prevails in most industries. Sustained competitive advantage is rare. Over the decade from 1992 to 2002, a scant 3 percent of the top 1,000 U.S. companies consistently delivered returns that bettered the average of their industry. Only 6 percent of the top 1,000 consistently underperformed industry averages. *What are the distinctive traits of the big winners that an organization should seek to emulate to reap the rewards of consistent winning? What traits should an organization eschew to avoid the punishment borne by the big losers?*

Winners occupy **sweet spots** in the market, which are attractive market positions characterized by a lack of direct competition that present incumbents with the opportunity to control the five classic industry forces. Winners move to those positions with agility, demonstrate the discipline to protect those positions by developing hard-to-imitate capabilities, and focus on fully exploiting the position's potential. Losers are disadvantaged by being positioned in industry **sour spots**, which are highly contested market positions affording incumbents little opportunity to control the five classic industry forces. Losers are hindered in moving from those positions by their own rigidity and are inept in developing the capabilities that would allow them to protect their positions. Losers' efforts to exploit desirable positions they might occupy are too diffuse to be effective.

IDENTIFYING THE WINNERS AND LOSERS

Big winners and big losers were selected for study from the *Wall Street Journal*'s scorecard on the basis of stock market returns over the period from 1992 to 2002. A final screen was applied to determine whether the selected companies' performance during the turbulent first half of 2002

Alfred A. Marcus. *Big Winners and Big Losers: The 4 Secrets of Long-Term Business Success and Failure.* Pennsylvania: Wharton School Publishing, 2006.

was consistent with results over the preceding 10 years. The *Wall Street Journal*'s industry designations were used; pairs of winners and losers in nine industry sectors were selected for study.

A separate analysis of the Fortune 1000 list with consideration for minor differences in timing and composition affirmed the selections of big winners and big losers. Use of accounting data in lieu of market data was considered and rejected; market data were favored for being forward looking and less susceptible to company manipulation.

Winning company performance met the following benchmarks:

- As of January 1, 2002, 10-, 5-, 3- and 1-year market returns exceeded their industry average.
- Five-year average market return was two or more times the industry average.
- Return for the period January 1, 2002, to June 1, 2002, exceeded the industry average.

Losing company performance was described by:

- As of January 1, 2002, 10-, 5-, 3-, and 1-year market returns were less than the industry average.
- Five-year average market return was half or less than half the industry average.
- Return for the period January 1, 2002, to June 1, 2002, was less than half the industry average.

The screening process identified nine pairs of companies:

Industry Sector	Company	5-Year Average Annual Market Return (%)
Technology	Amphenol	34.0
	LSI Logic	3.4
Manufacturing/Appliance	SPX	28.8
	Snap-On	1.7
Software	FiServ	31.2
	Parametric	−21.2
Food	Dreyers	22.4
	Campbell Soup	−2.8
Drugs/Chemicals	Forest Labs	58.5
	IMC Global	−18.7
Manufacturing/Industrial	Ball	23.9
	Goodyear	−11.5
Financial	Brown & Brown	48.7
	Safeco	−1.0
Retail	Family Dollar	36.1
	Gap	9.8
Entertainment/Toys	Activision	24.1
	Hasbro	−0.1

THE ANALYSIS

Over 500 experienced managers, each trained and competent in strategic management, participated in the effort to identify what differentiated the big winners from the big losers. Five teams of five or six manager/analysts were assigned each industry pair and participated in an iterative process of analysis and peer review that sought to answer:

- What external challenges did the company face?
- How did the company's internal strengths and weaknesses relate to those challenges?
- What moves did the company make?
- Why were the moves of one company more successful than those of the company it was paired with?

As the analysis progressed, patterns began to emerge. Winners tended to be smaller than losers—on average, winners in the sample generated $3.49 billion in annual revenue and employed 14,000; losers on average generated $10.66 billion in annual revenue and employed 48,000. Winners tended to be less well known than losers. Winners tended to have a broad customer base; losers found their customers more concentrated.

SWEET SPOTS VERSUS SOUR SPOTS

Perhaps most significant, big winners were found in industry "sweet spots" where they faced virtually no direct competition. Because they had come to offer something rare, valuable, and nonsubstitutable to their customers, big winners had achieved control over the five classic industry forces. Winners bring a combination of low cost and differentiation to their customers in striking packages. The net result is exceptional value.

In contrast, big losers were found in industry "sour spots" where they faced multiple competitors offering similar or equally good products or services. As their products offered customers nothing special, the losers had little leverage with which to control industry forces. Losers often found themselves disadvantaged by prices too high for customers to afford, prices too low to be profitable, and/or processes too complex to be managed effectively.

GAINING THE SWEET SPOT

Winners found sweet spots in their industries by achieving significant alignment with their customers. By successfully providing unique solutions to complex customer needs and by embedding themselves in customer processes and operations, winners were in a position to identify and exploit unique opportunities. This accomplishment took various forms—for Ball, it was providing a process for producing specialty packaging meeting customer needs; for Dreyers, it was managing the grocer's difficult-to-manage freezer space; for Family Dollar, it was geographic, embedding stores in underserved urban neighborhoods. In each case, achieving significant alignment with customers opened opportunities for the winners in uncontested markets and allowed them to grow under their competitors' radar.

Three Traits of Winners

Knowledge of customer needs gave winners a place to go; three traits shared by the winners—agility, discipline, and focus—gave them the ability to get there.

AGILITY   Each of the big winners knew exactly where they wanted to go. They also displayed the agility to get there and the capacity to regularly reinvent themselves. Whether through merger, acquisition, or internal growth, they added businesses that showed promise. They showed no reluctance to divest those businesses that did not show promise. Hallmarks of agility include:

- Responding quickly to changes in the market, such as overcapacity and consolidations of competitors with new innovations
- Maintaining flexibility by controlling size, focusing on profitable growth, and building partnerships or outsourcing where others could contribute needed competencies
- Seeking growth in customers' changing needs, responding with products and services that become an intimate part of the customer's process
- Moving to markets that present specialized needs that only the company can satisfy, that are underserved, or that are perceived as unattractive and thus ignored by others
- Aggressively seeking acquisitions to exploit opportunities or to broaden and enhance product and service offerings
- Achieving sufficient diversification so that declines in one sector might be offset by improved performance in another

DISCIPLINE   Exercise of internal discipline allows big winners to protect their sweet-spot positions by maintaining the scarce, hard-to-imitate capabilities that create best-value propositions for customers. Evidence of organizational discipline is seen in:

- Effectively reducing costs and raising quality through applying technology, instituting process controls, achieving volume-driven efficiencies, and attaining best-in-class levels of service
- Controlling distribution through efforts ranging from employing aggressive globalization to serve new and existing markets efficiently and developing technology to track merchandise, to avoiding product deterioration in transit
- Smoothly integrating acquisitions, carefully selecting those targets that fit the organization's goals, quickly consolidating operations, and eliminating low- or no-profit components
- Creating a culture of employee involvement through selective hiring of skilled, aggressive individuals given the training, recognition, and respect that support their ability to make a difference to the company
- Monitoring and influencing regulatory changes—winners willingly comply with regulations, have good environmental records, and promote ethical behavior and integrity

FOCUS   Big winners do more than just defend their sweet-spot positions; they are actively committed to growth by broadening and deepening the sweet spot. Risk of failure was reduced by focus on core competencies. Big winners demonstrated focus by:

- Concentrating on core strengths by spinning off noncore activities; avoiding activities with high risk of failure; allowing others to assume risks (such as research and development [R&D]), consistent with their own competencies; and demonstrating total dedication to selected customer categories, developed brands, and related products
- Developing high-growth, application-specific products for growth markets, deepening relationships with customers to offer solutions driven by emerging customer needs rather than by a particular product or technology
- Extending reach globally, capitalizing on growth opportunities overseas through acquisition or internal development to extend the organization's global presence

While big winners demonstrated these three traits in a variety of ways, *all demonstrated consistent mastery of the one competence most difficult to replicate: balance.* A tension exists among the three key traits. In the extreme, focus and discipline can impair agility by closing off consideration of opportunities. The organization must at once defend and develop the space it holds while prospecting for new positions to occupy. Continual reinvention of the company produces stress between what the organization is and what it intends to become. The distinctive performance of the big winners is the result of achieving a unique balance of these attributes.

MIRED IN A SOUR SPOT

Losers found themselves competing in occupied sour spots in the market with products that were too expensive to be attractive to customers, products priced too low to be profitable, or business models that were too complex to execute effectively. They had, in short, lost contact with their customers and found themselves focused on products or internal processes rather than customer needs. Without the leverage provided by a unique value position, losers had little control over the classic industry forces.

Without the sense of direction that an intimate knowledge of their customers provided the big winners, when big losers moved (and they did), they moved in the wrong direction or at the wrong time. As a group, big losers demonstrated the traits of rigidity, ineptness, and diffuseness that prevented them from escaping their sour spots.

Rigidity—Like the big winners, losers sought movement. Their moves were often defensive and in reaction to a threat, however, rather than an offensive initiative to better align with customer needs. Their moves were characterized by a sense of rigidity that showed itself in:

- Exclusive reliance on expansion of core products for growth, sticking with the company's original business or current niche even as it lost potential, putting effort into expanding unprofitable businesses, and ignoring the prospects of noncore brands or holdings
- Reliance on commoditized products sold on the basis of price, or on concentrated buyers who because of that concentration hold pricing power
- Accumulating excess capacity at times of stagnant or declining demand; losers tended to expand too rapidly, buying weak or commodity businesses at inflated prices with debt that later became a burden
- Failing to mount a vigorous response such as new product development, capacity adjustments, or new market entrance to declines in the core business
- Failing to recognize and respond to changes in customer tastes or competitors' innovations
- Favoring size over agility and consequently becoming burdened with bureaucracy, losing the ability to anticipate and exploit changes in demand, profitable new niches, and competitors' blunders

Ineptness—Losers lacked the skills to create best-value propositions to offer their customers, finding themselves unable to defend what positions they did occupy from more adept competitors. Losers were unable to escape from the sour spots in part due to the following:

- Inability to provide best-in-class service or customized product offerings at low cost; losers exacerbated their disadvantages by failing to successfully correct even recognized inefficiencies or unwisely cutting the activities valued by customers in their efforts to reduce costs
- Failure to master their supply chain, alienating distributors and retailers of their products through ineffective performance and not developing the long-term relationships with customers that could be translated into leverage over suppliers

- Ineffective management of acquisition activities, resulting in overpayment, ineffective integration, and a failure to realize operational synergies
- Demoralizing employees by creating disarray and disruption when implementing new systems, developing an adversarial relationship with unions and ineffective (or nonexistent) incentive compensation plans
- Failure to maintain high ethical standards or to deal effectively with regulation, resulting in violations of environmental and accounting regulations.

Diffuseness—Without focus, losers' activities were ineffective in building competitive advantage that might have liberated them from their sour spots. The losing companies failed to reinforce the positions they occupied against attack from more competent competitors, failed to integrate disparate acquisitions to achieve common goals, and invested in R&D that was never destined to serve their customers. Evidence of the diffuseness infecting the big losers included the following:

- Lack of clear strategic direction meant that activities of both existing and newly acquired business units failed to coalesce around common goals or to exploit synergies among them; acquisitions were executed without a long-term plan, operations became needlessly complex or duplicative, and poorly executed attempts at vertical integration took one loser into value chain functions where it lacked competence.
- Focusing internally on products and marketing existing, diverse brands caused losers to ignore promising opportunities presented by the market; out of touch with customers and the market, they failed to identify growth opportunities or to adequately support the rapidly growing product lines they did hold.
- Looking to global markets as a fix for domestic problems only compounded losers' problems as they failed in the same ways in new markets: acquisitions failed, service levels fell short of customer requirements, local regulations were not dealt with effectively, and opportunities that did present themselves were not pursued aggressively.

LOOKING FOR PATTERNS

Each of the big winners built competitive advantage through combinations of traits demonstrating agility, discipline, and focus; their performance resulted from building difficult-to-copy combinations of these contrasting traits. Multiple positive traits were interwoven to reinforce one another. In no case was success the product of a single positive trait.

Success, then, is not the result of building the strengths separately, but of combining strengths into a larger whole. Achieving that whole requires making nontrivial trade-offs in achieving a balance between agility and discipline and focus.

Conversely, the prolonged poor performance of the big losers was in no case the product of a single weakness. Multiple weaknesses in a pattern that reinforced each other condemned the losers to failure. Big losers had difficulty managing tension. Under stress, one negative trait simply piled on top of another negative trait.

TURNAROUNDS

Updating the selection process to include the most recent five-year period (1999–2004) shows that for the most part, big winners have continued to win and big losers have continued to lose. Of the 18 companies, only 2 have seen a reversal of fortunes.

Insurer Safeco went from loser to winner, beating the performance of the Dow Jones Industrial Average beginning in 2001. Safeco began its turnaround by embracing focus, cutting back on acquisitions while determining what kind of company it wanted to be and what it could do well. Divesting businesses that did not fit the new definition of the company reduced its size and increased its agility. Discipline—to increase accountability and aggressiveness, reduce costs, and raise quality—completed the groundwork for Safeco's turnaround.

Manufacturer SPX saw its performance deteriorate. Alrthough it did not fall behind big loser Snap-On during the period, the former winner did slide into mediocrity, barely besting the Dow Jones Industrial Average for the period. At the root of SPX's decline was diffuseness, as the company lost its strategic direction and spread itself too thin. Weakness then piled on weakness. Without clear strategic direction, diverse acquisitions quickly bloated the company and rigidity replaced agility. The unraveling continued as a loss of discipline led to inept ethical breaches in setting executive compensation.

The turnarounds at Safeco and SPX offer confirmation of the observation that *success results from building a reinforcing pattern of positive traits—agility, discipline, and focus—and managing the tensions inherent among them.* Failure is the product of a pattern of negative traits: diffuseness, rigidity, and ineptness.

3

How the Mighty Fall

Jim Collins

Summary Prepared by Tanya Pietz

Tanya Pietz received her Bachelor of Business Administration degree from the University of Minnesota Duluth with majors in Human Resource Management and Marketing. She has worked extensively as a consultant in the health-care field and is currently coordinating the Physician Recruitment Program. She is also developing a systemwide employee engagement program with a focus on impacting bottom-line results at Riverwood Healthcare Center in Aitkin, Minnesota. Dedicated to the field of health care, she has spent the past 12 years in human resources, working with clients nationwide to build strong recruitment, employee engagement, and appreciation programs. She has a passion for training and continues to research and develop new strategies for increasing employee engagement within organizations.

INTRODUCTION

Why have some of the greatest companies in history fallen? What causes a great company to spiral toward demise? Do companies that fall from greatness have anything in common? Is there anything to be learned from researching these once-successful organizations?

A research-based perspective of how some of the greatest companies in history succumb to decline and peril allows today's leaders the opportunity to avoid these same pitfalls and learn from these companies' mistakes.

By understanding and being aware of the typical stages of decline, leaders can equip their companies with tools and strategies for minimizing the chances of falling all the way to the bottom. One key conclusion from research is that *it is possible to avoid decline if you can catch it early.* Not all companies that enter the stages of decline are destined to fall, and not all falls experience the exact same number of steps. A company may fall quickly through each stage or may have moments of recovery before again proceeding toward further decline.

FIVE STAGES OF DECLINE

Research has shown that there are typically five significant stages displayed in the decline of once-successful organizations. These stages are Hubris Born of Success, Undisciplined Pursuit of More, Decline of Risk and Peril, Grasping for Salvation, and Capitulation to Irrelevance or Death. Each stage will be discussed briefly.

James C. Collins. *How the Mighty Fall—And Why Some Companies Never Give In.* New York: HarperCollins, 2009.

Stage 1: Hubris Born of Success

In the first stage of decline, most companies in this category have no indication or suspicion they are starting on a path toward destruction—partially because of their past success. In contrast, leaders of organizations at this stage believe that all is going well, that they are on top of their game, and the company can do no wrong. They are guilty of the sin of **hubris** (excessive pride, pretentiousness, ambition, self-importance, or arrogance). This is the first assumption beginning the path to decline.

Common indicators of this stage may include:

- An attitude of arrogance
- Belief that success is an entitlement
- Assumption that past success will continue, no matter what the organization does
- Loss of inquisitiveness
- Loss of focus on learning and process improvement
- Neglect toward primary business line

In contrast, successful leaders maintain a learning curve as steep as when they first began their careers; they never stop learning. Successful companies also pay greater attention to improving and growing the core business, while not becoming overly distracted by the "latest and greatest" fad or product. Successful companies are able to find a balance between continuity and change.

Stage 2: Undisciplined Pursuit of More

The arrogant attitude demonstrated by companies in Stage 1 leads directly into Stage 2—the Undisciplined Pursuit of More. As leaders believe the company can accomplish anything, achieve anything, and be successful in anything, they embark down a path of pursuing more with disregard for strategic alignment with the core business values of the organization. We sometimes assume that companies fail because they become complacent, failing to make necessary changes and stay competitive in the market. Although this can be the case, research indicates little evidence of complacency when companies experience decline. In contrast, *overreaching better explains how once indestructible companies self-destruct.*

Indicators of this stage may include:

- More scale, more growth sought at the risk of undermining long-term value
- Growth occurs beyond the ability of the organization to fill key positions with the right people
- Obsession with growth
- Confusion of being big with being great
- Taking undisciplined leaps of growth
- Trouble grooming and growing internal future leadership

Stage 3: Denial of Risk and Peril

As organizations enter this stage, warning signs begin to appear. However, external results still remain strong enough that leaders are able to justify and explain away the declining internal indicators as temporary, cyclical, or just an anomaly. Negative data are dealt with by adding a positive spin. In general, leaders remain in denial regarding any possible risk or potential peril.

Indicators of this stage may include:

- Warning signs begin appearing within the organization
- There is a disproportionate focus on positive data
- Big bets are made that pose too great a risk
- Restructuring becomes a primary business strategy to create a sense of doing *something*
- Team dynamics begin to weaken
- Blame is placed on external factors (i.e., economy, bad market, competitors)
- Leaders become detached from the daily life of the organization
- Excessive pride, presumption, or arrogance

Stage 4: Grasping for Salvation

As struggling organizations continue to deny the impending peril seen in Stage 3, they will inevitably find themselves in a steep decline, unable to be ignored and visible to those within as well as external to the organization. Leaders confronted by this level of decline and peril will either return to the fundamentals and core business values that brought them to greatness or they will implement a strategy of grasping at any opportunity for salvation. In the 11 companies studied, 7 hired a CEO from outside the organization during their era of decline in a desperate effort to shake things up and save the company from certain demise. However, this action often comes too late to succeed.

Indicators of this stage may include:

- Grasping at silver bullets ("magical" solutions that will solve everything)
- Investing in an unproven technology, putting all hope in an untested strategy or a flashy new product
- Making a major acquisition that dramatically changes the focus of the company
- Seeking a "savior CEO"
- Exhibiting a desperation mentality
- Desiring quick solutions versus engaging in a slow, methodical process of rebuilding
- Making radical, revolutionary changes or initiating major transformations

Stage 5: Capitulation to Irrelevance or Death

There is a direct correlation between how long a company remains at Stage 4 (grasping for magic solutions) and the likelihood that it will spiral toward certain death or **capitulation** (ending all resistance; giving up; going along with or complying with irrelevance as an organization). The accumulation of failed strategies, flashy new products, desperate solutions, and attempts to save the organization erode financial strength and hope, causing many leaders to walk away or let the organization die.

Indicators of this stage may include:

- Failed strategies accumulate that erode financial strength
- Cash availability tightens
- Loss of the ability to make strategic choices
- Leaders are forced into implementing short-term survival decisions

Conclusion: Is There Hope?

In the midst of studying the causes of decline and stages of decline, one wonders if there is hope. Are there specific strategies to implement in order to avoid such demise? Perhaps learning from the struggles and challenges of companies facing decline offers us more information on how to avoid these pitfalls and remain a strong and viable company.

Although a lack of discipline correlates with decline of an organization, a strong adherence to management discipline correlates with recovery and ascent. *Research shows that those organizations that never give in, never give up on their core purpose, and never give up on the idea of building a great company have a much greater ability to maintain their greatness and strength.* Success is not as much about avoiding falling down, but the ability of a company to get up time after time after time.

PART FOUR

Organizational Strategy and Execution

Many of the authors represented in *The Manager's Bookshelf* suggest that organizations can benefit by defining their own standard of effectiveness, especially after examining other successful firms. An organization's external environment has a powerful influence on organizational success and needs to be monitored for significant trends and influential forces. In addition, effective executives—and CEOs in particular—need to recognize when internal changes are necessary to adapt to the external environment.

The two readings in this section are designed to stimulate thinking about management through a focus on the management and leadership of the organization from its very top. Taken together, these readings suggest that organizations can (and should) proactively take control of their destinies. One way of doing this is by *articulating a higher purpose* that, along with effective strategies well executed, can systematically guide them into the future. In effect, managers are urged to have a master plan that defines their mission, identifies their unique environmental niche, builds on their strengths, and adapts to changing needs. This overall vision is then converted into operational goals by applying several very specific management practices.

Michael Beer and his associates, in *Higher Ambition*, studied executives at organizations such as IDEA, Campbell's Soup, Infosys, Volvo, and the Tata Group to determine how they were able to deliver both superior economic results for their shareholders and beneficial social value for their communities. They found that higher-ambition leaders helped their organizations forge a clear strategic identity, built a shared commitment by employees to excel, drew upon diversity to create a tight-knit sense of community, shared power with others via collective leadership, and demonstrated extraordinary perseverance (Finnish "sisu") in their pursuit of goals in the face of risk and difficulty.

Michael Beer is the Cahners-Rabb Professor Emeritus of Business Administration at the Harvard Business School. He is the author of nine other books, including *Breaking the Code of Change* and *The Critical Path to Corporate Renewal*, and a consultant to many organizations. Russell Eisenstat was previously on the faculty at Harvard Business School and is currently the chairman of the TruePoint Center (a research-based consultancy). Nathaniel Foote is a former partner in the McKinsey & Co. consulting firm and currently a director of TruePoint. Tobias Fredberg and Flemming Norrgren are both on the faculty at Chalmers University in Gothenburg, Sweden; both are also affiliated with the TruePoint Center in Europe.

Corporate **downsizing**, sometimes euphemistically referred to as "rightsizing," has cost hundreds of thousands of employees their jobs in the past decade, while organizations sought to reduce their costs, redirect their resources, and improve their stock price. Wayne Cascio, in *Responsible Restructuring*, reports on the results of an 18-year study of major firms that destroys many common myths about downsizing's presumably positive effects. By contrast, Cascio found that downsizing has a negative impact not only on the morale and commitment of the survivors, but also on key indicators of productivity, profits, and quality. He presents an alternative to layoffs—a step-by-step blueprint that revolves around treating employees as assets to be developed, and demonstrates how responsible restructuring has worked effectively at Compaq, Cisco, Motorola, and Southwest Airlines.

Wayne Cascio is a Professor of Management at the University of Colorado—Denver, and also instructs in the Rotterdam School of Management. Cascio is a past chair of the Human Resources division of the Academy of Management and past president of the Society for Industrial and Organizational Psychology. A consultant and writer, he is the author of numerous other books, including *Investing in People*, *Applied Psychology in Human Resource Management*, *The Cost Factor, Costing Human Resources*, and *Managing Human Resources*.

1

Higher Ambition

Michael Beer, Russell Eisenstat, Nathaniel Foote,
Tobias Fredberg, and Flemming Norrgren
Summary Prepared by Cathy A. Hanson

Cathy A. Hanson is the Director of Human Resources for the city of Manhattan Beach, California. She is responsible for all aspects of human resources within a dynamic, full-service city environment. A majority of her career has been spent in the human resources departments of Fortune 100 companies (Mars, Disney, and Kraft). Her areas of interest include high-performance work teams (both public and private sectors), change management, team building, and taking principles from the private sector and applying them to the public-sector environment. She received an M.B.A. from the University of Southern California and a B.A. in Business Administration from the University of Minnesota Duluth.

INTRODUCTION

Imagine working for a company that values long-term financial health and *equally* values its social standing with employees, customers, the environment, and the community. Neither financial success nor **social values** (the benefits that the firm provides to employees, customers, communities, and the world) are deemed superior. This company is likely led by a **higher-ambition leader**. These leaders are defined as those who are able to see the organization in its totality, its possibilities and potential, and are able to communicate to all employees so their efforts are maximized to create an organization that equally values financial and social value. Leaders of all types can learn a lot from how these leaders think, problem solve, and manage their organizations.

HOW HIGHER-AMBITION LEADERS LEAD

Characteristics of Their Leadership

Thirty-six highly successful leaders from around the world were studied and interviewed to distinguish them from other leaders. The key characteristics of higher-ambition leaders include the ability to:

- See the entire organization—the good, the bad, and the ugly. These leaders were able to look objectively at their companies and see what had been, what was there now, and what was possible.
- See the possibilities of what the company could become.

Michael Beer, Russell Eisenstat, Nathaniel Foote, Tobias Fredberg, and Flemming Norrgren. *Higher Ambition: How Great Leaders Create Economic and Social Value*. Cambridge, MA: Harvard Business Review Press, 2011.

- Set key goals and communicate them simply throughout the organization.
- Never waver on issues that are important and that impact financial or social value. They are tough on issues, but softer on people.

Nature of Decision Making

As with any company, leaders who lead with higher ambition look at a variety of measures to determine if their company is successful. They work to develop a business strategy, develop goals and manage them, and build a company culture that understands these goals, and they get involved at all levels of the organization to inspire and lead the employees. One of the most striking things that distinguishes them, however, is that they look at all these things at the same time and do not compromise one over another. They practice **integrated decision making** by taking into account and weaving together information from various functions to create an outcome that is acceptable to all stakeholders. *They believe that social value and financial value are intimately linked and that decisions need to be made so that there is a positive outcome for all stakeholders.*

Higher-ambition leaders are incredibly persistent; they will "leave no stone unturned" to accomplish their goals and will work tirelessly to make sure everyone in the organization understands where the organization is headed. Once they believe they have attained a certain level of performance, they will challenge the organization to reach for more while continuously reinforcing the culture they have worked so hard to build. These leaders have an innate ability to take all key parts of the organization and integrate them for the greater good.

KEYS TO HIGHER-AMBITION LEADERSHIP

Developing a Shared Strategy

Higher-ambition leaders recognize that the organization's strategy cannot be separated from the feelings and desires of its employees. These leaders are capable of going into a business that by all standards is currently failing and instead seeing and believing in the organization's potential. *They have the ability to pass their inspired and dedicated belief in the organization to all of the employees by:*

- Developing a strategy that is understood by everyone in the organization. This is more than your run-of-the-mill strategy. These leaders find ways to engage their employees, listen to what they have to say, and create a strategy that connects employees' three major assets—their hands, heads, and hearts. In the end, the strategy resonates with the whole person.
- Evaluating the organization's capabilities and developing the strategy around them. These leaders spend a lot of effort determining what type of organizational structure will best fit the strategy they have developed for the future. Higher-ambition leaders are also involved deeply in their organizations and work hard to align all functions around the strategy, hold employees accountable for results, and find creative ways to make sure employees understand how the business is performing and how it's viewed externally so the organization can achieve its full potential.
- Practicing flexibility when needed. These leaders commit to the strategy but will adapt when needed. This allows them to make difficult decisions such as getting out of businesses that no longer fit. They have a keen ability to be committed to a strategy while

clearly seeing the realities they are dealing with and making the necessary changes. These leaders believe the strategy is dynamic and something that needs to be updated frequently and that the balancing act between commitment and flexibility is continuous.

Commitment to Exceed Expectations

The higher-ambition leaders that were studied also had a higher level of vision and expectations for how they managed employee performance. The typical result was a company that delivers high-performance results (both economic and social) year after year after year. When managing employee performance, these leaders:

- Hold employees at all levels in the organization accountable. The culture created at companies with higher-ambition leaders cultivates employees who deliver what they say they're going to deliver while holding each other accountable for achieving the long-term strategy.
- Hold themselves accountable and set high standards. The employees believe these leaders have earned the right to lead. These leaders remove any obstacles that get in the way of what they want to achieve. This is true even if they themselves have created the obstacle through prior decisions.
- Have an uncanny ability to manage short-term demands in a way that helps position the organization to meet its long-term goals.
- Focus on the basics that lead to long-term success. Higher-ambition leaders are able to tie goals and the management evaluation process to sustainable business success in a way that is clearly understood by employees.

Creating Strength and Shared Vision Out of Differences

Higher-ambition leaders believe that they can bring together employees from all over the world from different business units, functions, cultures, ethnicities, and nations, and form one global community. These leaders are able to get beyond the differences and build a common sense of purpose and culture across the organization. Although some of the differences are profound, these leaders find ways to develop commonalities and a shared sense of purpose.

Building Commonalities Across the Globe

Leaders build global commonalities from diverse and dispersed employees by:

- Allowing and encouraging employees to voice their personal values and ambitions and showing them how they tie to the organization as a whole, not just to a particular leader, product, division, and so forth.
- Giving employees a sense that they are working toward a higher purpose that aligns with their personal goals and values.
- Encouraging and enhancing cooperation and collaboration between individual employees, functions, and business units across the globe.
- Utilizing diversity to create a strategic advantage.

By doing the above, these companies have very dedicated employees with a defined common purpose who are focused on the success of the organization. The success of the organization goes above and beyond financial success and is taken personally by its employees.

Leading with Sisu

In addition to defining a strategy, developing committed employees, and utilizing diversity, these leaders display a will to succeed that transcends almost any obstacle. This extraordinary perseverance is best captured by the Finnish national characteristic of **sisu**, which is the unwavering ability to continue pursuing a goal even in the face of great adversity and high odds of failure. People displaying sisu will continue moving toward a goal even though the current environmental conditions are less than ideal and the goal may seem far away and hard to attain.

Although confronting various difficult obstacles, these leaders share common characteristics to their leadership approach, including:

- Being engaged with the workforce at all levels. This allows these leaders to develop a personal connection with the employees and thereby build a sense of lasting trust.
- Being fair in their approach to difficult decisions. Although they cannot avoid making difficult and even painful decisions, these leaders do it by being fair and showing a great deal of respect and care for those affected by the decision.
- Utilizing a "Keep It Simple, Stupid" approach to leadership. Employees in these organizations clearly understand the goals and how what they do directly impacts the goals the organization is striving to achieve. There is a clear understanding among the organization's employees as to what is expected of them and what is important.
- Persevering toward the clearly defined goals and not allowing the employees or organization to veer off course.

The bottom line is that these leaders are able to integrate all functions of the organization to achieve multiple tasks with dedication and tenacity.

Leading Together

To achieve the vision of higher-ambition leaders takes time, commitment, and a lot of combined effort on the part of the organization's leadership. The leaders who are successful at sustaining this type of leadership:

- Have a high-functioning team at the top. The top leadership team is accountable not only to the CEO but also to each other, respects each other, and stays together for a long time (five or more years).
- Align the leadership throughout the organization. Not only is the top leadership team a high-functioning collaborative team, but so are the leadership teams many levels down in the organization. These lower-level teams are able to make decisions in real time that are consistent with how the top leadership team would make the decisions, as well as take responsibility and accountability for these decisions.
- Commit to the career progression and development of employees at all levels of the organization. The higher-ambition leader will look for opportunities to develop the skills and abilities of the organization's leaders. This may come in the form of temporary assignments, detailed performance management, and/or career development planning.
- Have a passion to develop leaders at the lower levels of the organization because they realize these are the organization's future leaders and are the key to sustaining the organization's success.

Higher-ambition leaders are committed not only to the organization's vision, values, and goals, they are committed to the individual employees and leaders within the organization. They develop a culture that values and encourages continuous learning and development.

MOVING TOWARD HIGHER-AMBITION LEADERSHIP

Higher-Ambition Leaders

In order to become a higher-ambition leader, individuals evaluate and spend time engaging in four key practices:

1. They find an "anchor." Higher-ambition leaders learn early on and believe in what they stand for and why they are doing what they're doing. They develop self-confidence through self-awareness and make decisions based on their values and beliefs. They lead with a great deal of integrity.
2. They find appropriate mentors and partners. Higher-ambition leaders believe they can learn from others both at their same level within the organization as well as their own management team. These leaders believe continuous learning is key to their development and moving the organization forward. Higher-ambition leaders will understand their weaknesses and surround themselves with people who have strengths in these areas.
3. They learn from the past. Higher-ambition leaders learn from each and every experience and assignment. These experiences build their self-confidence and allow them to understand what they value and why they value it.
4. They encourage honest feedback. These leaders utilize various methods to encourage feedback from all levels of the organization and communities in which they find themselves. They listen to this feedback and find ways to learn from it to build a stronger organization.

Higher-Ambition Businesses

A **higher-ambition business** is an organization that utilizes and maximizes the strengths, talents, and energy of its employees. Additionally, these organizations have functions, business units, and employees who all work together to make decisions that benefit the organization as a whole while maximizing the financial strength and social value of the organization. One area is not more important or sacrificed for the other.

A lot of work still needs to be done in order for more organizations to operate as higher-ambition businesses. This includes a board of directors holding CEOs accountable for not only short-term performance, but long-term performance as well, encouraging their top management teams to work together for a higher purpose that emphasizes financial performance and social value, developing and choosing top leadership that leads with higher ambition, and ensuring that all levels of the organization understand and can participate in determining the values, goals, and mission of the organization so they have a passion for and stake in its success.

Importantly, business schools need to change their focus to include integrative decision making that teaches how to maximize not only financial return but also the social value to the community in which the organization operates. Only when these two components come together can we expect to see more higher-ambition leaders and businesses.

2

Responsible Restructuring

Wayne F. Cascio
Summary Prepared by Stephen Rubenfeld

Stephen Rubenfeld is Professor Emeritus of Human Resource Management at the Labovitz School of Business and Economics at the University of Minnesota Duluth. He received his doctorate from the University of Wisconsin–Madison and was previously on the faculty of Texas Tech University. His professional publications and presentations have covered a wide range of human resources and labor-relations topics, including job-search behaviors, human resources policies and practices, job security, and staffing challenges. He has served as a consultant to private and public organizations and is a member of the Society for Human Resource Management, the Academy of Management, and the Industrial Relations Research Association.

A highly competitive business context carries with it both boundless opportunities and daunting challenges. On one hand, organizations are stimulated to become better at what they do by economizing, innovating, and honing their competitive advantage. But at the same time, the very existence of a business can be threatened by pricing pressures, declining profit margins, and burgeoning capital investment needs. This is not a situation that calls for "just getting by," mediocrity, or hoping that things will work themselves out. Intense competition is a call to action that tests the mettle of organizations and their leaders. It is a situation that demands thoughtful and aggressive actions. The pressures attributable to the global marketplace, pervasive technology, and more assertive consumers are not going to abate. Decisive steps are necessary to ensure that the critical elements of competitive success—price, quality, and customer service—are in place and fine-tuned to support continued organizational vitality.

The active pursuit of efficiencies, effective operations, and customer responsiveness are all subjects of much organizational rhetoric, but in practice it is the cost-containment part of the equation that gets most of the attention. In fact, it is easier, faster, and more predictable to cut costs than it is to increase revenues or to fundamentally improve the organization's product or service. Whether driven by a current financial crisis or the desire to avoid future problems, actions directed at cutting or controlling costs, rooting out inefficiencies, and keeping prices in check have become almost universal. Unlike earlier times, this self-imposed pressure to focus on cost containment is not limited to organizations swimming in red ink; it has become a benchmark of good business practice.

Wayne F. Cascio. *Responsible Restructuring: Creative and Profitable Alternatives to Layoffs.* San Francisco, CA: Berrett-Koehler, 2003.

Because employment costs are the most visible and frequently an organization's largest variable cost, downsizing along with wage and benefit containment are at the heart of most efforts to enhance competitiveness. Often characterized euphemistically as **organizational restructuring**, the logic of these efforts to control expenses by having fewer employees is compelling: Reducing costs will increase profit margins, which will produce immediate bottom-line results and help ensure future success. But the promised benefits of cost containment through reducing headcount often are elusive. Whether couched in the verbiage of *downsizing, rightsizing,* or other emotionless synonyms for reducing the number of employees, the benefits tend to be fleeting. By themselves these methods rarely offer a sustainable solution to the barriers to competitiveness. Likewise, wage freezes and benefits cuts may have an immediate and visible bottom-line impact, but the true savings are often reduced by diminished productivity along with undesired turnover or other employee withdrawal behaviors.

The net effect is that *restructuring that is built primarily on downsizing or containment of compensation costs will not have a positive effect on the areas where real competitiveness is built: innovation, quality, and customer service.* In the end, this approach to restructuring does not achieve the forecasted cost savings and does not help to improve long-term competitive vitality of the organization. If downsizing is not the solution, how can an organization succeed in a competitive marketplace?

IS RESTRUCTURING BAD?

Restructuring can be constructive and even essential when a company is struggling to regain or achieve economic success. Similarly, evolving technologies, nonperforming assets, or even aggressive moves by competitors can be a powerful impetus to restructure. It is obvious that job losses, layoffs, and sometimes radical changes to the jobs that remain are integral to most restructurings, but as is often the case, the devil is in the details. The issue is *how* these employment changes are made. Experience carries with it the lesson that across-the-board layoffs and hiring freezes, or similar *slash-and-burn* downsizing strategies, rarely achieve the promised benefits. The hidden costs and secondary impacts may even worsen the competitive crisis.

Many of the costs of downsizing are obvious and calculable. The decision to restructure typically carries with it a recognition that costs associated with severance pay, accrued vacations, benefit costs, outplacement, and additional administrative expense will be incurred. In contrast, there are many indirect costs that may be ignored or not even recognized. Even where acknowledged as potential problem areas, their severity is often underestimated. Although it may be difficult to accurately estimate their future costs and impacts, these costs are real and can have a dramatic negative impact on competitiveness. Examples of such hidden costs include:

- Reduced morale
- Risk-averse behaviors by surviving employees
- Loss of trust
- Costs of retraining continuing employees
- Legal challenges
- Reduced productivity
- Loss of institutional competencies and memory
- Survivor **burnout**

Although these problems and costs may impede competitiveness efforts, restructuring is not inherently bad. Many businesses have successfully downsized and restructured to improve their productivity and financial success, but downsizing is not a panacea. Research conducted over the past 25 years indicates that *downsizing strategies for most organizations do not result in long-term payoffs that are significantly greater than those where there are stable employment patterns.*

MYTHS ABOUT DOWNSIZING

When confronted by the need to reduce costs, many employers (who self-righteously proclaim that "employees are our greatest asset") turn to layoffs first when responding to a competitive dilemma. This may be fueled by a number of myths and misunderstandings about downsizing. For example, the following six myths are refuted by research and experience (facts):

> *Myth 1:* Downsizing increases profits.
>
> *Fact 1:* Profitability does not necessarily improve.
>
> *Myth 2:* Downsizing boosts productivity.
>
> *Fact 2:* Productivity results are mixed.
>
> *Myth 3:* Downsizing doesn't negatively affect quality.
>
> *Fact 3:* Quality does not improve and may go down.
>
> *Myth 4:* Downsizing is a one-time event.
>
> *Fact 4:* The best predictor of future downsizing is past downsizing.
>
> *Myth 5:* Downsizing has few effects on remaining employees.
>
> *Fact 5:* Negative impacts on morale, stress, and commitment are common.
>
> *Myth 6:* Downsizing is unlikely to lead to sabotage or other vengeful acts.
>
> *Fact 6:* Such behaviors are not rare, and their consequences can be severe.

These findings should offer decision makers a note of caution about the potential consequences of restructuring efforts painted with a broad brush. An obvious conclusion is that restructuring should not be done blindly, and when restructuring does appear to be necessary, it should be approached strategically and responsibly.

RESPONSIBLE RESTRUCTURING

The approaches that employers take toward restructuring reflect significant differences in how they view their employees. Organizational decision makers can be thought of as falling into two camps concerning their view of employees—those who see employees as *costs to be cut* and those who see employees as *assets to be developed*. The *cost cutters* consider employees to be the source of the problem. They think of employees as commodities. Through the lens of the income statement they strive to achieve the minimum number of employees and the lowest possible labor expenditures needed to run the business successfully. In contrast, in **responsible restructuring**, employee expertise and contributions are viewed as central to any solution. They consider their employees as essential in fashioning and carrying forward sustainable answers to competitiveness challenges. The initial focus of the responsible restructurers is not on reducing headcount or shrinking the budget, but rather on enhancing effectiveness and empowering employees to overcome competitive challenges.

Responsible restructurers turn to broad-based layoffs and compensation cuts only as a last resort. Their initial and primary approach is to use a variety of developmental and effectiveness-oriented practices to achieve and maintain competitive viability. These organizations are likely to:

- Flatten their hierarchical structures.
- Create an empowered, team-oriented work environment.
- Seek labor–management partnerships.
- Share information.
- Make extensive use of training.
- Demonstrate a culture of continuous learning.
- Link compensation to performance and skills.

These employers do not advocate and use these responsible restructuring strategies primarily as acts of compassion or for other altruistic reasons. They truly believe that there are benefits that come from employment stability and that the best and most sustainable outcomes are achieved when employees are part of the solution.

These companies, which include in their ranks Southwest Airlines, SAS Institute, Cisco, Charles Schwab, Procter & Gamble, and 3M, share the following critical characteristics:

1. A clear vision of what they want to achieve and how to communicate this vision to stakeholders,
2. The ability to execute and develop employee-centered initiatives, and
3. Highly empowered employees who are committed to help the organization succeed.

These companies don't start with the premise that the minimal number of employees is the best number of employees. Rather, they ask how their employees can help them fashion a solution and meet the market challenge. They know that short-term downsizing does not solve long-term problems.

HOW DO WE MOVE FORWARD?

In addition to the basic elements of responsible restructuring already described, it is useful to keep these recommendations in mind as issues of competitiveness are confronted:

- Deal with the underlying competitive problem, not just the bottom line.
- Integrate staffing decisions with the strategic business plan and the drivers of success.
- Involve employees in shaping broad solutions as well as specific organizational responses.
- Consider the payoffs from employment stability.
- Communicate regularly, openly, effectively, and honestly.
- If layoffs are necessary, be logical, targeted, fair, and consistent.
- Give survivors a reason to stay and prospective employees a reason to join the organization.
- Empower survivors to succeed and encourage them to beware of burnout.

Conclusion

The ultimate payoff from successfully pursuing *responsible restructuring* rather than budget slashing in responding to competitive challenges is better and longer-lasting solution. The organization also is more likely to reap the rewards of higher customer satisfaction, have the ability to respond more quickly and more successfully to future challenges, maintain a recruiting and retention advantage over its labor market competitors, and have committed employees who are not unduly risk averse. Remove the barriers to effective competition and financial success will follow.

PART FIVE

Organizational Culture

Shared beliefs and values, coupled with the basic assumptions employed by a group as it struggles with its problems and its opportunities, comprise an organization's *culture*. A strong organizational culture has been described as a key ingredient of many of the great organizations in our society. One of the many challenges facing managers at all levels of the organization is to develop an appropriate culture. A sense of shared beliefs and values can help bind the organization together and provide a coherent sense of direction to organizational activities.

Unfortunately, culture has various meanings and usages to different people. Edgar H. Schein, in *Organizational Culture and Leadership*, develops a workable definition that focuses on valid assumptions about how to perceive, think, feel, and act that are then communicated and taught to employees—both new and old. Schein goes on to discuss the ways in which we can identify the existing culture of an organization, the relationship of that culture to organizational stages, and when to change it and how to manage it. Edgar Schein earned his Ph.D. in Social Psychology from Harvard University and is a Professor of Management Emeritus at the MIT Sloan School of Management. A creative thinker and pragmatic writer, he has published books on career dynamics, process consultation, organizational learning, and corporate culture.

One fascinating dimension of organizational culture is its transparency—the degree to which its leaders practice and exhibit candor, openness, and easy accessibility. Transparent leaders are genuine (without hidden agendas) and authentic (true to their word, while acting sincerely). They also speak the truth and provide credible information to those above them, even if it means acting as a whistleblower by reporting unethical or illegal behavior. In contrast to past practice, many organizations are moving consciously toward a culture of transparency for two reasons: (1) society is demanding it, and (2) it is effective for reducing disruptive office politics, while increasing employee collaboration and loyalty.

Transparency is a composite of thinking by three noted authors. Warren Bennis is Distinguished Professor of Business Administration at the University of Southern California, and a renowned scholar, consultant, and author. He has published numerous books across his career on topics such as visionary leadership, co-leadership, the unconscious conspiracy that prevents leaders from leading, and judgment. Daniel Goleman is a trained psychologist and a science journalist. He is best known for his *Emotional Intelligence* book, which sold over five million copies worldwide. The third author is James O'Toole, who is the Daniels Distinguished Professor of Business Ethics at the University of Denver. A former Rhodes scholar, he received his doctorate in social anthropology from Oxford University. O'Toole has published previous books such as *Leading Change*, *The Executive Compass*, and *The New American Workplace*.

1 Coming to a New Awareness of Organizational Culture

Edgar H. Schein

Edgar H. Schein is the Sloan Fellows Professor of Management at the Sloan School of Management, M.I.T. Dr. Schein holds the B.A. degree from the University of Chicago, the M.A. degree from Stanford University, and the Ph.D. degree in Social Psychology from Harvard University. He has extensive consulting experience in human resource planning and development, corporate culture, organization development, top *management* team building, and related fields. He is the author of *Organizational Psychology* and *Career Dynamics*, as well as numerous articles, and is currently writing a book on organizational culture to be published by Jossey-Bass.

If we really want to decipher an organization's culture, this author claims that we must dig below the organization's surface—beyond the "visible artifacts"—and uncover the basic underlying assumptions, which are the core of an organization's culture. To do this, he provides a tool—a formal definition of organizational culture that emphasizes how culture works. With this definition in hand, the author feels that one cannot only come to understand the dynamic evolutionary forces that govern a culture, but also can explain how the culture is learned, passed on, and changed.

The purpose of this article is to define the concept of organizational culture in terms of a dynamic model of how culture is learned, passed on, and changed. As many recent efforts argue that organizational culture is the key to organizational excellence, it is critical to define this complex concept in a manner that will provide a common frame of reference for practitioners and researchers. Many definitions simple settle for the notion that culture is a set of shared meanings that make it possible for members of a group to interpret and act upon their environment. I believe we must go beyond this definition: even if we knew an organization well enough to live in it, we would not necessarily know how its culture arose, how it came to be what it is, or how it could be changed if organizational survival were at stake.

The thrust of my argument is that we must understand the dynamic evolutionary forces that govern how culture evolves and changes. My approach to this task will be to lay out a formal definition of what I believe organizational culture is, and to elaborate each element of the definition to make it clear how it works.

ORGANIZATIONAL CULTURE: A FORMAL DEFINITION

Organizational culture is the *pattern of basic assumptions that a given group* has *invented, discovered, or developed in learning to cope* with its *problems of external adaptation and internal integration*, and that have *worked well enough to be considered valid*, and, therefore, to be *taught to new members* as the correct way to *perceive, think, and feel* in relation to those problems.

1. Pattern of Basic Assumptions

Organizational culture can be analyzed at several different levels, starting with the *visible artifacts*—the constructed environment of the organization, its architecture, technology, office layout, manner of dress, visible or audible behavior patterns, and public documents such as charters, employee orientation materials, stories (see Figure 1). This level of analysis is tricky because the data are easy to obtain but hard to interpret. We can describe "how" a group constructs its environment and "what" behavior patterns are discernible among the members, but we often cannot understand the underlying logic—"why" a group behaves the way it does.

To analyze *why* members behave the way they do, we often look for the *values* that govern behavior, which is the second level in Figure 1. But as values are hard to observe directly, it is often necessary to infer them by interviewing key members of the organization or to content analyze artifacts such as documents and charters.[1] However, in identifying such values, we usually note that they represent accurately only the manifest or *espoused* values of a culture. That is

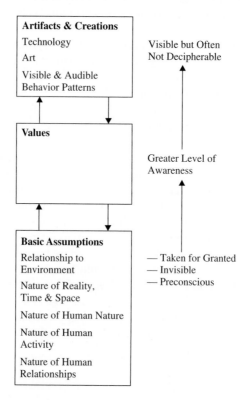

FIGURE 1   The Levels of Culture and Their Interaction

they focus on what people *say* is the reason for their behavior, what they ideally would like those reasons to be, and what are often their rationalizations for their behavior. Yet, the underlying reasons for their behavior remain concealed or unconscious.[2]

To really *understand* a culture and to ascertain more completely the group's values and overt behavior, it is imperative to delve into the *underlying assumptions*, which are typically unconscious but which actually determine how group members perceive, think, and feel.[3] Such assumptions are themselves learned responses that originated as espoused values. But, as a value leads to a behavior, and as that behavior begins to solve the problem which prompted it in the first place, the value gradually is transformed into an underlying assumption about how things really are. As the assumption is increasingly taken for granted, it drops out of awareness.

Taken-for-granted assumptions are so powerful because they are less debatable and confrontable than espoused values. We know we are dealing with an assumption when we encounter in our informants a refusal to discuss something, or when they consider us "insane" or "ignorant" for bringing something up. For example, the notion that businesses should be profitable, that schools should educate, or that medicine should prolong life are assumptions, even though they are often considered "merely" values.

To put it another way, the domain of values can be divided into (1) ultimate, non-debatable, taken-for-granted values, for which the term "assumptions" is more appropriate; and (2) debatable, overt, espoused values, for which the term "values" is more applicable. In stating that basic assumptions are unconscious, I am not arguing that this is a result of repression. On the contrary, I am arguing that as certain motivational and cognitive processes are repeated and continue to work, they become unconscious. They can be brought back to awareness only through a kind of focused inquiry, similar to that used by anthropologists. What is needed are the efforts of both an insider who makes the unconscious assumptions and an outsider who helps to uncover the assumptions by asking the right kinds of questions.[4]

CULTURAL PARADIGMS: A NEED FOR ORDER AND CONSISTENCY   Because of the human need for order and consistency, assumptions become patterned into what may be termed cultural "paradigms," which tie together the basic assumptions about humankind, nature, and activities. A **cultural paradigm** is a set of interrelated assumptions that form a coherent pattern. Not all assumptions are mutually compatible or consistent, however. For example, if a group holds the assumption that all good ideas and products ultimately come from individual effort, it cannot easily assume simultaneously that groups can be held responsible for the results achieved, or that individuals will put a high priority on group loyalty. Or, if a group assumes that the way to survive is to conquer nature and to manipulate its environment aggressively, it cannot at the same time assume that the best kind of relationship among group members is one that emphasizes passivity and harmony. If human beings do indeed have a cognitive need for order and consistency, one can then assume that all groups will eventually evolve sets of assumptions that are compatible and consistent.

To analyze cultural paradigms, one needs a set of logical categories for studying assumptions. Table 1 shows such a set based on the original comparative study of Kluckhohn and Strodtbeck.[5] In applying these categories broadly to cultures, Kluckhohn and Strodtbeck note that Western culture tends to be oriented toward an active mastery of nature, and is based on individualistic competitive relationships. It uses a future-oriented, linear, monochronic concept of time,[6] views space and resources as infinite, assumes that human nature is neutral and ultimately perfectible, and bases reality or ultimate truth on science and pragmatism.

In contrast, some Eastern cultures are passively oriented toward nature. They seek to harmonize with nature and with each other. They view the group as more important than the

TABLE 1 Basic Underlying Assumptions around Which Cultural Paradigms Form

1. **The Organization's Relationship to Its Environment.** Reflecting even more basic assumptions about the relationship of humanity to nature, one can assess whether the key members of the organization view the relationship as one of dominance, submission, harmonizing, finding an appropriate niche, and so on.

2. **The Nature of Reality and Truth.** Here are the linguistic and behavioral rules that define what is real and what is not, what is a "fact," how truth is ultimately to be determined, and whether truth is "revealed" or "discovered"; basic concepts of time as linear or cyclical, monochronic or polychronic; basic concepts such as space as limited or infinite and property as communal or individual; and so forth.

3. **The Nature of Human Nature.** What does it mean to be "human" and what attributes are considered intrinsic or ultimate? Is human nature good, evil, or neutral? Are human beings perfectible or not? Which is better, Theory X or Theory Y?

4. **The Nature of Human Activity.** What is the "right" thing for human beings to do, on the basis of the above assumptions about reality, the environment, and human nature: to be active, passive, self-developmental, fatalistic, or what? What is work and what is play?

5. **The Nature of Human Relationships.** What is considered to be the "right" way for people to relate to each other, to distribute power and love? Is life cooperative or competitive; individualistic, group collaborative, or communal; based on traditional lineal authority, law, or charisma; or what?

Source: Reprinted, by permission of the publisher, from "The Role of the Founder in Creating Organizational Culture," by Edgar H. Schein, *Organizational Dynamics*, Summer 1983 © 1983 Periodicals Division, American Management Associations. All rights reserved.

individual, are present or past oriented, see time as polychronic and cyclical, view space and resources as very limited assume that human nature is bad but improvable, and see reality as based more on revealed truth than on empirical experimentation.

In this light, organizational culture paradigms are adapted versions of broader cultural paradigms. For example, Dyer notes that the GEM Corporation operates on the interlocking assumptions that: (1) ideas come ultimately from individuals; (2) people are responsible, motivated, and capable of governing themselves; however, truth can only be pragmatically determined by "fighting" things out and testing in groups; (3) such fighting is possible because the members of the organization view themselves as a family who will take care of each other. Ultimately, this makes it safe to fight and be competitive.[7]

I have observed another organization that operates on the paradigm that (1) truth comes ultimately from older, wiser, better educated, higher status members; (2) people are capable of loyalty and discipline in carrying out directives; (3) relationships are basically lineal and vertical; (4) each person has a niche that is his or her territory that cannot be invaded; and (5) the organization is a "solidary unit" that will take care of its members.

Needless to say, the manifest behaviors in these two organizations are totally different. In the first organization, one observes mostly open office landscapes, few offices with closed doors, a high rate of milling about, intense conversations and arguments, and a general air of informality. In the second organization, there is a hush in the air: everyone is in an office and with closed doors. Nothing is done except by appointment and with a prearranged agenda. When people of different ranks are present, one sees real deference rituals and obedience, and a general air of formality permeates everything.

Nonetheless, these behavioral differences make no sense until one has discovered and deciphered the underlying cultural paradigm. To stay at the level of artifacts or values is to deal with the *manifestations* of culture, but not with the cultural essence.

2. A Given Group

There cannot be a culture unless there is a group that "owns" it. Culture is embedded in groups, hence the creating group must always be clearly identified. If we want to define a cultural unit, therefore, we must be able to locate a group that is independently defined as the creator, host, or owner of that culture. We must be careful not to define the group in terms of the existence of a culture however tempting that may be, because we then would be creating a completely circular definition.

A given group is a set of people (1) who have been together long enough to have shared significant problems, (2) who have had opportunities to solve those problems and to observe the effects of their solutions, and (3) who have taken in new members. A group's culture cannot be determined unless there is such a definable set of people with a shared history.

The passing on of solutions to new members is required in the definition of culture because the decision to pass something on is itself a very important test of whether a given solution is shared and perceived as valid. If a group passes on with conviction elements of a way of perceiving, thinking, and feeling, we can assume that that group has had enough stability and has shared enough common experiences to have developed a culture. If, on the other hand, a group has not faced the issue of what to pass on in the process of socialization, it has not had a chance to test its own consensus and commitment to a given belief, value, or assumption.

THE STRENGTH OF A CULTURE The "strength" or "amount" of culture can be defined in terms of (1) the *homogeneity* and *stability* of group membership and (2) the *length* and *intensity* of shared experiences of the group. If a stable group has had a long, varied, intense history (i.e., if it has had to cope with many difficult survival problems and has succeeded), it will have a strong and highly differentiated culture. By the same token, if a group has had a constantly shifting membership or has been together only for a short time and has not faced any difficult issues, it will, by definition, have a weak culture. Although individuals within that group may have very strong individual assumptions, there will not be enough shared experiences for the group as a whole to have a defined culture.

By this definition, one would probably assess IBM and the Bell System as having strong cultures, whereas, very young companies or ones which have had a high turnover of key executives would be judged as having weak ones. One should also note that once an organization has a strong culture, if the dominant coalition or leadership remains stable, the culture can survive high turnover at lower ranks because new members can be strongly socialized into the organization as, for example, in elite military units.

It is very important to recognize that cultural strength may or may not be correlated with effectiveness. Though some current writers have argued that strength is desirable,[8] it seems clear to me that the relationship is far more complex. The actual content of the culture and the degree to which its solutions fit the problems posed by the environment seem like the critical variables here, not strength. One can hypothesize that young groups strive for culture strength as a way of creating an identity for themselves, but older groups may be more effective with a weak total culture and diverse subcultures to enable them to be responsive to rapid environmental change.

This way of defining culture makes it specific to a given group. If a total corporation consists of stable functional, divisional, geographic, or rank-based subgroups, then that corporation will have multiple cultures within it. It is perfectly possible for those multiple cultures to be in conflict with each other, such that one could not speak of a single corporate culture. On the other hand, if there has been common corporate experience as well, then one could have a strong corporate culture on top of various subcultures that are based in subunits. The deciphering of a given company's culture then becomes an empirical matter of locating where the stable social units are, what cultures each of those stable units have developed, and how those separate cultures blend into a single whole. The total culture could then be very homogeneous or heterogeneous, according to the degree to which subgroup cultures are similar or different.

It has also been pointed out that some of the cultural assumptions in an organization can come from the occupational background of the members of the organization. This makes it possible to have a managerial culture, an engineering culture, a science culture, a labor union culture, etc., all of which coexist in a given organization.[9]

3. Invented, Discovered, or Developed

Cultural elements are defined as learned solutions to problems. In this section, I will concentrate on the nature of the learning mechanisms that are involved.

Structurally, there are two types of learning situations: (1) positive problem-solving situations that produce positive or negative reinforcement in terms of whether the attempted solution works or not; and (2) anxiety-avoidance situations that produce positive or negative reinforcement in terms of whether the attempted solution does or does not avoid anxiety. In practice, these two types of situations are intertwined, but they are structurally different and, therefore, they must be distinguished.

In the positive problem-solving situation, the group tries out various responses until something works. The group will then continue to use this response until it ceases to work. The information that it no longer works is visible and clear. By contrast, in the anxiety-avoidance situation, once a response is learned because it successfully avoids anxiety, it is likely to be repeated indefinitely. The reason is that the learner will not willingly test the situation to determine whether the cause of the anxiety is still operating. Thus all rituals, patterns of thinking or feeling, and behaviors that may originally have been motivated by a need to avoid a painful, anxiety-provoking situation are going to be repeated, even if the causes of the original pain are no longer acting, because the avoidance of anxiety is, itself, positively reinforcing.[10]

To fully grasp the importance of anxiety reduction in culture formation, we have to consider, first of all, the human need for cognitive order and consistency, which serves as the ultimate motivator for a common language and shared categories of perception and thought.[11] In the absence of such shared "cognitive maps," the human organism experiences a basic existential anxiety that is intolerable—an anxiety observed only in extreme situations of isolation or captivity.[12]

Secondly, humans experience the anxiety associated with being exposed to hostile environmental conditions and to the dangers inherent in unstable social relationships, forcing groups to learn ways of coping with such external and internal problems.

A third source of anxiety is associated with occupational roles such as coal mining and nursing. For example, the Tavistock sociotechnical studies have shown clearly that the social structure and ways of operation of such groups can be conceptualized best as a "defense" against the anxiety that would be unleashed if work were done in another manner.[13]

If an organizational culture is composed of both types of elements—those designed to solve problems and those designed to avoid anxiety—it becomes necessary to analyze which is which if one is concerned about changing any of the elements. In the positive-learning situation, one needs innovative sources to find a better solution to the problem; in the anxiety-avoidance situation, one must first find the source of the anxiety and either show the learner that it no longer exists, or provide an alternative source of avoidance. Either of these is difficult to do.

In other words, cultural elements that are based on anxiety reduction will be more stable than those based on positive problem solving because of the nature of the anxiety-reduction mechanism and the fact that human systems need a certain amount of stability to avoid cognitive and social anxiety.

Where do solutions initially come from? Most cultural solutions in new groups and organizations originate from the founders and early leaders of those organizations.[14] Typically, the solution process is an advocacy of certain ways of doing things that are then tried out and either adopted or rejected, depending on how well they work out. Initially, the founders have the most influence, but, as the group ages and acquires its own experiences, its members will find their own solutions. Ultimately, the process of discovering new solutions will be more a result of interactive, shared experiences. But leadership will always play a key role during those times when the group faces a new problem and must develop new responses to the situation. In fact, one of the crucial functions of leadership is to provide guidance at precisely those times when habitual ways of doing things no longer work, or when a dramatic change in the environment requires new responses.

At those times, leadership must not only insure the invention of new and better solutions, but must also provide some security to help the group tolerate the anxiety of giving up old, stable responses, while new ones are learned and tested. In the Lewinian change framework, this means that the "unfreezing stage" must involve both enough disconfirmation to motivate change and enough psychological safety to permit the individual or group to pay attention to the disconfirming data.[15]

4. Problems of External Adaptation and Internal Integration

If culture is a solution to the problems a group faces, what can we say about the nature of those problems? Most group theories agree it is useful to distinguish between two kinds of problems: (1) those that deal with the group's basic survival, which has been labeled the primary task, basic function, or ultimate mission of the group; and (2) those that deal with the group's ability to function as a group. These problems have been labeled socioemotional, group building and maintenance, or integration problems.[16]

Homans further distinguishes between the *external system* and the *internal system* and notes that the two are interdependent.[17] Even though one can distinguish between the external and internal problems, in practice both systems are highly interrelated.

EXTERNAL ADAPTATION PROBLEMS Problems of external adaptation are those that ultimately determine the group's survival in the environment. While a part of the group's environment is "enacted," in the sense that prior cultural experience predisposes members to perceive the environment in a certain way and even to control that environment to a degree, there will always be elements of the environment (weather, natural circumstances, availability of economic and other resources, political upheavals) that are clearly beyond the control of the group and that will, to a degree, determine the fate of the group.[18] A useful way to categorize the problems of survival is to mirror the stages of the problem-solving cycle as shown in Table 2.[19]

TABLE 2 Problems of External Adaptation and Survival	
Strategy:	Developing consensus on the *primary task, core mission, or manifest and latent functions of the group.*
Goals:	Developing consensus on goals, such *goals* being the concrete reflection of the core mission.
Means for Accomplishing Goals:	Developing consensus on the *means* to be used in accomplishing the goals—for example, division of labor, organization structure, reward system, and so forth.
Measuring Performance:	Developing consensus on the *criteria to be used in measuring how well the group is doing against its goals and targets*—for example, information and control systems.
Correction:	Developing consensus on *remedial or repair strategies* as needed when the group is not accomplishing its goals.

Source: Reprinted, by permission of the publisher, from "The Role of the Founder in Creating Organizational Culture," by Edgar H. Schein, *Organizational Dynamics*, Summer 1983 © 1983 Periodicals Division, American Management Associations. All rights reserved.

The basic underlying assumptions of the culture from which the founders of the organization come will determine to a large extent the initial formulations of core mission, goals, means, criteria, and remedial strategies, in that those ways of doing things are the only ones with which the group members will be familiar. But as an organization develops its own life experience, it may begin to modify to some extent its original assumptions. For example, a young company may begin by defining its core mission to be to "win in the marketplace over all competition," but may at a later stage find that "owning its own niche in the marketplace," "coexisting with other companies," or even "being a silent partner in an oligopolistic industry" is a more workable solution to survival. Thus for each stage of the problem-solving cycle, there will emerge solutions characteristic of that group's own history, and those solutions or ways of doing things based on learned assumptions will make up a major portion of that group's culture.

INTERNAL INTEGRATION PROBLEMS   A group or organization cannot survive if it cannot manage itself as a group. External survival and internal integration problems are, therefore, two sides of the same coin. Table 3 outlines the major issues of internal integration around which cultural solutions must be found.

While the nature of the solutions will vary from one organization to another, by definition, every organization will have to face each of these issues and develop some kind of solution. However, because the nature of that solution will reflect the biases of the founders and current leaders, the prior experiences of group members, and the actual events experienced, it is likely that each organizational culture will be unique, even though the underlying issues around which the culture is formed will be common.[20]

An important issue to study across many organizations is whether an organization's growth and evolution follows an inherent evolutionary trend (e.g., developing societies are seen as evolving from that of a community to more of a bureaucratic, impersonal type of system). One should also study whether organizational cultures reflect in a patterned way the nature of the underlying technology, the age of the organization, the size of the organization, and the nature of the parent culture within which the organization evolves.

TABLE 3 Problems of Internal Integration	
Language:	*Common language and conceptual categories.* If members cannot communicate with and understand each other, a group is impossible by definition.
Boundaries:	*Consensus on group boundaries and criteria for inclusion and exclusion.* One of the most important areas of culture is the shared consensus on who is in, who is out, and by what criteria one determines membership.
Power & Status:	Consensus on *criteria for the allocation of power and status.* Every organization must work out its pecking order and its rules for how one gets, maintains, and loses power. This area of consensus is crucial in helping members manage their own feelings of aggression.
Intimacy:	Consensus on *criteria for intimacy, friendship, and love.* Every organization must work out its rules of the game for peer relationships, for relationships between the sexes, and for the manner in which openness and intimacy are to be handled in the context of managing the organization's tasks.
Rewards & Punishments:	Consensus on *criteria for allocation of rewards and punishments.* Every group must know what its heroic and sinful behaviors are; what gets rewarded with property, status, and power; and what gets punished through the withdrawal of rewards and, ultimately, excommunication.
Ideology:	Consensus on *ideology and "religion."* Every organization, like every society, faces unexplainable events that must be given meaning so that members can respond to them and avoid the anxiety of dealing with the unexplainable and uncontrollable.

Source: Reprinted, by permission of the publisher, from "The Role of the Founder in Creating Organizational Culture," by Edgar H. Schein, *Organizational Dynamics*, Summer 1983 © 1983 Periodicals Division. American Management Associations. All rights reserved.

5. Assumptions That Work Well Enough to Be Considered Valid

Culture goes beyond the norms or values of a group in that it is more of an *ultimate* outcome, based on repeated success and a gradual process of taking things for granted. In other words, to me what makes something "cultural" is this "taken-for-granted" quality, which makes the underlying assumptions virtually undiscussable.

Culture is perpetually being formed in the sense that there is constantly some kind of learning going on about how to relate to the environment and to manage internal affairs. But this ongoing evolutionary process does not change those things that are so thoroughly learned that they come to be a stable element of the group's life. Since the basic assumptions that make up an organization's culture serve the secondary function of stabilizing much of the internal and external environment for the group, and since that stability is sought as a defense against the anxiety which comes with uncertainty and confusion, these deeper parts of the culture either do not change or change only very slowly.

6. Taught to New Members

Because culture serves the function of stabilizing the external and internal environment for an organization, it must be taught to new members. It would not serve its function if every generation of new members could introduce new perceptions, language, thinking patterns, and rules of interaction. For culture to serve its function, it must be perceived as correct and valid, and if it is perceived that way, it automatically follows that it must be taught to newcomers.

It cannot be overlooked that new members do bring new ideas and do produce culture change, especially if they are brought in at high levels of the organization. It remains to be settled empirically whether and how this happens. For example, does a new member have to be socialized first and accented into a central and powerful position before he or she can begin to affect change? Or does a new member bring from the onset new ways of perceiving, thinking, feeling, and acting, which produce automatic changes through role innovation?[21] Is the manner in which new members are socialized influential in determining what kind of innovation they will produce?[22] Much of the work on innovation in organizations is confusing because often it is not clear whether the elements that are considered "new" are actually new assumptions, or simply new artifacts built on old cultural assumptions.

In sum, if culture provides the group members with a paradigm of how the world "is," it goes without saying that such a paradigm would be passed on without question to new members. It is also the case that the very process of passing on the culture provides an opportunity for testing, ratifying, and reaffirming it. For both of these reasons, the process of socialization (i.e., the passing on of the group's culture) is strategically an important process to study if one wants to decipher what the culture is and how it might change.[23]

7. Perceive, Think, and Feel

The final element in the definition reminds us that culture is pervasive and ubiquitous. The basic assumptions about nature, humanity, relationships, truth, activity, time, and space cover virtually all human functions. This is not to say that a given organization's culture will develop to the point of totally "controlling" all of its members' perceptions, thoughts, and feelings. But the process of learning to manage the external and internal environment does involve all of one's cognitive and emotional elements. As cultural learning progresses, more and more of the person's responses will become involved. Therefore, the longer we live in a given culture, and the older the culture is, the more it will influence our perceptions, thoughts, and feelings.

By focusing on perceptions, thoughts, and feelings, I am also stating the importance of those categories relative to the category of *overt behavior*. Can one speak of a culture in terms of just the overt behavior patterns one observes? Culture is *manifested* in overt behavior, but the idea of culture goes deeper than behavior. Indeed, the very reason for elaborating an abstract notion like "culture" is that it is too difficult to explain what goes on in organizations if we stay at the descriptive behavioral level.

To put it another way, behavior is, to a large extent, a joint function of what the individual brings to the situation and the operating situational forces, which to some degree are unpredictable. To understand the cultural portion of what the individual brings to the situation (as opposed to the idiosyncratic or situational portions), we must examine the individual's pattern of perceptions, thoughts, and feelings. Only after we have reached a consensus at this inner level have we uncovered what is potentially *cultural*.

THE STUDY OF ORGANIZATIONAL CULTURE AND ITS IMPLICATIONS

Organizational culture as defined here is difficult to study. However, it is not as difficult as studying a different society where language and customs are so different that one needs to live in the society to get any feel for it at all. Organizations exist in a parent culture, and much of what we find in them is derivative from the assumptions of the parent culture. But different organizations will sometimes emphasize or amplify different elements of a parent culture. For example, in the two companies previously mentioned, we find in the first an extreme version of the individual freedom ethic, and in the second one, an extreme version of the authority ethic, *both* of which can be derived from U.S. culture.

The problem of deciphering a particular organization's culture, then, is more a matter of surfacing assumptions, which will be recognizable once they have been uncovered. We will not find alien forms of perceiving, thinking, and feeling if the investigator is from the same parent culture as the organization that is being investigated. On the other hand, the particular pattern of assumptions, which we call an organization's cultural paradigm, will not reveal itself easily because it is taken for granted.

How then do we gather data and decipher the paradigm? Basically, there are four approaches that should be used in combination with one another:

1. Analyzing the Process and Content of Socialization of New Members

By interviewing "socialization agents," such as the supervisors and older peers of new members, one can identify some of the important areas of the culture. But some elements of the culture will not be discovered by this method because they are not revealed to newcomers or lower members.

2. Analyzing Responses to Critical Incidents in the Organization's History

By constructing a careful "organizational biography" from documents, interviews, and perhaps even surveys of present and past key members, it is possible to identify the major periods of culture formation. For each crisis or incident identified, it is then necessary to determine what was done, why it was done, and what the outcome was. To the organization, one would then look for the major themes in the reasons given for the actions taken.

3. Analyzing Beliefs, Values, and Assumptions of "Culture Creators or Carriers"

When interviewing founders, current leaders, or culture creators or carriers, one should initially make an open-ended chronology of each person's history in the organization—his or her goals, modes of action, and assessment of outcomes. The list of external and internal issues found in Tables 2 and 3 can be used as a checklist later in the interview to cover areas more systematically.

4. Jointly Exploring and Analyzing with Insiders the Anomalies or Puzzling Features Observed or Uncovered in Interviews

It is the *joint* inquiry that will help to disclose basic assumptions and help determine how they may interrelate to form the cultural paradigm.

The insider must be a representative of the culture and must be interested in disclosing his or her *own* basic assumptions to test whether they are in fact cultural prototypes. This process works best if one acts from observations that puzzle the outsider or that seem like anomalies because the insider's assumptions are most easily surfaced if they are contrasted to the assumptions that the outsider initially holds about what is observed.

While the first three methods mentioned above should enhance and complement one another, at least one of them should systematically cover all of the external adaptation and internal integration issues. In order to discover the underlying basic assumptions and eventually to decipher the paradigm, the fourth method is necessary to help the insider surface his or her own cultural assumptions. This is done through the outsider's probing and searching.[24]

If an organization's total culture is not well developed, or if the organization consists of important stable subgroups, which have developed subcultures, one must modify the above methods to study the various subcultures.[25] Furthermore, the organizational biography might reveal that the organization is at a certain point in its life cycle, and one would hypothesize that the functions that a given kind of culture plays vary with the life-cycle stage.[26]

IMPLICATIONS FOR CULTURE MANAGEMENT AND CHANGE

If we recognize organizational culture—whether at the level of the group or the total corporation—as a deep phenomenon, what does this tell us about when and how to change or manage culture? First of all, the evolutionary perspective draws our attention to the fact that the culture of a group may serve different functions at different times. When a group is forming and growing, the culture is a "glue"—a source of identity and strength. In other words, young founder-dominated companies need their cultures as a way of holding together their organizations. The culture changes that do occur in a young organization can best be described as clarification, articulation, and elaboration. If the young company's culture is genuinely maladaptive in relation to the external environment, the company will not survive anyway. But even if one identified needed changes, there is little chance at this stage that one could change the culture.

In organizational midlife, culture can be managed and changed, but not without considering all the sources of stability which have been identified above. The large diversified organization probably contains many functional, geographic, and other groups that have cultures of their own—some of which will conflict with each other. Whether the organization needs to enhance the diversity to remain flexible in the face of environmental turbulence, or to create a more homogeneous "strong" culture (as some advocate) becomes one of the toughest strategy decisions management confronts, especially if senior management is unaware of some of its own cultural assumptions. Some form of outside intervention and "culture consciousness raising" is probably essential at this stage to facilitate better strategic decisions.

Organizations that have reached a stage of maturity or decline resulting from mature markets and products or from excessive internal stability and comfort that prevents innovation[27] may need to change parts of their culture, provided they can obtain the necessary self-insight. Such managed change will always be a painful process and will elicit strong resistance. Moreover, change may not even be possible without replacing the large numbers of people who wish to hold on to all of the original culture.

No single model of such change exists: managers may successfully orchestrate change through the use of a wide variety of techniques, from outright coercion at one extreme to subtle seduction through the introduction of new technologies at the other extreme.[28]

Summary and Conclusions

I have attempted to construct a formal definition of organizational culture that derives from a dynamic model of learning and group dynamics. The definition highlights that culture (1) is always in the process of formation and change; (2) tends to cover all aspects of human functioning; (3) is learned around the major issues of external adaptation and internal integration; and (4) is ultimately embodied as an interrelated, patterned set of basic assumptions that deal with ultimate issues, such as the nature of humanity, human relationships, time, space, and the nature of reality and truth itself.

If we are to decipher a given organization's culture, we must use a complex interview, observation, and joint-inquiry approach in which selected members of the group work with the outsider to uncover the unconscious assumptions that are hypothesized to be the essence of the culture. I believe we need to study a large number of organizations using these methods to determine the utility of the concept of organizational culture and to relate cultural variables to other variables, such as strategy, organizational structure, and ultimately, organizational effectiveness.

If such studies show this model of culture to be useful, one of the major implications will be that our theories of organizational change will have to give much more attention to the opportunities and constraints that organizational culture provides. Clearly, if culture is as powerful as I argue in this article, it will be easy to make changes that are congruent with present assumptions, and very difficult to make changes that are not. In sum, the understanding of organizational culture would then become integral to the process of management itself. The research on which this article is based was supported by the Chief of Naval Research, Psychological Sciences Division (Code 452), Organizational Effectiveness Research Programs, Office of Naval Research, Arlington, VA 22217, under Contract Number N00014–80–C–0905, NR 170–911.

Special thanks go to my colleagues Lotte Bailyn, John Van Maanen, and Meryl Louis for helping me to think through this murky area; and to Gibb Dyer, Barbara Lawrence, Steve Barley, Jan Samzelius, and Mary Nur whose research on organizational culture has begun to establish the utility of these ideas.

References

1. See J. Martin and C. Siehl, "Organizational Culture and Counterculture: An Uneasy Symbiosis," *Organizational Dynamics*, Autumn 1983, pp. 52–64.

2. See C. Argyris, "The Executive Mind and Double-Loop Learning," *Organizational Dynamics*, Autumn 1982, pp. 5–22.

3. See: E. H. Schein, "Does Japanese Management Style Have a Message for American Managers?" *Sloan Management Review*, Fall 1981, pp. 55–68; E. H. Schein, "The Role of the Founder in Creating Organizational Culture," *Organizational Dynamics*, Summer 1983, pp. 13–28.

4. See R. Evered and M. R. Louis, "Alternative Perspectives in the Organizational Sciences: 'Inquiry from the Inside' and 'Inquiry from the Outside,' *Academy of Management Review* (1981): 385–395.

5. See: F. R. Kluckhohn and F. L. Strodtbeck, *Variations in Value Orientations* (Evanston, IL: Row Peterson, 1961).

An application of these ideas to the study of organizations across cultures, as contrasted with the culture of organizations can be found in W. M. Evan, *Organization Theory* (New York: John Wiley & Sons, 1976), ch. 15;

Other studies of cross-cultural comparisons are not reviewed in detail here. See for example: G. Hofstede, *Culture's Consequences* (Beverly Hills, CA: Sage Publications, 1980); G. W. England, *The Manager and His Values* (Cambridge, MA: Ballinger, 1975).

6. See E. T. Hall, *The Silent Language* (New York: Doubleday, 1959).

7. W. G. Dyer, Jr., *Culture in Organizations: A Case Study and Analysis* (Cambridge, MA: Sloan School of Management, MIT, Working Paper #1279–82,1982).

8. See: T. E. Deal and A. A. Kennedy, Corporate Culture (Reading, MA: Addison-Wesley, 1982); T. J. Peters and R. H. Waterman, Jr., In Search *of Excellence* (New York: Harper & Row, 1982).

9. See: J. Van Maanen and S. R. Barley, "Occupational Communities: Culture and Control in Organizations" (Cambridge, MA: Sloan School of Management, November 1982); L. Bailyn, "Resolving Contradictions in Technical Careers," *Technology Review*, November-December 1982, pp. 40–47.

10. See R. L. Solomon and L. C. Wynne, "Traumatic Avoidance Learning: The Principles of Anxiety Conservation and Partial Irreversibility," *Psychological Review* 61,1954, p. 353.

11. See D. O. Hebb, "The Social Significance of Animal Studies," in *Handbook of Social Psychology*, G. Lindzey (Reading, MA: Addison-Wesley, 1954).

12. See E. H. Schein, *Coercive Persuasion* (New York: Norton, 1961).

13. See: E. L. Trist and K. W. Bamforth, "Some Social and Psychological Consequences of the Long-Wall Method of Coal Getting," *Human Relations*, 1951, pp. 1–38; I. E. P. Menzies, "A Case Study in the Functioning of Social Systems as a Defense against Anxiety," *Human Relations*, 1960, pp. 95–121.

14. See: A. M. Pettigrew, "On Studying Organizational Cultures," *Administrative Science Quarterly* (1979): 570–581; Schein (Summer 1983), pp. 13–28.

15. See: Schein (1961); E. H. Schein and W. G. Bennis, *Personal and Organizational Change through Group Methods* (New York: John Wiley & Sons, 1965).

16. See: A. K. Rice, *The Enterprise and Its Environment* (London: Tavistock, 1963); R. F. Bales, *Interaction Process Analysis* (Chicago, IL: University of Chicago Press, 1950); T. Parsons, The Social System (Glencoe, IL: The Free Press, 1951).

17. See G. Homans, *The Human Group* (New York: Harcourt Brace, 1950).

18. See: K. E. Weick, "Cognitive Processes in Organizations," in *Research in Organizational Behavior*, ed. B. Staw (Greenwich, CT: JAI Press. 1979), pp. 41–74; J. Van Maanen, "The Self, the Situation, and the Rules of Interpersonal Relations," in *Essays in Interpersonal Dynamics*, W. G. Bennis, J. Van Maanen, E. H. Schein, and F. I. Steele (Homewood, IL: Dorsey Press, 1979).

19. See E. H. Schein, *Process Consultation* (Reading, MA: Addison-Wesley, 1969).

20. When studying different organizations, it is important to determine whether the deeper paradigms that eventually arise in each organizational culture are also unique, or whether they will fit into certain categories such as those that the typological schemes suggest. For example, Handy describes a typology based on Harrison's work that suggests that organizational paradigms will revolve around one of four basic issues: (1) personal connections, power, and politics; (2) role structuring; (3) tasks and efficiency; or (4) existential here and now issues.
See: C. Handy, *The Gods of Management* (London: Penguin, 1978); R. Harrison, "How to Describe Your Organization," *Harvard Business Review*, September-October 1972.

21. See E. H. Schein, "The Role Innovator and His Education," *Technology Review*, October-November 1970, pp. 32–38.

22. J. Van Maanen and E. H. Schein, "Toward a Theory of Organizational Socialization," in *Research in Organizational Behavior*, Vol. 1, ed. B. Staw (Greenwich, CT: JAI Press, 1979).

23. Ibid.

24. See Evered and Louis (1981).

25. See M. R. Louis, "A Cultural Perspective on Organizations," *Human Systems Management* (1981): 246–258.

26. See: H. Schwartz and S. M. Davis, "Matching Corporate Culture and Business Strategy," *Organizational Dynamics*, Summer 1981, pp. 30–48; J. R. Kimberly and R. H. Miles, *The Organizational Life Cycle* (San Francisco: Jossey Bass, 1981).

27. See R. Katz, "The Effects of Group Longevity of Project Communication and Performance," *Administrative Science Quarterly* (1982): 27, 81–194.

28. A fuller explication of these dynamics can be found in my forthcoming book on organizational culture.

2

Transparency: How Leaders Create a Culture of Candor

Warren Bennis, Daniel Goleman, and James O'Toole

Summary Prepared by Patrick Heraty

Patrick Heraty is a native of Chicago, Illinois. He earned a Bachelor of Science degree in Finance at Marquette University, a Master's degree in Business Administration, and a Master's degree in Business Education from Canisius College in Buffalo, New York. He has achieved Six Sigma Black Belt certification, served as a trainer and organizational development consultant, and done extensive research on the automobile industry. His interviews on Six Sigma have been cited in print, television, and radio. He is currently a Professor of Business at Hilbert College and teaches courses in strategic planning, leadership, and management.

INTRODUCTION

When Mohandas Gandhi wanted to inform the world of injustices committed by imperialist Great Britain toward South Africa and India in the early twentieth century, he relied on the written word. His journals and those of his colleagues, as well as first-hand observations by journalists, provided details of wrongdoing. Looking through the lens of the twenty-first century, Gandhi's message traveled slowly and only to limited parts of the world. Fast forwarding to a century later, citizens protesting a planned petro chemical plant near the Chinese city of Xiamen organized their forces by using cell phones, text messaging, e-mails, and blogs. Images of the protest were virtually available to the world in real time. In response to this negative publicity, the Chinese government postponed construction of the petro chemical plant, acceding to the protestors' demands that an environmental impact study be completed.

The situation in China illustrates how technological advancements can lead to greater transparency in government. Organizational **transparency** is the desirable state of being able to be seen through, and is achieved through leadership behaviors involving candidness, openness, and accessibility. The China scenario serves as a lesson to anyone paying attention: Like it or not, institutional practices are more transparent than ever, and they will become more transparent in the future.

Warren Bennis, Daniel Goleman, and James O'Toole. *Transparency: How Leaders Create a Culture of Candor*. San Francisco: Jossey-Bass, 2008.

WHAT IS A CULTURE OF CANDOR?

Recognizing that knowledge is power, organizations can capitalize on this new transparency by sharing meaningful information (both good and bad) with their stakeholders, including the communities in which they operate. The prudent use of organizational information is similar to an effective central nervous system; they both promote optimal performance.

Choosing Transparency

As with most factors contributing to effective or dysfunctional organizations, *leadership creates the culture*. Leaders must continuously make it crystal clear that openness is not just desirable, but it is expected. Management must promote discussion of unpleasant news, disagreement, and contrarian views. Such a commitment will lead to a norm of effective communication, thereby empowering employees and maintaining optimal information management. For example, many municipalities, attempting to foster better communication with citizens, have instituted 311 phone lines to enable their citizens to report their concerns.

Whistleblowers, Then and Now

There was a time when employees who witnessed and desired to report unethical behavior would not speak out for a variety of reasons (e.g., fear of reprisal or risk of being branded as a troublemaker). They often chose the safest route, which was silence. Savvy organizations today realize that if they do not provide listening mechanisms for reports of illegal and/or unethical behavior, *whistleblowers will find and use their own medium* (e.g., blogs). Modern technology enables online **whistleblowing**, the act of reporting behavior that is unethical and/or illegal. When whistleblowing exposes internal problems to the public, organizations are placed in a much worse position than if they had proactively found, confronted, and exposed potentially bad news.

Transparency, Ready or Not

Whole Foods is an organization that is committed to transparency. Consistently recognized as one of America's best places to work, Whole Foods follows a "no-secrets" policy that includes posting every employee's pay. Reports about actions that would undermine the Whole Foods' culture are not only encouraged, but expected. Leaders who continuously strive for openness and transparency build up human capital. Because no organization is totally immune to unethical behavior by employees, the capital that has been built up through transparency provides some insulation to the organization as it recognizes the wrongdoing and confronts it aggressively.

The New Transparency

The Internet and its sources of information, including cell phones, cameras, and blogs, have created a transparency never previously thought possible. No longer do whistleblowers need to jump through bureaucratic hoops to report unscrupulous behavior. If organizations do not provide venues for employees to speak out on important matters, those voices will be heard on the blogosphere. In a global context, government violations of human rights can be captured and instantaneously made available to the world. At the extreme, digital technology can reform or overthrow governments, as was witnessed in the "Arab Spring" of 2011.

IMPEDIMENTS TO TRANSPARENCY

With such compelling arguments for transparency, why is it so challenging to put it into practice? Here are a few reasons:

- *A "need-to-Know" Culture:* Leadership that lacks confidence in its employees hoards information, unwittingly creating a mind-set of secrecy throughout the organization.
- *Structural Barriers:* Some organizations have unknowingly created clearly delineated silos, whereby functional areas at best barely recognize each other and at worst compete against each other. A by-product of this structural separation is the absence of the effective flow of information.
- *Charisma:* Leaders are sometimes seen as almost mythical figures, possessing a charisma that reflects well on the organization and its reputation. This charisma sometimes creates a **shimmer factor**—a glow emanating from the leader that can also lead to isolation and unapproachability. Followers may be reluctant to share problems or bad news with these charismatic leaders, thus isolating them from information that ultimately may prove harmful to the organization.

Fortunately, there are remedies for these obstacles to transparency. The prerequisite to making the remedies effective is a philosophy on the part of the leaders that *knowledge and information need to be shared in order to have an engaged workforce.* This requires a belief in people—a confidence that they can absorb information and use it in a way that strengthens the organization. This view of people must be authentic. Attempting to fake it will undermine collaboration.

Genuine leaders can overcome obstacles to transparency by:

- Engaging in "managing by wandering around"—periodically cruising around the organization to take the pulse of the culture.
- Demonstrating an "open-ear" policy—asking questions, listening purposefully, and sending the message that the upward flow of information contributes to organizational success.
- Promoting constructive conflict—modeling the behavior of respectful disagreement, and focusing on the issue rather than the person.

SPEAKING TRUTH TO POWER

Truth has no power if it remains unspoken. Martin Luther King observed that "our lives begin to end on the day we become silent about things that matter." **Speaking truth to power** (bringing credible information—even bad news—to those in authority) has been a challenge for as long as power structures have existed. In the play *Antigone,* from the fourth century B.C., Sophocles speaks of guards who are fearful of bringing bad news to King Creon. They understand that the king finds negative information disruptive, and will fault those bringing the information. This play introduced us to the "kill-the-messenger" syndrome that ultimately victimized Thomas a' Becket and Thomas Moore.

Effective leadership enables (and encourages) "messengers" to share bad news. Alfred Sloan, CEO of General Motors in its early years, promoted dissent as a way of undermining groupthink and getting all aspects of an issue out into the open. The message from the top was that employees were expected to speak their minds and to test assumptions. This type of transparency promotes a deep understanding of issues critical to organizational performance and fosters insightful and open decision making.

Even in the best organizations, speaking truth to power is often easier said than done. Bad news is easier to ignore than to confront, and is certainly easier to keep to oneself than it is to share with supervisors. If an organization is truly committed to empowering its employees to speak truth to power, it will provide training to do so and will design metrics to keep score of its commitment. For example, through role-playing and storytelling, leadership can convey its willingness to hear bad news, citing specific examples. These examples can be captured and shown during employee-orientation sessions. The quality of speaking truth to power can be quantified by administering periodic surveys, a section of which would contain a graphic response scale to capture the extent to which employees feel comfortable reporting bad news.

SPEAKING TRUTH . . . RESPONSIBLY

Speaking truth to power must be done in a manner that Aristotle called virtuous. Employees can be frustrated for a variety of reasons (e.g., job insecurity, perceived unfairness), and they may vent by lashing out at the organization. The effective organization will design a process for speaking truth to power and will identify criteria that legitimize the content being reported.

The act of speaking truth to power must:

- be based on facts.
- protect innocent parties.
- have a legal or ethical context.
- be motivated by doing what is right for the organization.

RESPONSIBILITIES OF LISTENERS

Have you ever heard a leader dare to proclaim, "I have a closed-door policy"? Of course not! So it is hard to be impressed with the mere proclamation of an open-door policy. The objective is not to have an open door, but rather to have employees feel safe coming through that door to share information, both positive and negative. Leaders need to model an "open-ear" policy by demonstrating a genuine interest in what employees have to say. This can be done by hard-wiring time into the schedule to wander around with the sole purpose of meeting and listening to employees. The two keys to making sure that there is a return on that investment of time are:

1. **Authenticity** (acting sincerely and genuinely without a hidden agenda). The leaders cannot fake this desire to listen to employees; if they do, the fraud will be identified quickly, and the result is a further erosion of trust.
2. *Humility.* Leaders must possess a core belief that every employee is valuable (both as a human being and as an employee) and has vast potential. Then they must listen to, and respect, their employees.

THE DOWNSIDE TO TRANSPARENCY

Because the Internet is a medium for storing and sharing information, there is considerable risk that information may be accessed by those for whom it was not intended. Digital announcements to internal employees, although candidly intended to keep them informed, can easily be modified and distributed widely on the Web. Social security numbers and consumer buying habits float around cyberspace. Every person and organization must be cognizant of the real and potential violations of privacy. There is a principle that may be helpful as individuals and organizations consider their vulnerability to misinformation. Although leaders cannot control what others say about them, they do have control over their actions and behaviors. *Conducting themselves in an honest and transparent manner minimizes the risk of damaging news.*

THE IRONY OF TRUST: IT IS BOTH STRONG AND FRAGILE

Employees are most likely to be open and candid after they have developed strong relationships, and trust is the essential element underlying relationships. Organizational trust is established through a series of positive behaviors, and sustained by a culture of integrity in which leaders and followers hold each other accountable for living up to the highest standards of behavior.

The elements of trust—integrity and openness—strengthen the fabric of organizational culture and empower its stakeholders. Ironically, this dynamic is quite fragile, and needs to be handled with great care. A single, serious breach of integrity or violation of trust may erode the culture in a way that undermines the collaboration required to optimize performance.

Effective listening conveys the message that what employees have to say matters, for they are stewards of the organization. Once they believe in the culture of candor, they will serve as *de facto* internal auditors, reinforcing transparency so as to enrich the organization for its next generation.

PART SIX

Motivation

A number of readings contained in this edition of *The Manager's Bookshelf* focus the manager's attention on the social-psychological side of the organization. New concepts and suggestions for proactive management call our attention to the importance of recognizing that all organizations have a natural (human) resource that, when appropriately motivated, can lead to dramatic performance effects.

This part has four readings, each of which takes a different but complementary path toward the same objective. In *The Enthusiastic Employee*, authors Sirota, Mischkind, and Meltzer describe ideal employees. Their unbridled enthusiasm helps them outperform others, strive to achieve the impossible, and rally each other to work hard and make unusual contributions. Unfortunately, unenlightened managers often *dampen* the enthusiasm of these stellar performers and *demotivate* them. The answer to this problem lies in a three-pronged approach involving equitable treatment, opportunities for achievement, and the experience of camaraderie.

David Sirota holds a doctorate in Social Psychology from the University of Michigan; Louis Mischkind received his Ph.D. in Organizational Psychology from New York University; and Michael Meltzer received his J.D. from Brooklyn Law School. All three are associated with Sirota Consulting, and they share background expertise in various aspects of opinion surveys, behavioral science research, and management assessments.

Fred Luthans, Carolyn Youssef, and Bruce Avolio are the authors of *Psychological Capital: Developing the Human Competitive Edge.* Luthans is the George Holmes Distinguished Professor of Management at the University of Nebraska, a former president of the Academy of Management, editor of *Organizational Dynamics*, and a prolific author. With Bruce Avolio (who holds a Ph.D. from the University of Akron and is currently the Executive Director of the Foster Center for Leadership), he published *The High Impact Leader: Moments Matter in Authentic Leadership Development.* Carolyn Youssef holds a Ph.D. from the University of Nebraska and teaches at Bellevue University.

Psychological capital is the study of how to make healthy people happier at work. It draws upon positive organizational behavior (POB), whose attributes must be theory based, measurable, developmental, and positively related to work performance.

The key attributes of positive organizational behavior are self-efficacy, hope, optimism, and resilience. The presence of psychological capital has been found to correlate with rated performance, objective performance, and employee satisfaction.

Based upon his observations of a large number of organizations (e.g., Southwest Airlines, the U.S. Marines, and General Motors), Jon R. Katzenbach, in *Why Pride Matters More Than Money*, tackles the question, "How do I motivate my employees?"—the question most frequently asked by supervisors, managers, and leaders. Whereas conventional wisdom, as practiced in most organizations, suggests that money and intimidation are the keys to sustained performance, Katzenbach asserts that the real answer is to be found in the word *pride*. He asserts that neither money nor intimidation contributes to the long-term sustainability of an organization. With regard to money, Katzenbach states that it is not a motivator and that pay-for-performance programs lead to self-serving behavior and ephemeral commitment to the organization. Instead, he notes that most employees are motivated by meaningful work, feelings of accomplishment, recognition/approval, and a sense of belonging and being a part of others in the work environment.

The author, Jon R. Katzenbach, was a senior partner and director of McKinsey and Company, a large U.S.-based consulting organization. He now directs his own firm, Katzenbach Partners, assisting organizations in such areas as workforce performance, team building, and leadership. Mr. Katzenbach is the author of several other books, including *Peak Performance, Teams at the Top, The Wisdom of Teams*, and *Real Change Leaders*. With Zhia Khan, Katzenbach published *The Informal Organization*.

Marshall Goldsmith continues the emphasis on the internal dimension of motivation in his book *MOJO: How to Get It, How to Keep It, How to Get It Back If You Lose It*. He defines *Mojo* as "that positive spirit toward what we are doing now that starts from the inside and radiates to the outside," and suggests that it is closely connected to being on a roll, in the zone, and having no gap or difference between internally positive feelings and others' perceptions of us. Goldsmith suggests that there are four key ingredients to great Mojo: identity, achievement, reputation, and acceptance of reality.

Goldsmith teaches executive education at Dartmouth's Tuck School, writes regular blogs for *BusinessWeek* and other publications, and has been named by *Harvard Business Review* as the most influential leadership thinker in the world. His previous book *What Got You Here Won't Get You There* focused on ways to cure self-destructive executive behaviors, and the book remained on best-seller lists for several years.

Readers interested in exposing themselves to a contrarian view of motivation might be interested in examining Charles Jacobs's book *Management Rewired*. Jacobs argues that many traditional approaches to motivation (e.g., rewards and punishment, criticism and praise) are blunt tools that are ineffective, and managers are better advised to use more subtle tactics.

The Enthusiastic Employee

David Sirota, Louis A. Mischkind,
and Michael Irwin Meltzer
Summary Prepared by Shelley Ovrom

Shelley Ovrom is a human resources professional, having started her career in the private sector working as a recruiter for Walt Disney Studios and Universal Studios. She then made the transition to the public sector, and is currently working as a human resources analyst for the city of Azusa in California. In her current position, she is responsible for risk management, recruitment, and workers' compensation, as well as daily support for city employees, department heads, and the public. She is passionate about the importance of human resources in an organization and is thrilled to be working in a capacity that benefits not only an employee population but also an entire community.

Most people begin a new job with a sense of enthusiasm. They are typically excited about their work and their organization, eager to be part of a productive team, and reasonable in how they expect to be treated. This is the case for approximately 95 percent of any employee population. The other 5 percent should never have been hired, and managers spend an inordinate amount of time with these difficult employees. However, an even bigger problem lies in the vast number of workers who are not openly troublesome; they are individuals who have become indifferent to the organization and its purpose. They have learned not to expect too much and not to give too much. The most significant decline in employee morale typically begins about six months after being hired and occurs in approximately 9 out of 10 companies.

There are various approaches and theories of how to best tackle this problem. However, a strong argument can be made that the first step is to determine what workers really want. *The key question is not how to motivate employees, but how to sustain—and prevent management from destroying—the motivation and enthusiasm employees naturally bring to their jobs.* **Employee enthusiasm**, a state of high employee morale that derives from satisfying the three key needs of workers, results in significant competitive advantages for companies with the strength of leadership and commitment to manage for true long-term results. A highly effective method of creating and maintaining high levels of long-term organizational performance is a **partnership relationship**, in which employees work collaboratively; share common, long-term goals; and feel a genuine concern for other employees at work.

David Sirota, Louis A. Mischkind, and Michael Irwin Meltzer. *The Enthusiastic Employee: How Companies Profit by Giving Workers What They Want.* Philadelphia, PA: Wharton School Publishing, 2005.

WORKER MOTIVATION, MORALE, AND PERFORMANCE

Many theories exist as to the differences in what employees want, explained by generational, racial, gender, or economic differences. Research indicates, however, that the percentage of people satisfied with their work is high for every group, with an average of 76 percent of all workers across all organizations generally enjoying the work they do.

Three-Factor Theory of Human Motivation in the Workplace

According to the **three-factor theory of motivation**, three primary sets of goals of people are at work:

EQUITY   Employees want to be treated justly—in comparison to others—in relation to the three basic conditions of employment. These conditions are unrelated to a position in the company or to performance. The three basic conditions are:

- Physiological—decent working conditions and working environment
- Economic—satisfactory compensation and benefits
- Psychological—respectful and consistent treatment by management

ACHIEVEMENT   Employees want to take pride in their achievements; they want to do things that matter and do them well; they desire to receive recognition for their accomplishments; they want to take pride in the organization's accomplishments. Statistical analysis shows there are six primary sources that contribute to a sense of **achievement**:

- Challenge of the work itself
- Acquisition of new skills
- Ability to perform
- Perceived importance of the job
- Recognition received for performance
- Feeling proud of their employer

CAMARADERIE   Members of the workforce wish to experience **camaraderie**—the feeling that they have warm, interesting, and cooperative relations with others on the job. This includes the extent to which an organization functions not only as a business entity but also as a community that satisfies the social and emotional needs of its employees. The impact that camaraderie can have on performance is often not recognized.

The overall relationship between morale and performance is reciprocal; each is both a cause and an effect of the other.

ENTHUSIASTIC WORKFORCES, MOTIVATED BY FAIR TREATMENT

Three important areas, as viewed by employees, define the issue of fair treatment:

- *Job security:* In general, 60 percent of workers are confident in the security of their jobs, but this ranges widely across organizations, from a high of 90 percent to a low of 6 percent. Many workers have experienced layoffs and typically do not view them as a prudent business decision, but rather as simply inequitable treatment. Many U.S. companies now seem to use downsizing as a strategic maneuver rather than as a last resort compelled by economic necessity. This "strategy" violates a fundamental need of workers and, in doing so, severely damages the sense of equity that is necessary for effective organizations.

Companies genuinely committed to their employees adhere to five basic principles in doing their best to provide employees with stable employment:

1. They exhaust all possible alternatives before laying people off.
2. When layoffs cannot be avoided, they first ask for volunteers.
3. When layoffs cannot be avoided and there are no more volunteers, they act generously and decently. From an organizational standpoint, they're not doing it just for those who are let go, but for those who will stay.
4. They communicate honestly, fully, and regularly throughout the entire process.
5. They recognize the impact of downsizings on the survivors and take steps to minimize the negative impact.

- *Compensation:* This factor is extraordinarily important for worker morale and performance. Pay provides the material wherewithal for life and is also a measure of respect, achievement, and the equitable distribution of the financial returns of the company. It is a satisfier of both the equity and achievement needs.
- *Respect:* This is the nonfinancial component of equity, with *equality* being at the heart of respect—the treatment of each individual as important and unique without regard to any other characteristics, such as gender, race, income, or even perceived performance or contribution to the organization. This is a fundamental human need that has enormous consequences for human behavior and the effectiveness of organizations. Three broad levels of respectful treatment in organizations can be distinguished:

  1. *Humiliating treatment*: This treatment is rare in most organizations at the present time. When it does occur, however, it can be devastating to people and their performance. This treatment comes in two forms: interpersonal, such as an employee's work being ridiculed by an immediate boss; and structural, such as formal organizational controls that allow workers absolutely no decision-making authority in the performance of their jobs. The consequences of this treatment show up most dramatically in labor conflict.
  2. *Indifferent treatment:* This treatment is more common than blatant humiliation and is often better termed *benign neglect*. It implies that workers are not worthy of management's time and attention, thereby making workers feel insignificant. Indifferent managers are solely focused on the bottom line. The response of workers to indifference is less anger than it is disappointment and withdrawal.
  3. *Positive treatment:* There are many factors that contribute to the positive treatment of employees, including physical working conditions, job autonomy, and communication. Ultimately, employees need to feel that they are not just being tolerated but are made to feel welcome and genuinely included.

ENTHUSIASTIC WORKFORCES, MOTIVATED BY ACHIEVEMENT

A critical condition for employee enthusiasm is a clear, credible, and inspiring organizational purpose. Research reveals a strong correlation between pride in the organization and the overall satisfaction of workers with that organization. The four main sources of pride, all of which reflect different facets of excellence, are:

- Excellence in the organization's financial performance,
- Excellence in the efficiency with which the work of the organization gets done,
- Excellence in the characteristics of the organization's products, and
- Excellence in the organization's moral character.

Success in this area consists of a combination of *purpose* (how an organization serves its customers) and *principles* (the moral character of the company). Any judgment about a company's principles must be based on its behavior in relation to *all* of its key constituencies.

One of the most important components of providing leadership is providing an organization with a purpose and principles of which employees can be proud, and to which they will willingly and enthusiastically devote their skills and energy. The basic points to keep in mind are:

- Purposes and principles must emanate from strongly held convictions of senior management.
- Statements of purposes and principles will be exercises in futility unless they are accompanied by a serious implementation plan.

In studies of group functioning, a useful distinction between three types of leadership exists: autocratic, laissez-faire, and participative. Of the three, research most strongly supports the participative method, which is an active style that stimulates employee involvement. A successful participative method is **self-managed teams (SMTs)**, which are teams of workers who, with their supervisors, are delegated various functions and the authority and resources needed to carry them out. The team operates like a small business whose members are highly involved in its management and in the sharing of its rewards. Effectiveness and job satisfaction are greatly enhanced by organizing teams, when possible, around identified customers and setting the primary goal of the teams to meet the needs of their customers.

External sources of satisfaction are feedback, recognition, and reward. Employees want to perform well, learn how to improve, and be recognized and rewarded for their achievements, which is among the most fundamental of human needs. There are four major means to recognize employees:

1. Compensation—differential compensation based on performance levels
2. Informal recognition—day-to-day recognition of performance
3. Honorifics—special awards for performance
4. Promotion—advancement to higher-level positions for superior performance

To be most effective, organizations must think of recognition as a cluster of components that need to be used consistently with each other and with the organization's goals and values in mind.

ENTHUSIASTIC WORKFORCES, MOTIVATED BY CAMARADERIE

The quality of social relationships in the workplace—its social capital—is of enormous importance, not only because of the general need people have for camaraderie but also because cooperative relationships are critical for effective performance, and therefore for a sense of achievement in one's work. An employee's greatest sense of satisfaction and accomplishment can come from interacting as a team toward common performance goals. Teamwork is needed for just about every job at every level. This cooperation is the glue that binds together the different parts of the organization. Groups, when structured and managed correctly, allow for the emergence and consideration of different perspectives, which is vital to solve problems and make good business decisions.

BRINGING IT ALL TOGETHER: THE TOTAL ORGANIZATION

To create and implement a truly significant and lasting organizational change, the various components discussed cannot be thought of individually, but only together as a system, one that is governed by an organization's culture. The essence of the system and culture discussed is a partnership relationship. Partnership has both a vertical dimension, which consists of the relationships between workers and management, and a horizontal dimension, which consists of the relationships between individuals and between work units. Essentially, a partnership is people working together toward common goals. The partnership method is a high-involvement model, with the successful hallmarks including:

- Win–win—all parties recognize they have key business goals in common and that the success of one depends on the success of the other.
- Basic trust—intentions of all parties are trusted.
- Excellence—high performance standards are set for all parties.
- Competence—the parties have confidence in each other.
- Joint decision making—key decisions are made jointly.
- Open communications—parties communicate fully with each other.
- Mutual influence—parties listen to and are influenced by each other.
- Mutual assistance—parties help each other perform.
- Recognition—contributions by each party are recognized.
- Day-to-day treatment—parties routinely treat each other with consideration and respect.
- Financial sharing—parties share equitably in results.

Partnership is highly effective because it harnesses the natural motivation and enthusiasm that are characteristic of the overwhelming majority of workers. Although some conditions may make partnership inappropriate, such as extremely contrasting individual differences, there is no evidence that the approach does not work when it is applied to certain types of work or in certain cultures. Certain adaptations may obviously need to be made, but the fundamental concepts are applicable everywhere as long as the actions for a partnership organization begin with, and are sustained by, senior management.

Psychological Capital

Fred Luthans, Carolyn M. Youssef, and Bruce J. Avolio
Summary Prepared by Cathy A. Hanson

Cathy A. Hanson is the Director of Human Resources for the city of Manhattan Beach, California. She is responsible for all aspects of human resources within a dynamic city environment. A majority of her career has been spent in the human resources departments of Fortune 100 companies (Mars, Disney, and Kraft). Her areas of interest include high-performance work teams (both public and private sectors), change management, and team building. She received an M.B.A. from the University of Southern California and a B.A. in Business Administration from the University of Minnesota Duluth.

GAINING A COMPETITIVE EDGE THROUGH PSYCAP

In today's competitive work environment, employers need to find innovative and creative ways to gain and maintain a competitive advantage. One such way currently being explored is gaining a competitive advantage through human resources. This competitive edge has been termed **Psychological Capital (PsyCap)** and is defined as a positive psychological state that is characterized by a person displaying several key attributes.

The recent volatility in the economy has forced the corporate world to change dramatically through acquisitions, mergers, and business closures. It has left current and prospective employees with a generally lower level of commitment, loyalty, and feeling of ownership. In order for employers to maximize their competitive advantage now and in the future, they need to find ways to capitalize on "PsyCap." When done correctly, this can affect work performance and profitability.

An important prerequisite for PsyCap is the study of positive psychology—the study of how to help healthy people become happier. What separates positive psychology from the latest trend or fad is that it bases its conclusions on science. From positive psychology two parallel and important movements have begun. These are:

1. **Positive organizational scholarship (POS)**, which focuses on the macro-organizational level and deals with attributes such as compassion. These traits may not be open to development or even relate to an individual's performance.

Fred Luthans, Carolyn M. Youssef, and Bruce J. Avolio. *Psychological Capital: Developing the Human Competitive Edge.* New York: Oxford University Press, 2007.

2. **Positive organizational behavior (POB)**, which focuses on the micro-individual level and deals with positive attributes that can be developed and directly relate to an individual's work performance.

Recent focus has been on POB in order to develop and maintain a competitive edge through human resources. For an attribute to be identified as a POB, the scientific research approach is used to ensure the attribute meets specific criteria. It must be:

- Theory based
- Measurable
- Developmental
- Positively related to work performance

Self-Efficacy
Hope
optimism
Resiliency

FOUR ELEMENTS OF POB

Several positive attributes have been considered for inclusion in POB, but four have been identified that best meet the criteria. These are self-efficacy, hope, optimism, and resiliency. Each one not only impacts individual performance on its own but may work in concert for an even greater impact. Additionally, these attributes appear to improve with relatively short but focused training and development efforts, which is very appealing to most organizations.

Self-efficacy

Self-efficacy is the confidence that one will be successful given difficult circumstances. In addition to having various levels of confidence or self-efficacy in specific areas of one's life, an individual can have a generalized level as well. There are five key discoveries regarding efficacy:

1. It is area specific. For example, a manager may be very confident when giving positive feedback, but much less confident talking with one who is having performance issues.
2. Areas practiced and mastered lead to high levels of efficacy. Utilizing the previous example, the manager may have given many positive performance evaluations and very few requiring giving constructive feedback.
3. It can be improved even within an area of high confidence.
4. It is influenced by others.
5. It can be variable, and influenced by things within and outside an individual's control. For example, by acquiring skills, abilities, and knowledge in a subject area, one's efficacy can be enhanced. On the other hand, a serious illness can detract from efficacy.

Characteristics of Employees with Efficacy

People with high levels of confidence or efficacy typically exhibit five distinct characteristics. They:

1. Set challenging goals that require themselves to grow, and they choose to participate in difficult tasks.
2. Consistently look for challenges.
3. Are highly self-motivated.
4. Put forth the necessary effort to reach goals.
5. Persevere despite difficult conditions and early failures.

COGNITIVE PROCESSES NECESSARY FOR EFFICACY   Five cognitive processes necessary for developing high levels of efficacy are as follows:

1. Ability to "see" the desired outcome ("symbolizing"), analyze how to get there, and use this knowledge for future interactions.
2. Ability to plan future actions based on the expected outcomes ("forethought").
3. Ability to learn from observing mentors in similar situations and internalize it for one's own use.
4. Ability to set goals and standards for oneself and to determine where one stands in relation to them.
5. Ability to reflect on past performance, successes, and failures and learn from them.

Research has shown that self-efficacy and work performance are strongly related. Of particular interest to organizations, self-efficacy can be developed through work experience, learning opportunities, social situations, feedback, day-to-day life experiences, and self-reflection. There have been four major identified sources of efficacy and ways in which they can be developed.

FOUR SOURCES OF SELF-EFFICACY DEVELOPMENT   Self-efficacy can be developed through:

1. Experiencing success on tasks important to the area in which one wants to build it. This can be accomplished through various training scenarios and/or on-the-job experiences.
2. Participating in vicarious learning through observing coworkers attaining success (or failure) in the desired area and reflecting and internalizing these lessons.
3. Receiving positive feedback and individual recognition.
4. Having a positive emotional state and a generally positive sense of well-being.

In addition to developing an employee's level of self-confidence, an organization can look to build the organization's collective confidence through use of cross-functional teams, shared goals, and collaborative decision making.

Hope

Hope is the optimistic belief that challenging goals can be successfully achieved, and if one way doesn't work another one will. Early research supports a positive relationship between hope, work performance, and profitability. Hope can be developed through several approaches, including the following:

- Effective goal setting (joint goal setting where goals are internalized and the individual is allowed to determine the means to achieve them).
- Presence of goals that are realistically attainable but require the individual to "stretch" (go above and beyond).
- Breaking large goals down into manageable pieces ("stepping"). This allows employees to experience success and develop a belief that the larger goal can be reached.
- Involvement in decision making. By allowing employees to participate in decision making and giving them the freedom to determine *how* to achieve the organization's goals, they experience successes that can translate to other experiences.
- In addition, employees are likely to have a higher degree of hope if they believe that they have an appropriate reward system, have necessary resources available to them, are well matched to their jobs, and have training and development experiences available that focus on building employee strengths that can easily be applied to a variety of situations.

Optimism

Optimism is the belief that positive events will happen now and in the future, and the reasons for those events are permanent and attributed to one's actions. An optimistic employee uses this belief system to explain why positive things happen and also believes negative events are caused externally, are temporary, and are situational. These employees believe they have the power and control to perform successfully despite the temporary setbacks.

On the other hand, pessimistic employees will attribute positive performance to factors outside their control and as the result of pure luck, and negative performance to the failure of other employees, or low expectations of supervisors. Pessimistic employees will continue to believe they have little power and control over positive events and believe these events are unlikely to happen in the future.

POTENTIAL DOWNSIDE OF OPTIMISM   At the extreme, using blind optimism to explain events can lead to undesirable consequences. These include:

- Exposing employees, coworkers, and organizations to higher risk.
- Underestimating the consequences of a risky action.
- Failing to learn from mistakes.

Additionally, extremely optimistic individuals may falsely believe they control the outcome of all events if they just work hard enough. At the extreme these individuals cannot correctly analyze negative events as external to themselves and will suffer both psychologically and physically.

In order to avoid these potential pitfalls, the employee needs to be able to use "flexible-optimism" and "realistic-optimism" approaches, where the individual analyzes the situation and appropriately utilizes the optimistic or pessimistic style to explain a given situation.

Optimistic employees welcome change and work toward maximizing that change for the good of the organization. Because they believe they greatly influence their performance, optimistic employees tend to be more flexible, adaptable, proactive, and independent.

Optimistic leaders are more effective than pessimistic ones by being more effective interpersonally, more able to utilize relevant information to make better decisions, and more flexible when faced with roadblocks. They are realistic and know what risks to take and when to take them. They can act independently and understand their strengths and vulnerabilities. They take responsibility for their actions and work hard to develop their subordinates to build their own realistic, flexible, optimistic approach.

DEVELOPING OPTIMISM   Optimism can be developed by either enhancing a currently optimistic style or altering a pessimistic style. For example, employees can learn to

1. Forgive the past.
2. Acknowledge or appreciate the present.
3. Recognize future opportunities.

Resiliency

Resiliency is the ability to bounce back and encourage/inspire others to bounce back in the face of extreme adversity or from positive occurrences such as quick business growth.

Several factors have been identified as contributing to or hindering the development of resiliency. These are as follows:

- *Resiliency assets:* These include "cognitive abilities, temperament, positive self-perceptions, faith, positive outlook, emotional stability, self-regulation, insight, independence, relationship initiative, creativity, humor and morality." When these are present, individuals and groups of individuals are more likely to develop and demonstrate resiliency when faced with adverse conditions.

- **Resiliency risk factors:** These are elements that cause an increased probability of an unwanted outcome. These risk factors can take several forms, such as substance abuse, exposure to violence, stress, unemployment, and so on. Because each individual experiences these risk factors differently, the mere presence of them does not always lead to a lack of resiliency. By using the resiliency assets identified earlier, these risks can be overcome and may actually allow an individual or group of individuals to identify potential that they didn't know they had. Resiliency assets and risk factors work together to determine overall resiliency.

DEVELOPING RESILIENCY   Several strategies have been identified to develop resiliency in the workplace. These include increasing the perceived and/or actual level of assets and resources to positively affect outcomes, looking for ways to prevent/reduce risk factors that lead to undesirable outcomes rather than avoiding them, developing systems and processes that can adapt to the situation at hand, and identifying the effective mix of assets in order to manage various risk factors.

RESILIENT LEADERS AND EMPLOYEES   Leaders play a key role helping their employees to become resilient. By utilizing transformational leadership skills, leaders can help their subordinates learn to view challenges as opportunities and can help them take charge of their future. Leaders do this by encouraging open communications, building trust, developing employees, and giving them the necessary independence to encourage them to feel that they make an impact and that their work has meaning.

RESILIENT ORGANIZATIONS   A resilient organization is able to bounce back from setbacks and extreme adversity. Similar to resilient individuals, the organization must utilize its assets, manage its risk, and have effective processes in place to determine the effective mix of assets to employ in order to manage these risks.

Other processes have been shown to affect/enhance organizational resiliency. These include developing a strategy (goals and objectives), aligning the strategy within the organization, and being aware of the corporate culture. Allowing employees to participate in decision making also enhances organizational resiliency, as the employees feel they have a stake in the outcome.

POTENTIAL PSYCAPS

Recent research has identified four additional broadly defined categories as potential PsyCaps. Although these do not meet all the criteria (theory based, measurable, developmental, and related to work performance) for inclusion as PsyCaps yet, they are worth mentioning. The four categories are cognitive processes (creativity and wisdom), affective/emotional (subjective well-being, flow, and humor), social (gratitude, forgiveness, emotional intelligence, and spirituality), and higher order (authenticity and courage).

Conclusion

With today's fierce competition between organizations and the high levels of volatility in the economy, organizations need to explore innovative ways to differentiate their businesses from those of the competition. Although the PsyCaps of self-efficacy, hope, optimism, and resiliency best meet the scientific criteria for inclusion, several others are promising. Psychological capital appears to be a powerful and promising option for today's organizations.

3 Why Pride Matters More Than Money

Jon R. Katzenbach

Summary Prepared by AnneMarie Kaul

AnneMarie Kaul is the Development Director for the North Central Chapter of the Arthritis Foundation in St. Paul, Minnesota. She previously served as the Donor Recruitment Manager for the North Central Blood Region of the American Red Cross in St. Paul, Minnesota. She also has several years of experience managing financial services operational departments. Her business expertise has been in the areas of leadership and customer service. She has a B.A. from the University of Minnesota Duluth and an M.B.A. from the University of St. Thomas in St. Paul, Minnesota.

Pride can be the key to unlocking the motivational spirit of any employee at any level and within virtually any enterprise. At the base of this building of pride is emotion. More specifically, it is critical to obtain the emotional commitment of associates, which in turn can lead to both positive and negative forms of motivation. The positive form of motivation is called **institutional-building pride** and the negative form is **self-serving pride**.

Companies that rely solely on monetary incentives to motivate employees will only realize short-term successes, because they are not taking advantage of the easily accessible building of pride that is a powerful motivating force. *Enterprises today must move beyond egos and monetary incentives to sustain not only employee satisfaction but also economic performance and long-term growth.*

WHY INSTITUTIONAL-BUILDING PRIDE WORKS

In the long run, a person who is allowed to pursue worthwhile goals and endeavors will be more motivated to work harder than a person only receiving monetary incentives. When associates take pride in their work, their job satisfaction increases, their productivity is higher, and the enterprise ultimately is more likely to succeed. One of the best reasons for using pride as a motivator is that it can be quickly learned and easily applied. Before leaders use pride to

Jon R. Katzenbach. *Why Pride Matters More Than Money: The Power of the World's Greatest Motivational Force.* New York: Crown Business, 2003.

motivate, it is important that they understand the other reasons why instilling pride works so well to motivate others:

- The skills and knowledge for instilling pride are mostly teachable and can be readily learned.
- Pride begets pride; there is a closed loop of energy linking pride to work performance. The anticipation of higher performance feels good and generates the emotional commitment to obtain better results.
- The fundamental correlation between pride and performance can be found in any company that depends on humans.
- Leaders don't have to wait for real success before instilling pride in others. They can tap into past accomplishments as well as future expectations to trigger emotions.

DIFFERENCES BETWEEN SELF-SERVING PRIDE AND INSTITUTIONAL PRIDE

In companies that consistently perform better than their competition, pride is a primary driver of their higher performance. There is clear evidence indicating that in traditional larger companies, managers who instill pride also have better economic and market performance than their competitors.

Both categories of pride—self-serving and institutional building—can be a factor in the production of good and bad results, but typically self-serving pride only produces short-term success.

Self-Serving Pride

Self-serving pride is all about power and money. The individual's thought process goes something like this: "The more you can earn, the more visible you are, the more powerful and well-off you become." Power and control are believed to be all-important, so typically a person who is motivated by this type of influence will switch allegiances such that there is no loyalty or commitment to the company. However, there *are* some advantages of self-serving pride, especially in situations such as in individual sports. Monetary awards not only serve as indicators of talent and achievement but are also a simple way to distinguish between performers and nonperformers.

Institutional-Building Pride

This type of pride is based on the character and emotional commitment of associates. With institutional-building pride, people are motivated to help others and work for the good of the enterprise. They place their efforts on more basic performance factors such as customer satisfaction, peer and mentor approval, developmental opportunities, and quality of work. These in turn build self-worth, group cohesion, and personal developmental happiness—factors that lead to success.

When further comparing the two types of pride, it is important to note that institutional pride has real strength because it can work across different types of organizations, even in companies where money is not a realistic source of motivation. For example, organizations such as the U.S. Marine Corps and Kentucky Fried Chicken (KFC) have been very successful because they have integrated institutional-building pride into the workplace. It has been demonstrated over and over again that money may attract and keep people, but it does not continue to motivate them to excel. At the end of the day, it is the feeling of pride (self-serving or institutional building) that prompts employees to do well.

SOURCES OF INSTITUTIONAL PRIDE

Institutional pride can come from many sources. The primary origins fall into three main categories—work results, work processes, and coworkers/supervisors.

- *Pride in the results of one's work:* This is often exhibited when employees feel good about what they have accomplished. This can arise from the product or service delivered or the kind of work done.
- *Pride in how work is done:* Employees can take pride in "doing something right." This refers to the set of values, standards, work ethic, and commitment that is applied to one's job.
- *Pride in coworkers and supervisors:* The people that an employee works with—supervisors, subordinates, or peers—can all provide job satisfaction.

Given the fact that these sources of "good" pride can be easily directed and controlled by leaders within corporations (as opposed to money), institutional-building pride should be the primary source of pride for the broader base of employees. *It is important to remember that what motivates upper-level executives is very different from what motivates frontline employees, especially during difficult times.*

Why is this true? Top executives not only possess the business savvy in terms of schooling in business fundamentals, typically their individual goals are stated in terms of economic results and market share. As a result, their motivation is a function of performance logic and many rational factors. On the other hand, at lower levels, simple emotional factors from everyday occurrences are more important as a motivating source because on the front line, the performance statistics of the company are often less meaningful. The six most important nonfinancial elements of enterprise success that influence *all* associates are:

- Local company reputation
- Product/service attributes
- Customer satisfaction
- Work-group composition
- Peer approval
- Competitive position

The good news is that these sources of pride result in the emotional commitment that motivates employees, leading to enterprise-wide success. Understanding the motivational differences between the top and the other levels of an organization is a critical challenge, but it can be learned. The enterprises that excel at engaging emotions employ leaders who are masters at cultivating institutional-building pride.

THE FIVE PATHS TO HIGHER PERFORMANCE

There are five distinct applications or paths that motivate higher-performing groups in companies that have successfully developed emotional commitment:

- *Mission, Values, and Collective Pride (MVP):* This is where companies use their rich histories of past accomplishments to instill pride.
- *Process and Metrics (P&M):* Delivering value by measuring the right things and maintaining effective processes is a powerful source of pride.
- *Entrepreneurial Spirit (ES):* High-risk/high-reward opportunities typically provide motivational direction on this path.

- *Individual Achievement (IA):* Individual performance and personal advancement, rather than team performance, are the primary motivational sources.
- *Recognition and Celebration (R&C):* Giving recognition and holding celebrations and special events are used to motivate others.

All of these paths lead to an emotionally committed **workforce**, which leads to a higher level of performance. Companies that desire to sustain an emotionally committed environment will be more successful if they integrate two of these paths, rather than concentrating on one. But what if you work for a company that does not appear to comprehend these concepts? What can a leader do as an individual to motivate the workforce?

IDEAS FOR INDIVIDUALS NOT IN AN INSTITUTIONAL-BUILDING COMPANY ENVIRONMENT

What if the company you work for is not a well-established enterprise—one whose size, market position, and growth prospects are not highly attractive? A manager in this situation can use the case study results of General Motors to identify successful key motivating features. The following three methods are not only useful but also easy to apply:

1. *Keep it simple:* Use one or two concentrated themes and place great significance on local sources of pride that employees can easily understand.
2. *Develop one's own unique pride-building formula:* Strong pride-influenced managers should connect to their employees in any way they can (e.g., by tapping into their pride in the community, pride in their families, and pride in a legacy).
3. *Make pride a priority:* Using pride on an everyday basis to motivate is the key to obtaining long-term results.

Pride-building people are aware that instilling pride along the way is the *only way* to gain long-term success from it. Therefore, it is more important for people to be proud of what they are doing every day than it is for them to be proud of accomplishing their goals and getting the wanted results. Good leaders appeal to emotions rather than rational compliance; that is why their internal compass is always pointing to pride.

Conclusion

The really good news is that a person does not have to work for a **peak-performance** enterprise to experience pride and the motivation that comes with it. Institutional-building pride motivates people in almost any environment—from top-performing firms to traditional organizations to financially challenged companies.

The ability to instill pride can be learned and utilized, just like any basic performance management technique. What a manager must look out for, however, is trying to motivate employees solely by using sources that are more self-serving, such as monetary incentives and ego building. Although money is economically necessary, it does not motivate one to excel in the long run. When a manager uses institutional-building pride sources, such as recognition, accomplishments, entrepreneurship, and team support, the general population of the workforce, especially people on the front line, is more likely to produce consistent and high-quality results.

At the base of pride-instilling motivation is emotional commitment. Employees want to feel connected to the cause, such as providing the best customer service or not letting the team down. It is this connectedness to an overall objective that gives institutional-building pride its powerful force. *Managers must think beyond the compensation package.*

There are many peak-performing enterprises, such as KFC, General Motors, and the Marine Corps, that have clearly demonstrated that motivating by pride can lead to successful results. We should continue to look at these organizations for guidance. Pride is a powerful motivating force—one that has proven to result in improved success.

4   Mojo

Marshall Goldsmith, with Mark Reiter
Summary Prepared By Meghan Brown

Meghan Brown obtained her bachelor's degrees in Human Resource Management from the Labovitz School of Business and Economics and Political Science from the College of Liberal Arts at the University of Minnesota Duluth in 2008. She is currently working as a Store Team Leader at Target Corporation in Minneapolis, Minnesota.

INTRODUCTION

Mojo is the positive spirit aimed toward what we are doing now that starts from the inside and radiates to the outside. This is the moment where we feel we've made a difference or done something with purpose, the moment we've done something powerful, or achieved something we're proud of and that rest of the world recognizes. Mojo produces harmony between internal feelings and external appearances.

There are four vital ingredients that, when combined, allow your Mojo to be at its highest: identity, achievement, reputation, and acceptance. To achieve these, you should first assess how prevalent each is in your current life and then explore ideas of how you can change either *yourself* or *it* to start achieving more meaning and happiness in your life.

The first step in sustaining or increasing your Mojo is to determine your current Mojo Score. Where do you excel and where do you need to focus? Ten qualities, five related to your Professional Mojo and five related to your Personal Mojo, make up the **Mojo Scorecard**. This scorecard helps determine what day-to-day tasks are contributing positively (and negatively) to your current Mojo.

After identifying your current Mojo, a **Mojo Tool Kit** can be used. It contains 14 useful tools to help you achieve your *peak* Mojo by helping you to close the gap between the way you perceive yourself and how others perceive you. Ultimately, the goal is to find (or create) an extended answer to a common workplace question: "What is the *one* quality that differentiates truly successful people from everyone else?"

Marshall Goldsmith, with Mark Reiter. *Mojo: How to Get It, How to Keep It, How to Get It Back If You Lose It*. New York: Hyperion, 2009.

Four Mojo Ingredients

1. Identity—*Who do you think you are?* The element of identity is not to be confused with how others perceive you or to answer with what you *think* those closest to you would say, but instead to focus on your own self-image. Who *are* you? This may be difficult to assess, but without it, you may never be able to fully understand why you gain (or lose) your Mojo.

2. Achievement—*What have you done lately?* This is the act or process of finishing something successfully—an accomplishment that has meaning, impact, or power as defined by you. Achievements are often looked at from two perspectives: (1) What we bring to the task, and (2) what the task gives to us. Understanding what we've accomplished and/or what we've awarded value to recently is the second important part of creating or finding your Mojo.

3. Reputation—*Who do other people think you are?* In contrast to identity and achievement (where you develop your own definition), your reputation is defined by those around you, whether it is your friends, family, coworkers, or a stranger walking down the street. They are grading your performance and reporting your scores to the world, and although you are not directly in control of your reputation, there are a variety of things you can do to preserve or change it that can have a big impact on your Mojo.

4. Acceptance—*What can you change and what is beyond your control?* On a surface level, acceptance should be the easiest of the four to achieve. To assess the situation, "take a deep breath and accept it" sounds a lot easier than creating a whole new identity or changing how you do things in order to change the reputation you have with others. However, acceptance is often the biggest challenge. Why? This is because failure to accept what is and move on often stands in the way. In doing this, our Mojo often fades.

Measuring Your Mojo

The next step is to determine where you individually score on the Mojo Scoreboard. You need to measure how much Mojo you currently possess, and in what areas you are strong and weak, in order to know what you have to change. To do this an operational definition is necessary to ensure both parties (i.e., teacher and student) are discussing the same thing. The operational definition of *Mojo* is "an expression of the harmony—or lack of harmony—between what you feel inside about whatever you are doing and what you show on the outside." The opposite of Mojo is **Nojo**. This is the "negative spirit toward what they are doing now that starts from the inside and radiates to the outside. In brief, it means 'No Joy!'"

As noted, in order to assess your current Mojo, a Mojo Scorecard can be used. This scorecard measures both your **Professional Mojo** (the five skills and attitudes that you *bring* to any activity) as well as your **Personal Mojo** (the five benefits that a particular activity *gives back* to you). The test involves logging your daily activities and rating yourself on a scale of 1 to 10, with 10 being the highest, in regard to each of the 10 qualities. A perfect Mojo score would be 100.

Professional Mojo Qualities

- Motivation: How well do you *want* to do this activity?
- Knowledge: What is your current *understanding*? Do you understand what to do and/or how to do it?
- Ability: Do you have the *skills* required to complete the task well?
- Confidence: How well do you feel you *will* perform this activity?
- Authenticity: How *sincere* are you about engaging in this activity?

Personal Mojo Qualities

- Happiness: How *happy* does doing the particular activity make you?
- Reward: Does this activity provide you with an emotional or material *outcome* that is important to you?
- Meaning: When completed, does the end result of this activity *mean* something to you?
- Learning: What do you "get" from this activity that has helped you learn something new or *grow* in some way?
- Gratitude: Do you believe this activity to be a good use of your time? Were you *appreciative* for being able to participate?

Although this self-assessment seems like an easy and simple test, remember that you determine your own score. Ensuring you are honest and accurate in your assessment of yourself is pivotal to your Mojo success.

Mojo Tool Kit

The last step is determining how to create significant positive change in the areas that you've identified as having low Mojo. To do this, a Mojo Tool Kit should be used. First, however, you must ultimately understand (and agree) that to create this change, you need to either *change yourself or change it.*

Changing "yourself" means changing your thoughts, your words, your feelings, or anything else that you control. Changing "it" means just the opposite. It includes everything that you are not in control of—other influences within your life that are not *you,* such as, relationships, another person, or a place. This "you-or-it" way of thinking puts matters into the individual's hands. To positively impact your Mojo, you can either change you or change it, but inherently no one else can make this decision for you. It's your life, making it your decision. Fortunately there is a tool kit to help with these decisions.

The Mojo Tool Kit is made up of 14 specific actions, broken down into the four building blocks of Mojo: Identity, Achievement, Reputation, and Acceptance. This allows you to pinpoint which tool or tools will help you improve your Mojo based on where your Mojo (Personal or Professional) is most deficient.

- Identity Tools

  Tool #1 Establish Criteria That Matter to You. What brings meaning and happiness to your life? The odd thing about this tool is that for most other people in our lives we apply criteria to judge them, but we don't always set similar criteria for ourselves. Establish your criteria and then hold yourself accountable to them; this will often help you make many of the major choices in your life, and help bring you meaning and happiness.

  Tool #2 Find Out Where You're "Living" (Emotionally). Whether we realize it or not, we often run everything through two filters: short-term satisfaction (or happiness) and long-term benefit (or meaning). These two filters, when combined on two dimensions, together form five modes: Surviving, Stimulating, Sacrificing, Sustaining, and Succeeding (the best combination of short-term and long-term satisfaction). These modes help identify how individuals experience meaning and happiness at work and at home.

  Tool #3 Be the Optimist in the Room. Optimism (as a practiced behavior) is contagious. When setting goals, be aware of the negative forces that could negatively impact you reaching your goal. Knowing these factors and realizing when one or more of them may be getting in the way of achieving your goal will help you maintain your optimism. Optimism tends to be self-fulfilling, and often increases your influence in a room.

Tool #4 Take Away One Thing. Don't wait until it's too late to subtract something. Most often we don't change until we are forced to, such as continuing to work at doing something we hate until we are laid off. It's at this point that we decide to find our "dream job." Although this is not the most obvious strategy, taking away something (instead of adding or changing) could reshape your life for the better.

- Achievement Tools

Tool #5 Rebuild One Brick at a Time. Aim at serial achievements. Remember that a brick wall cannot be built overnight but instead brick by brick, layer by layer. This is the same mentality you must use when the thought of something seems like a daunting task. Reputations are rebuilt through continuity—a sequence of successes.

Tool #6 Live Your Mission in the Small Moments, Too. Give yourself a mission, but remember that you can't just talk about it; you need to actually live it. Multiple small moments can create a big impact on who we are—oftentimes more impactful than that one big moment!

Tool #7 Swim in the Blue Water. Don't be afraid to differentiate yourself. Going about something in a completely different way can be a game changer and/or a game winner. Embrace the impulse to do things differently.

- Reputation Tools

Tool #8 Decide When to Stay, and When to Go. If it's time, jump! Don't wait to be pushed. Use the Mojo Scorecard to distinguish what needs to change—you or it?

Tool #9 Say Hello, or Say Good-bye. How do you start a new job or leave an old one? Always keep your reputation in mind. Consider how you enter into a new job and give the same amount of attention to your exit strategy when/if necessary.

Tool #10 Adapt a Metrics System. Create your own personal stats. Using a personal metrics system is a way for us to obtain specific feedback so that we do not have to rely on impressions or hunches. Measuring what we're not doing well is just as important as measuring positive progress if we want an accurate assessment of our reputation.

Tool #11 Reduce This Number. Reduce the amount of time spent singing your own praises or passing judgment on others. Reduce the number of unproductive minutes that are lost every day in meaningless and oftentimes damaging conversations.

- Acceptance Tools

Tool #12 Influence Up as Well as Down. Treat those who make the most important decisions as you would your best customers. Every transaction has a buyer and seller, and this includes your relationship with your boss. Leaders who are successful at influencing upward are much more likely to get the support or resources needed to meet their goals.

Tool #13 Name It, Frame It, Claim It. To better understand something, someone, or a situation, give it a name. In doing this, we can better recognize and deal with the situation. The names we use are oftentimes referred to as "jargon." Naming can help in two ways: It can provide a private understanding as well as help define a common understanding for a group of people.

Tool #14 Give Your Friends a Lifetime Pass. Make a list of the people who have had a significant impact in your life. This should help you realize that you have not achieved everything on your own, but that you've had friends, family, coworkers, and bosses who have helped you achieve your goals. You are better off because you know them. Give them a "lifetime pass" from criticism! Chances are they've been more forgiving, sometime during your relationship, than they should have been.

Conclusion

Whether you are finding your Mojo for the first time, trying to keep your Mojo during a difficult time in your life, or looking to get it back after losing it, your success can be positively influenced by enlisting someone to help you. Your odds of successfully finding and keeping your Mojo are greatly increased by finding a friend who is genuinely interested in helping you succeed.

Strive to increase and exhibit your Mojo (the positive spirit toward what you are doing now that starts from the inside, and radiates to the outside). Study its four key factors: Identity, Achievement, Reputation, and Acceptance. Pinpoint where to focus, and decide which of the 14 tools to use to improve your overall Mojo.

PART SEVEN

Leadership and Power

Leadership has been a popular and enduring theme in the twenty-first century. Notably in the recent U.S. presidential elections, voters seemed to be looking for the hero who could turn the country around; establish a new direction, instill hope, and create change; and pull us through tough times. Organizations, too, are searching for visionary leaders—people who by the strength of their personalities can bring about a major organizational transformation. We hear calls for charismatic, transformational, and visionary leadership. Innumerable individuals charge that the problems with the U.S. economy, declining organizational productivity, and lost ground in worldwide competitive markets are largely a function of the lack of good organizational leadership.

What do positive leaders do? What do bad leaders do? How do (should) leaders utilize their power? These are some of the key questions addressed in the three readings in this section.

Kim Cameron is the William Russell Kelly Professor of Management and Organization at the University of Michigan's Ross School of Business. He has conducted research on downsizing, corporate quality culture, leadership excellence, and virtuousness in organizations. His published books include *Making the Impossible Possible*, *Leading with Values*, *Diagnosing and Changing Organizational Culture,* and (with Gretchen Spreitzer) *The Oxford Handbook of Positive Organizational Scholarship.*

Drawing on the fields of positive organizational scholarship and positive psychology, Cameron contends that *Positive Leadership* suggests three things—dramatically positive deviant performance; emphasis on strengths, optimism, and supportive communication; and facilitating the best of the human condition. Four associated leadership strategies are positive climates, relationships, communication, and meaning. This requires a diagnosis of current practices, careful role definitions, and measurement of progress toward positive leadership.

Barbara Kellerman received her Ph.D. from Yale University and subsequently held professorships at Fordham, Tufts, Fairleigh Dickinson, and George Washington Universities. She is currently the James MacGregor Burns Lecturer in Public Leadership at Harvard University's John F. Kennedy School of Government. In addition to writing

Bad Leadership, she has also published *Followership, The End of Leadership,* and three previous books on leadership in the public sector.

Bad Leadership dispels the simplistic notion that all leadership is positive. Bad leaders can be either ineffective (inappropriate means or ends) or unethical (failure to distinguish right and wrong). Kellerman identifies seven types of bad leadership: incompetent, rigid, intemperate, callous, corrupt, insular, and evil. She proceeds to identify a wide variety of ways in which leaders can improve their behavior, and tactics for followers to engage in self-help. In short, bad leaders can still become good leaders if they are willing to attempt making personal changes.

Leadership power (the ability to exert influence over others) is explored by Jeffrey Pfeffer in his book *Power: Why Some People Have It and Others Don't*. He explores three primary obstacles to building one's power—a false belief that the world is fair, superficial books and personal stories about gaining power, and pervasive self-sabotage (along with an excessive desire to be liked). Pfeffer then discusses four key bases of influence: control of resources, social networks, development of communication skills and personal appearance, and enhancing one's personal reputation. He concludes with an analysis of the costs of having power, and how power can be lost if it is not monitored and developed.

Jeffrey Pfeffer has taught at the Graduate School of Business at Stanford University for over 30 years, where he is the Thomas D. Dee II Professor of Organizational Behavior. He is the author or coauthor of 13 books, including *Hard Facts, Hidden Value, What Were They Thinking*?, and *The Human Equation*. The author of numerous articles, Pfeffer received the Richard I. Irwin Award for scholarly contributions to management.

1

Positive Leadership

Kim Cameron
Summary Prepared by Jodi Nelson

Jodi Nelson is the Chief Operating Officer for SISU Medical Solutions, LLC, in Duluth, Minnesota. SISU Medical Solutions, LLC, is an information technology (IT) organization with a focus on the IT needs of health-care organizations. She concentrates her efforts in the areas of human resources management, organizational operations, and leadership. Prior to joining the SISU organization, Jodi worked in the human resources department at Miller-Dwan Medical Center in Duluth, Minnesota. Jodi has a bachelor's degree from the University of Minnesota Duluth in Business Administration, with a concentration in human resources.

INTRODUCTION

Leadership style within an organization can greatly impact the results that an organization strives for. Although our society as a whole tends to focus on the negative outcomes of a given action, a person who is able to think outside of that box and provide a positive leadership style will be successful. Leadership in any organization can be a delicate balance of many outside forces. When dealing with decisions and adversity through use of a positive leadership style, the organization will more likely reap the desired results.

POSITIVE LEADERSHIP

Three key belief systems underlie positive leadership:

- *Positively deviant performance:* the belief that results will exceed expectations and go above and beyond them.
- *Affirmation bias:* the belief that the focus should be on the positive assets and strengths of people.
- *Facilitating the best of the human condition:* the belief that people are intrinsically good and simply need nurturing.

Organizations will improve themselves through the belief and practice of these three positive **leadership characteristics**.

Kim Cameron. *Positive Leadership: Strategies for Extraordinary Performance.* San Francisco, CA: Berrett-Koehler Publishers, 2008.

FOUR POSITIVE LEADERSHIP STRATEGIES

For an organization to achieve positive leadership through a positive deviant performance, affirmation bias, and facilitating the best of the human condition, there are four leadership strategies to promote within an organization. Managers should focus on fostering the four positive leadership strategies that enable positive deviance. Those four strategies are positive climate, positive relationships, positive communication, and positive meaning.

Positive Climate

The positive climate in an organization is a direct reflection of the emotions of the employees working there. Leaders looking to achieve a positive deviance will embrace the concept of a positive climate or atmosphere and work to achieve it. This positive climate can be attained through consistent demonstration of compassion, forgiveness, and gratitude. Employee emotions within an organization will create the desired climate.

Positive Relationships

Positive relationships within an organization focus on both the relational value of the experiences among staff as well as extending to the more physical, mental, and emotional health of relationships within the organization. Ensuring that the organization fosters the relations of the individuals involved will enhance the strengths that each individual brings to the table as well as enhance the physical and mental health of those individuals.

Positive Communication

Positive communication within an organization should be fostered to ensure positive deviance. Managers should focus on supportive communication and feedback. This is especially important during critical points within an organization's existence. Supportive communication is important to keep lines of communication open. Feedback must be provided, whether it be of a negative or positive nature. Leaders within an organization who foster communication will ultimately help individuals as well as the organization to grow.

Positive Meaning

Managers should strive for positive meaning within an organization while looking for a balance between the work being done and the outcomes associated with that work. Work and meaningfulness come together when:

1. The work has an important positive impact on the well-being of individuals.
2. The work is associated with an important virtue or personal value.
3. The work has an impact that extends beyond the immediate time frame or creates a ripple effect.
4. The work builds supportive relationships or a sense of community in people.

To ensure positive deviance within an organization, managers should recognize the importance of positive meaning.

IMPLEMENTING POSITIVE STRATEGIES

Providing positive leadership within any organization can be a delicate balance to ensure positive deviance. Initially, *managers should diagnose their current practices.* Before leaders can begin to instill a positive leadership style within an organization, it is mandatory that they understand where their leadership style has come from. After identifying current practices, leaders should plan for the implementation of change within their organization. A concerted effort needs to be made to ensure a positive leadership style is adopted by all.

As a portion of the implementation plan, managers should determine a strategy to build a positively deviant organization. To accomplish a positive leadership style within an organization, managers should pursue a Personal Management Interview (PMI) program. The first step in the PMI program is to define roles and responsibilities. Members within an organization must understand their role is to be successful and feel good about what it is that they do. Second, it is paramount that leaders revisit the individual role definitions and measure progress on a regular basis with their direct reports within the organization. Leaders need to communicate with all individuals and coach them as they move forward and grow.

Conclusion

Effective leaders inherently strive for greatness. Through the implementation of a positive leadership style and the achievement of a positively deviant organization, leaders *will* succeed.

2

Bad Leadership

Barbara Kellerman
Summary Prepared by Warren Candy

Warren Candy was Senior Vice President for Allete/Minnesota Power, a diversified electric services company headquartered in Duluth, Minnesota, where he was responsible for the electric, water, gas, and coal business units in Minnesota, Wisconsin, and North Dakota. His interests include high-performance organizational systems, sustainable organizational design, leadership development, and sociotechnical systems implementation. He received his diploma in Production Engineering from Swinburne Institute of Technology in Melbourne, Australia.

INTRODUCTION TO BAD LEADERSHIP

What does **bad leadership** mean? Is bad leadership automatically immoral or unethical? Or does it mean leadership that is incompetent or ineffective? What is to be done to maximize good leadership and minimize bad leadership? Can we fully understand the impact and role of leadership within our organizations without acknowledging its dark side? What role do followers play in supporting and enabling bad leadership? Why do people hold idealized visions of their leaders and defer power and control to them? Why do competent people sometimes behave badly when leading? Finally, can there ever be any form of "leadership" without "followership"?

Over the past several decades a "leadership industry" has developed within the United States that is based on the proposition that leadership, as a body of knowledge, is a subject that can be studied and a skill that can be learned by any and all people. To support this industry, definitions of leadership have evolved to the point where they are always undeniably positive and always have leaders as people of competence and character.

For example, in 1978, James MacGregor Burns stated that leadership occurs when people use resources to attain goals by engaging their followers and satisfying their needs. Warren Bennis, in 1989, suggested that a leader creates shared meaning through integrative goals, speaks in a distinctive voice so as to differentiate himself or herself, exhibits the capacity to adapt, and demonstrates his or her integrity. John Gardner noted that leadership is different from coercion. People who use coercion are judged as bad.

Therefore, all "leadership" has become synonymous with "good" leadership. This should not be surprising, as there is a natural preference to want to go through life accentuating the

Barbara Kellerman. *Bad Leadership: What It Is, How It Happens, Why It Matters.* Boston, MA: Harvard Business School Press, 2004.

positive and eliminating the negative in order to be as healthy and happy as possible. Recognizing and accepting the negatives of human nature goes against this tendency and is not something we naturally or easily acknowledge.

However, we need to think more broadly about the concept of leadership, not so much as a "thing" to be learned, but as an integral part of the human condition. It has not only a positive side but also a "dark side," or in the context used here, a bad side!

Leadership is a complex interaction that needs to be thought of in shades of gray and black and in terms of how people actually go about exercising power, authority, and influence.

Additionally, we need to understand that *leadership does not exist in isolation* or in the abstract. Without followers there is no leadership; leaders and followers are interdependent. There cannot be "good" leadership without "good" followers or, conversely, bad leadership without bad followers.

WHAT IS BAD LEADERSHIP?

Often leaders are assumed to be all powerful and independent. However, we must remember that leaders do not act alone. A leader chooses a particular course of action and then in some way gets others to go along, or, more subtly, encourages the led to "choose" the course that the group will follow. That followers matter is a presumption that is now widely shared.

There's something odd about the idea that somehow leadership can be distinguished from coercion, as if leadership and power were unrelated. There is no leadership without followership. Leaders cannot lead unless followers follow, either passively or actively.

Two fundamental categories of bad leadership exist—ineffective and unethical. *Ineffective leaders* are generally judged ineffective because of the inappropriate means they employ (or the appropriate means that they fail to employ) rather than the ends they pursue. *Unethical leadership* occurs when people fail to distinguish between right and wrong. Ethical leaders put their followers' needs before their own; unethical leaders do not. Ethical leaders exemplify private virtues such as courage and temperance; unethical leaders do not. Ethical leaders exercise leadership in the interest of the common good; unethical leaders do not. Most people are familiar with ineffective and unethical leaders. These leaders tend to disappoint us because they are inept or corrupt, and not because they are inherently evil.

Bad Leadership

Bad leadership is mainly a result of leaders behaving poorly because of who they are and what they want, and then acting in ways that do harm. This harm can be intentional or can occur as a result of carelessness or neglect. Seven types of bad leadership have become prevalent in today's organizations: incompetent, rigid, intemperate, callous, corrupt, insular, and evil.

- Incompetent leadership—the leader and at least some followers lack the will or skill (or both) to sustain effective action or to create positive change.
- Rigid leadership—the leader and at least some followers are inflexible and unyielding. Although they may be competent, they are unable or unwilling to adapt to new ideas, new information, or changing times.
- Intemperate leadership—the leader lacks self-control and is aided and abetted by followers who are unwilling or unable effectively to intervene.
- Callous leadership—the leader and at least some followers are uncaring or unkind. Ignored or discounted are the needs, wants, and wishes of most members of the group or organization, especially subordinates.

- Corrupt leadership—the leader and at least some followers lie, cheat, or steal. To a degree that exceeds the norm, they put self-interest ahead of the public interest.
- Insular leadership—the leader and at least some followers minimize or disregard the health and welfare of "the other"—that is, those outside the group or organization for which they are directly responsible.
- Evil leadership—the leader and at least some followers commit atrocities. They use pain as an instrument of power. The harm done to men, women, and children is severe rather than slight. The harm can be physical, psychological, or both.

WHAT IS BAD FOLLOWERSHIP?

To fully understand the role of leadership in organizations of today, we must understand leadership as two contradictory things: good and bad. Just as we have bad leaders, we also have bad followers; just as we have good leaders, we have good followers.

Bad followers commit themselves to bad leaders. They do so knowingly and deliberately, and generally mirror bad leaders for a variety of complex reasons.

Good followers are true partners with leaders. They think independently, engage in self-direction and self-control, follow through on their own, and fulfill their responsibilities willingly.

Individual Versus Group Needs

People do not exist in organizations in isolation, so they are driven to satisfy a wide variety of both individual and group needs and expectations. Among the most compelling explanations for the willingness of followers to obey authority is the need that people have to *keep things simple*. Even bad leaders often satisfy the most basic human needs, in particular safety, simplicity, and certainty. Leaders, even bad ones, can provide a sense of order and certainty in a disordered and uncertain world. The construct of the leader itself is a manifestation of our preference for simple as opposed to complex explanations.

Groups also go along with bad leaders to gain important benefits for themselves collectively. Leaders maintain order, provide cohesion and identity, and do the collective work. Hierarchy, it turns out, is the natural order of things, because as societies increase in size, they become even more dependent on leaders to order, organize, and carry out their collective activities. There will always be leaders, and there will always be those tasked with getting the group's work done.

For reasons that are now quite clear, followers have good and sound reasons for following, even when their leaders are bad. To meet their needs as individuals and as members of groups, followers usually conclude that it's in their interests to go with the flow.

FROM BAD TO BETTER, HOW LEADERS AND FOLLOWERS CAN IMPROVE

We cannot stop, slow, or change bad leadership by attempting to change human nature. Exhortations to do good works are often ineffective. And we cannot expect to reduce the number of bad leaders until we reduce the number of bad followers.

Leaders and followers will change only when they decide that it is in their best interest to do so. When the cost/benefit ratio of bad leadership tips in favor of good leadership, then change will occur!

From the research and analysis of many real-life examples of bad leadership, specific actions have been identified that can be used by leaders and followers alike to limit, correct for, and prevent bad leadership and followership.

Ideas for Leadership Self-Help

- Share power and work with others collaboratively in meaningful ways.
- Don't believe your own hype: "For leaders, to buy their own publicity is the kiss of death."
- Get real, stay real, and stay in touch with reality.
- Compensate for your blind spots by acquiring in-depth knowledge, or support, in areas of weakness.
- Stay balanced, because balanced leaders develop healthier organizations, and make more thoughtful and effective decisions.
- Remember the mission, your reason for existence, and use it as your compass during difficult times.
- Stay healthy; physical and mental health are critical.
- Be reflective and develop self-knowledge, self-control, and good habits through quiet contemplation.
- Establish a culture of openness in which diversity and dissent are encouraged.
- Bring in advisers who are both strong and independent.
- Avoid groupthink, encourage healthy dissent, minimize excessive cohesiveness, and strive for frank and open discussions to realistically appraise alternative courses of action.
- Get reliable and complete information, and then disseminate it.
- Establish a system of checks and balances. For example, limit the tenure of leaders, rotate responsibilities, hold regular performance reviews, and use multiple metrics.
- Strive for stakeholder balance by connecting with all constituencies and not just a chosen few.

Ideas for Follower Self-Help

- Empower yourself to take action and don't merely "go along."
- Be loyal to the whole, and not to any single individual.
- Be skeptical, realizing that leaders are not gods and are subject to errors and omissions that need to be highlighted and discussed.
- Take a stand.
- Pay attention; do not contribute to bad leadership through deliberate or inadvertent inattention.
- Find allies, as there is always strength in numbers when working with other like-minded individuals.
- Develop your own sources of information to verify correct and complete information, remembering always that the interests of leaders and followers do not always coincide.
- Take collective action.
- Be a watchdog; do not abdicate responsibility for oversight and for minding the store.
- Hold leaders accountable to all stakeholders through transparency, open discussions, and meaningful participation.

3 Power

Jeffrey Pfeffer
Summary Prepared by Kristie J. Loescher

Dr. Kristie Loescher is a Senior Lecturer in the McCombs School of Business at the University of Texas at Austin, where she teaches management, leadership, human resources, and business communication courses. She earned her doctorate in Business Administration, specializing in human resources management. Prior to her career in academia, she earned a master's degree in Public Health and worked in the health-care industry for 15 years in the areas of quality assurance, utilization management, and clinical research. Her academic publications focus on ethical education, organizational ethics, change management, and diversity management. Dr. Loescher is also a coauthor of the book *Communication Matters: Write, Speak, Succeed*, now in its second edition.

POWER: ITS NATURE, OBSTACLES, AND ROLE

Building **power** (influence over others) and using it effectively is related to career success in three key ways. First, power gives you more control over your work environment, which leads to better health and happiness. Second, power can lead to monetary success. Finally, power is necessary for leaders to accomplish their goals; if you want to change the world, you will need to develop a strong **power base** (support from others) to succeed.

Obstacles to Power

There are three major obstacles to building power. The first is the mistaken belief that the world is fair. If you expect a fair world, you will be less likely to take advantage of relationships and learning opportunities with people you don't respect. This choice will limit your potential and access to power-building relationships. You will also be more likely to wait for the rewards you "deserve" to come to you instead of actively seeking the power needed to obtain those rewards.

The second obstacle to building power is leadership literature. Books by top executives tend to paint an unrealistic picture of what it takes to attain top power positions by focusing on a more ethical and righteous portrait of the leader and neglecting to detail the power plays and less politically correct actions that played a role in the leader's success. These books focus on the positive aspects of the leader and ignore or downplay his or her negative traits and make it seem

Jeffrey Pfeffer. *Power: Why Some People Have It and Others Don't*. New York: HarperBusiness, 2010.

like the leader gained the top position entirely through fair play and hard work, which can encourage a belief in "the-world-is-fair" fallacy.

The final obstacle is often the most damaging: self-sabotage. People will undermine their own chances of success out of a fear of failure and a desire to maintain a positive self-image. An example of self-sabotage is failing to research the requirements of a new job, giving you a handy excuse for not getting it that deflects the blame for failure from you onto an action (or nonaction), and thus protecting your self-esteem (i.e., "If I just study more, I can get the job; I remain inherently worthy of the job").

Power Matters More Than Performance

Many of us believe that if we work hard and produce high-quality work, we will be successful. *However, in reality, performance is not the key to success—power is.* Actually, pleasing your boss is the biggest key to success. If your boss is happy, performance is not as important, but if your boss is unhappy, good performance will not save your job. If you have a good relationship with your boss, then he or she will be more likely to help you meet your career goals.

In fact, if your performance is highly effective, it may trap you in your current position. If there is nothing to be gained by your promotion and a high cost to replace you, your boss is less likely to support or help you advance. In contrast, according to a study by Melvin Lerner, CEOs who had several years of poor operations and led firms that went into bankruptcy only faced a 50 percent chance of losing their jobs. If the CEO was powerful, he or she was more likely to keep the job despite poor performance.

Additionally, to build and maintain power, make sure you are visible and noticed by your superiors, control how your performance is measured or perceived, and help those already in power achieve their goals and feel good about themselves. These actions will lead to a desire on the part of powerful people to help you succeed.

SOURCES OF POWER

Personal Qualities That Help You Build Power

To build and maintain power, change your behaviors and adapt to new situations and people. *To support your changeability, make identifying and pursuing optimal behaviors a high-priority goal throughout your career.* You also need to evaluate yourself objectively and have people in your life that can help you identify your blind spots. To begin, you can focus on evaluating yourself against the *seven personality traits that are helpful in building power: ambition, energy, focus, self-knowledge, confidence, empathy, and conflict tolerance.* Finally, you need to accurately prioritize the personal changes that are most important for your success in your particular situation.

Organizations and Positions That Can Help You Build Power

When you start your career, from the perspective of building power, you have two choices: start in a position where there is less competition and more opportunity to build a power base and rise quickly without a lot of opposition, or enter an inherently powerful position (or join an already powerful department), knowing these positions and departments will attract many other capable people and you will face stiffer competition for promotion. The first choice makes building power faster but more risky, the second makes it a harder (and probably longer) struggle, but with more assurance of success.

How to Get High-Power-Potential Jobs

To succeed in your quest for power, ask for what you need to gain access and proximity to powerful people. Although you risk being turned down, you will stand out from your more timid colleagues, and you are more likely to get the projects and personal access needed to build the relationships that will, in turn, help you build a power base. *Standing out by asking for access to power is part of getting noticed, differentiating yourself from the competition, and showing confidence—traits mentioned earlier as keys to building power.*

If you are afraid that asking for "too much" will hurt your **likeability** (pleasant qualities noticed by others), note that likeability increases influence only among those who are fairly equal in power. When you are dealing with those who have more or less power than you, *competence* is equally or even more important than likeability; coming across as competent usually requires an appearance of toughness, or even meanness. People who focus solely on being nice can come across as weak or even unintelligent. When people make a decision on whether to support and help you, they are far more interested in your standing or position in the "pack" and your ability to beat the competition than with your charm.

Bases of Influence

There are four critical sources of power that you can use to build your influence base: resources, social networks, communication skills, and reputation. You should develop a strategy for building each.

1. *Resources.* Controlling access to scarce resources such as money and jobs is a source of power as long as you use it to help curry favor to increase your power base. It is the relationships resources can buy that build the power, not the resources themselves. Because of this link between resources and relationships, positions that have a bigger budget or bigger staff have a greater potential for building power. Hence, line positions are typically a surer path to power than staff positions, where resources are fewer. Don't forget that your time and attention is also a resource that you can give away judiciously to help those in power feel better about themselves and, by extension, about you.

2. *Social networks.* Building, maintaining, and using social ties, both inside and outside your organization, helps you be more visible and gets you noticed, increasing your power and status. As you build your network, remember to pay careful attention to adding those people to your network who can add to your power base and support your career development. Having outside connections can also give you the opportunity to provide critical links for powerful people in your organization with those on the outside whom they value. If you are the one who gives them this important connection, it will be a favor they will pay back with support for your career advancement. *The best networking strategy is to know a lot of people at an acquaintance level*, as opposed to knowing a few people at a deeper social level. You want to focus on building diverse, high-status contacts, not merely friends.

3. *Communication skills.* Act and speak with power. Assume that people are always watching you. For example, focus on looking interested in meetings and at other public events; yawning through a meeting or surreptitiously checking your cell phone could leave a lasting bad impression on the very people you need to impress to build your power base. Men can use anger to stand out and create an impression of strength and intelligence, whereas being quiet and nice can be interpreted as weak and/or stupid. Many people do not like confrontation, so displaying a temper can be a useful tool to get what you want. Women, however, have a harder time using anger without coming across as abrasive and harsh as opposed to strong. Women have to be careful to express anger forcefully (mostly verbally) as opposed to submissively (mostly nonverbally with body language and expression). In situations where you have to choose between appearing likeable or appearing competent (yet abrasive), choose to appear competent. To gain power, you need to learn to convey emotions you may not feel in the moment—such as confidence. Use the device that many stage actors employ in these situations: Remember a time when you *did* feel confident and use that memory to help you choose your body language and demeanor.

In terms of dress and comportment, look like you belong one or two more rungs up the ladder; dress for your next job, not your current one. *Always use your posture, gestures, and facial expressions to communicate confidence and self-assurance.* For example:

- Stand up straight.
- Keep your hand gestures open and forceful.
- Use personal space strategically (invade space when trying to out-power or to persuade another).
- Maintain direct eye contact.
- Take time to react to questions (to appear more forceful, reflective, and intelligent).
- Use interruption strategically; people with power often interrupt others.

Although you should use forcefulness in your nonverbal communication and tone of voice, your word choices should be driven by the goals of connection and affiliation to successfully persuade others. There are six techniques for improving the persuasiveness of your word choice:

1. Define cultural boundaries by using us-versus-them references to create a connection among "us."
2. Pause to encourage approval or applause.
3. Focus your talks around three succinct points. A three-point list creates the impression of intelligence, preparedness, and objectivity. Repetition is also key—mention your main points several times to increase retention and support.
4. Use contrasting pairs presented with similar grammatical structure to highlight the idea you want to persuade others to adopt.
5. Avoid using notes or sounding too scripted when you present. Memorize your key ideas, but let the specific words flow naturally, so as to appear prepared and avoid sounding robotic or insincere.
6. Use extensive humor when appropriate to help create a bond between you and your audience and to increase retention and support of your message.

Finally, pay attention to your surroundings and their reflection on your status; set the stage for critical discussions with others to maximize your power potential.

4. Reputation: Associate with high-status people and organizations to improve your reputation. First impressions are developed within the first few seconds someone meets you, and these impressions tend to remain consistent over time. Strive to make a good impression on everyone you meet and carefully choose the image you want to project in these situations to reflect the culture and values of where you want to move. Build your reputation, because this image creates the "reality" people will perceive and act on in regard to their interactions with you.

PROBLEMS WITH POWER

How to Deal with Opposition and Impediments

Meeting force with more force is typically not a successful strategy for dealing with opposition. Instead, work to include your opponents in your plans and to identify their needs to win them over to your side. *A sure way to turn enemies into allies, or at least remove them from the picture, is to help them get a better job elsewhere.* Be careful to avoid pushing opponents to a point where they have nothing left to lose and can only gain by beating you.

Keep your actions focused on your strategic priorities. Do not be tempted by emotions to fight battles that are tangential to your goals. In addition to strategic focus, you will also need to control your reactions to people. Regardless of how you feel, there will be people you have to work with to get access to the resources and the people you need to build your power base. Learn to build constructive relationships with people who have hurt you, angered you, and disrespected you—without giving these people any hint that you do not like them. Build the maturity and self-discipline required to remain focused on your goals and the role each person plays in helping you meet your goals.

If you see a power struggle emerging, act fast and act first. Use your power base to remove or isolate opponents before they have a chance to organize against you. Your access to resource control will be key to surmounting challenges to your position; use it to reward your friends and helpers and to punish your enemies. Another helpful tactic to overcome opposition is to *connect your goals to a higher purpose*, such as quality service for customers or shareholder interest, which will compel others to support you (i.e., if they do not support you, they will look like the bad guys).

Costs of a Power Position

Holding a position of power brings rewards, but at a price. You must be comfortable paying this price to maintain your power. The costs of power include:

- Intense scrutiny of your work and personal life.
- Loss of autonomy. When you are in a powerful position, you lose control over how you spend your time.
- Extreme amount of time and effort. Achieving and maintaining a powerful position will require focus and commitment and will leave little time for a personal life. This cost is particularly high for women.
- Being unable to trust anyone. The higher your position, the less likely it is that people will be honest with you. To survive and maintain your power position, you will need constant vigilance to identify those who are likely to challenge or undermine you.
- Becoming addicted to it. Because having power is so exciting and flatters our egos, losing it can be devastating. The addictive nature of power has driven many people to abandon their values and original goals in order to maintain it at all costs. Although it is tough to leave a powerful position, the reality is that everyone has to leave at some point.

How Power Is Lost or Maintained

As the historical adage reminds us, power corrupts. *People lose power when it begins to corrupt them into a state of overconfidence, lack of self-control, and insensitivity to the interests and needs of their supporters.* The addictive nature of power changes everyone, and that change is typically the cause of power downfalls. If you manage to keep your head and not fall victim to arrogance and **hubris** (foolish pride and egotism), your downfall may still be brought about by trusting the wrong people. If you want to maintain power, you cannot afford a lack of vigilance and paranoia about others' intentions.

Power is also lost when we lose patience and forget the valuable lesson of dealing with opposition by **co-opting** opposers (drawing them into your group or position). Because power tends to decrease our self-control, we are more likely to respond out of anger and frustration, offending the people whose support we need to maintain power, or pushing our enemies to a point where they will stop at nothing to see us fail.

Ignoring changing conditions is another reason people lose power. Maintaining old techniques that worked well 10 years ago and ignoring their decreasing efficacy in today's environment will leave you weak and easy prey for your opposition. Because power tends to decrease our attention, we do not listen to the people who could help us build the new skills or gain the new perspective that could maintain our supremacy.

Finally, the long hours and intense focus required to acquire and maintain power can be exhausting. As a consequence, we make mistakes and lose focus. If you feel burned out and too tired to maintain the focus and energetic time commitment required to be in a powerful position, it is better to resign; you will not have the resources to resist opposition for very long anyway.

Power and Organizational Effectiveness

The pursuit of power may be good for your career, but is it helpful for the organization? In short, *no; power plays and struggles reduce job satisfaction, organizational commitment, and productivity within a company while increasing people's intentions to quit.* However, the pursuit of power is a universal aspect of human beings living in a hierarchical community. Regardless of the impact on organizations, wherever there are people living in a community, power and its political struggles will be there too.

PART EIGHT

Teams and Teamwork

Some employees work as individuals, whereas others find themselves in groups; some employees are part of teams, whereas others merely think they are. Teamwork has become a widespread mantra espoused by consultants and a frequent practice among organizations in the twenty-first century, but the question remains—"How does a collection of interdependent individuals meld their efforts into true teamwork?"

J. Richard Hackman has studied teams for many years, and most recently focused his research on organizations in the intelligence community. In *Collaborative Intelligence* (not summarized here), he identifies six preconditions for a high-performing team; it must be real, have a compelling purpose, consist of the right members, establish and follow clear norms of conduct, work under a highly supportive context, and receive the benefits of competent coaching for success. When these factors are in place, a team can demonstrate true collaboration, allowing it to solve complex problems, share scarce resources, and achieve its objectives on a timely basis.

Beyond Teams lays out a simple premise based on research and case studies—that high-performing organizations stem from collaborative work systems. The authors (Beyerlein, McGee, Moran, and Freedman) identify 10 major principles that define collaborative organizations, including an emphasis on personal accountability, facilitation of dialog, managing trade-offs, and "exploiting the rhythm of divergence and convergence." They also demonstrate the applicability of the 10 principles across manufacturing, product development, service, and virtual office settings.

Michael Beyerlein is the author or editor of numerous books on collaboration. He is the Director of the Center for the Study of Work Teams at the University of North Texas. Craig McGee is a principal with Solutions; Linda Moran works for Achieve Global; and Sue Freedman is President of Knowledge Work Associates.

Beyond Teams

Michael M. Beyerlein, Sue Freedman, Craig McGee, and Linda Moran
Summary Prepared by David L. Beal

David L. Beal is a retired Operations Manager and Vice President of Manufacturing for Lake Superior Paper Industries and Consolidated Papers, Inc., in Duluth, Minnesota. Under his leadership, the all-salaried workforce was organized into a totally self-reliant team system using the principles of sociotechnical design to create a high-performance system. Dave teaches in the Labovitz School of Business and Economics at the University of Minnesota Duluth, where his areas of interest include designing and leading self-directed team-based organizations, teamwork, and production and operations management. He received his B.S. in Chemical Engineering from the University of Maine in Orono, Maine, with a fifth year in Pulp and Paper Sciences.

INTRODUCTION

The challenges organizations face today continue to grow as a result of a rapidly changing environment, not the least of which includes the proliferation of new technology, a dynamic global marketplace, and (more recently) the threat of terrorism. Contemporary organizations must be structurally flexible, capable of adapting to changing markets, and able to compete and win on a national and frequently international scale. **Collaborative work systems** (CWSs) provide the fundamental principles and means to meet these challenges. Collaboration and CWSs are not new; they are simply the principles and practices that make organizations and teamwork succeed. There are 10 major principles for successful collaboration and a set of characteristics that collaborative organizations have that effectively apply these principles. Organizations that fail to embrace the CWS approach exhibit a contrasting set of defining characteristics.

Managers and employees at all levels working together can outperform individuals acting alone, especially when the outcome requires a variety of creative abilities, multiple skills, careful judgments, and the knowledge and experience that different employees possess in achieving organizational goals. CWSs are the means to achieve these goals and not an end in and of themselves.

Michael M. Beyerlein, Sue Freedman, Craig McGee, and Linda Moran. *Beyond Teams: Building the Collaborative Organization.* San Francisco, CA: Jossey-Bass/Pfeiffer, 2003.

RATIONALE FOR COLLABORATIVE WORK SYSTEMS

Collaborative work systems put into practice a disciplined, principle-based system of collaboration necessary to be successful in a rapidly changing environment. All organizations collaborate to some extent in order to achieve their goals, including how the organization serves its customers and meets its financial objectives. CWSs carry collaboration to a much higher level and therefore outperform organizations that do not consistently apply the principles of collaboration as a disciplined practice, or do not make collaboration the means to achieve business objectives and the goals of the organization.

Organizations that not only value collaborative practices, but consciously apply and nurture these practices with passion and conviction at all levels create a definite competitive advantage over organizations that simply assume collaborative practices will occur. Strategic direction and leadership at the top of the organization are paramount to achieving a CWS. Although team-based organizations and self-directed work systems depend on collaborative practices, these organizations may not go far enough in the degree or variety of collaboration to reach the full potential that CWSs have.

Collaborative work systems are a key strategy for achieving superior business results. Although employees create value through collaborative practices, their ability to perform and to be highly productive is often limited by the barriers the organization creates. These barriers stifle the collaborative practices employees are expected to have. Key employees at all levels solve problems, make and act on important decisions, invent new practices and improved methods of doing business, build relationships, and strategically plan for the future. The effectiveness of their processes and practices and the work system the employees are in determines the degree to which they reach their full potential. A high level of collaborative capacity will stimulate both formal and informal learning and enhance the effectiveness of work done at all levels.

When collaboration becomes both a strategy and competency for achieving business goals and a major part of the organizational culture, then:

- Organizational barriers to a collaborative work system are broken down.
- Employees at all levels know when and how to collaborate to achieve business results without wasting valuable time and resources.
- Managers and leaders in the organization create systems that are highly flexible, functionally adaptable, and fast to react to a changing environment.
- The waste that occurs within a functional silo and between functional silos diminishes and is replaced with a high level of cross-functional cooperation.
- Teams become accountable for their results and hold themselves to a high standard.
- The organization becomes a highly interdependent, interacting, and interconnected system of processes and functions that continuously performs at a high level.

Collaborative work systems do not require formal teams or a team-based system (i.e., an organizational arrangement where teams are the basic unit of organizational structure), but their collaborative capacity and competency are enhanced by the use of these structures. Because teams are frequently the most common form of business collaboration, the design, management, and work processes that make collaboration within and between teams successful are important features to discuss.

THE PRINCIPLES OF COLLABORATIVE ORGANIZATIONS

The 10 principles of collaborative work systems are as follows:

1. *Focus Collaboration on Achieving Business Results:* Collaboration is necessary to achieve the goals and strategies necessary for long-term success. It is not an end in itself, but a means to an end. This principle focuses the organization on a common goal where everyone understands their role in the broader context of achieving intermediate and overall corporate objectives. When collaboration is focused on achieving business results, everyone is focused on common goals and objectives and is in the business of getting results with very few self-serving obstacles. Employees know what needs to be done and can go about doing it in an efficient and effective manner. When collaborative efforts are not focused on business results, conflicts and disagreements will occur and employees may suboptimize their own functional areas, sometimes at the expense of achieving overall organizational goals.

2. *Align Organizational Support Systems to Promote Ownership:* This principle stems from an understanding that all systems of support must be congruent with the goals and principles of the organization. If a collaborative work system is a defined strategy to achieve the goals of the organization, then all systems must support the who, when, where, and why of collaborative practices. These systems include management systems, organizational design, performance management systems, and information and communication systems. Support systems that create a sense of ownership have a much greater chance of success in creating a competitive advantage. When these systems are aligned, employees are rewarded for acting in a predictable and consistent manner toward achieving individual, intermediate, and overall corporate goals and objectives. When it is not working, employees are sent mixed messages that collectively produce organizational chaos and poor performance.

3. *Articulate and Enforce a Few Strict Rules:* This principle applies to the policies, practices, and methods that drive decision making within organizations. Everyone needs to understand what needs to be done within a framework of a few highly understood rules. These rules must be consistently applied and individuals held accountable for their application. The application of this principle gives individuals and teams of individuals a common understanding of what needs to be done without limiting their ability to accomplish it. It also allows them to break down barriers and make and act on important decisions toward the accomplishment of the goals and objectives. Organizations with too many rules suffer from inaction and an unwillingness to take risks, whereas an organization with too few rules struggles from a lack of direction and consistency.

4. *Exploit the Rhythm of Divergence and Convergence:* This principle provides a balance between creating new and exciting ways of getting the job done, and the discipline necessary to get the job done. Both of these are processes by which participants are allowed to diverge with their ideas and generate different ways of getting the job done, and also converge to a level of agreement necessary to move forward to get the job done. Managing the process of divergence and convergence is important to goal accomplishment. The process also has a rhythm that is recognizable. As collaboration within and between teams and individuals at different levels and across functional boundaries occurs, complex activities take place toward the accomplishment of the stated goals and objectives. Each cycle accomplishes an intermediate objective that allows the next step or iterative cycle to occur. When the rhythm of divergence and convergence is effectively managed, new ideas and ways of getting the job done naturally occur, while the disciplined commitment to accomplish the objective in the expected time frame is achieved.

5. *Manage Complex Trade-Offs On A Timely Basis:* Making timely and effective decisions requires the skills, knowledge, and a process for effective decision making. When the collaborative unit is faced with complex, interrelated, or interdependent decisions, trade-offs frequently have to be made between contradictory criteria or information. Managing these trade-offs for effective decision making sometimes requires specialized skills, knowledge, and information that the collaborative unit must recognize and acquire on a timely basis. When complex decisions are made on a timely basis, the collaborative unit can move forward with increased confidence.

6. *Create Higher Standards for Discussion, Dialogue, and Information Sharing:* Collaborative processes can be very complex and highly important to goal attainment. These processes must be well managed by leaders that recognize the need for good organization, coaching, and facilitation skills. Higher standards mean that participants have direct access to relevant information, expert opinions, and advice; new and improved capabilities for effective decision making; and a sense of excitement and commitment to be involved in CWS. When the collaborative capacity of an organization is not increased through coaching or training of the participants, decision making suffers, deadlines and expectations are more difficult to meet, and participants seek a safe haven by sticking to their own opinions and perspectives. Getting "out of the box" and taking a risk will become a rare event.

7. *Foster Personal Accountability:* When organization members are personally accountable for their own role and responsibilities in the collaborative process, the capability of the collaborative unit will improve. Accountability means that participants will build capability to achieve goals by breaking down the barriers to goal attainment, putting the goal ahead of self-serving considerations, and tackling the tasks of getting the job done with confidence, risk taking, and timeliness. Participants simply do what needs to be done and act in support of the collaborative process. When there is a lack of accountability, participants fail to acknowledge their responsibility or mistakes, and they will usually act in support of their own self-serving interests.

8. *Align Authority, Information, and Decision Making:* This principle means that teams and participants have all the tools, including the authority to make important decisions; the skills, knowledge, and information for effective decision making; and the resources and support to act and carry out the decisions they make for effective goal attainment. When these tools are present, decisions are timely and well executed, and participants are committed with a high degree of responsibility for their participation in the collaborative unit. When authority, information, and decision making are not aligned, participants experience a loss of both support and direction, a lack of ownership in the process, and chaos or confusion when decisions and plans have to be revisited.

9. *Treat Collaboration as a Disciplined Process:* This principle means that CWS organizations must recognize and support the principles as a strategy for goal accomplishment. Making collaboration a disciplined process requires the skills, knowledge, and training of a critical mass of participants who can pass on their expertise in successfully conducting collaborative processes. When organizations are competent at collaboration, they are able to manage multiple interdependent and interacting processes at the same time. These organizations will have good organization skills, the ability to quickly hurdle obstacles and break down barriers, easy access to relevant information, excellent communication skills, and the ability to make good decisions and act on those decisions in a timely manner. When collaboration is not treated as a disciplined process, meetings are not very productive or

goal oriented, participants are frustrated by the lack of goal accomplishment, and managers with authority may try to micromanage the activities of the collaborative unit.

10. ***Design and Promote Flexible Organizations:*** The successful organization today must be quick to respond to all sorts of changing business conditions and structurally flexible in its ability to get the work done and compete in a dynamic business environment. Flexible organizations respond with different structures, both formal and informal, to maximize the speed and effectiveness of what needs to be done to be successful. The increasing complexity and dynamic nature of competing in a global marketplace requires that organizations react with different structures based on the situation. These organizations break down the barriers that traditional organizations have in a way that improves their ability to compete and respond to changing business conditions. Information and decision making are moved to those who have to take action, rather than those who control the action of others. Flexible organizations have leaders who decentralize decision making for maximum effectiveness and manage the organization with a high level of cross-functional capability. When organizations are structurally inflexible, their collaborative activities are less effective, they waste valuable resources, and decisions take a lot longer to make and implement.

APPLICATIONS OF THE PRINCIPLES

Manufacturing facilities produce tangible products from physical materials with the support of functionally based staff organizations. They have become flatter in organizational structure, more flexible in their ability to get the work done in many different ways, and faster to react to the marketplace and remain competitive. As manufacturing organizations integrate vertically and horizontally to achieve a competitive advantage, they have also integrated new work systems such as "team-based organizations," "high-performance systems," "self-reliant teams," and "sociotechnical systems." When properly applied, these principle-based systems can produce superior performance. All of these systems represent changes in how work is organized and how the empowerment of employees has moved leadership down to the productive process or shop floor. As organizations become flatter and more flexible, the opportunities to collaborate become more numerous. The leadership in organizations must make clear expectations of the "how" and "when" to formally and informally collaborate. The "when" occurs when more than one person is required to make a decision and when effective implementation requires the acceptance or the decision is executed by a group of employees.

Collaboration in service settings needs to occur when the skills, knowledge, and expertise needed reside in more than one employee, when the decisions or tasks are interdependent with other employees or parts of the organization, when decisions require the acceptance of a group of employees for effective implementation, and when multiple teams or areas need to share resources or have a common understanding for goal accomplishment. On the other hand, collaboration can be wasteful when there is not good direction or leadership for collaborative processes, when the practice of "command and control" of employees makes the empowerment of employees an abstract thought, and when management fails to share important information with employees or give employees direct access to information necessary to accomplish their tasks.

New product development creates unique and creative opportunities. Expertise in functional organizations is organized into silos as opposed to product- or customer-based organizing structures. Another design is the team-based model, in which integration teams oversee the coordinated efforts and assignments of new product development teams. Global pressures, the threat of declining profit margins if new products are not developed, and the time to produce new products to preempt the competition are challenges these organizations face. The question is when, where, and who should collaborate to maximize the use of the valuable resources. It is also important to establish the training, expectations, and the time frame for effective collaboration.

The 10 principles can also be applied in "virtual work settings." **Virtual organizations** are "groups of individuals working on shared tasks while distributed across space, time and/ or organizational boundaries." They are unique in that they traverse organizational and functional boundaries that exist at multiple national and sometimes international locations. The participants in virtual settings are not located at the same site, but it is still possible to apply the principles of CWS to virtual work settings.

Conclusion

Collaborative work systems are principle-based systems that are consciously designed and nurtured for high performance. CWSs allow the creative capacities and talents of their employees to continuously increase through knowledge sharing and mutual support.

Individuals collaborating effectively in pursuit of common goals and objectives will consistently outperform individuals acting alone or in functional silos, especially when the task requires multiple skills, knowledge, different experiences, and creative abilities. As the work and the accomplishment of tasks become more complex, flexible organizational structures and collaborative practices must be carefully thought out and executed to meet the varied challenges the organization faces. When organizations apply the 10 principles of collaboration, employee ownership and involvement increase, decision making is more consistent and execution is more effective, positional power is replaced with knowledge and leadership, and employees learn and grow at a much faster rate. The organization is also quicker to respond to the business environment, more flexible in its ability to accomplish objectives in different ways, and flatter in an organizational structure that values cross-functional competencies.

PART NINE

Organizational Change

A Greek philosopher (Heraclitus of Ephesus) once noted that a person never steps into the same river twice, for the flowing current is always changing (as well as the person). Contemporary organizations have their own "river"—a turbulent environment around them. Consequently, managers of today's organizations are being called on to integrate their operations with a rapidly changing external (e.g., social, economic, political, and ecological) environment. To bring about this integration, they must often adapt their organization's internal structure, processes, and strategies to meet these environmental challenges. The ability to manage change effectively is far different from the ability to manage and cope with the ongoing and routine operational side of the organization.

Experts frequently advise American managers to invest in research and development (R&D) to keep their product mix current. Some companies (e.g., 3M) derive as much as 25 percent of their revenues from products introduced in the past five years. Nevertheless, many critics charge that one of the reasons for the decline in the competitiveness of U.S. industry revolves around its failure to innovate at sufficiently high levels. Clearly, organizations need to manage change, stimulate renewal, and develop organizational cultures in which change can thrive.

Robert E. Quinn is the M. E. Tracy Collegiate Professor of Organization Behavior and Human Resource Management at the University of Michigan, and also the cofounder of the Center for Positive Organizational Scholarship. He has written a trilogy of books that focus on the positive tensions associated with excellent performance—*Deep Change, Change the World*, and *Building the Bridge as You Walk on It.*

Quinn believes that understanding change is the foundation for building a better world. He suggests that each of us faces a core dilemma: Make deep and significant changes within ourselves, or face a slow but certain death. The solution to this dilemma lies in practicing the "fundamental state of leadership," which involves eight practices of increasing integrity—reflective action, authentic engagement, appreciative inquiry, grounded vision, adaptive confidence, detached interdependence, responsible freedom, and tough love. To effect change, Quinn says, requires that leaders become results centered, internally driven, other focused, and externally open.

John P. Kotter is the Konosuke Matsushita Professor of Leadership Emeritus at Harvard Business School and author of numerous books on leadership and change, including *The Heart of Change, Leading Change, Buy-In*, and *Our Iceberg Is Melting*. One of his newest books, *Buy-In*, identifies ways in which constructive ideas for change get shot down—and then proposes counterstrategies for overcoming those barriers. Collectively, his books have sold over two million copies and have been printed in 120 languages.

Kotter's *A Sense of Urgency* argues that the real nemesis of change is complacency, but an even more insidious threat is a *false* sense of urgency that drives frenetic activity. Instead, it is imperative that managers stir feelings and emotions powerful enough to drive employees to overcome obstacles to change. Four key tactics for creating true urgency are described—bring the outside (various stakeholders) in through questions and listening, behave with urgency every day, find opportunity in crises, and deal promptly and firmly with perpetual naysayers.

1

Building the Bridge as You Walk on It

Robert E. Quinn

Summary Prepared by Peter Stark

Peter Stark has taught strategy, managing change, entrepreneurship, and international marketing courses in the Labovitz School of Business and Economics at the University of Minnesota Duluth. Peter is an ABD doctoral student in organizational change at Pepperdine University. He has previously taught at several institutions in the United States, Mexico, and China, and is a frequent visiting instructor with the Helsinki School of Economics in Finland. He is an international consultant working with many global companies. His research interests include the application of systems theory and chaos theory to the process of understanding and dealing with the embedded ontological archetypes that inhibit culture change in organizations.

THE BASIC IDEA AND CONCEPT PATH

Leadership, rather than being a set of tool-like behavioral patterns to be enacted through emulation, is best portrayed as a state of *being* ("who we are") rather than a means of *doing* ("what we do"). Many people spend most of their time in the "normal life state." They tend to be comfort centered, externally driven, self-focused, and internally closed. As a consequence, many organizations reflect the embedded selfishness, insecurity, and lack of courage inherent in this state of being. Fortunately, anyone can transform his or her state of being and enter the extraordinary **fundamental state of leadership** in which they become results centered, internally directed, other focused, and externally open. These individuals become role models for others to emulate, and hence they stimulate positive organizing approaches and more productive social systems.

There is a strong link between an individual's personal transformation to the fundamental state of leadership and subsequent organizational transformation. *Anyone who aspires to leadership must engage in a continuous and, perhaps most important, courageously and consciously intended learning journey.* This requires that they wed their individual ability to let go of ego-needs-based control and venture into uncharted territory with their capacity for inspired, authentic leadership. Leaders who undertake this journey of self-transformation enable the positive creation of a more productive community capable of creating, leveraging, and enduring change.

Robert E. Quinn. *Building the Bridge as You Walk on It: A Guide for Leading Change.* San Francisco, CA: Jossey-Bass, 2004.

Five major conclusions about leadership can be offered:

1. Extraordinarily positive organizations (productive, flourishing communities) are reflections of (and are brought about by) extraordinary states of being among their members; they are consequently capable of creating, leveraging, and enduring great change. Without such states of being present among an organization's leaders, organizations will entropy (decline).

2. Leadership has nothing to do with position and power. It is about your fundamental "state of being" (who you are), not what you do or what you have. Leadership is realized not in what the leader does but in what others do as a consequence of the leader's state of being.

3. The normal state of being for most individuals is comfort centered, externally driven, self-focused, and internally closed. Leadership in the "normal state" isn't really leadership at all—it is a self-interested rationalization in support of socially normed organizational coping strategies. The fundamental state of leadership is results centered, internally directed, other focused, and externally open.

4. Entering the "fundamental state of leadership" requires those who aspire to leadership to experience deep, revitalizing personal change in which they challenge and change many, if not all, of their basic beliefs and assumptions in pursuit of greater awareness and authenticity.

5. Organizations change only when the leaders among their members change. The creation of extraordinarily positive organizations/productive communities is contingent upon a leader's acceptance of and engagement in a process of deep personal change.

How, then, should one fundamentally "be" in the context of a catalytic and systemic organizational process? It must be noted that human beings are complex paradoxes of qualities, attributes, and behaviors. Leadership, then, is the effect on others that emerges from the confluence of these creatively tense paradoxes. Positive traits and tensions tend to exist and operate as part of a larger, more complex, reciprocal system. Integrating the oppositions of eight polarities of being (spontaneous/self-disciplined, compassionate/assertive, mindful/energetic, principled/engaged, realistic/optimistic, grounded/visionary, confident/flexible, and independent/open) suggests eight creatively tense states from which a more dynamic and more accurately representative view of the state of leadership emerges. These practices serve as "guard rails" on the path and are both realistic and idealistic in conception and application. In *striving* for the integrated path, one is in the fundamental state of leadership.

PRACTICES FOR ENTERING THE FUNDAMENTAL STATE OF LEADERSHIP

The eight integrated but creatively tense and seemingly paradoxical practices individuals can engage in for entering the fundamental state of leadership are as follows:

- *Reflective Action:* the practice of integrating the realm of personal identity (who we are) with the realm of action (what we are doing). This person acts and learns simultaneously.
- *Authentic Engagement:* the practice of increasing our integrity by engaging the world of action with genuine love for what we are doing. This person is authentically engaged (ethical, while also highly involved).
- *Appreciative Inquiry:* the practice of gaining the capacity to see the best in the world and what is possible. These persons are optimistic, constructive, realistic, and questioning, which allows them to help others surface possibilities that previously have been less recognized.

- *Grounded Vision:* the practice of integrating the present with an image of a positive future. Such leaders are grounded, factual, hopeful, and visionary.
- *Adaptive Confidence:* the practice of letting go of control and moving into a state of action learning. The adaptively confident person is concurrently flexible, confident, secure, experimental, and open to feedback.
- *Detached Interdependence:* the practice of considering one's relationships from a very high level of maturity. This leader combines independence, a strong sense of purpose, and strength with humility and openness.
- *Responsible Freedom:* the practice of being aware of and acting in regard to the intimate connections between freedom and responsibility. The practitioner of responsible freedom is spontaneous, expressive, self-structuring, self-disciplined, empowering to others, and responsible.
- *Tough Love:* the practice of living in the balance of being both simultaneously compassionate/ concerned and assertive/bold. The **tough love** practitioner is assertive, challenging, bold, compassionate, and concerned.

DEVELOPING LEADERS

Leaders are developed through a two-step process: changing ourselves and choosing to enter the fundamental state of leadership. In the first step, all change requires and begins with self-change and requires making a personal choice to change. The second step is helping others to do the same. Leadership development similarly involves these interdependent, mutually reinforcing phenomena. Developing leaders is not just imparting a set of concepts or teaching a tool kit of strategies and behaviors; *it is encouraging people to engage in the process of deep change in themselves and then inviting others to do the same.*

Self-change can be viewed as a nine-stage path or spiral:

- Precontemplation: increasing information about one's self—one's own problems (self-deceptions), negative routines, and self-defeating behaviors. This involves consciousness raising (becoming aware that we don't know what we don't know).
- Social liberation: increasing social alternatives for behaviors that are not problematic.
- Emotional arousal: experiencing and expressing feelings about one's problems and solutions.
- Self-reevaluation: assessing feelings and thoughts about one's self with respect to a problem.
- Commitment: choosing and committing to act; belief in one's own ability to change.
- Countering: substituting new and positive alternatives for problem behaviors.
- Environment control: avoiding stimuli that elicit problem behaviors.
- Reward: rewarding one's self, or being rewarded by others, for making appropriate and positive changes.
- Helping relationships: enlisting the help and support of someone who cares to aid in preventing you from relapsing.

The fundamental state of leadership has significant implications. First, it redefines what leadership means. It is not authority and not a set of easily imitated attributes or skill sets. It is, instead, a state—a way of being that has the ability to profoundly change the systems that it is a part of. Second, it redefines what it means to develop leaders. Leadership development is first and foremost self-change, which requires an understanding of the stages and strategies inherent in this process as well as the ability to support others as they go through them.

There really is no way to teach what it means to be in a fundamental state of leadership. The best way is simply to be what you wish to evoke from others. However, the fundamental state of leadership is an inherently fragile and episodic phenomenon; it is difficult to get into and difficult to stay in.

We attract others into the fundamental state of leadership, then, by our own change process in pursuit of our own uniqueness and ever-increasing integrity. *It is one's courage to engage in the process and not one's success in mastering it that attracts others.*

2

A Sense of Urgency

John P. Kotter
Summary Prepared by David L. Beal

David Beal is a retired Operations Manager for Stora Enso, formerly Consolidated Papers, Inc., and Vice President of Manufacturing for Lake Superior Paper Industries in Duluth, Minnesota. Under his leadership, an all-salaried high-performance work system was organized into a totally self-reliant team system using the principles of sociotechnical design (STS). Dave teaches in the Labovitz School of Business and Economics at the University of Minnesota Duluth, and his areas of interest include designing and leading self-directed team-based organizations, teamwork, organizational studies, and production and operations management. He received his B.S. in Chemical Engineering from the University of Maine in Orono, Maine, with a fifth year in Pulp and Paper Sciences.

INTRODUCTION

Managers need to understand the psychology of creating a true sense of urgency in organizations to solve problems and address issues that will achieve strategic and financial objectives. If they focus on capturing the hearts and then the minds of a critical mass of employees, that will create this **true sense of urgency** necessary to succeed in a fast-moving, turbulent environment. When **a true sense of urgency** is not present, either complacency or a false sense of urgency gives people enough sense of security to believe that the organization will survive and be able to address any real threat.

Complacency exists to a certain extent in all organizations and is much more common than we believe. **Complacency** is often not seen or recognized by the employees involved because it is the product of success or perceived success. Unfortunately, it can still be part of the culture long after great success has disappeared.

The perception of success does not have to be accurate nor do the complacent rarely believe they are complacent. *The fear of what change might do to the organization or the complacents' involvement can drive irrational behavior.* The complacent are satisfied with the *status quo* and want predictability, as they have known it more than anything else. Because of this, they pay more attention to what is happening internally than externally and ignore real competitive

John P. Kotter. *A Sense of Urgency.* Boston, MA: Harvard Business Press, 2008.

threats to the organization. Although the opposite of urgency is complacency, an even more insidious threat is a **false sense of urgency**—thinking that frenzied activity alone can produce success. However, that type of activity is not likely to address real issues or threats occurring outside the organization. This false sense of urgency is as prevalent today as complacency, and it is dangerous because employees believe that the activities that occur are moving the organization into the future when in fact the opposite may be true. False urgency comes from a belief that there is a real threat to the organization when past experience has failed to achieve intended results or from others in the organization applying extreme pressure on the group. Employees with a false sense of urgency think the situation is a mess, and their frantic attempt to deal with it makes them angry, frustrated, and exhausted.

The issues of complacency and having a false sense of urgency are easily illustrated by some examples of organizations that have both succeeded and failed. Learning from these and many other case studies combined with decades of studying organizations, a strategy has emerged for increasing a true sense of urgency that is exceptionally alert, inclusive of the external environment, and relentlessly aimed at achieving success by making incremental progress each and every day. This strategy includes getting rid of seemingly important activities that do not win over the heart for change and instill a compulsive determination to act now. The actions that really matter are about *creating feelings essential for the change process to succeed.* When it comes to changing the behaviors of people, feelings are more powerful than thoughts. Feelings will motivate people to achieve more ambitious objectives despite seemingly insurmountable obstacles. Feelings will create timely actions that move the organization forward and do so every day.

THE STRATEGY FOR INCREASING TRUE URGENCY

The primary way to develop a true sense of urgency is to aim at the heart first. This can be done by creating thoughtful human experiences, such as bringing in a customer who has a passion for quality and performance, or visiting a successful competitor's place of business. Managers need to rely on all the senses to make the experience move people to address real issues and threats. Not all experiences create the desired emotional reaction. Effective experiences should move people from their day-to-day comfort zone to actions that address real problems and issues that do not have to be explained. These experiences do need to be carefully crafted so they develop a true sense of urgency that will embrace strategic goals and model desirable and observable behaviors. Strategies should be designed to empower employees by giving them access to important information and the ability to decide and act on critical issues. In short, strategies need to be created that address real issues and problems by winning, by making continuous progress every day, and by appealing to the heart as well as the mind.

THE FOUR TACTICS FOR CREATING A TRUE SENSE OF URGENCY

There are four tactics for creating a true sense of urgency:

1. Bring the outside in.
2. Behave with urgency every day.
3. Find opportunity in crises.
4. Deal with the NoNos.

Bring the Outside In

Success creates an inward focus and a false sense of security that diminishes the critical influence and reality of serious threats from the outside. To **bring the outside in** to the organization, top management needs to listen to those employees who have regular contact with customers, suppliers, and the business community. More and more enterprises need to listen to the valuable information that front-line employees bring into the organization. This requires establishing a trusting relationship that values their input and ability to understand the customer in a changing environment. Asking the right questions, closely listening to the responses, and appropriately acting on the information will become increasing valuable. When important data become available, they should not be shielded from employees, especially if the data are troubling. Data made available to those who have the ability to make important decisions and act in service of their customers will address critical issues and problems if a true sense of urgency is instilled in the culture.

The initiative to act starts at the top when management sees an opportunity and not just a problem. The primary objective is to transition from complacency to urgency without creating a flurry of activity that makes people anxious and angry. Information should be freely disseminated and direct access given to those who have the ability to act. Successful management clearly reinforces the importance of bringing the outside in to strengthen the organization. As top managers act with confidence, they make it clear that the focus is on urgency for creating the future and not blaming employees for the past. Managers need to predict how the organization will react so that fear and anger will be defused by a conviction that a sense of true urgency will produce future success.

Behave with Urgency Every Day

The information revolution and proliferation of electronic communications have added to the often-unrelated busy activities that fail to address real threats and bring the outside into the organization. Adding more hours in the day or working harder simply adds to fatigue and clutters the mind with pressure and activities that add little or no value in achieving true urgency. So why would anyone behave in a way that is contrary to their belief that they are modeling a true sense of urgency? The answer is usually complex, with a combination of forces at work. These forces may include being pushed in the wrong direction by the organization's culture; being unapproachable by peers and subordinates; not seeing the problem because of complacency; or being trapped in a set of behaviors that created past successes.

In order to **behave with urgency** every day it is important to:

- Free uptime by eliminating low-priority activities and busy appointment books that prevent acting with a true sense of urgency every time the opportunity arises.
- Delegate by empowering employees with the ability to make and act on decisions that increase a true sense of urgency. Hold employees accountable and do not allow them to delegate up.
- Leave enough free time during the day to respond immediately to high-priority issues, and bring closure to conversations and meetings by clarifying the next steps with a true sense of urgency.
- Leave at least one hour each day to talk to subordinates with feeling and passion about the importance of having a true sense of urgency and what it means to the success of the

organization. Listen, listen, listen, and respond with true urgency by identifying the strategic issues and activities that will move the organization into the future.

- Make sure you "walk the talk" by modeling behaviors that are supportive of the passion you have for a true sense of urgency. Bring the outside world into your actions in various ways that appeal to the multiple senses that people have.
- Be as open and visible as possible, using your personal strengths effectively.

Find Opportunity in Crises

Managers can often **find opportunities in crises** if the situation is used effectively to create a true sense of urgency. The following principles will guide the effectiveness of using crises productively:

- Look for potential solutions that turn crises into opportunities. A crisis can be a valuable opportunity for change that appeals to the heart and reinforces supportive behaviors.
- Recognize that crises do not by themselves reduce complacency. They must be used as opportunities to create the kind of behaviors that address real business problems and demonstrate a true sense of urgency for everyone to see.
- When using crises to reduce complacency, predict how people will react so that specific plans will be timely and effective.
- If the organization is highly complacent and hurting deeply, never depend on a crisis to create a true sense of urgency. The issue needs to be addressed with paramount importance by bringing the outside in and developing critical urgent behaviors that address real issues every day.
- Great care should be taken in creating a crisis because of the backlash others might have if they feel manipulated or less secure. Their reactions will not be supportive.
- If you are in the middle of the organization and see a looming crisis that others do not see, try to work open-mindedly and communicate that information with someone who is in a position of power and influence.

Deal with NoNos (Perpetual Naysayers)

NoNos are those few individuals in the organization who are against change in any form. They are far more dangerous than we want to believe, and frequently their negative behavior is not fully seen by their superiors. Their peers and subordinates know who they are, and by using a nonthreatening questioning approach, their identity can be revealed. NoNos are highly effective urgency killers who will do almost anything to discredit others who are trying to create a sense of urgency. Their negative impact by undermining the efforts of others can have a damaging, even disastrous effect on the organization. They must be dealt with effectively and with a true sense of urgency.

There are three strategies that work and two that are rarely successful. The three strategies that are most successful are as follows:

1. Keep the NoNos fully occupied with value-added responsibilities and activities that do not allow them to have a negative effect on the change process.
2. Eliminate NoNos from the organization and give them an appropriate severance package.
3. Expose their negative behaviors and allow the force of peer pressure to reduce or eliminate their effectiveness.

The two strategies that usually do not work are (1) making a NoNo part of the change process that will move the organization forward with the hope that the NoNo will change and support a sense of urgency and (2) isolating the NoNos from the change process. This latter strategy almost never works because the NoNo can create a great deal of damage behind the scenes that may not be observable to top management.

Conclusion

Organizations today need a true—not a false—sense of urgency to survive and prosper. Fortunately, there are strategies available for creating this, but managers must focus on the hearts of employees to stimulate them to buy into that passion. Four techniques—bringing the outside in, behaving with urgency, finding opportunity in crises, and dealing strongly with naysayers—are vital to the success of programs for change.

PART TEN

"Undiscussable" Issues at Work

Organizational culture is all about the relationships that exist among organizational members, and how people connect and interact with one another as they carry out their organizational roles. However, there is an *intended* (or aspirational) culture and an *actual* culture in many cases—and the two can be vastly different. In this section, three book summaries (*Workplace Survival*, *The No Asshole Rule*, and *It's All Politics*) are presented, with each one providing insight into what are often and unfortunately the negative and harmful internal and interpersonal workings of people in organizations.

Three dysfunctional elements in any organization can lead to its downfall: bad bosses, bad employees/colleagues, and bad jobs. Bad bosses, according to Ella and David Van Fleet, use heavy-handed threats to abuse their power, show favoritism, micromanage, are insecure and/or incompetent, and cannot accept criticism. Bad employees don't carry their own weight and may bully, harass, threaten, or sabotage others. Bad jobs create an unpleasant or unsafe workplace. Any of these factors can cause workplace turmoil, dissatisfaction, or even violence.

Dr. Ella Van Fleet is the founder and President of Professional Business Associates and has been an educator, trainer, and consultant for over a quarter century. Dr. David Van Fleet has been a faculty member, fellow of the Academy of Management, and editor of prestigious business journals. He has published several previous books, including *Contemporary Management*, *Behavior in Organizations*, and *Organizational Behavior*.

Dr. Robert Sutton holds a Ph.D. in Organizational Psychology from the University of Michigan and serves on the faculty in the Stanford Engineering School. He is an award-winning writer, the former editor of *Administrative Science Quarterly*, and a member of the *Academy of Management Journal*'s Hall of Fame. His previous books include *Weird Ideas That Work, Good Boss, Bad Boss,* and *Hard Facts, Dangerous Half-Truths, and Total Nonsense.*

Sutton confronts a previously taboo topic—the ubiquitous and persistent presence of mean-spirited jerks who are bullies and tyrants and make other people miserable and fearful. He provides two key tests for whether an individual qualifies as an asshole—whether the target of the abuse feels belittled and humiliated (via insults, shaming, rudeness, and sarcasm), and whether there is a power differential between the two parties. Sutton proposes a simple solution—the banning of assholes via strict policies, careful monitoring, constructive confrontation, and saying "good riddance" to incorrigible jerks.

In *It's All Politics*, Kathleen Kelley Reardon notes that hard work and potential are not the only keys for an individual's movement upward and ultimately to the top of the organizational hierarchy. Those who make it—the winners—and those who don't—the losers—differ from one another in terms of their political skills and the use of those skills. Those who make it upward successfully manage their relationships with those who are capable of rewarding them with key organizational moves.

Kathleen Kelley Reardon is a Professor of Management and Organization in the Marshall School of Business at the University of Southern California. She holds a Ph.D. in Communications from the University of Massachusetts in Amherst and is an expert in the areas of persuasion, negotiations, and politics. Dr. Reardon is the author of nine books, including *The Secret Handshake* and *The Skilled Negotiator*.

1

Workplace Survival

Ella W. Van Fleet and David D. Van Fleet
Summary Prepared by Kelly L. Nelson

Kelly L. Nelson earned her Bachelor of Business Administration from the University of Minnesota Duluth and her M.B.A. from Xavier University. She is currently General Manager of Human Resources with AK Steel Corporation. Kelly strives to avoid being known as a bad boss or a bad coworker by following the guidance provided in *Workplace Survival: Dealing with Bad Bosses, Bad Workers, Bad Jobs.*

BAD BOSSES

Three key elements in the workplace have a profound effect on everyone: bosses, workers, and the tasks that make the job. Bosses in particular, through the course of their duties, have a significant effect—for better or worse—on employees in the workplace. **Bad bosses** can demonstrate their effects in a number of ways:

- Abusing their power. Threats can include any number of subjects, but some common threats include threatening to give a difficult (or distasteful) assignment to keep employees in line, threatening to fire employees if even a minor mistake is made, threatening to withhold raises unless the employee follows questionable directions, and so on. Bosses can also abuse their power by defending actions "because I am the boss," and setting poor examples by requiring employees to follow rules that the supervisor doesn't feel he or she needs to follow. Bad bosses take the power they have over workers to exploit them.

    Furthermore, insecure bosses can attempt to withhold promotions from competent employees whom they feel may pose a threat to their own job security/promotional opportunities, treat employees as their own personal servants, abuse employees in order to force them to resign, act inappropriately or illegally, and lie or exaggerate. In short, bosses who abuse their power rely on using a "whip" instead of a "carrot" and subsequently cause misery for those who report to them.

- Failing to control their anger. Most people have worked for a "screamer" at one point in their career. Bosses who yell provide public embarrassment to the subject of their rant, and this flies in the face of the good management axiom to "praise in public; correct in

Ella W. Van Fleet and David D. Van Fleet. *Workplace Survival: Dealing with Bad Bosses, Bad Workers, Bad Jobs.* Baltimore, MD: Publish America, 2007.

private." As a part of their responsibilities, supervisors should display maturity and level-headedness. However, bad bosses don't control their behavior; instead, they fly off the handle and react emotionally over business-related issues.

Bad bosses who fail to control their anger often use foul language habitually, curse at bearers of bad news, and use snide remarks to intimidate workers. This offensive language creates an unprofessional workplace and unhappy, unproductive workers. Foul language may be considered degrading behavior, but it is not the only method. Nor is degrading behavior always done in person. It can be accomplished through e-mails or by talking about someone when he or she is not present. Furthermore, behavior that belittles others can be done under the guise of teasing or intimidating an employee due to race, gender, or cultural differences. Behavior that demeans is done to instill fear in employees and "to keep them in line."

- Exhibiting poor management skills. Nothing screams "bad boss" as loudly as the insecure manager who micromanages, focuses on activity instead of results, or constantly checks on his or her employees to ensure they are staying on task. Poor management skills are also demonstrated by providing poorly done, unconstructive, and/or inaccurate performance appraisals. Inaccurate appraisals can be used in the future to "prove" the employee is a poor employee, even when the appraisal is not an accurate depiction of the employee's true contribution to the organization. Finally, bosses who fail to let others do their job and fail to provide strategic leadership to the organization are content to have a rudderless ship.
- Being insecure and/or incompetent. Bad bosses often try to cover up their incompetence by refusing to participate in the work to be done, relying on the reason "because I'm the boss," and, in extreme instances, deliberately sabotaging operations in order to be the hero by providing the solution to the problem. Incompetent or insecure bosses often show their lack of ability by failing to manage the employees who work for them. They ignore problems that exist, fail to solve even simple problems, and act like a friend instead of a boss. Insecure bosses show their stripes when they are unable to accept criticism, surround themselves with only those who agree with them, and refuse to accept any blame when problems occur. They often use their employees for scapegoats and spread the blame to everyone but themselves.
- Being backed by weak/poor upper management. Higher levels of management play a crucial role in the behavior of bad bosses. The problem can be exacerbated when upper management either ignores the bad behavior or, worse yet, affirmatively supports the bad behavior. They can also cause the bad boss behavior by failing to train bosses, criticizing the boss but doing nothing to correct the behavior, or rewarding the wrong behavior from the boss. Bad bosses have the ability to affect the work lives of their employees, but they are not necessarily the only "bad" element that can impact others' work lives.

BAD EMPLOYEES

Bad employees (coworkers) can also make others miserable. They may:

- Lack interpersonal skills. Not only can a coworker's bad attitude be difficult to endure, it can also shape the attitude of workers around him or her, spreading the poor morale. However, employees don't have to have a bad attitude to affect others; they can also be so self-focused that they are actually inconsiderate to coworkers, and this can directly affect team outcomes. Finally, appearance or hygiene problems can be a nightmare. Who wants to work next to an employee who thinks toothpaste and deodorant are not necessary?

- Take or subject others to unnecessary risks. Taken to the extreme, an employee who subjects others to risks may actually cause the death of a coworker. At the very least, this risky behavior can damage assets and decrease productivity. In addition, the bad worker can also be a danger to himself or herself, leading to injuries, or worse.
- Manipulate, threaten, harass, bully, or sabotage others. Similar to the bad boss who uses threats and manipulation to accomplish goals, coworkers can do the same. They may lie, deliberately undercut others' work, or threaten coworkers to make themselves feel like successes on the job—at the expense of all of the others around them.
- Don't carry their own weight. Not only do coworkers depend upon their fellow workers to be at work when expected, they also need for them to do their fair share of the work. Some good workers actually perform more than their fair share in order to make the operation successful; however, others' performance can be negatively affected when they feel they are expected to make up for the bad employee's lack of productivity, particularly when the bad worker's behavior is not corrected because there is a bad boss in the picture.

BAD JOBS

As if bad bosses and bad workers weren't enough of a problem, there is a third element that can make the workplace miserable—the bad job. A number of factors can make a job a "bad" job:

- Unpleasant or unsafe workplaces. Not only can unsafe or physically demanding work take its toll on workers, the environment also can be uncomfortable and inconvenient. In addition to the environment, the tasks themselves can be changed or unexpected, leading to disappointment for the workers.
- Low rewards and poor security. Workers and bosses both may suffer from insecurity caused by unstable employment prospects and lack of compensation. It is difficult for employees to perform at their highest level when plagued by doubts about the organization's survival or haunted by their own ability to make ends meet with their current level of compensation.
- Bad customers. As if bad bosses, bad coworkers, and bad jobs aren't bad enough, the employee may also need to deal with unpleasant or "bad" customers, which makes the job even more difficult in which to function.
- Poor organizational culture/climate. If the organization is filled with bad workers and bad bosses, the probability is high that the organizational culture actively or passively supports this behavior. Some organizations are so "bad" that they create a threatening environment throughout all levels of the organization.

WHAT CAN BOSSES AND WORKERS DO TO BECOME "GOOD"?

Bosses should make a determined effort to not abuse their power, control their anger, learn new management skills, refuse to micromanage employees, provide timely performance feedback, not show favoritism, be an effective role model (and find one for themselves), use meetings appropriately, become competent and secure, learn to make good decisions, learn to accept criticism, hire and keep the right employees, and communicate effectively.

At the same time, workers should analyze their own job performance, seek constructive criticism from coworkers, analyze and address their personal problems, obtain others' perceptions of their boss, and choose to exercise one or more of these options:

Option #1: Talk with your boss (prepare by listing your complaints, then ask others for their inputs, consider your boss's lack of experience, assess your boss's personality, narrow your list of complaints, schedule a meeting, and meet with the boss to resolve issues).

Option #2: Report the situation.

Option #3: Get another job.

HOW CAN JOB SEEKERS AVOID JOINING AN ORGANIZATION WITH BAD BOSSES AND BAD COWORKERS?

First, job seekers need to find out as much as possible about the organization, its people, and the job in advance of the interview and certainly before accepting the job. Talk to people who work in the organization or live in the area. Search for relevant information on the Internet—both from the employer and from observers and commentators.

Second, take advantage of the job interview. Use it to evaluate everything you see and hear. Analyze the questions you are asked. Ask questions yourself that probe the issues you might be concerned about.

If you are given the opportunity to talk with people other than the person who will be your boss, find out how well the supervisor communicates, and ask about the supervisor's interpersonal style.

Finally, follow up. While the details are fresh in your mind, write them down, including impressions of interactions, the "feel" of the workplace, and the apparent culture of the organization.

WHAT CAN BOSSES DO TO AVOID HAVING BAD WORKERS?

1. Hire the right employees (know what skills you need, recruit the right people, and evaluate applicants to gather maximum information).
2. Be aware of employees' behavior through direct observation and second-hand reports.
3. Reinforce your expectations consistently.
4. Take action with bad workers promptly.
5. Provide feedback to employees.
6. Provide remedial training.
7. If the employee doesn't correct the unacceptable behavior, assist the exit.

WHAT CAN COWORKERS DO ABOUT BAD WORKERS?

Resolve to be polite and professional, but don't ignore the problem. Identify your values so that it will be easier to determine what is acceptable and what is not. Practice avoidance behaviors so as to not become irritated. Focus on your life off the job. Carefully try to change the behavior of the person, but pick your battles carefully. Identify the bad behavior, and analyze your feelings about it before deciding what you want. Talk with the coworker, and assertively specify how the bad behavior impacts you. Most critically, avoid potentially violent coworkers, and report your assessment of their behavior to several other persons.

WHAT CAN BOSSES DO ABOUT BAD JOBS?

1. Improve undesirable workplaces, by asking employees for suggestions.
2. Ensure employees' safety is your top priority all of the time. Implement rules to keep employees safe, and hold employees accountable to follow the rules. Engineer solutions that eliminate safety problems. Keep employees safe from criminal behavior. Eliminate workplace violence. Ensure employees are properly trained for job tasks. Do not tolerate unsafe behavior.
3. Try to modify a dysfunctional organizational culture.
4. Select better workers and outside contacts.
5. Explore increasing pay, job security, and advancement opportunities.
6. Redesign jobs to make them more desirable.

WHAT CAN WORKERS DO ABOUT BAD JOBS?

1. Change or adapt to the workplace.
2. Try to deal with the organizational culture.
3. Change or adapt to bad bosses, coworkers, and outside contacts.
4. Reevaluate your career.

Conclusion

There are many challenges to developing and living a satisfying career; however, it is not impossible. Success begins with the attitude of the individual and maintaining a positive outlook, no matter what the circumstances. Bosses, workers, and job seekers all have choices to make. Each individual should commit to avoiding the characteristics that make people "bad" at their jobs and should make positive steps to improve shortcomings. Furthermore, each person should be proactive enough to provide suggestions to make the job better, more efficient, and more satisfying. However, if an employee realizes that he or she is faced with challenges that are not within one's control and that will prevent him or her from having a satisfactory career, the employee must accept the reality that not every job (and not every boss) is going to be a good match for every worker, and decide to move on. After all, *life is too short to work in an atmosphere filled with bad bosses, bad workers, and bad jobs.*

2

The No Asshole Rule: Building a Civilized Workplace and Surviving One That Isn't

Robert I. Sutton

Summary Prepared by Stephen Rubenfeld

Stephen Rubenfeld is a Professor Emeritus of Human Resource Management in the Labovitz School of Business and Economics at the University of Minnesota Duluth. He received his doctorate from the University of Wisconsin—Madison and was previously on the faculty of Texas Tech University. His professional publications and presentations have covered a wide range of human resources and labor-relations topics, including workplace accommodations, compensation, human resources policies and practices, job security, and staffing challenges. He has served as a consultant to private and public organizations and is a member of the Society for Human Resource Management and the Academy of Management.

INTRODUCTION

"Who hired this jerk?" is a frequently asked question. *Unfortunately, almost all organizations have some mean-spirited employees who are bullies, tormentors, tyrants, egomaniacs, and weasels— bluntly speaking, assholes—who make our lives miserable.* In many cases, however, formal policy prohibitions and informal or unwritten codes of civilized interactions serve as *no-asshole rules* to make offensive behaviors unacceptable in the employment setting. Nevertheless, these antisocial interactions exist and flourish. This is not a culture-bound phenomenon; they are found across the globe. Likewise, they are not unique to particular industries or cultures. The problem is ubiquitous and persistent. Organizations and their denizens seem to overlook and forgive, and, at times, even encourage abusive and boorish behaviors.

WHY ARE THERE SO MANY OF THEM?

The terminology is used widely and frequently, perhaps indiscriminately, and without an agreed-upon definition. We know one when we see one. People that annoy us, that cross us, and even those who show us up are often tagged with the label of *asshole*. Although researchers have explored the nature of conflict, hostility, and psychological abuse, most of us assign this label to a guilty party spontaneously, emotionally, and vindictively. But to better understand the

Robert I. Sutton. *The No Asshole Rule: Building a Civilized Workplace and Surviving One That Isn't.* New York: Business Plus, 2007.

implications for organizations and how to cope with (and hopefully reform) these social misfits, there must be some metric to operationalize this construct. Answers to the following questions are a start:

1. Does the *target* of the abuse feel oppressed, humiliated, de-energized, or belittled by the person?
2. Is the venom directed at people who are *less powerful* rather that at those with greater stature and hierarchical power?

Affirmative responses to both questions provide a strong indication that we are dealing with an *asshole* (jerk). If we are completely honest, every one of us has the potential to act in ways that might earn us the title when we are placed in high-stress situations, are blindsided, are dealing with people who are socially inept, or immersed in a culture that encourages and reinforces such behaviors. We might temporarily regress and commit a social *faux pas*, but the *certified asshole* demonstrates ongoing and persistent patterns of behaviors that are overt and hurtful.

There are strategies and techniques that are frequently found in the quiver of everyday actions that such individuals use. They include the following:

- Personal insults
- Sarcastic teasing
- Two-faced attacks
- Humiliation
- Public shaming
- Threats
- Intimidation
- Rude interruptions
- Treating people as if they are invisible

These are but a few of the tools used to accomplish their inhumane deeds—particularly when dealing with subordinates and other who are less powerful in the work setting.

The answer is not to ban people who are forceful and driven to accomplish valued outcomes. Hiring only sycophants cannot be the answer. Tension, pressure, and high expectations can be constructive and perhaps essential to achieving excellence. Strong-willed, forceful, and even argumentative people can contribute to **constructive confrontation** (using evidence and logic to deal with problems) but not at the expense of engaging in character assassination and abusive personal conflicts. Research on bullying, workplace incivility, and psychological abuse tells us that there are many—way too many—occurrences in the workplaces of today. The preponderance of issues arises in dealings with subordinates and others seen as lower in the organizational pecking order. Doctors and their treatment of nurses, CEOs and their interactions with administrative assistants, and senior professors and their untenured colleagues are frequently cited situations of destructive work relationships.

EVERY WORKPLACE NEEDS *THE RULE*

All organizations need a no-asshole rule, or **the rule**, *to offset the harm caused by mean-spirited and abusive people.* These jerks cause damage to the targets of their venom as well as to bystanders and colleagues, and their actions are detrimental to the success of the organization and to themselves.

The **victims** of this abusive treatment suffer psychologically, physiologically, and through damage to their careers. Demeaning, hostile, and overly aggressive treatment by abusive supervisors leads victims to exhibit less commitment to the organization and its goals, suffer burnout, and possibly to quit or withdraw. Likewise, the ramifications go beyond the employee's work life. Overall life satisfaction diminishes, people develop sleep problems, issues of mental health and depression may arise, and marital relations may be affected as well. As one office administrator reported, he "dies a little" with every meeting with his boss. These insensitive and demeaning interactions are damaging and pervasive. Too many of the perpetrators are oblivious to the disproportionate impact that negative interactions have on employees.

Innocent **battered bystanders** also are affected by the acts of these misguided managers and colleagues. Coworkers who cringe in fear of future interactions based on what they have observed or heard second hand are also less likely to take prudent risks and follow unproven paths. They, too, may question the wisdom of investing so much of themselves in the organization, and therefore may be more receptive to opportunities to escape. But the ripple effects felt by the *innocents* are not necessarily limited to work colleagues; spouses, children, and friends also pay a price.

The direct and indirect effects (and costs) to organizational performance can be enormous, although not always obvious. The costs of increased turnover, absenteeism, lowered commitment, distraction, and reduced individual contributions can be quite substantial. Other risks including the increased probability of litigation involving harassment and other violations of employment law are lurking behind each boorish act and are greatest for organizations that ignore or cover up the inappropriate actions of their managers. Likewise, protective behaviors and revenge can have a tremendously negative impact. Protecting oneself becomes a priority and may push aside efforts directed toward organizational improvement. Human nature may lead victims to get even and achieve equity in a bad situation, which rarely works to the advantage of the employer. The risks are tremendous.

Finally, the *assholes* themselves may suffer as victims of their own abuses. Although they are unlikely to get much sympathy from victims and bystanders, they often do pay a real price. They suffer career setbacks and, eventually, humiliation and ridicule. Although our vindictive human nature may lead us to gloat when an abuser falls, there are elements of a Greek tragedy in this story line. Moreover, the perpetrators also may take some innocent bystanders down with them.

The effects are many, and the total costs can be tremendous. Some are obvious and others nearly invisible. Some are felt directly and immediately, whereas others are indirect and felt over the long haul. Some are easily quantifiable, whereas others are well below our budgetary radar. Some of the less obvious effects on organizations are as follows:

- Low levels of innovation and quality improvement
- Reduced cooperation
- Lower individual contributions "at the margin"
- Impaired ability to recruit high-caliber employees
- Higher health insurance costs
- Time spent appeasing, calming, and counseling
- Cultural changes that detract from performance

IMPLEMENTING AND KEEPING ALIVE *THE RULE*

If an employee is extremely successful, our societal norm is to overlook *little* imperfections in conduct and the lack of cultural fit. But even organizations that seem to relish (or at the very least tolerate) having some arrogant jerks in their midst do have limits. Some organizations have tightly enforced zero-tolerance policies, but most have a combination of rules, policies, and cultural norms that provide guidance but allow discretion and *wiggle room*. Most large organizations have behavioral conduct policies that capture the spirit of the *no-asshole rule*. However structured, successful rules share a number of characteristics and implementation guidelines:

1. Make it public: Having official policies buried in handbooks, sentiments posted in the hallways, and intranet reminders is necessary but not sufficient. What you say and what you do—consistently—are what really matters.
2. Integrate the *rule* into hiring: Left to their own devices, people making hiring decisions will hire people similar to themselves. The potential for bad outcomes is obvious when we hire our clones. To escape this dilemma, references are essential, especially those that go beyond technical competence. Likewise, interviews and other face-to-face elements of the selection process should focus on human qualities. All job candidates should be interviewed by people who will work with and be subordinates of the new hire.
3. Apply the *rule* to customers and clients: Organizations that really care about their employees expect their customers and clients to uphold comparably high standards of behavior.
4. Status and rank shouldn't matter: Rules are not just for mortals—the powerful and the high producers must be held to the same standards.
5. Enforce the rule and walk the talk:
   - Write it down and use it.
   - Recognize that *assholes are incompetent*, so just get rid of them.
   - Be aware that power breeds nastiness.
   - Manage moments; don't simply engage in policy enforcement.
   - Legitimize constructive confrontation.

HOW TO SURVIVE NASTY PEOPLE

Don't become one of the jerks; recognize that *assholes are contagious*. Anyone can catch the disease, so don't let your **inner jerk** (innate ability to be caustic and cruel) surface. But even if you keep yourself pure, you *will* come in direct contact with jerks in all facets of your life. You have to find ways to **reframe**, or change your mind-set regarding what is happening to you. Here's how:

1. Hope for the best, but expect the worst.
2. Develop indifference and emotional detachment.
3. Look for small wins; you're not going to change the world.
4. Limit your contact and risk.
5. Develop a support network.

Even if you *can* endure abusive behavior, the question remains, should you? This is a personal decision, but the reality is that we can't (and probably shouldn't) go on the attack or pick up and run every time adversity rears its head.

DO *ASSHOLES* HAVE ANY VIRTUES?

Much to the annoyance of their peers and subordinates, jerks often are successful—sometimes, very successful. They gain personal power, intimidate their rivals, and motivate fear-driven performance. Even the good guys may find it useful to temporarily use jerklike strategies. Some people are so clueless or lazy that a tantrum and a little noise might help to bring them to their senses. Despite the sometime successes and the selective usefulness of out-of-character behaviors, most defenses of being an asshole are misguided. Many jerks assume their successes are driven by their abusive ways, when in fact it is just as likely to be despite the way they treat others. *Most assholes suffer from delusions of effectiveness.*

THE RULE AS A WAY OF LIFE

The following lessons shown will not cure the ills of the world or suddenly turn jerks into model citizens. They are, however, constructive steps to achieve incremental improvement and help victims cope with bad situations. The seven key lessons are as follows:

1. A few jerks can overwhelm the good of a large number of civilized people.
2. Policies and rules are a start, but successes are built on day-to-day actions.
3. The *rule* lives or dies by dealing with problems immediately and directly.
4. A few bad people, if managed properly, can be helpful in demonstrating how *not* to behave.
5. Enforcing the *no-asshole rule* is *not* just management's job; everyone should step up to the plate and support the goal of eliminating unacceptable behavior.
6. Embarrassment can be a powerful learning tool, so jerks must be put on the spot.
7. Remember, there are times when WE are the *assholes*.

Conclusion

It would be nice if we never had to deal with people who treat us like second-class citizens and offend our sensibilities. But because this isn't the case, we must continuously strive to create a civilized, jerk-free workplace.

It's All Politics

Kathleen Kelley Reardon
Summary Prepared by AnneMarie Kaul

AnneMarie Kaul is the Development Director of the North Central Chapter of the Arthritis Foundation. Previously, she served as the Donor Resources Manager for the St. Paul Blood Center of the American Red Cross. She also has several years of experience managing financial services departments at Securian Financial, Inc. Her business expertise has been in the areas of leadership and customer service. She has a B.B.A. degree from the University of Minnesota Duluth and an M.B.A. from the University of St. Thomas in St. Paul, Minnesota.

POLITICS: IS IT REALLY A BAD THING?

Most people consider workplace politics as a necessary evil. The words themselves are usually associated with negative feelings, such as anger, anxiety, and fear. Moreover, people usually attribute politics to a whole host of problems, including missed promotional opportunities, terminations, and even smaller decisions such as who gets the best office. In fact, many people sling around the word *politics* as if it was mud. But truth be told, it is a well-known fact that politics, in general, is a part of life, and those who can overcome their fear and learn how to be more politically astute have a higher rate of success and satisfaction. The downside is that even though politics plays an important role in one's life, rarely do we see a college class focused on learning how to become politically skilled. However, the good news is that we can learn how to enhance our political competencies on our own. Politics can be a positive influence in our lives; we just need to observe and practice it.

THE DEFINITION OF POLITICS

Quite simply, politics is the positioning of ideas in a favorable light by knowing what to say, and how, when, and to whom to say it. There are five key areas of political development: intuition, insight, persuasion, power, and courage. To increase one's political acumen, developing and strengthening skills in these five areas is essential.

Kathleen Kelley Reardon. *It's All Politics: Winning in a World Where Hard Work and Talent Aren't Enough.* New York: Broadway Business (Crown), 2005.

Letting Intuition Be the Guide

People who are born with natural intuition are a very rare breed. The good news, however, is that anyone without natural instincts can develop them just by observing those who are intuitive and then replicating certain behaviors. Therefore, it is important to be able to identify these general characteristics of an intuitive person.

A person using intuition is constantly *unpredictable* and does not work on the premise of going with the *status quo*. For example, instead of the typical greeting, "Hi, how are you?" an intuitive person would more likely quickly assess the social level of the passing individual and customize a more appropriate response. If the other person is more reserved, a simple head nod would suffice. An intuitive person will make others feel comfortable, yet keep them guessing by varying his or her behavior.

Another trait of an intuitive person is the ability to use **gut feelings** to make quick decisions. This person acts on a hunch or a feeling versus analyzing the facts. The trouble with pure intellect is that it allows us to take in only a small portion of the relevant information. On the other hand, intuitive people tend to multitrack, which means taking in information from gestures, tone of voice, and other nonverbal cues in addition to the words. They process the message at a deeper level, resulting in more effective communication.

In addition to unpredictability and the use of feelings, being empathetic is another key ingredient to enhance political intuition. **Empathy** is being sensitive to the changing feelings of another person. Getting connected to people and how they think will place a person in a better position to guide future outcomes of almost any interaction.

Here are some common, straightforward guidelines to improve your intuition skills:

- Ask a lot of questions.
- Don't make assumptions.
- Learn how things are normally done.
- Read between the lines.
- Look for differences between verbal and nonverbal communication.

Political Insight: It's About Thinking

Another component of politics is knowing what to do after you predict what is about to happen. This is called **political insight**. Political insight is typically 99 percent perspiration and 1 percent inspiration. Essentially, it is using creativity to respond to typical situations. Insightful people demonstrate the following behaviors:

- Being patient
- Looking at problems from all angles (using the **mind-mapping** technique)
- Choosing the best option after considering the positives and negatives
- Considering possible **choice points** or reactions of others
- Using the concept of framing to position ideas in an appealing manner to others
- Not making assumptions

More specifically, it is important to develop political insight *before* and *during* interactions with others. Advance work primarily involves managing the perception of others and being prepared for different reactions. Some tactics to include in this prep work are as follows:

- Getting to know people and forming alliances
- Testing an idea or concept on a select audience

- Preparing a response prior to negative reactions
- Possessing a solid track record in your field of work

During an interaction, thinking on your feet helps to glean political insight. Responding in the moment is critical, but many people feel inadequate in this area of political interaction. In the context of political strategies, responding properly to problems, personal attacks, and hidden agendas holds the key to creating a favorable outcome. The following guiding principles can be used to defuse negative conversations:

- Know when to confront, when to back off, and when to ask for support.
- Recognize when to apologize.
- Give credit to others.
- Divert attention away from sensitive or unresolvable issues.
- Paraphrase what was said in a favorable context.

Understanding how to proceed in a politically charged environment by doing up-front homework can virtually save a person's job and, at a minimum, a person's credibility and reputation.

Understanding Persuasion

Political influence can be more important to bring about change in the workplace than the standard methods of authority, culture, or expertise. **Persuasion**, one of the most important components of influence, is the ability to position ideas in an appealing manner so others will accept them. Interestingly, whether specifically at work or generally in life, many people consider persuasion as the "high road" of manipulation, which is actually a form of deception. To be an astute student of politics, both persuasion and manipulation techniques should be well understood.

Listening to really understand the actual meaning of a message and taking time to formulate thoughts *before* responding wields great power and influence. Knowing when the content of a message is relevant, called **conversational coherence**, and how to introduce a new topic, called **topicality shift**, are also necessary skills to enhance persuasive ability.

These preparation steps are critical to enhance political persuasion:

- Understanding what motivates the other person so as to connect the message to those interests
- Determining how much should be said and the way it should be said
- Ensuring that the information is reliable and relevant

Common Persuasion Strategies

There are many methods and approaches to persuade others. The approach that is most effective will depend on each person and situation. Typically, however, the three more commonly used strategies are reciprocity, scarcity, and authority.

Reciprocity is doing a favor for someone *now* in order to have it returned *later*. Skilled politicians are very good at giving help up front to get things accomplished in the future. **Scarcity** is the ability to create a high demand by providing scarce resources. People want what they can't have. An example of this strategy was the Tyco Beanie Baby craze of the late 1990s. **Authority** is becoming an expert in a certain field, preferably in a field that is inadequately filled. Thus, a person becomes a "niche" player.

Whether a person's strategy encompasses any of the three just described or a combination of others, it is helpful to keep the following suggestions in mind:

- Keep your work visible to the right people.
- Be in a position to be noticed.
- Make sure the project goals are in line with the company's goals.

How Does Political Power Work?

In order to get ahead in the workplace it is paramount to understand how political power works and to learn how to gain this power. Accomplishments alone are not enough; selling yourself is the key.

Power can easily be gained and lost, so cultivating and maintaining it should be a continual process. During this process, it is important to keep in mind that it is the *perceptions* of others that essentially create and sustain the somewhat nebulous power. In other words, if a person feels powerless, it is because that person has allowed someone else's perception to influence how he or she thinks, feels, and behaves. Fortunately, by following these power strategies, people can improve and maintain their power base:

- Maintain appearances, including attire, office décor, handshaking, gestures, and so on.
- Maintain relationships by getting to know the people who can help you (be charming and humorous).
- Enhance communication by listening and then adapting one's style to fit another's style.
- Assess the power of your position within the hierarchy of the organization.
- Seek out advisers.
- Be sure to thank people who help you and remember to help them, too.
- Increase knowledge by learning about the company's culture and real goals.
- Manage your reputation by acquiring the skills to do the job well, and ensuring that others know about it.

Political Power: Courage Versus Suicide

Most people would agree that in order to increase power, a person must take risks and not be afraid to make misjudgments or mistakes. *But the question is: When does political courage become political suicide?* The answer lies in one's intentions. If a person is taking a stand based on true beliefs and feelings, then showing courage by speaking out is the smart and necessary option. On the other hand, if the intent is artificial or self-centered, eventually these actions will lead to career suicide. Of course there are varying degrees between doing what is best for the company and what is best for the person. Political courage should not lead to self-destruction or the destruction of others. *One must assess the real risks and rewards before moving too quickly, keeping in mind that achieving the goal is not always as important as the way it is reached.*

Before jumping into a politically charged situation, the following questions should be evaluated and answered honestly:

- Do I have the needed support?
- Is my track record sufficiently developed?
- Am I up for the challenge right now?
- What are the win–win and no–win options?

Ultimately, having the strength and stamina to proceed with caution is the key. It is up to each individual to personally reconcile his or her motives with the risks and rewards to make this type of decision.

POLITICAL BOUNDARIES

To some extent, all organizations mold and shape their political direction by the nature of their culture. A company's political environment should be carefully analyzed prior to employment whenever possible. By doing this up-front work, a person will be in a better position to react when faced with political choice points. It is good practice to establish a personal "comfort zone" when dealing with politics, as many individuals who do not do so end up confused and misunderstood.

From a corporate culture perspective, smart organizations will intentionally influence their political direction. Good organizations encourage positive politics. They develop and communicate a set of values that can be adopted at every level—from the mailroom clerk to the CEO. Two examples of politically smart companies are Mars and Nokia. Both of these firms put a high priority on rewarding associates who demonstrate a strong work ethic. They also support workplace principles such as responsibility, mutuality, and freedom of expression.

THE POLITICAL GAME

Staying on top of the political game can make all the difference between hiding out on the bench (frightened to take risks) and getting out on the field to score the necessary points to stay ahead. The good news is that anyone can nurture and strengthen their political savvy to actually win the game. The process to improve political know-how requires only two simple actions: observing and practicing. Equipped with enhanced intuition and persuasion skills, a not-so-politically adept person can take more control over his or her life and make some highly astute political decisions and useful connections. Moreover, having the knowledge of the political culture in the workplace and the courage to abide by personal political boundaries will provide the necessary strength to face and overcome political adversity. The opponent is no longer a threat but an adversary.

PART ELEVEN

Managerial Decision Making

Managers at all levels of organizations make decisions. Some of these are relatively trivial and some are powerfully significant. Some managers make decisions frequently, and others engage in the process more infrequently. Some managers make decisions intuitively (e.g., using gut feelings or their "adaptive unconscious"), and others follow a more systematic process. Nevertheless, from a systems perspective, all decisions eventually affect the success of the enterprise. It is critical to discover useful frameworks for how managers should approach the decision process so as to avoid common errors and increase the probability of success. This becomes increasingly true for decisions with large potential payoffs or when managers are faced with crisis situations.

The author of the first reading in Part 11, Daniel Kahneman, is a 2002 winner (with Amos Tversky) of the Nobel Prize in Economic Sciences for his pioneering work on the psychology of judgment and decision making. Kahneman is currently the Eugene Higgins Professor of Psychology Emeritus at Princeton University, where he wrote *Thinking, Fast and Slow*.

Kahneman envisions two primary thinking styles of decision makers. The first (System 1) is active and rapid, automatically processing information in an instinctive and intuitive fashion. The second (System 2) is the slower, more rational element that exhibits self-control. In general, decision makers should seek to limit their System 1 approach and develop their System 2 skills. The author then proceeds to discuss a variety of biases (e.g., availability, anchoring, hindsight, and outcome) that can creep into decision processes unless we are aware of them.

Ian Ayres draws on two unique backgrounds—a law degree from Yale and a Ph.D. in Economics from M.I.T. He holds a joint appointment as William K. Townsend Professor of Law and Anne Urowsky Professorial Fellow at Yale, after previous positions at Illinois, Stanford, Virginia, and Northwestern. He has published nine books, including *Carrots and Sticks*, *Straightforward*, *Optional Law*, and *Insincere Promises*. He is the editor of *the Journal of Law, Economics, and Organization*.

In his book *SuperCrunchers*, Ayres puts forward a powerful proposition— *managerial decision makers need to become statistically literate*, while relying less on their intuition and anecdotal experiences. Huge amounts of data are now available, and this phenomenon, combined with rapid computers and common statistical tools and ideas such as regression and Bayes' Theorem, allows managers to analyze the impact of prior events and decisions and even update predictions as new data become available. An excellent example of statistical tools in action is provided by the emergence of evidence-based medicine.

Gerd Gigerenzer has been both a Professor of Psychology (University of Chicago) and Visiting Professor in the School of Law (University of Virginia). He is currently a Director at the Max Planck Institute for Human Development in Berlin. His published books include *Calculated Risks*, *Bounded Rationality*, and *Rationality for Mortals*.

Gigerenzer contends, in *Gut Feelings*, that decision makers might consider discarding their propensity to acquire more and more data. Instead, he proposes that they seek to use their intuition, hunches, and unconscious intelligence. Rules of thumb (heuristics) are useful aids; these rely on trust, identification, deception, wishful thinking, and cooperation. The operating definition of a gut feeling is one that arises spontaneously, is not fully understood, and yet is strong enough to be acted upon. (Note that Dan Ariely's popular book *Predictably Irrational* shares a similarity with *Gut Feelings* in the argument that human behavior is often irrational. Whereas Ariely may see this as a flaw, Gigerenzer views this as an asset to be capitalized upon via intuition.)

1

Thinking, Fast and Slow

David Kahneman
Summary Prepared by Amber Christian

Amber Christian is consulting partner at Phoenix Endeavors, LLC. She assists clients in implementing and enhancing financial systems processes. She received her M.B.A. from the University of Minnesota Carlson School of Management and her undergraduate degrees in Management Information Sciences and Organizational Management from the University of Minnesota Duluth.

TWO PROCESSING SYSTEMS

The mind has two different systems to process our thoughts. The active system, *System 1*, automatically processes information from our environment. This system never shuts off and is continuously providing information to System 2 on immediate reactions, thoughts, feelings, and judgments. This system is our intuition. *System 2* normally operates in a passive mode, becoming mobilized only when necessary. This system exhibits our self-control. It catches us when we are about to make a mistake or when the automatic system cannot process information in our environment. Each of these systems has its own strengths and limitations.

The automatic system (System 1) constructs stories from the information it gathers. Any information it does not retrieve does not exist, as it cannot allow for information it does not have. Even if we possess the information but choose not to retrieve it, the information effectively does not exist. This system is also able to completely ignore our own ignorance. Therefore, our automatic system follows a simple rule: What You See Is All There Is (**WYSIATI**). System 1 is remarkably adept at jumping to conclusions as it tries to simplify the world and make it more coherent. As we make observations, System 1 generates a halo effect. This bias magnifies positive and negative reactions based on its initial observations. For example, when we like someone we are more likely to focus on their positive attributes and discount anything negative. For someone we do not like, we focus on their negative attributes and tend to disregard positive attributes. Given this propensity, we need to control this tendency and be careful that the halo effect does not unduly sway our thoughts and judgments.

Daniel Kahneman. *Thinking, Fast and Slow*. New York: Farrar, Straus and Giroux, 2011.

HEURISTICS AND BIASES

Heuristics and biases are processed with ease by the automatic system. The information comes quickly and intuitively, and this makes it difficult for us to separate skilled assessments from biased ones. Two specific problems we encounter are availability bias and the anchoring effect.

An **availability bias** occurs when we can easily recall information. When we are able to easily recall information, this leads us to specific belief. A good example of this occurs in marriages. When each spouse is asked for an estimate of his or her personal contribution of the percentage of housecleaning tasks performed, the total of the two estimates usually amounts to more than 100 percent. The explanation? Each person is able to remember his or her efforts more clearly than the efforts of the spouse. The same bias occurs due to frequency of events. For example, fear of flying after hearing about an airplane crash often occurs because airplane crashes are now on people's minds. Decision makers need to remember that availability bias can influence their decisions; consequently they should strive to make balanced decisions based on more than just readily available information. Individuals must recognize the signs that they are rushing and adjust accordingly. Slowing down and engaging System 2 for reinforcement can help us limit the effects of availability bias.

Another type of bias is the **anchoring effect**. This effect occurs when a value for an unknown quantity is presented to us before we estimate it ourselves. It is a powerful influence on our judgments, and is used to influence desired results. A perfect example of this arises when we are about to give money to a charitable cause. Research shows that a higher suggested value for donations results in a higher overall donated amount, whereas a lower suggested value results in lower donated amounts. An experiment for sentencing of crimes in Germany also demonstrated this effect. Judges with 15 years of experience read the description of a woman caught shoplifting. They then rolled a loaded die that produced either a 3 or a 9. After rolling the die and seeing the specific outcome, they were asked to specify their sentence. On average, judges that rolled a 9 sentenced the woman to 8 months in prison. Those that rolled a 3 sentenced her to 5 months in prison. The result was a 50 percent greater sentence based on the anchoring effect. It is critical, therefore, to recognize when anchoring is being used, so that we may actively diminish its ability to influence our judgments.

BIASING EFFECTS

Overconfidence results from our belief that we can understand and validate most situations. The automatic system introduces a narrative fallacy through inaccurate stories that we tell ourselves about the past; these in turn, shape our beliefs about the future. We are likely to make our stories about the past simple and concrete. Facts are assumed as if the story was a foregone conclusion; we believe in our intuition in spite of missing facts. The automatic system does not account for variables that *could* have influenced or changed a given situation. There are numerous illusions and biases that can occur as a result.

Hindsight bias occurs once we adopt beliefs; we cease to recognize our old beliefs and are unable to reconstruct them. The old axiom of "hindsight being 20/20" applies here. We often even believe that we knew of an event before it ever happened. We forget how surprised we were by events that occurred, as they have become part of our memory.

Outcome bias occurs when we are unable to properly evaluate outcomes due to our hindsight bias. When we do not like an outcome, we blame others for not seeing the obvious outcome. When the outcomes are good, we do not give those decision makers credit for the successful moves that were not readily apparent at that time. Outcome bias often occurs when we utilize third-party experts. We should make judgments based on how the decisions were made, not how they turned out.

Our stock market industry is built on an illusion of skill. The industry accepts that a stock price incorporates all the available knowledge from the market within the price. If everything in the market is priced correctly, no one should have any gains or losses. In spite of this, trades are still made, with millions of stocks being bought and sold daily. Traders expect that the shares they sell will perform worse than the shares they buy. However, research shows that the reverse was actually true: shares sold did better than those purchased by an average of 3.2% above trading costs. The same is true for professionals in the industry, as more than two out of three mutual funds perform worse than the industry average. In addition, the year-to-year correlation for mutual fund results is barely higher than zero. Individual investment professionals fared no better. Year-over-year results showed no correlation for persistence of investing skill. Within this industry, the outcome of investments often determines the compensation received. It appears based on the correlations that individuals are receiving compensation more based on luck in a given year than skill.

CHOICES

The principle of **loss aversion** (our innate desire to avoid losses and setbacks) governs how we make our choices. Our aversion to loss increases as the stakes rise. When the stakes are high enough to ruin our lives, loss aversion can grow to infinite values, as there are certain risks we simply will not accept.

The **endowment effect** (the desire to hold onto something once it is in your possession) occurs for items that are not traded on a regular basis. An example of this is the purchase of concert tickets. If you have purchased a ticket for a sold-out concert, you are not likely to sell your ticket. Standard economic theory suggests that, as a rational person, you would sell your ticket once a legitimate offer reaches a certain threshold. However, most people do *not* sell their tickets despite a lucrative offer, as they are unwilling to give up what they already have in their possession.

A fourfold pattern of our behaviors exists when risk probabilities are compared to gains and losses. This is illustrated by the following chart:

	Gains	Losses
High Probability	Risk Averse	Risk Seeking
Low Probability	Risk Seeking	Risk Averse

When we are faced with a low probability of success coupled with the potential for high gains, we become risk seekers. Millions of people purchase lottery tickets every week even if they know their odds of winning are tiny. We enjoy dreaming that we may win the lottery despite the statistical facts regarding its probability.

We are also risk seekers when there is a high probability of losses. If our choices are between two options that both constitute large losses, we choose the option that would allow us the least losses regardless of the probability. This situation can lead to desperate gambles, where we accept a high probability that could make a situation worse in exchange for a small chance of avoiding a large loss. We accept this gamble instead of cutting our losses because defeat is too painful. We should recognize that, at times, *cutting our losses is the best course of action even if it is painful.*

Perhaps surprisingly, we are risk averse when there is a high probability for high gains. We are willing to accept less in order to lock in a sure thing. Where there is a low probability for high losses, insurance is purchased. Limiting our exposure is the most important factor. We are willing to pay more than something is worth in order to limit our potential losses.

TWO SELVES

People act as though they are differentiated into two selves—the experiencing self and remembering self. Our experiencing self (System 1) is busy living, while our remembering self (System 2) keeps score and makes choices. To demonstrate the difference between the two selves, an experiment was conducted. Participants put one hand in cold water until they were asked to remove it and place it in a warm towel. The free hand was used to record their level of pain during the experiment. There were two episodes for the experiment:

- During the first episode, participants immersed their hands in 14° Celsius water for 60 seconds. After this time, a warm towel was offered.
- During the second episode, participants immersed their hands in 14° Celsius water for 60 seconds. At the end of that time, the experimenter opened a valve that allowed in warmer water. Over the course of 30 seconds, the water temperature rose by 1° Celsius. This allowed participants to feel slightly less pain, but the elapsed time totaled 90 seconds.

Participants were then asked which of the experiments they would repeat. Fully 80% of those who reported diminishing pain during the second trial opted to repeat it, even though it meant 30 seconds more of pain. *Individuals must learn to look beyond an immediate experience of pleasure or pain when assessing choices.* It is easy to label a project or experience as bad or good simply because of what occurred at the end, instead of balancing what occurred for the duration.

The **focusing illusion** occurs when a particular aspect of life takes precedence over everything else. This is captured by the statement that "Nothing in life is as important as you think it is when you are thinking about it." We must learn to see beyond the item that draws our primary focus and dominates our thoughts.

Conclusion

As the active system continually processes thoughts, we need to be aware of the ways in which it can influence our decisions. Attaching a name to these effects gives us a framework to describe them. Although it is not always possible to prevent all biases or effects, awareness of the effects can help us mitigate their influence.

Super Crunchers

Ian Ayres
Summary Prepared by Brian Russell

Dr. Brian Russell is a psychologist, an attorney, and an M.B.A., whose management consultancy focuses on the use of psychological assessment data to facilitate executive-level employment decisions, primarily in health-care organizations. Experienced in the practice of both psychology and law, he also serves as a mediator, litigation consultant, and expert witness in a varied range of civil and criminal cases. In addition, he has become a national television personality, frequently providing psychological and legal analysis on multiple networks. Dr. Russell is a Lecturer at the University of Kansas School of Business.

THE ERA OF THE SUPER CRUNCHERS

Conventional decision makers tend to rely on textbook axioms, anecdotal experience, and intuition. **Super Crunchers**, by contrast, are people who use the best data available and then carefully apply statistical analyses to make real-world decisions. Head-to-head comparisons of the two methods repeatedly demonstrate that overreliance on intuition can lead to inefficient, ineffective, and even disastrous outcomes. Super Crunching optimizes both the effectiveness and efficiency of decisions.

For the most part, Super Crunchers' statistical methods are not new; they have been utilized by social science researchers for decades. Fortunately, just when global competition has made it economically necessary for businesspeople to adopt these methods, technological advancements have made it economically feasible for almost anyone to accumulate, assimilate, and manipulate the vast quantities of data that give Super Crunching its power. According to **Moore's Law**, data *processing* power has been doubling every two years, but even more critical is **Kryder's Law**, which holds that data *storage* capacity has been doubling every two years as well. Our days of thinking in terms of gigabytes are numbered, as today's Super Crunchers are already thinking in terms of **terabytes** (1 terabyte = 1,000 gigabytes).

The ability to take vast quantities of data into account enables Super Crunchers to profit from the "wisdom of crowds," whereby they predict future behaviors of both individuals and groups by aggregating and analyzing past behaviors of many individuals. Behavioral predictions derived from the collective observations of large numbers of people are frequently more

Ian Ayres. *Super Crunchers: Why Thinking-by-Numbers Is the New Way to Be Smart.* New York: Bantam Books, 2007.

accurate than both intuitive predictions and predictions derived from observations of relatively small numbers of people. A survey of numerous illustrations of Super Crunching at work in business, medicine, and government makes a compelling case for its utility—more accurately, its necessity—in today's globally competitive environment while raising intriguing questions about its ultimate consequences, both intended and unintended.

Super Crunching with Regression

If you like wine and have at least eighth-grade math skills, you can predict the quality of a given vintage (harvest year) of French Bordeaux wine more accurately than wine experts can, by simply inserting the previous winter's total rainfall, the growing season's average temperature, and the harvest season's total rainfall into a mathematical formula. Similarly, if you are an armchair Major League Baseball team manager, you may be interested to know that the 2011 movie *Money Ball* realistically illustrates how you—armed with a given player's total numbers of hits, walks, and bases inserted into a mathematical formula—can predict the total number of future runs to be generated by that player more accurately than professional talent scouts can. Although predictive formulae such as these may excite oenophiles and sports fans, employers who are trying to predict job interviewees' future productivity and turnover rates may be more interested to know that both are stronger functions of certain personality traits than of conventional aptitude test scores. Based not on general gut feelings, but rather on specific traits that have been associated with high productivity and low turnover in the past, employers can predict interviewees' future job behaviors with superior accuracy. Similarly, based on past inventory data rather than managers' experience and intuition, manufacturers and retailers can predict their supply needs with superior accuracy, minimizing both storage costs and backorder delays through **just-in-time purchasing** (a technique that minimizes inventory storage time and carrying costs, while avoiding backorders).

Regression is the primary statistical method that facilitates these kinds of predictions of the future based on the past. Developed over a century ago by Charles Darwin's cousin, Francis Galton, *the regression method measures the extent to which various historical factors are associated with particular past outcomes and then generates a formula whereby future outcome predictions can be extrapolated from past observations.* In consumer lending, for example, the role of a lending officer's personal judgment in predicting whether a specific loan applicant will faithfully repay a loan has been virtually supplanted by mathematical formulae, derived through regression, that dispassionately measure numerical characteristics of the prospective borrower (such as income, credit score, and years of education) and compare those against the same characteristics of profitable and unprofitable borrowers in the past. Sometimes, regression reveals powerfully predictive factors that may not have been obvious or even intuitive. For example, poor credit scores do not just predict loan defaults; rental car companies and automobile insurers have found that poor credit scores also predict heightened probabilities of automobile accidents. Other times, regression reveals that factors previously believed to have been obvious or intuitive actually have little predictive power. For example, airlines that once re-ticketed their frequent fliers ahead of other passengers when flights were canceled now routinely re-ticket other passengers first. The airlines learned that the other passengers are more likely to choose a different airline in the future (unless they receive special treatment during a time of difficulty).

Super Crunching with Randomization

As powerful a Super Crunching method as regression is, a major weakness of its reliance on historical data is its difficulty establishing causation. For example, when redesigning a website for your business, there may not be sufficient historical data from which to extrapolate whether your customers will spend more time on your site if you change the background color. Fortunately, thanks to the low cost of altering virtual reality and the availability of a second Super Crunching method, **randomization**, you do not have to simply accept an axiom about background colors from an advertising textbook. Instead, you can test alternatives on real customers in real time. The idea behind randomization is that you can profit from the "wisdom of crowds" by learning what relatively large numbers of people prefer. Although each customer has unique characteristics, as you randomly assign increasing numbers of customers to groups that are then presented with different colored backgrounds, the average characteristics of the groups—gender, income, responsiveness to colors, and son on—should become increasingly identical. Thus, as the size of each of your "crowds" or, as Super Crunchers call it, your sample size, increases, *you can infer with increasing confidence that any persisting difference between the groups' average times spent on your site was caused by the way in which you treated the groups differently*—in this case, by presenting them with different background colors–the **treatment effect**.

Super Crunchers gauge the strengths of treatment effects using **standard deviations**. If a measurement is normally distributed among the population from which your samples are drawn, then there is a 95 percent chance that measurements of that characteristic will fall within two standard deviations of their average. Thus, if a measurement is farther than two standard deviations from the average, there is less than a 5 percent chance that it happened by accident. If, for instance, the average time spent on your website by all customers is three minutes, with a standard deviation of one minute, then 95 percent of visitors to your site spend between one and five minutes there. So, if visitors who see a red background linger for an average of 5 minutes and 30 seconds, there is a strong indication that the red background is the reason.

Businesses, both on- and off-line, are discovering the power of randomization to improve their bottom lines. Craft retailer JoAnn Fabrics more than tripled its average online sale, in part, by randomly testing the effectiveness of different promotions. Google's "AdWords" specializes in this kind of Super Crunching, and as it crunches, it automatically steers visitors to the most effective versions of its clients' websites. Lender Capital One runs similar randomized experiments to decide, for example, whether it is more effective to mail credit-card solicitations with "Limited Time Offer" or an attractive introductory interest rate prominently printed on the envelopes. Likewise, a short-term lender using randomization found that **priming** customers (suggesting a particular desired response) with photos of attractive, smiling women at the tops of solicitation letters raised male customers' response rates just as effectively as a 4.5 percent interest-rate reduction! And Continental Airlines found, through randomized experimentation, that sending apology letters to customers who had experienced delays while traveling on Continental resulted in millions of more dollars in repeat business than the airline received from similarly inconvenienced customers who did not receive the letters.

Still, randomization seems to be taking longer than regression to proliferate around the business world, perhaps because randomization requires more proactivity to design and implement experiments. In fact, the U.S. government actually seems to have embraced randomization ahead of many private-sector institutions, with hundreds of policy experiments currently running. For example, the now-complete "Project Follow Through" analyzed the academic achievement levels of nearly 80,000 children from low-income communities across the United States. It compared the effectiveness of 17 different teaching methods over a 20-year period, including methods that emphasized basic skills, problem-solving skills, and self-esteem, respectively. A method known as Direct Instruction (DI)—in which basic skills such as arithmetic and vocabulary are emphasized in cumulative, carefully scripted lessons—proved most effective at promoting the acquisition of both basic and problem-solving skills, and it even promoted self-esteem more effectively than some methods which emphasized that as a primary goal. As a result of such randomized trials, federal law now requires educational programs that receive federal funding to be scientifically based.

Super Crunching with Hybrid and Other Methods

Regression and randomization are not the only statistical methods employed by Super Crunchers. Often, Super Crunching requires the analysis of cumulative decisions, and in such cases, Super Crunchers employ **Bayes' Theorem**, which updates predictions as additional data become available.

The latest (and perhaps the most novel) Super Crunching method, though, is the **neural network**. Named for its mimicry of the human brain's ability to process data on multiple levels and in multiple directions simultaneously, *the neural network utilizes programming algorithms that continuously analyze far more parameters than traditional regression and update both their predictions and their predictive models as the underlying data changes.* For example, a company called Epagogix has developed a neural network that has demonstrated the ability, six out of nine times, to accurately predict a movie's total ticket sales based on certain characteristics of the movie's script.

Super Crunching Versus Intuition

A substantial body of research accumulated over decades and across multiple fields suggests that predictions derived from Super Crunching are often more accurate than predictions derived from the intuition of subject-matter experts. This has been documented in the diverse fields of medicine, law, and purchasing management. In a meta-analysis (aggregation) of 136 such studies, the statistical predictions were accurate 73.2 percent of the time, whereas the experts' predictions were accurate just 66.5 percent of the time. *Predictions derived from Super Crunching are at least as accurate and often more accurate than predictions based on experts' intuition.*

One explanation for Super Crunching's edge is the susceptibility of intuition to the interference of emotion, resulting in biased and overconfident predictions. Humans tend to overestimate the likelihood of emotionally evocative occurrences such as murder and to underestimate the likelihood of relatively mundane occurrences such as falling from a ladder. For example, if a child's home has both a handgun inside and a swimming pool outside, people might assume that the handgun poses a greater threat to the child's life. Statistically, however, the child is roughly 100 times more likely to drown in the pool than to be shot with the gun.

The optimal scenario is for Super Crunching and human intuition to be in dialogue with one another. One way to achieve such interaction is for a human's intuitive prediction to be included as one factor in the derivation of multifactorial statistical predictions. Another method is to seek agreement between statistics and intuition (but when there is disagreement, it tends to be safer, in terms of predictive accuracy, to defer to the statistics). In any case, statistics and intuition are more like complements than substitutes. Humans have to determine what to predict or to test statistically, discern which factors should be taken into account, and gather or create the necessary data. Human participation, then, is both a necessity and a potential weakness of Super Crunching. After all, a data input error could render a Super-Crunched prediction meaningless, which is why decision makers who rely on Super Crunching generally should not rely on a single Crunch or Cruncher!

The Case of Evidence-Based Medicine

The debate over Evidence-Based Medicine (EBM) is about the extent to which Super Crunching should be used in the diagnosis and treatment of diseases. For centuries, academic medicine has almost exclusively relied on the centuries-old Aristotelian methodology, striving first to understand how a given disease progresses and then, from that understanding, to derive interventions likely to stop and reverse the disease process. Although quite logical, this methodology has two important weaknesses:

1. If a disease is either misunderstood or misidentified, then the presumptive interventions are likely to be ineffective.
2. If a particular intervention is not intuitively related to the conventional conceptualization of a disease, then that intervention is unlikely to be tried.

Fast-forward to 2004, when Don Berwick, president of the Institute for Healthcare Improvement, championed the "100,000 Lives Campaign," challenging hospitals to prevent 100,000 deaths in 18 months by implementing six basic protocols (e.g., verification of correct drugs and dosages; systematic hand washing; updated heart attack response procedures).

After 18 months, the "100,000 Lives Campaign" actually prevented over 122,000 deaths.

Proponents of EBM do not advocate the abandonment of the Aristotelian methodology in medicine; rather, they advocate the appropriate consideration of empirical data in making diagnostic and treatment decisions. But in order for empirical data to be considered, the data need to be widely and readily accessible. Fortunately, a number of Super-Crunching search engines now enable doctors to access empirical data relevant to their patients. One such program takes doctors' input regarding patients' symptoms and returns lists of probable causes, including the side effects of over 4,000 drugs.

Just as too *little* data can be a problem for doctors and their patients, *data overload* can be a problem, in that doctors rarely have time to sift through the entirety of the data now available online. For example, over 3,500 new studies are published each year on the subject of heart disease alone! Accordingly, in response to a doctor's query, today's Super-Crunching medical search engines not only locate summaries of potentially relevant studies, they also report the likely relevance of each study and where else each study has been referenced since its original publication. Thus, the latest medical search engines also now assess the quality of the Super Crunching that went into each of the studies that they locate (based on the designs of the studies, the methods employed, the sample sizes, etc.).

The next generation of medical search engines is likely to Super Crunch not just the data relevant to diagnoses but also the data relevant to the interventions most likely to be effective under given sets of circumstances. Our doctors will then be able to obtain and present us with predictions of the outcomes that we are likely to experience from utilizing a range of available interventions for whatever ails us, enabling us to participate in data-driven decisions about our health care. Thus, EBM does not spell the end of intuition in medicine, but rather the empowerment of intuition through Super Crunching.

Pros and Cons for Consumers

Super Crunching can be viewed as both a benefit and a detriment to consumers. It can benefit consumers by helping businesses and governments to better understand people's wants and needs. For example, websites like Pandora.com, eHarmony, and Netflix use "collaborative filtering" to help people find new music, potential relationships, and movies that they enjoy based on the types of music, people, and movies that they have enjoyed in the past.

A significant consumer concern, however, is the capability of retailers to Super Crunch the maximum prices that we will pay for goods and services. For example, randomized testing on a website can be used to test customers' responses to different prices for the same thing and to find an individual customer's pain point (the price at which the customer decides not to buy more of a particular thing). Casinos already compute pain points to determine how much money individual gamblers can lose and still be repeat customers. A grocery store chain could use that same concept to send personalized coupons—with different-sized discounts—to you and to your next-door neighbor, depending on your respective pain points. *Although it is certainly true that Super Crunching can give an edge to retailers, it is also true that Super Crunching can give an edge to consumers.* Just as Super Crunching can reveal the highest price points at which consumers will be willing to make purchases, websites like Farecast.com, E-loan, and Priceline use Super Crunching to reveal the *lowest* price points at which retailers are willing to make sales.

Conclusion

Super Crunching is here to stay, and, on balance, it is improving the effectiveness and efficiency of business, government, and medicine while empowering individuals to obtain what they want and need. The rise of Super Crunching is not, however, the fall of intuition. Rather, *in the era of the Super Crunchers, a successful decision maker must be adept at blending intuition with data.*

3

Gut Feelings: The Intelligence of the Unconscious

Gerd Gigerenzer

Summary Prepared by Rebecca M. C. Boll

Rebecca M. C. Boll is employed with Central Minnesota Federal Credit Union (CMFCU) as a Financial Analyst with responsibilities for asset–liability management, financial analysis, competitive analysis, and strategic analysis. Prior to joining CMFCU, Boll worked as an Equity Research Analyst at Piper Jaffray; during her tenure, she covered medical device and diagnostic companies in the health-care sector. Ms. Boll received her B.B.A. in Organizational Management and Finance from the Labovitz School of Business and Economics (LSBE) at the University of Minnesota Duluth. During her undergraduate career, she participated in the LSBE Financial Markets Program and in the university's Undergraduate Research Opportunities Program, resulting in a paper entitled "Interorganizational Trust: Trust, Routines, and Institutionalization." For recreation, she enjoys spending time with friends and family, traveling, and participating in outdoor activities.

INTRODUCTION

A driver slows her car as she approaches the four-way stop at the upcoming intersection. She does not use deliberate calculation in order to react, nor does she weigh the pros and cons of continuing through the intersection; instead, she relies upon an automated response based on evolved capacities in order to slow, stop, and offer the right-of-way to the oncoming driver. Her driving accuracy is guided by her unconscious intelligence, as there is not enough time for her to safely conduct complex calculations for every decision she makes on her drive to work.

UNCONSCIOUS INTELLIGENCE

Intelligence is often thought of as deliberate and guided by the ideas of logic, but it is also based on gut feelings and intuition. Managers traditionally consider intelligence as conducting complex calculations, weighing pros and cons, and analyzing before acting. However, the mind also relies upon **unconscious intelligence**—rules of thumb and evolved capacities in order to save time while making accurate decisions. In order to fully understand total intelligence, managers should learn how employees, teams, and organizations utilize both conscious intelligence

Gerd Gigerenzer. *Gut Feelings: The Intelligence of the Unconscious.* New York: Viking Press (Penguin), 2007.

and unconscious intelligence to solve problems, determine strategy, and execute business decisions in dynamic environments. Managers should acquire many mind tools, including both logic and gut feelings. Gaining a solid understanding of both types of intelligence is necessary for managers to become effective in today's organizational setting.

Gut Feelings and Intuition

Gut feelings (hunches or intuition) are judgments that appear quickly in consciousness and are strong enough to be acted on, although the individual may not be aware of the underlying reasons for doing so. Gut feelings steer people in life because intelligence is not solely based on deliberate reasoning. Managers should recognize that the question is not *if* they should trust their gut, but *when* they should trust their gut.

Good intuitions ignore nonapplicable information and manifest gut feelings from rules of thumb that extract only a few pieces of information from a complex world. In order to understand and best utilize both types of intelligence, managers should

- explore rules of thumb underlying intuition,
- pinpoint when these rules will succeed or fail, and
- acquire many mind tools, including logic and gut feelings.

Simple rules of thumb, also known as heuristics, take advantage of the **evolved capacities** of the brain, which are a function of both genetics and the learning environment one has encountered and drawn from. Nature (genetics) gives people capability, practice turns it into a capacity, and the rule of thumb solves the problem. The recognition heuristic is one example of a simple rule of thumb. It indicates that what one recognizes is the right decision. An example of this is traveling to the supermarket in order to pick up peanut butter and laundry detergent. In both cases, people purchase what they recognize, or what they know.

Less Is (Sometimes) More

The concept of "less is more" stems from the benefits of forgetting, the importance of starting small, and the speed–accuracy trade-off. The benefits of forgetting prevent detail from slowing people down; in a dynamic world, remembering all details would weigh them down. When a manager is training a new employee, the importance of starting small prevails just as it does when a parent is teaching a child to speak. Finally, the speed–accuracy trade-off suggests that the faster a task is completed, the less accurate it becomes. However, this depends on one's evolved capacities and ability to know when to use gut feelings. If experts take too long to complete a task, they'll perform worse than if given a time limit because their expertise is executed by unconscious intelligence. However, if a novice lacks instruction, he or she will not perform optimally.

Managers should internalize that less is more under these conditions:

- a beneficial degree of ignorance exists,
- unconscious motor skills are at play (trained experts' gut feelings outperform overdeliberation),
- cognitive limitations exist, and
- the freedom-of-choice paradox occurs.

In addition, the costs associated with information often make "having less" a better choice, whereas the benefits of simplicity indicate that simple rules of thumb may be better predictors of successful decisions than complex rules in an uncertain world.

How Intuition Works

Unconscious inferences combine sensory information and depend on prior knowledge that is accumulated about the world. Intuition allows people to focus on a few pieces of information and ignore the rest. It is based on an adaptive toolbox, mentioned previously as rules of thumb. Moreover, minds fill in missing information based on the information that is available; in other words, they make perceptual bets. *Specifically, intuition occurs when a manager experiences a rule-of-thumb move from unconscious to conscious.* Evolved capacities are the building blocks of rules of thumb, and rules of thumb produce gut feelings; the environment helps determine whether a rule of thumb will succeed. Furthermore, gut feelings help apply the correct rule of thumb under the most appropriate circumstances. Managers should remember the three parts of an intuition, which suggest that intuition is

- strong enough to act upon,
- inflexible, and
- triggered automatically by external stimuli.

Evolved Brains

Brains are a function of their genes and learning points from the environment. Important business decisions often rely on more than complex calculation of pros and cons; managers often also rely on a "gut check," which is based on evolved capacities from prior experiences. Additionally, managers should be forward thinkers by reflecting on their experiences to further build their evolved capacities and sharpen their gut feelings.

Adapted Minds

Managers should accept the fact that gut feelings help shape an organization's culture. In their jobs, employees develop rules of thumb to aid decision making, which ultimately expedites workflow and saves precious organizational resources. These rules of thumb are absorbed into the organization's bloodstream and are sometimes adopted or possibly forgotten. In either case, an organization's culture may shift. Therefore, organizational leaders should think carefully about the values their rules communicate and realize how these rules shape the organization. Periodically, managers should conduct an inventory of conscious and unconscious intelligence demonstrated by employees, teams, and the organization as a whole. They can then use this information to align rewards with rules of thumb that shape the desired team or organizational culture.

Adapted minds are necessary for navigating uncertainty as an organization executes its strategies. Complex calculation often relies too heavily on historical information, and only portions of this information are suitable predictors of the future. In a dynamic operating environment, organizations will ignore some information and base strategic initiatives on one good reason because even if problems are well defined, ideal solutions may not be obtainable. Hence, *good rules of thumb become irreplaceable.*

Why Good Intuitions Shouldn't Be Logical

Rigid logical norms ignore volatility in the environment, whereas unconscious intelligence goes beyond the information given and makes reasonable guesses. People often frame logical information in different ways, yet people decipher information often overlooked by logic. For example, when a man is told by his doctor that there is a 90 percent chance of survival associated with a surgery, he acknowledges this statistic but also considers the 10 percent chance that complications or death may occur. Therefore, managers should recognize that intuition is richer than logic and often helps solve a problem.

GUT FEELINGS IN ACTION

American culture has embraced the belief that more information is better and more choices are best; however, managers also should study gut feelings, which include recognition, recall, "one-good-reason" decision making, moral behavior, and **social instincts**. These gut-feeling applications also belong in a manager's intelligence toolbox because they save time, prevent information overload, and predict well while operating under uncertainty. The next section analyzes these gut feelings individually.

Ever Heard of . . .?

Recognition memory is the ability to tell the novel from the previously experienced, or to decipher the old from the new. It is an evolved capacity that the recognition heuristic utilizes. Recognition shapes intuitions and emotions in everyday living. It reinforces reciprocity by aiding recognition of names and faces. This evolved capacity leads people to rules of thumb that generate gut feelings about which brand of a product should be purchased and which business partner has been fair and is likely to continue to be fair.

Managers should discover that the recognition heuristic is one simple tool in the adaptive toolbox; it guides intuitive judgments, including both inferences and personal choices. If one object is recognized but the other is not, people infer that the recognized object has higher value. Furthermore, this heuristic is impacted by quality, publicity, and validity. High-quality products are mentioned more often, those mentioned more often are recognized more frequently, and those recognized more often are thought to have higher quality. Therefore, by measuring the impact of quality and publicity, managers can predict in which situations recognition is informative versus misleading.

Effective use of the recognition heuristic depends on recognition and automatic evaluation. It is important for managers to note that evaluation is absent in automatic rules of thumb; however, scientists have studied the human brain and have discovered that specific neural activity is observed when unconscious intelligence, or automatic evaluation, occurs. People follow the recognition heuristic intuitively when it is valid.

One Good Reason Is Enough

Recall memory takes recognition memory one step further by recalling episodes, facts, reasons, cues, and/or signals to assist with decision making. Sequential decision making is part of recall memory, whereby cue after cue is considered until a decision can be made. There are three fundamentals behind this heuristic, and they include:

- a search rule, where reasons are looked up in order of importance;
- a stopping rule, which stops a search as soon as alternatives differ; and
- a decision rule, which chooses the alternative that this reason suggests.

The "take-the-best" heuristic is efficient and accurate because less information and computation is needed. The intuition underlying this heuristic is exemplified when two friends are viewing a football game and are trying to predict the winner: "If the Minnesota Vikings won last season, they will win this season too. If this is not the case, then bet on the team leading at half time." Another sequential decision was discussed in the introduction; weighing the pros and cons in heavy traffic could be unsafe. When one is leaving a crowded stadium after a football game, he or she obeys the police officer directing traffic rather than the stoplight. This person's unconscious intelligence tells him or her not to question the police officer but to follow his or her instructions instead of the stoplight when the police officer is present. Continually making conscious trade-offs would turn the world into a risky place; decisions would be made too slowly.

LESS IS MORE IN THE REAL WORLD   Physicians' judgments are usually based on the highest expected utility, statistical aids, or intuition. Simple rules of thumb can be faster, less costly, and more accurate than computer-driven strategies, but oftentimes the fear of litigation drives physicians to make deliberate and complex calculations. Fast and frugal trees should be used by managers when solving a problem of classifying one object into two or more categories.

A "fast-and-frugal" decision tree asks a few "yes" or "no" questions, places the most important factor on top, and is transferable from managers to employees. A real-world example of this is found in the emergency room where physicians are trying to determine whether a patient's severe chest pain is related to cardiac problems or another health problem. If the former is determined, that patient should be taken to the coronary care unit, and if the latter is found, he or she should be taken to the general hospital ward. In this case, a fast-and-frugal tree has been devised to focus on what is important and to improve decision making, thereby freeing up scarce and costly emergency room resources.

MORAL BEHAVIOR   Managers should also study the three principles of moral intuition, as follows:

- *Lack of awareness* symbolizes that gut feelings appear quickly and are strong enough to act upon.
- *Roots and rules* suggest that intuition is attached to the individual, family, or community and to an emotional goal described by a rule of thumb.
- *Moral behavior* is also contingent upon the social environment, which triggers a rule of thumb. Putting these principles together, moral intuitions are based on rules of thumb and rely on one-reason decision making.

To use an example of organ donation, people utilize a *default rule of thumb* (versus stable preferences) as a basis for their decision. In countries where people have to consciously "opt in," (i.e., choose to become organ donors) few are donors; in countries where people must "opt out," many more are donors. Default rules of thumb are often viewed as the reasonable recommendation.

Managers should recognize that defaults set by their companies have considerable impact on economic and moral behavior. When managers know both the unconscious and conscious mechanisms underlying moral behavior as well as environmental triggers, they will prevent or reduce moral dilemmas and increase ethical behavior within the organizational setting.

SOCIAL INSTINCTS   Special gut feelings lead to social interaction and include family and community instincts that are based on trust and reciprocity. Imitation is another gut feeling that lends itself to social instincts; for example, each generation does not begin from scratch; it learns from the previous generation and adapts. Imitation of the majority therefore satisfies the community instinct. However, when the world changes too quickly, imitation can be inferior to individual learning. Because organizational systems are continuously changing, managers should rely on unconscious intelligence, or the ability to know without thinking which rule to rely on and in what situation it applies.

Conclusion

Unconscious intelligence is about gut feelings taking advantage of evolved capacities, which are based on rules of thumb. It enables people to act fast while maintaining accuracy. Meanwhile, the quality of intuition lies in the intelligence of the unconscious, that is, knowing without thinking which rule to rely on and what situations are appropriate. Managers are encouraged to study and apply gut feelings because they can be faster than and equally as accurate as deliberate reasoning and complex computation. From screening patients with chronic chest pain to branding and marketing peanut butter in supermarkets, managers should realize the importance of understanding unconscious intelligence and recognize that there are good reasons to trust their own guts on occasion.

PART TWELVE

Ethics and Authenticity in the Workplace

Almost daily, newspaper and television reports appear that document unethical activities engaged in by organizations, their executives, and their employees. The corporate world has been rocked by reports of scandal and corruption. Simultaneously, the past several years have seen an increase in the number of schools of business that have introduced ethics courses into their curricula. Large numbers of organizations are actively discussing ethical behavior, developing codes of conduct or codes of ethics, and making statements about the core values of their organizations.

Many books have explored the ethical dilemmas that managers face, the core principles that guide ethical decision making, and the need for linking corporate strategy and ethical reasoning. However, questions still surround which values ethical leaders should hold and how those values could be conveyed to their employees. The readings in this part address the need for managers to be ethical, credible, and authentic.

Behavioral ethics—the understanding of the actions of people when faced with ethical dilemmas—is the topic of Bazerman and Tenbrunsel's *Blind Spots*. The authors point out that people generally think they are ethical, but are typically less so (due to personal biases) when the opportunities arise. This gap is the result of ethical fading— conveniently forgetting actions that don't match one's self-image. The authors go on to discuss concepts such as motivated blindness, "should" versus "want," outcome bias, and a variety of ways to reduce one's blind spots.

Max Bazerman is the Jesse Isidor Straus Professor Business Administration at the Harvard Business School. He is the author of numerous books, including *Judgment in Decision Making, Conflicts of Interest, Negotiation Genius,* and *Cognition and Rationality in Negotiation*. Coauthor Ann Tenbrunsel is the Rex and Alice A. Martin Professor of Business Ethics at the Mendoza College of Business, University of Notre Dame. She has participated in the preparation of several books, such as *Codes of Conduct, Groups and Ethics, Social Decision Making*, and *Behavioral Business Ethics*.

Authentic Leadership is the second reading in this section on ethics, values, and authenticity. Drawing upon his 20-year leadership position at Medtronics, a world-leading medical technology company, Bill George offers lessons on leading with heart and compassion—a guide for character-based leadership. He identifies what he believes to be five essential dimensions of authentic leadership—purpose, values, heart, relationships, and self-discipline—and discusses how they can be developed.

Bill George is the former chairman and CEO of Medtronic. The Academy of Management recognized Mr. George as Executive of the Year, and the National Association of Corporate Directors and *Business Week* recognized him as Director of the Year. Currently, he serves as a Professor of Management at Harvard Business School and has sat on the boards of ExxonMobil, Goldman Sachs, Novartis, and Target, as well as several nonprofit organizations. The author of *True North* and *Finding Your True North*, his newest book is *7 Lessons for Leading in Crisis.*

1

Blind Spots

Max H. Bazerman and Ann E. Tenbrunsel
Summary Prepared by Linda Hefferin

Linda Hefferin is a Professor of Business at Elgin Community College, in Elgin, Illinois, where she teaches business ethics, organizational behavior, and other business management courses. Hefferin completed her master's and doctoral degrees at Northern Illinois University. As a founding member of her college's Multicultural and Global Initiatives Committee, Hefferin is a firm supporter of global ethics and social responsibility.

THE IMPORTANCE OF ETHICAL SELF-AWARENESS

How ethical are you? On a scale of 0 to 100, with 0 representing *least* ethical and 100 representing *most* ethical, how would you rate yourself? Research indicates that most of us believe we are more ethical than we really are. A gap exists between how ethical we *think* we are and how ethical we *really* are. Despite our good intentions, we often act differently than we planned when actually facing an ethical dilemma. More important, we are often blind to the obstacles that prevent us from behaving the way we want or expect to behave. In addition, our moral blind spots prevent us from seeing the need to improve our ethicality, so the pattern repeats itself over and over.

These blind spots are the reason why we overestimate our ability to do what is right. **Blind spots** are ethical vulnerabilities that exist outside of our conscious awareness. *When we fail to recognize our moral blind spots, we surrender to our personal biases.* Our biases affect our reactions in ethical situations, but in most cases we do not realize this is the case. We engage in unethical behavior that influences our decisions as a result of biases; these are biases that we may not even be aware we possess. Our biases make illusions about our ethicality appear to be reality.

Our biases help hide our unethical actions and cause us to become "revisionist historians." We remember behaviors that support our self-image and conveniently forget those actions that do not so as to rationalize our unethical behavior. This process is known as **ethical fading**. Ethical dimensions are eliminated from our decisions in order to justify our choices. This moral disengagement allows us to behave contrary to our ethical beliefs yet still maintain that we are ethical people. We are motivated to see ourselves as ethical people, so we remember actions that were ethical and forget those that were not. We forgive ourselves for an unethical act and then allow ourselves to commit increasingly more unethical infractions as time passes.

Max H. Bazerman and Ann E. Tenbrunsel. *Blind Spots: Why We Fail to Do What's Right and What to Do About It.* Princeton, NJ: Princeton University Press, 2011.

Decision makers often fail to see "ethics" in an ethical dilemma. The field of **behavioral ethics** seeks to understand why people behave the way they do when facing ethical dilemmas. *Behavioral ethics examines how blind spots affect our decision-making processes in both our personal and professional lives.* Over 10 million individuals have completed the computer-based Implicit Association Test (IAT), where they examine the way they might discriminate against others without their own awareness. Individuals are asked to quickly classify people's faces by pressing one of two computer keys. Researchers have concluded that even honest people hold biases that equate white-skinned faces as "good" while equating black-skinned people as "bad" when they say they do not possess racial bias in their conscious minds. The results of the IAT predict unconscious biased treatment of blacks when they interview for jobs, apply for loans, or receive treatment from medical doctors.

Behavioral Forecasting Errors

Why are we so blind to our personal biases and their consequences? We often analyze a situation prior to it actually happening to us, and we intend to act ethically. Somehow, our biases get in the way.

Biases occur during several stages of the decision-making process. Before facing an ethical dilemma, individuals predict that they will make an ethical choice. But when faced with the ethical dilemma, individuals sometimes make an unethical decision.

Our biases lead to erroneous perceptions that prevent us from seeing the need to improve our ethicality. This process is known as **behavioral forecasting errors**. As an example, when patients are diagnosed with an illness, they may be offered the choice to participate in a clinical trial. The goal of clinical trials is to assess the effectiveness and safety of certain medical treatments. Using control groups, different treatments are administered to each experimental group. When asked if you would participate in a clinical trial, most likely you would come to the conclusion that it is the "right" thing to do. You would be making a contribution to the greater good of advances in medicine. So you predict that you would engage in a clinical trial should the occasion arise.

Then your child contracts a life-threatening illness. A newly approved but risky treatment will be administered to one group. The other group will receive the traditional, less risky treatment. Your doctor asks if you will agree to place your child in a clinical trial where a computer determines which treatment your child receives. You quickly decline to have your child participate in the trial. When a decision is purely theoretical, individuals make decisions compatible with their ethics. But when the decision becomes a reality, we typically choose the decision that best serves our self-interest.

"Want" Versus "Should"

When making decisions, we experience conflict regarding our actions. Ethical conflict occurs between the "want" self and the "should" self. The "should" self represents actions we believe we should take. Our "want" self signifies how we wish to behave. *We predict how we will behave in an ethical dilemma based on our "should" self, but the "want" self dominates when actually facing the situation.* Further, when reflecting back on our decision, we often believe that we acted according to our "should" self.

The "want" self is considered emotional, impulsive, self-centered, and hotheaded. The "should" self is rational, cognitive, thoughtful, and cool-headed. Whether the "want" self or the "should" self responds varies across time. The "should" self dominates before and after we make a decision. We predict we will make "should" decisions, such as participating in clinical trials for the greater good of humankind. At the time of a decision, thoughts of how we "should" behave fade and the "want" self usually wins.

Consider New Year's resolutions. Many people set goals for expected behavior, including actions within their moral domain. They vow to quit smoking, get out of debt, volunteer to assist charities, or spend more time with family. As the year comes to a close, the majority of people have not kept their resolutions. Another new year begins, and they make another set of erroneous predictions about their behavior for the following year. Somehow, though, their "want" self has replaced the "should" self that was present when setting the resolutions. In many people's minds, they believe they have met their goals for the prior year at least in part; and they are ready to set new resolutions.

ORGANIZATIONAL AND SOCIETAL BLIND SPOTS

Although blind spots can originate with individuals, they are compounded at the organizational level. In 2009, the *Chicago Tribune* printed a story stating that despite the objections of admissions officers, hundreds of underqualified students were admitted to the University of Illinois (U of I) after receiving special consideration from high-ranking officials. Many university administrators, including U of I president B. Joseph White, were accused of cooperating in admitting privileged, unqualified applicants over more qualified applicants. When several of the wrongdoers were questioned about their granting of favors, they said they were just doing their job and helping people close to them. In the end, a number of university trustees and administrators resigned, but the reputation of the U of I had already been damaged. Clearly, blind spots within the organization existed and resulted in ethical sinkholes.

Blind spots also multiply exponentially at the societal level. For example, take the debate over climate change. Developing countries such as China have blamed the West for its industrialization and excessive consumption, whereas the United States tends to blame emerging nations such as China for their overpopulation and uncontrolled urbanization. The United States may wish to sign a climate change treaty that is fair to both the United States and China, but its view of what is "fair" is likely biased. The same is likely to be true for China. Society at large is vulnerable to blind spots as a result of unconscious biases.

Motivated Blindness

Why do people frequently look the other way when it should be evident that someone is doing something wrong? Our self-interest in a situation makes it difficult to approach a decision without bias. **Motivated blindness** is the tendency for people to overlook unethical behavior when it is in their best interest *not* to notice the behavior.

We are blind not only to our own unethical actions but also to the unethicality of others around us in organizations and society at large. We are seldom rewarded for noticing or preventing the unethical behavior of others. Motivated blindness comes from many sources: fear, incentives, organizational loyalty, and/or organizational culture.

One of the most striking examples of motivated blindness is the 2001 case of Enron. Arthur Andersen, Enron's auditing firm, earned millions of dollars in fees from Enron. Andersen auditors had a strong motivation to vouch for Enron's financial health, even when it was evident Enron was concealing billions of dollars in debt from its shareholders. Motivated blindness results in our classifying a decision as a "business decision" rather than an "ethical decision."

Motivated blindness also appears to be responsible for the widespread use of steroids in Major League Baseball (MLB). Steroid use led to more home runs; these led to increased attendance and greater profit for the league, the teams, and the players. The MLB Commissioner, individual teams, and the players' union all benefited financially from the steroid use of players, and even those who were not using performance-enhancing drugs were motivated to cover for those who were. Thus, the steroid problem persisted for many years before it finally became public. Motivated blindness causes people at all levels of society to engage in behaviors that they would never condone if there were greater awareness.

Outcome Bias

Outcome bias involves judging a decision based on its eventual outcome rather than the quality of the decision at the time it was made. People too often judge the ethicality of an action based on whether harm follows rather than the ethicality of the decision itself. Consider the example of two brothers, neither of which has a criminal record. A man confronts the two brothers and insults their family. The first brother vows to kill the man, pulls out a gun and shoots, but misses the man. The second brother only wants to scare the man, so he pulls out a gun but accidentally shoots the man and kills him. Which brother is guiltier? In most U.S. states, the second brother who accidentally killed the man would receive a far longer prison sentence than the first brother. The law pays more attention to the outcome of the action rather than the intention.

As a result of outcome bias, we ignore bad decision making if it happens to lead to desirable results, which can then encourage future bad decision making.

On a societal level, outcome bias may partially explain why many people reserved judgment over the Bush administration's decision to invade Iraq in 2003 until they knew what the outcome would be. Criticism was limited in much of the United States early in the invasion when it appeared that the United States was winning the war. As the war began to drag on for years, people became more vocal about unfounded claims of weapons of mass destruction in Iraq. Many people now question the ethics of going to war, including the misrepresentation of facts that prompted the invasion. As a result of outcome bias, we often condemn behavior only after a harmful outcome occurs.

ACTIONS TO REDUCE BLIND SPOTS

How can you bring your decision making into closer alignment with your ethical views? Moreover, how can you help your organization—and society in general—to do the same thing?

*The first step in making ethical decisions is **ethical self-awareness**.* We must recognize our vulnerability to our unconscious biases. We need to acknowledge our tendency to act based on how we "want" to behave rather than on how we "should" act. One way to counteract the "want" self is to think about motivations that are likely to influence us when actually facing an ethical decision. By projecting ourselves into a future situation as if we were there, we can better anticipate our actions.

Another strategy is to anticipate the influence of your impulses and learn how to accurately assess and learn from your past behavior. Training individuals on how their biases impede accurate evaluation of their behavior can help mitigate the effect of these biases.

Finally, think about what you would like to have written or said about yourself in a eulogy at your funeral. What principles will people say guided your life? Try using the "mom litmus test." When faced with an ethical dilemma, ask if you would be comfortable sharing your decision with your mom (or dad, or someone else whom you really respect). These strategies will give your "should" voice more power in decision making.

Conclusion

Adopting a behavioral ethics perspective can help create a more ethical society. First, at the individual level, we must recognize our vulnerabilities to our unconscious biases in order to overcome our blind spots. When we are able to more clearly see the ethical implications of our actions, we will make choices that better align with our values. Next, at the organizational level, leaders must be aware of how the decisions they make affect the ethicality of their colleagues and subordinates. In addition, the organization's formal and informal systems and values must be aligned to promote ethical behavior.

Finally, at the societal level, we want individuals and organizations that represent us to act ethically. Especially in a time of globalization, we hold a moral responsibility to contribute to the creation of a better society. *By removing our ethical blinders, we can improve the morality of decision making at the individual, organizational, and societal levels.*

2

Authentic Leadership

Bill George
Summary Prepared by Randy Skalberg

Randy Skalberg is an Associate Professor of Taxation and Business Law at the University of Minnesota Duluth, where he has taught courses in corporate and individual tax, business law, and corporate ethics. He holds a B.S.B. in Accounting from the Carlson School of Management at the University of Minnesota, a J.D. from the University of Minnesota Law School, and an L.L.M. in Taxation from Case Western Reserve University in Cleveland, Ohio. He has served as an in-house tax counsel to Fortune 500 corporations, including Metris Companies and The Sherwin-Williams Company, and also served in the tax department at Ernst & Young's Minneapolis office. He is admitted to practice law in Minnesota, as well as before the U.S. Tax Court.

AUTHENTIC LEADERSHIP

Authentic leadership involves those actions taken by people of high integrity who are committed to building enduring organizations relying on morality and character. It means being your own person as a leader. A leader's authenticity is based not only on differentiating right and wrong (the classic "moral compass") but also on a leadership style that follows qualities of the heart and mind (passion and compassion) as well as by intellectual capacity. All too often, society has glorified leaders based on high-style and high-ego personalities instead of personal qualities that provide for true quality leadership.

DIMENSIONS OF A LEADER

An authentic leader practices the five dimensions of leadership: purpose, values, heart, relationships, and self-discipline. *Purpose* focuses on the real reasons people choose to become leaders—not the trappings of power, the glamour, or the financial rewards that go with leadership. *Values* provide the "true north" of a leader's moral compass. Failure of leadership values lies behind the failure of Enron, but more important, leadership values have been critical in the growth of virtually all of America's long-term corporate success stories. An example of *heart* in leadership is provided by Marilyn Nelson, CEO of Carlson Companies. She took over an organization bordering on crisis from previous years of "hard-nosed" management and created a program called

Bill George. *Authentic Leadership: Rediscovering the Secrets to Creating Lasting Value.* San Francisco, CA: Jossey-Bass, 2003.

"Carlson Cares," which has resulted in both corporate growth and an improved bottom line. The *relationship* dimension debunks the myth that a great leader needs to be distant and aloof to prevent the relationship from interfering with "hard" decisions. An authentic leader creates close relationships as part of leadership. The existence and fostering of such relationships is actually a sign of strength in leadership, not an indicator of weakness. Consistency is the hallmark of *self-discipline* in a leader. Consistency enables employees who work with the leader to know where he or she stands on important issues and to rely on even the most difficult decisions the leader has made.

LEADING A BALANCED LIFE

One of the key characteristics of authentic leadership is the focus on the journey rather than the destination. The leader must recognize that a career is rarely a straight-line path to success (and most likely should not be), but rather it is a journey wherein all of the leader's experiences contribute to overall success.

This concept of success implies not merely financial or professional success, but the overall success that comes from leading a **balanced life**—one that recognizes the importance of work, family, friends, faith, and community service, with none of them excluding any of the others. Leaders who subordinate everything else in life to their work do not develop organizations as well as those who live a more balanced life. Living such a life and allowing their employees to do so as well creates higher levels of commitment to the organization and, in turn, improves the organization's bottom line. *Balancing work, family, social, and spiritual aspects of your life and providing a meaningful amount of time to each provides the leader with richness in life* that is unavailable to someone who chooses an 80-hour week and is simply a "company person." The balance between work and family life is a substantial challenge, especially in today's two-career families. One of the challenges every leader will face is the impact of increased time demands from the organization on his or her family. The "delicate balance" between work and family life continues to be very difficult to achieve.

In addition to work/family balance, friendships are important. True friendships offer a place to share your emotions outside your family and without workplace involvement. This sharing process is an important part of the process of personal development. Equally important is the mentoring process. Contrary to the traditional view of mentoring, where an older person provides one-way advice to a younger person, true mentoring is a two-way process where both parties learn from each other. This two-way process acknowledges that mentoring is not merely the older generation telling "war stories," but a process where younger employees and students can provide insight into the questions that young leaders have about the business world. Finally, community service is an essential part of authentic leadership. Through community service, leaders have an opportunity to work with people of lesser economic means. *Getting in touch with people helps develop both the heart of a leader and sensitivity for the difficulties of the lives of others.*

ORGANIZATIONAL MISSION AS MOTIVATION

A common phrase in today's business world (some would say almost a mantra) is "maximizing shareholder value." Although that might be an appropriate goal for a company seeking a white knight in a takeover battle, it is fundamentally flawed as a long-term business model. The best way to create real long-term value for a company's shareholders is to be a **mission-driven**

organization—one that utilizes its mission statement as an integral part of managing the organization, not merely as a plaque that hangs on the CEO's wall. The best organizations have a corporate mission that inspires creative employees to develop innovative products and provide superior service to the customer. This strategy creates a self-sustaining business cycle. In Medtronic's case, this mission is to "alleviate pain, restore health, and extend life" of the patient consumer, which creates demand from physicians, who are the immediate customers.

CUSTOMER FOCUS

Every company's purpose boils down to serving its customers well. If it does this better than any of its competitors, and does it over the long term, it will ultimately create more shareholder value than its competitors. **Customer-focused quality** relies for its success on measurements that focus externally on customers and uses customer feedback as the ultimate measurement of quality. The role model for customer focus must be senior management. If senior management is focused on internal operations instead of on customer service, the company will eventually fail to an environment that empowers and rewards employees who provide high-quality sales and service to the customer.

TEAM-FOCUSED MANAGEMENT

CEOs are given credit when companies succeed, but it is largely a myth that the CEO is primarily responsible for the success of a company. Many of the great corporate success stories of the past 25 years—for example, Intel, Nokia, Hewlett-Packard, Microsoft, Coca-Cola, and Pepsi—have all been managed by a team at the top, not merely by a single high-powered CEO. Upon being named CEO of Medtronic, Bill George immediately proposed a partnership (as opposed to a traditional boss–subordinate relationship) with Vice Chair Glen Nelson. This was critical to Medtronic's success. Nelson, an M.D., brought a critical perspective on the relationship of the practice of medicine and technology to the management team, whereas George brought experience in high technology management from his previous employer, Honeywell.

PITFALLS TO GROWTH

There are seven key pitfalls to sustainable corporate growth: lack of mission, underestimation of core business, single-product dependence, failure to spot change, changing strategy with changing culture, ignoring core competencies, and overreliance on growth through acquisition. Avoiding each of these pitfalls requires disciplined leadership to recognize the problem and aggressively solve it without immediately retreating into a dangerous cost-cutting mode. This type of leadership in the face of inevitable criticism from securities analysts and the media will provide inspiration to the organization and rejuvenate its growth.

OVERCOMING OBSTACLES

A key obstacle for Medtronic involved litigation in the implantable defibrillator market. A former Medtronic employee held patent rights to the first implantable defibrillator and went to work for Eli Lilly, a Medtronic competitor. Lilly used the patents to prevent Medtronic from developing its own defibrillator, a product that was critical to its core pacemaker business.

Medtronic and Lilly litigated this patent claim to the U.S. Supreme Court, where Medtronic won the right to develop its implantable defibrillator. Even after this victory, though, Medtronic still had to negotiate a cross-licensing agreement with Lilly, clear Food and Drug Administration (FDA) approval, and face the challenge of another competitor (Guidant) that reached the market with a dual-chamber defibrillator prior to Medtronic. This 15-year struggle proved worthwhile, however, as Medtronic now enjoys a greater than 50 percent market share in the implantable defibrillator market.

ETHICAL DILEMMAS

Socially responsible organizations need to confront directly the issue of ethical standards in international business. Medtronic discovered shortly after acquiring the Italian distributor of Medtronic's Dutch pacemakers that the distributor was depositing large sums in a Swiss bank account, presumably to pay off Italian physicians who were Medtronic customers. George confronted the recently hired president of Medtronic Europe about the account and terminated him for violating Medtronic's corporate values. The termination caused uproar within Medtronic Europe, but in the 12 years since this incident, the Dutch pacemaker subsidiary has responded with outstanding performance.

A second crisis arose in Japan, where two Medtronic-Japan managers were arrested and put in jail for giving airline tickets to a physician so that he could give speeches at two international transplant conferences. The arrests were part of a series of arrests of executives of foreign pacemaker manufacturers apparently based on the Ministry of Health's frustration at its inability to force the manufacturers to reduce prices in the Japanese market. The two managers were eventually released from jail following a guilty plea and returned to work. But George took the critical step in visiting Japan to reestablish confidence in Medtronic-Japan's employees and meet with officials from the Ministry of Health. This visit led to the creation of an industry-wide code of conduct approved by the Ministry of Health. Medtronic continues to be a leader in the medical device industry in Japan and has not agreed to mandated price concessions.

GROWTH BY ACQUISITION

In the fall of 1998, Medtronic engaged in a series of acquisitions costing a total of $9 billion. Medtronic's growth had been in sharp decline, so George decided to make a series of bold moves. These included the acquisition of Physio-Control, a manufacturer of manual defibrillators used in hospitals. George had to overcome internal resistance to the Physio-Control deal, as well as others, based on a poor history of acquisition integration at Medtronic. After overcoming that resistance in the Physio-Control deal, the groundwork was set for two more acquisitions in 1998 and 1999—Sofamor Danek, the world's leading spinal surgery company, and AVE, the leader in the U.S. stent business.

By late January 1999, Medtronic had completed five acquisitions at a total cost of $9 billion. Next Medtronic faced the more difficult task of integration. Most acquisitions that fail do so not from financial issues or lack of strategic vision, but rather from cultural clashes within the newly merged entities. Medtronic took a proactive approach to integration focusing on four key issues: leadership of the business, financial leadership, business integration, and cultural integration. George formed integration teams for each company led by a Medtronic executive and including Medtronic employees and employees from the acquired company.

SHAREHOLDERS COME THIRD

George's executive philosophy was described in an article in *Worth Magazine*, quoting him as saying, "Shareholders come third." George expected some backlash from the article, but surprisingly received none. The theory is simple. Customers are first, employees are second, and shareholders come third. Only by truly meeting the needs of the first two stakeholder groups does the successful company have any chance of satisfying the shareholders. *The key to meeting shareholder expectations is transparency.* Medtronic is completely transparent about every corporate event inside the company with respect to shareholders, a policy that can be contrasted with the Kozlowski-led Tyco, which hid major corporate expenditures from its own board of directors, much less the shareholders.

CORPORATE GOVERNANCE

The key to improved corporate governance is to restore power to boards of directors to govern corporations. The board should play an important role as a check on the company's executives and a means of ensuring long-term as opposed to short-term focus. One key to creating this type of board is to have a majority (perhaps two-thirds) of truly independent board members who have no business relationship to either the corporation or the executives. This will ensure that the directors can truly act independently of the CEO, not merely as "inside" directors who serve at the pleasure of the CEO.

PUBLIC POLICY AND RISK TAKING

Medtronic found itself cast in a leadership role in the reform of the U.S. FDA. The key issue in the reform movement was the steadily increasing approval time for new drugs. Drugs that were already in use in foreign countries were taking months, and in many cases years, to be approved in the United States, and American patients were dying without access to life-saving medications. George presented his ideas about the need for reform at the Food & Drug Law Institute in Washington, D.C., and went on to work with the late Senator Paul Wellstone to generate bipartisan support for the Food and Drug Modernization Act of 1996. Today, new drugs are approved in less than 6 months, as opposed to 29 months at the height of the FDA's delay problems.

SUCCESSION PLANNING FOR THE CEO

One of the most critical and often overlooked steps in a CEO's career is succession. Almost as many CEO succession processes fail as succeed. If the board working with the incumbent CEO fails to identify a qualified and appropriate internal candidate, board members are often forced to look outside the organization for a "star" CEO, a process that more often than not fails, as happened at Xerox and Maytag. One of the key factors is a lack of clarity on the CEO's part about how and when he or she will step aside. The CEO should identify a retirement date well in advance (Bill George announced his retirement date one year in advance), develop a succession plan, and make the transition as seamless as possible. This transition method is critical not only to employees and shareholders who desire consistent leadership but also to the new CEO, who knows when he or she will take over. This prevents the new CEO from being forced to choose between waiting around and moving on to other opportunities.

PART THIRTEEN

Emotions: Positive, Negative, and Irrational

Topics of interest to managers encompass a wide array of themes, and these are constantly changing and evolving. This part includes a sampling of topics that have received substantial attention in recent years, all focusing on employee emotions, feelings, and attitudes. The topics in this part include the need for employees to find meaning in their (work) lives, toxic experiences at work, and the ways in which people sometimes act irrationally. These readings are designed to raise issues, provide an opportunity to reflect on oneself, and stimulate conversations regarding the balance between emphasis on corporate profits and employee (and personal) needs.

Viktor Frankl is one of the world's best-known survivors of the Holocaust's Nazi concentration camps in World War II. He attributed his survival under horrifying conditions to a driving search for meaning in a seemingly hopeless situation and reported his lessons learned in his book *Man's Search for Meaning* (named by the Library of Congress as one of the 10 most influential books of the twentieth century). Alex Pattakos, in *Prisoners of Our Thoughts*, has distilled Frankl's 30 books down into seven core principles: choose your attitude, commit to meaningful goals, find meaning wherever you are, recognize how you work to defeat yourself, search for insight and perspective while laughing at yourself, learn to shift your focus of attention, and make a difference in the world. Pattakos shows us how to connect with others so as to create and experience meaning in our lives.

Alex Pattakos is the founder of the Center for Personal Meaning in Santa Fe and also a principal of the Innovation Group. He is a speaker, writer, facilitator, and consultant to corporate clients on the Fortune 500. He is a strong advocate of "community building" in a wide range of settings, an Adjunct Professor at Penn State University, and author of the books *Intuition at Work* and *Rediscovering the Soul of Business*.

Toxic bosses and organizational cultures exist in many workplaces even in this enlightened era, and their impact is often compounded by the presence of combative customers, impossible deadlines, and unexpected tragedies. The results of this insidious organizational toxicity include lower productivity, job stress, workplace sabotage, and labor–management disputes. *Toxic Emotions at Work* by Peter J. Frost provides a description of the positive roles that toxin handlers can engage in to reduce and minimize the adverse impacts of toxic pain. They can listen with compassion, facilitate the discussion of emotions, intercede on behalf of colleagues, and reframe painful situations. Frost concludes his book with a three-stage model for managing toxicity that identifies strategies for prevention, intervention, and restoration.

Peter J. Frost received his Ph.D. from the University of Minnesota and served as the Edgar F. Kaiser Professor of Organizational Behaviour on the Faculty of Commerce of the University of British Columbia. In addition to *Toxic Emotions at Work*, he is the coauthor of many other books, such as *HRM Reality, Doing Exemplary Research, Organizational Reality*, and *Reframing Organizational Culture*. Peter Frost received the George R. Terry Book Award from the Academy of Management for *Toxic Emotions at Work.*

Dan Ariely, in his closely related books *Predictably Irrational* and *The Upside of Irrationality*, raises the rhetorical question, "Are we rational or irrational?" He uses that provocative beginning to introduce his discussion of behavioral economics (the study of environmental factors that ultimately bias the outcomes made by decision makers). Borrowing from social psychology, Ariely uses Festinger's theory of cognitive dissonance, the phenomenon of assortative mating, and the "not-invented-here" bias to help explain how people who believe they are rational are not always so, and how they respond when faced with disparities between their beliefs and their actions. He concludes that actions that appear to be irrational are not always so; in reality they are "systematic and predictable" and thus predictably irrational.

Dan Ariely earned two doctorate degrees—one in cognitive psychology from the University of North Carolina and one in business administration from Duke University. He is currently the James B. Duke Professor of Psychology and Behavioral Economics at Duke, where he holds appointments in the areas of economics, medicine, business, and cognitive neuroscience areas. Ariely is also the founding member of the Center for Advanced Hindsight, and the author of two business best sellers. His most recent book is The (Honest) Truth about Dishonesty.

1

Prisoners of Our Thoughts

Alex Pattakos
Summary Prepared by Gary P. Olson

Gary P. Olson is CEO of the Center for Alcohol and Drug Treatment, Duluth, Minnesota. He is responsible for the overall direction of this regional not-for-profit corporation. He received his M.B.A. from the University of Minnesota Duluth.

INTRODUCTION

How many of us have worked at jobs we didn't really like? Perhaps we were happy to be making a living, but were unfulfilled by the work itself. We found ourselves asking, "Isn't there more to life than this?"

Sometimes we are frustrated when we seem to have little control over our work situation and feel that there is little we can do to change our circumstances. These common experiences often lead us to ask ourselves fundamental questions about the way we live, work, and play.

Viktor Frankl, the world-renowned psychiatrist and Nazi concentration camp survivor, saw these questions as part of a fundamental human drive he called "man's search for meaning." Frankl believed that *the meaning of a person's life can only be determined by your own life, not the circumstances you find yourself in.* Dr. Frankl's theory was put to the test during his incarceration by the Germans during World War II at the Auschwitz and Dachau death camps. He survived these horrific conditions with his humanity intact and the certainty that his ideas had universal application.

The following principles use Dr. Frankl's work to guide our search for meaning no matter what job or situation we are in, and to connect our work with the meaning in other parts of our lives. These principles are as follows:

1. Choose your own attitude.
2. Commit to meaningful values.
3. Find meaning in the moment.
4. Don't work against yourself.
5. Practice self-detachment.
6. Use creative distraction.
7. Transcend your personal interests.

Alex Pattakos. *Prisoners of Our Thoughts: Viktor Frankl's Principles at Work.* San Francisco, CA: Berrett-Koehler, 2004.

MEANINGFUL WORK

The basic principle of Viktor Frankl's work is that *we are entirely free at all times to choose our response to the circumstances of our lives.* Frankl's **logotherapy** was a method by which the therapist helped the client become fully aware of this freedom of choice. Frankl believed in the unconditional meaningfulness of life and the intrinsic dignity of every person. He also believed every person had the capacity to search for meaning under any conditions. In other words, no one is off the hook.

When we search for meaning, we are looking for that which is meaningful for ourselves in relation to our own core values. Situations that may "try our souls" can become opportunities to help us clarify our own values. The way we accept the things we cannot control can lead to a deeper sense of personal meaning.

If we view our jobs as somehow apart from our "real" lives, we shut ourselves off from a large portion of our life experience. This often happens when we fall into the habit of constantly complaining about our work, our bosses, and our coworkers. When we choose to search for meaning and acknowledge our freedom to choose our responses, work becomes a rich opportunity.

CHOOSE YOUR OWN ATTITUDE

The freedom to choose is not always easy to exercise in practice. Our personal ability to cope and adapt is often tested. In order to effectively exercise this freedom, we must be able to look at a situation differently, even if this leads us to choose a path that is at odds with other people's expectations of how someone in our position normally responds.

No one can choose our attitude for us. Everyone knows someone who relentlessly complains about his or her working conditions, but does nothing to change them. It is when we take responsibility for exercising our freedom to choose our attitude that we move from being part of the problem to becoming part of the solution.

When we choose our attitude, we

- can choose to bring a positive attitude to the situation,
- adopt a creative approach to imagining what is possible, and
- unlock the passion or enthusiasm that makes the possible actual.

When we abstain from the responsibility for choosing consciously, we are choosing instead to remain locked in habits of thought that may no longer serve our search for meaning. We have the freedom, but we must make a conscious decision to exercise it. Out freedom is limited by conditions, but we *can* take a stand.

COMMIT TO MEANINGFUL VALUES

Frankl described the **will to meaning** as the authentic commitment to meaningful values and goals that only we as individuals can actualize. He believed *the will to meaning is a basic human drive.* Other drives may be more externally apparent, such as the will to power (or superiority) and the will to pleasure. Frankl believed these "drives" were actually efforts to mask a void of meaning that exists in many people's lives.

It is not difficult to find examples of what Frankl meant. It is obvious that no amount of power or pleasure can fill such a void when it exists. If it did, the most powerful and pampered among us should be the most fulfilled and satisfied, but this is not the case. Only the sustained search for meaning can lead to the sense of fulfillment that most of us desire from our work and our lives.

Values that are primarily related to power and pleasure are not those values that lead us to meaning in our lives. The will to power, for example, is always contingent on external conditions. Power relies on a cooperative set of subjects and circumstances to be meaningful at all, and because change is the only constant, power tends to dissipate over time despite our efforts to sustain it. The will to meaning, on the contrary, comes entirely from within us. Only we can discover and realize it.

Some modern, progressive companies attempt to create the illusion of freedom in the workplace, but fail to connect with the emotional, intellectual, and spiritual values of their employees, customers, or communities. Yet business and economics are connected with all aspects of our lives, communities, and planet. The inability to honor meaning at the top of any organization often leads to demoralization, dissatisfaction, and, ultimately, decreased productivity.

FIND MEANING IN THE MOMENT

If we could live life over for a second time, would we make different choices? Although meaning may exist in every second, we have to make an effort to find it. Meaningful moments often slip by without notice only to be realized months or even years later. Meaning does not exist within our own minds, and it is not created; it is discovered in the world around us. *The search for meaning requires a conscious effort.*

The pace of modern life and work conspires against the search for meaning. Unless we stop to consider why we are doing what we are doing and what our lives and work mean to us and to examine the reasons we do what we do, we cannot expect to find meaning. This requires time for serious reflection, time without a cell phone to our ear or a list of e-mails to check. Technology, which is designed to make life easier, can instead become a relentless, demanding set of obligations. It may take a serious effort to disconnect from these tools long enough to find time to reflect.

Finding meaning in our lives and work is our personal responsibility and rests on our ability to achieve a certain level of awareness or mindfulness. To be aware means to stop and consider our situation and discover what life lessons it may hold. When we become aware of the many possibilities open to us, we become open to meaning. We can be creators or complainers, for example, for both of these potentials exist within us. Which potential is realized depends on our decisions, not our external conditions.

DON'T WORK AGAINST YOURSELF

How satisfied can we be if we achieve a lofty goal at the expense of a friendship, loss of respect, or our own health? Meaning exists in appreciation of the moment, the present, or the process—not in a particular outcome!

Sometimes our efforts to create meaning, particularly in our work, can lead us away from meaning. This is because the meaning and value in our work are acquired not simply through our own performance, but in the way our work contributes to society. We do not work in a vacuum. Our bosses, coworkers, and customers have their own agendas that may be at odds with our own. Like the football coach whose plan went awry because the opponent did not follow it, we can't ignore the others on the field.

Our jobs are never just *our* jobs. We work within a fabric of relationships that extends far beyond our immediate workspace. These relationships have meaning individually and collectively. Becoming too focused on ultimate outcomes and results can cause us to overlook the meaning that exists moment to moment. Our anxiety about a successful outcome can actually undermine our ability to "get it right." Instead, we need to focus on the meaning in the process.

Our good intentions can become the cause of failure. This happens when we overlook and neglect the relationships that are integral to the process of accomplishing a larger goal or project. Ignoring the opportunity to experience meaningful moments with others at work undermines the chance for success because business issues and people issues are usually intertwined. Even a desired promotion at work can, in the end, depend more on your relationship with your coworkers than it does on pleasing the boss. Your boss may understand that *your ability to relate in a meaningful and positive way with coworkers is a key indicator of your ability to lead.* Your knowledge of what your coworkers value and care about can be a more important asset in leadership than your job knowledge. The more meaning we experience in the process, the more satisfied we will feel *irrespective* of the outcome.

PRACTICE SELF-DETACHMENT

Humor is an excellent way of distancing ourselves from something—even our own predicament. It can be a form of self-detachment. Our ability to laugh at ourselves can make a serious situation more bearable, not just for us, but for those around us. When we can laugh at mistakes, we can own up to them, learn from them, and move on.

Even in a concentration camp, Frankl was able to find humor, and he believed it was an important weapon in the fight for self-preservation. Nevertheless, it is important to distinguish between detachment and denial. *Detachment* is a conscious choice to create psychological distance that opens the door to action, learning, and growth. *Denial* of our experience involves disconnecting from ourselves and others who may share an experience with us. Detachment permits us to acknowledge a mistake, a poor decision, or even fear, but not be paralyzed into inaction.

USE CREATIVE DISTRACTION

Thinking itself can become an obsession, particularly when it is focused on negativity and complaint. Venting frustration can become a habit of blaming and complaining that saps our energy and ultimately leads nowhere. There are times when we need to shift our focus and distract ourselves from something we don't like in order to see the possibilities in a situation. This is the principle of creative distraction.

When we are too focused on something—a demanding boss, a boring task, an unproductive coworker—we can lose sight of the meaning in our lives. The principle of creative distraction allows us to ignore some aspect of our lives that *should* be ignored. In doing so, we may perceive our situation in an entirely new way. We can then transcend the limits in our condition, avoid becoming self-absorbed, and direct our attention toward discovering new meaning in our lives.

TRANSCEND YOUR PERSONAL INTERESTS

Real success, like happiness, is not a goal or a target. It is a by-product of a dedication to a cause or purpose greater than one's self. When we reach beyond the satisfaction of our own limited needs, we enter the realm of ultimate meaning.

This personal transcendence is for some a religious or spiritual relationship. For others it is our connection with a greater good or with the human spirit. It is sometimes experienced when we are part of a team—doing and being with others. On a team with "team spirit," for example, the greatest reward is being part of the team, part of the process, and not necessarily contingent on the final result of our efforts.

No matter who we are or where we work, the opportunity to go beyond our own interests is almost always present. Companies that can look beyond the bottom line and bring meaning to the business at hand also bring meaning to everyone who works there. It takes more than good intentions to grow meaning in a corporation. For one thing, corporations are not in business to grow meaning! It requires courage and a deep commitment to meaningful personal values on the part of corporate leaders to place meaning before quarterly profits.

LIVING AND WORKING WITH MEANING

The opposite of meaning is despair—a condition brought on by the apparent meaninglessness of life. Each of us has the freedom and responsibility to place ourselves somewhere along a continuum that connects the two. Success or failure in the eyes of others has no bearing at all on where we stand with regard to meaning. A low-profile, low-paying job in a setting filled with meaningful purpose or one where we are able to fully realize our personal values in relationship to our work can fill us with a sense of meaning and purpose. It can truly make life worth living.

When we connect with ourselves, our coworkers, or to the task at hand, we experience meaning. When we continuously adjust our attitudes and reflect on the choices and possibilities open to us, we will be led to discover meaning. No matter what our job or our personal situation is, we can transform it with meaning.

2   Toxic Emotions at Work

Peter J. Frost

Summary Prepared by Gary J. Colpaert

Gary J. Colpaert received a B.A. in Business Administration from the University of Minnesota Duluth and a master's degree in Health Care Administration from the University of Wisconsin in Madison. He worked for the U.S.S. Great Lakes Fleet, with his responsibilities there including marketing, sales, and running the day-to-day operations of the commercial fleet. After leaving Duluth, Gary held the position of Vice President of Clinical and Support Systems at the Children's Hospital of Wisconsin and then became the Executive Vice President of the Blood Center of Southeast Wisconsin. Gary is currently the Administrative Director of the Eye Institute in Milwaukee. He has developed and implemented internal coaching programs, a Winning at Work program, and a Leadership Intensive program. He leads a men's group whose members are interested in leading an authentic life of leadership and service and also has a meditation practice that includes a yearly 10-day period of silence.

OVERVIEW

Work organizations and their leaders sometimes take actions—intentional and unintentional—that cause emotional pain to their employees. That pain can become toxic and thus have a negative effect on the organization. Alternatively, there is a meaningful role for compassion in an organization, and managers face the task of handling toxic emotions and their consequences for those people who experience pain in the workplace. In short, *compassionate companies can improve their toxin-handling practices.*

Organizations by their very nature create a regular supply of emotional pain. New bosses, mergers, layoffs, stifling or confusing policies, salary decisions, and even the way that changes are communicated can all be sources of emotional pain felt by all organizational members. If the pain cannot be dissipated, it will, at a minimum, become a source of decreased productivity and a toxic condition that renders significant negative consequences for the organization and its staff.

Most organizational leaders lack the awareness to encounter and neutralize toxins, and therefore an informal structure of **toxin handlers** emerges that takes on the difficult (often unsupported) work of maintaining emotional homeostasis. The large amount of emotional pain

Peter J. Frost. *Toxic Emotions at Work: How Compassionate Managers Handle Pain and Conflict.* Boston, MA: Harvard Business School Press, 2003.

caused by organizations, the unrecognized value of engaging this pain, and the already heavy workload of toxin handlers put the organization at risk for not having the capacity to deal with the emotional pain it creates.

SPECIFIC SKILLS NEEDED BY AN EFFICIENT TOXIN HANDLER

A Gallup poll of two million employees revealed the value of compassionate managers, finding that most people value having a caring boss higher than money or the fringe benefits they receive. It takes some basic skills to be an effective toxin handler:

- Reading emotional cues of others and themselves
- Keeping people connected and in communication
- Acting to alleviate the suffering of others
- Mobilizing people to deal with their pain and get back to a stable state
- Building a team environment that rewards compassionate action

The impact of using these skills to diminish the emotional pain of even one person in the organization can have a significant positive impact on the whole organization.

USEFUL PRACTICES

Compassionate organizations promote a healthy, productive culture through a set of policies, procedures, and belief systems that produce generative responses from people at all levels of the organization. Useful compassionate practices include the following:

- Identifying a link between the emotional health of the organization and the bottom line;
- Recognizing and rewarding managers who are good at handling emotional pain;
- Using hiring practices that emphasize attitude as well as technical skill;
- Maintaining fair-minded practices consistent with loyalty, responsibility, and the fostering of community in the workplace;
- Implementing intervention strategies during times of distress and initiating rehab strategies to ensure long-term vitality; and
- Building a culture that values compassion.

Studies reveal a direct correlation between harmony in the workplace (as a result of these compassionate practices) and company profits. For example, there is a 20 percent increase in survival probability for firms that are one standard deviation above the mean as compared to organizations one standard deviation below the mean on the dimension of valuing human resources.

TOXIN HANDLERS

The work of the toxin handler is to respond compassionately to pain in the organization, reduce its impact, and enable people to return to constructive behaviors. Toxin handlers have complex profiles. They are caregivers, leaders, social architects, and builders of productive systems of relationships. Their work reflects five major themes:

- *Listening:* providing moments of human compassion by giving attention and consideration to the pain of others;
- *Holding Space for Healing:* providing support and time needed for healing;

- *Buffering Pain:* reframing communications, using political capital, building relationships, displaying personal courage;
- *Extricating Others from Painful Situations:* making the decision to get people out of the situation causing the pain; and
- *Transforming Pain:* framing pain in constructive ways by changing the view of painful experiences and coaching.

BURNOUT CAN OCCUR

The potential toll on toxin handlers is, not surprisingly, burnout. Without support and the ability to "decompress," the toxin handler can suffer psychological, physical, and professional setbacks. Often anger and guilt are the first symptoms of problems developing within the toxin handler. It is imperative for a toxin handler to manage negative emotions because the effects of stress last a significant period of time. Stress impairs the immune system and has been shown to influence the brain's neurological pathways.

Paying attention to others more than themselves has its costs, and the potential for becoming addicted to helping others is real. A trap that toxin handlers may frequently fall into is having an agenda for the person being helped. Another particular problem that handlers often face is that they may not know how to handle their own pain. If they overidentify with the role, they may have the incorrect perception that there is no one else they can count on for help. It may be difficult to maintain their perspective or manage their time when results of this type of work are ambiguous. Adding to the potential for burnout is that all of this work is in addition to the stress and strain of their life experience outside of work.

PROVIDING ASSISTANCE

Healing the handlers is possible when there is a clear personal vision of why they are helping someone, when they are provided with the tools and skills to protect themselves, and when conversations are held that recognize and bring into consciousness the intention to not get overly involved emotionally with the people in pain.

A game plan for self-protection that includes options for action is critical for long-term success. World-class athletes, for example, overcome stress through methods including hydration, physical movement, mental change of channels, balanced eating programs, and emotionally changing channels. It is also necessary to build up one's reserves in advance, and this can be fostered by:

- *Increasing One's Physical Strength:* keeping fit; getting a massage.
- *Boosting One's Emotional Capacity:* staying positive; not taking things personally; accepting what you can't change.
- *Regenerating Mental Capacity:* refocusing the mind; creating personal space; developing mental sanctuaries; learning to say no.
- *Building Spiritual Capacity:* being clear on values; revering one's life balance.

AIDING AND SUPPORTING TOXIN HANDLERS

What handlers and their organizations can do at the interface between the handler, the organization, and the person in pain is to generate an increased level of organizational understanding, respect, and language for the role and work of toxin handling. This results in the toxin handler's feeling connected and less isolated. There is power in naming this work as a positive, contributing factor in the organization's success. The way in which this work is spoken about is a critical factor in building a compassionate organization. For example, the question "What did you do at work today?" is typically difficult for a toxin handler to answer. A positive way for the toxin handler to answer this question is to acknowledge that there is a lot of pain in the office and to express feeling that progress is being made toward shifting the situation. Other positive actions for the handlers to systematically manage and diffuse the emotional pain in organizational life include the following:

- Acknowledging the dynamic, by naming the work, giving it legitimacy, and creating a forum to talk about it.
- Offering support, by encouraging toxin handlers to meet with professionals/experts for assistance.
- Assigning handlers to **safe zones**, by sending toxin handlers to an outside conference.
- Modeling healthy behavior, by having top leaders demonstrate and reinforce the behaviors.
- Creating a supportive culture, by allowing them to learn from each other.

WHAT DO COMPASSIONATE LEADERS DO?

Leaders sometimes create painful messes by themselves. When this happens, they need a repertoire of personal pain-handling skills. Compassionate leaders:

- Pay attention, because there is always pain in the room.
- Put people first, so as to keep the feelings and the well-being of staff in mind when decisions are made.
- Practice **professional intimacy** by empathizing without clouded judgment or overidentification.
- Plant seeds, by thinking long term and noticing the power of leadership's compassionate actions.
- Push back, by addressing the toxic sources, whether they be people or systems.

Leaders must be willing to place responsibility where it belongs (with whoever is accountable for the toxicity) and then sharpen the practices just listed so that the organization is responsive to pain.

THREE MAJOR STRATEGIES

The compassionate company is more than just the leaders and gifted people who excel at handling toxic situations. The institutional venues and structures necessary to create healthy and productive workplaces can be compared to a biological system. Toxins are natural by-products in a biological system. Using the metaphor, three sets of strategies become apparent for use before, during, and after the toxic situation:

1. *Prevention* can be accomplished by choosing new people wisely, developing existing staff, being fair minded, and setting a healthful tone.
2. *Intervention* can be implemented by dealing with downturns, dealing with acute trauma, being visible, creating meaning for the pain, and providing a context to talk about the pain.
3. *Restoration and recovery* occur when managers demonstrate patience and trust, provide guidance, acknowledge pain, and then focus on constructive actions for resolving it.

ORGANIZATIONAL AND INDIVIDUAL CAPACITY FOR HANDLING TOXIC SITUATIONS

The following list of questions can help the organization make an assessment of its organizational capacity and individual capacity for compassionate response(s).

For *organizational* capacity, consider the following:

- What is the breadth of resources that can be provided to the people in need—money, work flexibility, or physical aid as well as others' time and attention?
- What is the volume of resources (time and attention) required by the people who are suffering?
- How quickly can a response to the suffering be delivered?
- How specialized is the need in the organization?

For *individual* capacity, consider the following:

- Can you listen and be aware of grief and maintain awareness of your own and others' response to it?
- Do you know how to support initiatives that come from subordinates that may be outside of organizational norms?
- Have you expressed sympathy to others in the past, and can you imagine doing that in the context of your work life?
- Can you deal with fast-moving changes in circumstances that have an emotional focus?

Conclusion

Paying attention to these kinds of questions and pondering how the person or the organization would answer them is an effective initial response. This can lead to a greater acknowledgment of the emotional toxicity and pain, broader self-awareness in the organization, and (hopefully) utilization of the strategies for increasing the capacity for compassionate responses within the organization.

3

The Upside of Irrationality (and) Predictably Irrational

By Dan Ariely

Summary Prepared by Fred J. Dorn

Dr. Fred J. Dorn has had a broad and varied career related to the disciplines of management, psychology, and counseling. Presently he is a Clinical Professor of Psychology teaching industrial and organizational psychology on behalf of the University of Mississippi while serving as the managing principal of a boutique management consulting firm he founded more than 20 years ago known as Career Management Resources. Prior to teaching industrial and organizational psychology courses, he served as a Clinical Professor of Management with the School of Business at the University of Mississippi. From a practice, research, and theoretical perspective he is most interested in all things related to career management and vocational psychology.

THE 64,000-DOLLAR QUESTION

Here is a question for you to consider. When it comes to removing a bandage from a wound, do you pull it off quickly or slowly? Some would say that it is better to get through the pain in a short period of time, whereas others would argue for a slower action. Both that question and some other very interesting questions of both a business and personal nature can be answered from the perspective of behavioral economics.

Are We Rational or Irrational?

Many people, in their everyday lives as well as in the world of business, take personal and professional pride in the decisions they make—obtaining the best price for the goods and services they purchase, how they manage their relationships, or the manner in which they utilize their time. They even take pride in the people they establish relationships with, and at the most significant level the persons they choose to spend their lives with as a mate or significant other. They tell themselves as well as those around them, "Look at me—I have made decisions in a reasonable and rational manner." In reality, however, this is not necessarily so.

    Behavioral economics seeks to understand the underlying reasons why human beings function as they do. This emerging discipline attempts to identify and assess the numerous influences in the environment that creep into the decisions humans make (which ultimately bias the

Dan Ariely. *The Upside of Irrationality: The Unexpected Benefits of Defying Logic.* New York: Harper Perennial, 2011

Dan Ariely. *Predictably Irrational: The Hidden Forces That Shape Our Decisions.* New York: Harper Perennial, 2010.

outcomes). Behavioral economists are interested in understanding human weakness and determining how people can be taught to avoid temptation, increase self-control, and become more efficient in reaching their long-term goals. It is conceivable that more control can be achieved over people's careers, their investments, the distribution of their resources, the allocation of their time, and the opportunity for relationships—be it with a friend, spouse, or significant other.

The Yerkes-Dodson Law and the Theory of Cognitive Dissonance

Behavioral economists borrow from other disciplines in an attempt to build an integrated and persuasive case for some of the conclusions they reach. Psychology is one such discipline, and two well-known concepts from psychology are particularly applicable: the Yerkes-Dodson Law and the Theory of Cognitive Dissonance.

The **Yerkes-Dodson Law** is best exemplified by an experiment addressing the issues of incentive and performance. Laboratory rats were administered three levels of electrical shock— low, medium, and high. The levels of shock were administered in an attempt to teach rats certain tasks, such as navigating their way through different mazes. Experimenters predicted that the rats would learn quicker or demonstrate motivation to avoid being shocked (which in this case was learning) if the intensity of the shock was greater. Stated another way, performance level was predicted to increase (learning the maze) if sufficient incentive was present (avoiding being shocked). Therefore, the higher the level of shock, presumably the greater would be the incentive to perform.

Contrary to advance expectations, performance peaked at a certain level of shock (around the medium level) and then tapered off as the shock levels increased. In short, *(negative) incentives to perform only work up to a certain level and then performance drops regardless of the incentive present.* CEO pay provides a good example of this as well. Logic suggests that the higher the incentive to perform, the greater would be the organization's performance. But time and time again, when CEO pay reaches a certain level, the firm's financial performance tends to drop and shareholders are disappointed.

The Theory of Cognitive Dissonance

Human beings take pride in making sure that their attitudes and their behavior are consistent—or at least appear that way. When they become out of alignment, humans tend to feel uncomortable.

Leon Festinger, a noted social psychologist, articulated the powerful concept of the **Theory of Cognitive Dissonance**. He suggested that *the experience of a simultaneous contradiction between one's own contrasting attitudes, values, or emotions will generate a certain level of discomfort* (e.g., surprise, guilt, or embarrassment), which then motivates the person to find some way to reduce the discomfort or anxiety. This change usually comes in the form of creating an explanation (rationale) for the divergent attitudes, or by creating a more consistent value system by modifying one's attitudes.

Physical Attractiveness

The phenomenon of "birds of a feather flock together" is another area of intrigue. Known as **assortative mating** by social scientists, the concept under study is physical attractiveness. To the dismay of many, physical attractiveness in our society, more than any other attribute, tends to define our place in the social hierarchy.

Of course, if you are sitting on the top rungs of the ladder of attractiveness, life can be good. But what if you are not? Do people who are "aesthetically challenged" (people who are less attractive than those who are defined as physically attractive) adjust or adapt to a world that for all intents and purposes emphasizes one's physical attractiveness over other attributes?

Some people do a better job than others. Initially, for example, men do a poorer job of realizing that some dating or matchmaking opportunities are beyond their grasp.

Some of the research on this topic generated the following conclusions:

- Men are less selective about the overtures or expressions of interest they make than are women.
- Men are more concerned with "physical attractiveness" (or, in more contemporary language, "hotness").
- Men are less concerned with their own attractiveness (and yet you might think they would or should be more concerned).
- Men are more hopeful or even unrealistic, as they are far more likely to seek out women who are "out of their league" aesthetically.

   Woman do not exhibit this tendency nearly as often. Of course, as some men experienced more and more rejection in these thwarted efforts, they began to temper their expectations and adjusted their level of reaching out so that they eventually met with greater success.

Eventually, however, things work out for just about everyone. After a while almost everyone begins to realize at some level what their own overall (true) rating is within a point or so in either direction. For example, a "6" male (on a 10-point scale) comes to accept that he is in the 5–7 range and begins to seek out women who fall within this same range. Realistic females tend to respond (of course, far more selectively and probably not consciously) to men that fall in the 5- to 7-point range as well. Eventually, everyone finds someone, and more often than not whom they find falls within the scope of their own self-rating or the rating assigned to them by an independent group.

Research conducted with couples who have been together for 15 years or more reinforces this point. Asked independently of each other, they rated themselves and their significant other within two points of where they rated themselves in the first place. So, a 6 moving one point in either direction between 5 and 7 rated his or her spouse or significant other between 5 and 7 as well.

Cake Mixes Without Eggs?

Pride in creation and ownership is a quality we see in both business and in other human endeavors. Common examples include the inventor who starts a business or the amateur chef who takes great pride in an innovative recipe.

When semi-prepared foods, such as "instant" cake mixes (that simply require adding water) were introduced to the market around mid-century, the response from housewives of the day was less than enthusiastic. However, mixes requiring only water for piecrusts and biscuits did quite well. The apparent difference lies in the fact that when cakes are served they are often served alone. Therefore, those who are eating the pastry chef's creation of a cake are eating it as a complete reflection of the cook. Biscuits and piecrusts, however, are part of a much larger picture or display. Biscuits are usually served with a meal or as part of a complete meal and piecrusts are nothing without pie-filling and whipped-cream or meringue toppings.

Ernest Dichter, a marketing and psychology expert in the 1940s, is credited with the realization that women were feeling not only guilty but less involved with the cake mixes when all they had to do was add water. They unconsciously wanted more pride of ownership and less guilt about the ease of using a cake mix. Dichter applied Freudian concepts to business problems and is credited with resolving this dilemma by simply suggesting that the manufacturers of cake mixes keep the eggs out of the mix as well. This became known as the **egg theory**, meaning that women felt better about using cake mixes if they had to add more than one ingredient to the recipe—such as eggs, oil, and water. The women of that era wanted to feel as though they weren't shortchanging their guests. The lesson from the egg theory? *People want to feel involved, and have a sense of contribution, pride, and psychological ownership.*

The "Not-Invented-Here" Bias

Many years ago, Sony Corporation achieved great success by introducing innovative and well-received products such as the transistor radio, the Walkman, and the Trinitron Tube. However, in response, other companies began introducing products such as the iPod and the Xbox. Sony held firm, believing outside ideas such as MP3 players and flat-screen TVs were not of much value, as Sony had not created them. The outcome of this strategy, of course, was disappointing. Many of the products Sony continued to focus on were of little interest to customers, including cameras that were not compatible with most of the forms of memory storage that eventually became popular. In effect, Sony fell victim to the **Not-Invented-Here (NIH) bias**—the tendency to like one's own ideas and to discount or reject those of others.

The NIH bias, like many other findings in behavioral economics, presents us with a double-edged sword, and so it should be examined carefully. On the one hand, there is tremendous merit to the pride of ownership that results from development of something new. It can inspire a group of employees (such as those at Apple Corporation who worked under the late CEO Steve Jobs), pushing them to extremes in terms of commitment and performance. However, there are times when creative groups become fixated on their idea or solution to the exclusion of a more obvious, simpler, and less expensive approach to the problem. At that point, the NIH bias imposes dangerous blinders on those persons and organizations.

Returning to the Bandage Question

Remember the question about how rapidly bandages should be removed from a patient? The presumptive answer was that it is better to remove them rapidly rather than slowly. What was the long-held rationale for this approach? Because it presumably causes the patient less discomfort. But what is the surprisingly real answer to this behavioral question? The rapid removal of bandages from patients became standard practice because it reduced the discomfort level of the *caregivers.* They could rip off the bandages, move on to the next patient, and avoid having to hear the cries of pain for very long. Like many other issues in human behavior, *what we first believe to be true (or have historically been taught) may not be consistent with the results of scientific studies.*

PART FOURTEEN

Social Technologies at Work

One of the most powerful and pervasive trends affecting employers that has emerged in the twenty-first century is the dramatic growth in the use of social technologies. These are in addition to the previous and still-dominant factors of information technology development. Both readings in this section address this phenomenon—the first by suggesting ways in which to capitalize on the "groundswell," the second by offering down-to-earth advice for preparing powerful content via those social technology channels.

Josh Bernoff and Charlene Li are the authors of *Groundswell.* Bernoff is Senior Vice President for Idea Development at Forrester Research, where he created an approach to classifying customers according to how they approach technology. He has written for the *New York Times, Wall Street Journal*, and *Advertising Age.* Charlene Li was Vice President and Principal Analyst at Forrester Research and has served as a consultant with Monitor Group in Boston and Amsterdam. Her ideas on interactive media, social technologies, and marketing appear in her blog, The Altimeter.

In *Groundswell*, Li and Bernoff identify three key trends—emerging interactive technologies, a strong desire among people to connect with each other, and online economics (through online advertising)—that combine to produce an unprecedented opportunity for businesses. The dominant groundswell is "a social trend in which people use a variety of technologies to get what they need from each other." These technologies include those used in MySpace, Facebook, YouTube, Wikipedia, eBay, Craigslist, LinkedIn, blogs, and Twitter. Bernoff and Li advocate using one or more of five progressive approaches to engage the groundswell: listening, talking, energizing, supporting, or embracing.

Ann Handley and C. C. Chapman, the coauthors of *Content Rules*, are business writers, speakers, and consultants to major corporations. Handley is the Chief Content Officer of MarketingProfs and a blogger about online business and marketing issues. Chapman is the creator of DigitalDads.com (an online parenting space), an online marketing expert, as well as an entrepreneur and media creator.

Handley and Chapman focus on technological content—anything that is uploaded to a website, such as photos, blogs, FAQs, videos, webinars, and written words. They believe that it is critical to have highly engaging content in order to build a recognizable brand and strong relationships with customers. Strong content should exhibit energy, demonstrate a clear purpose, and add value to the message. The authors provide practical suggestions for brand building, choosing the best format, and communicating through engaging stories, authenticity, humor, and originality. The principles they espouse are equally applicable to webinars, podcasts, videos, blogs, e-books, and the entire spectrum of social technologies in vogue today (e.g., Facebook, LinkedIn, Twitter).

1

Groundswell

Charlene Li and Josh Bernoff
Summary Prepared by Amber Christian

Amber Christian is consulting partner at Phoenix Endeavors, LLC. She assists clients in implementing and enhancing financial systems processes. She received her M.B.A. from the University of Minnesota Carlson School of Management and undergraduate degrees in Management Information Sciences and Organizational Management from the University of Minnesota Duluth.

INTRODUCTION

As online technologies evolve, it is easier than ever for individuals to connect with each other. This trend began simply with e-commerce and grew as more people gained Internet access and comfort levels. Critical mass was reached as the majority of North America and Europe began using the Internet. The transformation of technologies has now created a world where a consumer can be online virtually anywhere, at any time. Today the consumer also has the ability to obtain information without relying on traditional sources, and increasingly makes purchasing decisions without input from the seller of the goods and services. This has far-reaching implications for companies today and into the future.

Groundswell represents the major trends in online technologies and shifting consumer behavior that are forcing companies to reexamine their traditional marketing and customer interaction models. As these new models emerge, it is easy for a company to place its focus on any one online technology as the answer to interact with the customer. The technologies enabling the groundswell are viewed by many businesses as a problem to be solved. However, they are really only intended to be the medium used to reach customers in order to build relationships. Horror stories abound of bad public relations generated from dissatisfied customers in the online community. The inability to completely control a message about a brand or a company makes many businesses nervous, as significant time and money have been expended to build brands and reputations. It is difficult to understand how to engage this groundswell, but a description of the major online trends and recommendations for addressing the online community can help substantially. Each trend identified is supported with case studies to demonstrate how companies can be successful when engaging their customers.

Charlene Li and Josh Bernoff. *Groundswell: Winning in a World Transformed by Social Technologies.* Boston, MA: Harvard University Press, 2008.

SOCIAL TECHNOGRAPHICS PROFILE

Who is participating in the groundswell? Why do they participate? These are the first two fundamental questions to answer. *Understanding why your customers participate provides direction on how to engage them to participate with you.* The **Social Technographics profile** was created with the central idea that not all participants in the groundswell will participate in the same way. This profile groups participants into six different types: creators, critics, collectors, joiners, spectators, and inactives. *Creators* are the most active participants and typically generate original content. This group includes people who post articles, write blogs, and upload their own videos to YouTube. As a much larger group than creators, *critics* generate content through responding to the content generated online by others. Critics participate in online forums, respond to blogs and articles, and write product or service reviews. *Collectors* aggregate information to centralize in one place. They typically use services such as **Really Simple Syndication (RSS) feeds**—a technological process that allows readers to subscribe to areas of content interest and automatically receive updates in a standardized form from a site when new content is published. *Joiners* participate in social networking. They are found on Facebook, MySpace, LinkedIn, and other social networking sites. Joiners are a large group with continued growth trends. However, the largest online group is *spectators*. This group reviews the content generated by others, reads blogs and product reviews, and watches online media. Finally, the last group is the nonparticipants. These *inactives* include both those customers who are online and offline. This group does not participate in the groundswell and is served through traditional marketing.

A company can align each of the types with different age groups and genders to provide a mechanism to refine the classification of its customers. This helps explain why customers participate in a particular way. These classifications help direct the focus of marketing efforts to reach customers. Marketing budgets typically include online and more traditional sources, and expenditures must be prioritized. There are a variety of options when moving to online sources, depending upon the available budget. The process to begin engaging the groundswell does not have to be expensive. Monitoring customer feedback through existing channels is one inexpensive way to begin the process. Other efforts such as creating an online community will require significantly more time and money and must be prioritized against other marketing objectives.

TAPPING THE GROUNDSWELL

It is very easy to become trapped in the "me, too" phenomenon, where anything a competitor does online must be responded to equally and immediately. This is often done regardless of whether the strategy and logic behind the competitor's actions are well understood or should even be replicated. Instead of simply copying a competitor's strategy, a four-step process called the POST method can be used to plan a groundswell strategy. This process consists of the following steps:

- *People:* What is the Social Technographics profile of my customers? Do they even participate in the groundswell? Are they more likely to create content, or respond to content? This profile will provide both the motivation behind a customer's actions and ideas on the features and functionality required in the technology that is used to address them.
- *Objectives:* What is our company's purpose in participating? Are we going to energize our customers to drive sales, gain insights to help market our products, or simply listen to what

our customers say about us and our products? The objectives clarify goals against which to measure progress.

- **Strategy:** How do we want to interact with our customers? How will we measure our progress? How will we manage changes within our company after the relationship with our customers begins to deepen? Engaging the customer in a deeper relationship over time will require your company to change.
- **Technology:** This should be addressed only after the previous three steps are in place, to ensure that the appropriate technologies are selected. Technology identifies what applications are necessary to engage customers, meet the objectives, and support your online strategy.

The POST method is very important to understand because *there is no one right way to engage the groundswell.* This method helps guide the planning to begin engaging your customers in new ways. There are five main approaches to use when engaging your customers: listening, talking, energizing, supporting, and embracing. One of the five typical approaches to successfully engage the groundswell should be selected in order to provide focus. Over time, the additional methods can be added. The approaches are progressive, with those first in the list requiring less commitment. *Companies should start small, learning how to work with the groundswell to build success.* Success in that step can then be used to progress to the next step. As a company actively engages the groundswell, it will shape the direction of the company.

Listening

Listening helps clarify what the market is saying about your brand. Traditionally, companies conduct focused market research to understand customer perceptions of their brand. Traditional marketing is presented with the concept that a company owns its brands. According to groundswell theory, *it is actually the customers who own your brand.* Customers will speak vocally about your brand virtually anywhere online. The sheer volume of different mediums (blogs, online forums, Web pages, etc.) makes it difficult to obtain actionable information. There are two primary strategies for listening: private communities and brand monitoring.

Private communities are an active strategy for listening. These communities offer a two-way conversation between the company and the customer. Although this is important, an even more powerful connection can be forged in these communities between your customers. These connections can provide insights to questions a company may never think to ask! Through listening on a private community, Memorial Sloan-Kettering Cancer Center learned that reputation was not the deciding factor for choosing a cancer center. A cancer diagnosis is frightening, and most people are not aware of how the treatment process begins, or where to go for treatment. The Center learned that the recommendation of the primary care doctor whom the patient trusts is more important than any national rankings. This helped the Center realize that advertising its ranking is less important than making sure primary care doctors understand its services.

Brand monitoring is a passive strategy for listening that seeks primarily to hear what the groundswell is saying about your brand. Has someone started a fan group on Facebook? Are blogs speaking about products and services positively or negatively? Are videos posted about products on YouTube? Given the sheer volume of media content available on the Internet, brand monitoring may best be outsourced. Firms have been created to specialize in the aggregation of this information. They can provide aggregated data that are more actionable in order to minimize the time required for this activity.

Talking

Traditionally, talking with customers is fulfilled through advertising and public relations. Marketers create messages aimed at the mass market through television commercials and print ads. Public relations departments seek free publicity through news and magazine coverage. This publicity may be related to company sales, new product launches, or anything else that increases positive exposure of the company in the mass media. Traditional advertising and public relations typically focus on traditional sources. To engage the groundswell, the focus needs to move to online advertising. Although there are several ways to do this, two potential approaches include utilizing social networking sites and creating blogs. Utilizing social networking sites requires joining sites such as Facebook and MySpace. This allows a company to create content aimed at the specific audience that uses these sites. Depending upon the objectives previously determined using the POST method, for example, a page on Facebook could be used to allow customers to provide input on a particular product design. However, a clear strategy will need to be in place first due to the interactive content on these sites. Some questions to consider include: How will your fans connect with you? How will you respond to their postings? This approach works well when there is already strong brand loyalty for your product and your target audience utilizes these sites.

Creating blogs is another approach that can be used to reach your audience. Before launching a blog, carefully consider the process involved in creating and maintaining a blog, and ask a series of questions. Why will this blog be created? (Understanding the goals for the blog gives direction to shape the blog.) What will be accomplished by publishing on this blog? (There is a difference between blogging to announce new products for a company and blogging about a particular product or product line.) Who will write for the blog? (Finding an executive sponsor who is willing to commit the time to write for the blog and sponsor it are key components to this process.) Finally, how often will content be published, and how will the target audience know your blog exists? *None of the goals for blogging can be reached if your core audience does not even know you are there!*

Energizing

Energizing is used to start the word-of-mouth engine. Word of mouth succeeds because it is credible and self-spreading. The same characteristics that can work against a company when spreading negative publicity can be channeled to create a positive message when a customer has a good experience. Positive "spin" has been used in politics for many years. In the online space, creators are typically the group to focus on if energizing is used because they generate original content. There are three main considerations in energizing your customers. What is the Social Technographics profile of my customers (i.e., how do I engage them)? What is the problem my customers are trying to solve? Can I afford to stick around for the long haul? The final question is the most important. Once customers are engaged in a community, it is difficult to take that community away without generating negative backlash.

Supporting

Allowing the groundswell to support itself by enabling people to connect with each other is another key approach. Traditional customer support models are built to deal with issues after a product has been sold. If support systems are being utilized, it means there is an issue with the product. Proper levels of staffing to maintain support for products already sold can be very expensive. Creating the ability for customers to support each other can translate into cost savings for product support. Dell embarked on creating a community support forum to allow users to support each other. This allows customers to post questions, and other customers are able to answer questions. So why would anyone take the time to answer questions for a complete stranger? Dell learned that *customers who answer questions value the mental rewards they receive for helping people.* Some of these customers will spend many hours helping others without receiving any compensation from Dell. All parties benefit in this case: The customer with the question receives an answer, the customer assisting receives mental rewards, and Dell receives fewer support calls. This has translated to significant cost savings for Dell in the area of customer support. Systems that allow supporting each other should be designed with mental rewards in mind. This entices customers to participate in helping others.

Embracing

Embracing utilizes the groundswell to innovate with help from potential or existing customers. There are currently no unique technologies specifically used for embracing. This objective is the culmination of engaging the groundswell. The previous methods begin to shape a company, and embracing brings the customer more fully into the development life cycle. Customers want to be engaged and provide feedback. They will ask for products and services that a company may not even have designed yet. After a company is able to successfully engage the groundswell, it is more likely to continue to do it as part of its business. The evolutionary process for a company has now begun, and this becomes part of the company's identity over time.

THE GROUNDSWELL TRANSFORMS

The journey to engage the groundswell influences a company from the outside. Although this is important, an internal groundswell can also be leveraged to change from the inside out. Just as listening and talking can be used with customers, they can also be used with employees. Best Buy, for example, successfully created an internal site called blueshirtnation.com to help engage employees. With over 1,200 stores, there are many employees in blue shirts at the stores. Employees have different levels of commitment to the company. This site was created to help these employees feel connected on a day-to-day basis and help each other solve problems. An associate at one store can post product questions or issues and get answers from an associate at another store. This saves the company time and money.

What is the future of the groundswell? How does a company prepare for the changes in the groundswell itself that will require the company to respond? The best strategy for addressing these continuous changes is not found in technology. Remember, the groundswell is not about technology—it is about people and relationships. *Listening to your customers, developing relationships with them, and being collaborative will provide a solid long-term foundation as the groundswell continues to evolve.*

2

Content Rules

Ann Handley and C. C. Chapman
Summary Prepared by Richard Kimbrough

Richard Kimbrough is a Senior Lecturer in the College of Business Administration at the University of Nebraska—Lincoln. He has taught in high schools and colleges from Illinois to California and has served as a visiting professor in several republics of the old Soviet Union. In 1991 he received the Leavey Award for Excellence in Free Enterprise Education. Through his own company he has provided more than 1,000 entrepreneurship programs in schools around the nation. He is the author of 11 books, including a national-prize-winning juvenile novel.

CONTENT IS THE KEY

With the use of online technological tools the ability of businesses to reach customers and potential customers has vastly increased and been greatly enhanced. Marketing success for online businesses can be significantly improved by creating "killer" content, which is compelling content that grabs the viewer, is of interest and of use to the viewer, and, in many instances, might be shared with others by the initial viewer.

What Is Content?

Content is broadly defined as any writing, photos, graphs, charts, and the like produced for not only business websites, but also for any other social media, including blogs, Twitter, Facebook, LinkedIn, and more. The purpose of creating engaging and useful content is to convert passive viewers into active purchasers by developing relationships with viewers so that they know, trust, and like a company's product or service even to the extent that many will share the company's content with other potential buyers.

One important benefit of producing strong content is the elimination of the possible—and often probable—annoyance of customers and would-be customers caused by bombarding them with advertisements, phone calls, and direct mail. Properly done, content is not simply "copywriting." It is relating stories.

Ann Handley and C. C. Chapman. *Content Rules: How to Create Killer Blogs, Podcasts, Videos, Ebooks, Webinars (and More) That Engage Customers and Ignite Your Business.* New York: Wiley, 2010.

Publishing

Publishing content on websites is similar to what book and magazine publishers do; *they learn the interests and needs of their prospective readers and then publish material that addresses those interests and needs.* Therefore, a **targeted approach** is needed to determine the profile of customers and potential customers and write content for them. Before publishing any online content, a business must answer the following questions:

- What is your purpose in creating content?
- Whom are you trying to reach?
- How will the content be created?
- On what online sites will the content be placed?

To succeed in publishing, *a business must differentiate its message;* it cannot be the same as its competitors. The online business must develop a distinct identity that will set it apart. The most effective way to differentiate online is through unique content—through *stories that are appealing, creative, and bold*—stories that viewers find engaging and useful.

The Art of Effective Storytelling

The stories developed and used as online content *must fit the targeted audience.* As an example, a speaker addressing high school students about driving safely and another speaking to a group of senior citizens about the same topic might have an identical objective in mind—to reduce auto accidents—but each speaker would use different examples, language, voice, tone, and gestures to illustrate similar points. *Content stories* are the most effective way for a company to create and build a **brand**, that is, the image that viewers have of the company. Successful branding is crucial to developing customer relationships. These brand-building stories should:

- Be original and bold (definitely not bland).
- Be written conversationally in a "human" voice. Do not attempt to dazzle with a "professional" vocabulary. Be authentic.
- Show passion in the content and enthusiasm for your product or service.
- When appropriate, demonstrate a sense of humor or inject your personality.
- Show clearly how the company's product or service can help the viewer.

Who Creates and Develops Content?

It is important to include all departments of a company in creating and developing content. Although the marketing department might appear to be the logical creator of content, every other department should play a contributory role.

Depending on several factors (e.g., the size of the company, knowing how to create compelling content, the writing ability of the management and staff), a business may need someone to fill the position of "**Content Creator**." This person must possess several skills, including:

- The ability to recognize a good story, and know how to make it interesting.
- A thorough knowledge of all social media and how they mesh and blend.
- The capacity to build and nurture relationships (be a "people person").

What Format Should Be Used for Content?

Content should be created around a **major theme**—a basic storyline or dominant underlying message. Thus, much of the content can be used in the larger social media sites—e-books, company websites, case studies, webinars, white papers—and shorter versions can be used for blogs, newsletter pieces, and on such sites as Twitter, Facebook, and LinkedIn. It is desirable to have as many content sources available for use as possible.

A Publishing Schedule

Content should be produced on a predetermined schedule. Some content may be offered daily through tweets, Facebook, or replies to blogs. More content, but still based on the major theme, may be sent weekly, including new blogs, helpful how-to advice, and updates on the company website. Once a month an e-mail newsletter may be sent, or perhaps a video podcast, a guest posting, or a variety of other relevant materials. Content may be sent quarterly or even yearly.

Although the major theme should be kept in mind and a publishing schedule created, it is best to start small using only two or three social media sites. Starting small permits a company to gauge the success of its initial content efforts and tune and tweak as needed.

Content Is a "Help" Tool

Content must be of real value to the business's customers and potential customers. Although a company's ultimate storytelling objective is to drive up revenues, first and foremost it must connect in a human way with customers and potential customers by demonstrating its humanity and caring philosophy. Thus, the stories should meet the following criteria:

- They should be factual, not made up.
- Each should have a clear message.
- People should be at the core of most stories.
- They should show that the company is a caring company.
- They should provide a fresh slant on things.
- They should surprise the audience with the unexpected.

Rather than advertising the superiority of their product or service through content on websites, companies should provide information about how others use their wares with a view toward meeting the needs of others and solving the problems of others.

Using Content from Other Sources

Often some appealing content written by customers or other viewers may appear on other websites and may be republished on a company's site; this is known as **user-generated content**. Several questions must be asked before using outside material, including:

- Is the content compatible with the company theme?
- Does the manner of presentation match the company's content?
- Is the outside content licensed?

Sometimes user-generated content may be suitable for inclusion on a company's site. Encouraging satisfied customers to provide content has the advantage of creating a virtual community that may enhance customer relationships. A negative side of user-generated content is that inevitably some customers will write negative reviews.

Where Is It; How Do I Get to It; Can I Use It?

A business's content must be easily found. Information given through the use of **multiple key words** makes it easier for users to find the content. Bearing in mind that today many instruments are available to browsers, a business should make sure that its content is available on as many instruments as possible. Finally, encourage viewers to share content on and across websites. This can increase the effect of a business's content.

B2B Content

All of the information previously given relating to content also applies to businesses selling to other businesses (B2B); however, some differences exist in B2B marketing. It is important for the seller to know the prospective buyer and how that person makes buying decisions. B2B buyers are unique. Some take a long time to make purchasing decisions; others are more direct and take less time. Some seek advice from associates; others are "lone ranger" purchasers. Some have only long-time "crony" businesses from which they buy; others are open to buying from a number of companies.

USING DIFFERENT SOCIAL MEDIA FOR CONTENT

Not only must a business understand how to develop strong content but it must also know where and how to place that content. Many social media avenues are available to businesses, including blogs, webinars, e-books, white papers, case studies, videos, podcasts, and photographs. The specific strengths of each of the social media sites are discussed here.

Blogs

Blogs are sites displaying comments (short or lengthy) on specific topics. Blogs are different from most other sites in that they are **interactive**—they can communicate back and forth with other websites. Because viewers can respond to them, they are a means of social networking. Therefore, if properly created and provided to readers on a regular schedule, blogs can serve as the foundation for a business's content. Several points are important to remember when creating and posting blogs, including:

- Identify the target reader.
- Be consistent in posting on a schedule.
- Use more than merely text; consider enlivening text with the use of graphics.
- Capture the reader's attention with provocative headlines.
- Classify each blog so that the reader can find similar blogs quickly.

Webinars

Web-based seminars in which online conferences may be held or lectures, training events, or other types of short presentations via the Internet are called **webinars**. Although webinars are often poorly done, when they are done in a relevant, zestful, fun way, they can be a very helpful marketing tool. The key points to focus on in doing webinars are:

- Decide what information the viewers need. (What problems do they have?)
- Illustrate the message with stories told in voice and visuals of how your business can help them attain their goals.
- Come up with great titles that cause the viewer to ask, "Hey! What's this?"
- Have dynamic presenters and moderators conduct the webinar.

E-books and White Papers

E-books are electronic books to be read on computers or on other social media sites. White papers provide information from experts in the field to help policymakers make decisions. In the business world, white papers have the ultimate objective of making sales. Although e-books and white papers may be quite similar, there are some differences. Usually both deal with one subject, but e-books are more loosely structured and present visuals as well as text. The key points relating to producing webinars are just as important in creating e-books or white papers.

E-books and white papers are most useful for businesses that:

- Need to clearly demonstrate their knowledge of a product or service.
- Need to appeal to potential customers who know little about their product.
- Have many customer success stories to tell.
- Can provide relevant and fresh information to specific industries.

Customer Success Stories

Creating a customer success story is fairly easy. It must be a *true* story, not fictional. It must be *interesting* to the recipient. It must have a *human side*—an approach that causes the reader to care what happens to the customer or business being portrayed.

The story should also emphasize the role that the business telling the story played in the customer's success. Customer success stories are best presented through videos.

Videos

Videos can provide very strong stories. They must tell *real stories*. They should feature *actual people* from the company doing the video. They should include testimonials or other positive material from a company's *customers and/or vendors*. It is imperative that all videos have a professional appearance. They lighting must be right; the camera must be steady; noise must be avoided; the microphone pick-up must be of high quality.

A company may produce several types of videos, including ones that show uses of its product or service, ones that show something about the production of its product, or ones that show event experiences.

Podcasts

Podcasts are programs to be played back on audio devices. For some desired outcomes they will serve a company's purposes better than videos. The rules for producing successful podcasts are similar to those for producing successful videos.

Photographs

A business can illustrate its operation, its people, its fun times, and more through still photos placed online, in brochures, or in other print marketing places. The photos must be tagged and described so that when they are shared the persons in the photos, the places they were taken, and other key information can be identified and verified.

EXAMPLES OF SUCCESSFUL CONTENT

Examples of strong, successful content developed for different forms of social media by a number of organizations are widely available, including a golf academy, the U.S. Army, Boeing, and an English enterprise that seeks to help young girls think positively. Businesses may adapt their own content and social networking based on these examples.

PART FIFTEEN

Management Fables: Lessons for Success

Two major interrelated phenomena in business book publishing emerged in the past quarter century. The first was to use the format of a brief "managerial fable" (fabricated storyline) to catch the reader's attention and as a format for presenting a few (usually four to eight) key lessons to readers in a simple, readable, straightforward form. The first book of significance to achieve substantial success with this format was *The One Minute Manager* (summarized in Part 2), followed by dozens of similarly structured books. The second phenomenon involved the explosion in demand (and products provided) for managerial "guidance" books that offered suggestions for personal success. The model of this genre of book in the modern era is unquestionably *The Seven Habits of Highly Effective People* (also summarized briefly in Part 2). This section of *The Manager's Bookshelf* brings you a sampling of these "fable-form" books.

Spencer Johnson (coauthor of *The One Minute Manager, The Present, "Yes" or "No": The Guide to Better Decisions, Peaks and Valleys,* and many others) is the author of *Who Moved My Cheese?*, which has sold over 10 million copies. This book catapulted to the top of best-seller lists for *USA Today, Publisher's Weekly,* the *Wall Street Journal,* and *BusinessWeek,* with some companies (e.g., Southwest Airlines and Mercedes-Benz) ordering thousands of copies to distribute to their employees. Written in the form of a fable about two mice and two small people living in a maze, Johnson suggests that change is rampant around us, and thus employees must anticipate, monitor, and adapt to change quickly in order to survive. Unfortunately, fear—and the tendency to cling to the familiar and comfortable past—prevents some people from letting go of old beliefs, attitudes, and paradigms.

The second book summarized in this section of *The Manager's Bookshelf* has a simple and surprisingly nonbusiness-sounding title: *Fish!* Like several other books (e.g., *The One Minute Manager, Zapp!, Heroz,* and *Who Moved My Cheese?*), which have also sold in large numbers, *Fish!* is short (about 100 pages), easy and quick to read, engaging, and written in the form of a parable. The authors (Lundin, Paul, and Christensen) provide a creative way to convey a central message—that work can (and should) be a joyful experience for all involved. Like any of the books summarized in this edition, we urge you to read the original source in its entirety and then reflect about what you have read. What are the roles of "fun" and "play" at work? Can such an environment be created? Is the conceptual foundation of the authors' message a solid one? Do negative implications as well as positive ones arise from creating a joyful experience at work?

Authors Lundin, Christensen, and Paul and Chart House Learning have also collaborated in the preparation of other products extending the Fish! philosophy and practice. Their follow-up books include *Fish! Tales, Fish! Sticks*, and *Fish! for Life*, and they also have a wide array of videos, calendars, training programs, apparel, and other related products available at their website, www.charthouse.com/home.asp. We think you will discover that despite the brevity, simplicity, and creative format of *Fish!*, useful ideas for action and debate can be found in this and almost any type of managerial literature. Like all ideas, of course, they need to be tested for their soundness, validity, and applicability.

Bob Pike, Robert Ford, and John Newstrom collaborated to produce a unique book, *The Fun Minute Manager.* They pick up on the theme that many organizations are actually toxic workplaces devoid of humor. Instead, they argue, managers should create a fun work environment that is characterized by humor, playful games, joyful celebrations, and recognition of achievements. Through an imaginative storyline, they develop nine key insights about fun at work, and offer 10 useful guidelines for new "fun minute managers."

Bob Pike, Chairman and CEO of the Bob Pike Group, is a member of the Speakers Hall of Fame. His creative presentations to annual conferences on participative approaches to training are legendary. Robert Ford holds a Ph.D. from Arizona State University and is currently a Professor at the University of Central Florida. His best-known book is *Managing the Guest Experience in Hospitality.* Dr. John Newstrom spent his academic career at the University of Minnesota Duluth, and is a self-styled funologist. He is the coauthor of over 45 books, including *Games Trainers Play, Transfer of Training*, and *The Manager's Bookshelf.*

Who Moved My Cheese?

Spencer Johnson
Summary Prepared by Gary Stark

Gary Stark is a faculty member at Northern Michigan University. He earned his Ph.D. in Management from the University of Nebraska, and subsequently taught at the University of Minnesota Duluth and Washburn University. Gary's research interests include recruiting, work–life balance, and the study of how and why people seek feedback on their work performance. Prior to his academic life, Gary earned his B.S. and M.B.A. degrees at Kansas State University and worked in Chicago as a tax accountant.

A REUNION

Several former classmates met in Chicago one Sunday, the day after their class reunion. After discussing the difficulties they had been having with the many changes in their lives since high school, one of the classmates, Michael, volunteered a story that had helped him deal with the changes in his life. The name of the story was "Who Moved My Cheese?"

THE STORY

The story revolved around four characters who spent their lives in a maze. The maze was a giant labyrinth with many dead ends and wrong turns. But those who persisted in the maze were rewarded, for many rooms in the maze contained delicious **cheese**. Two of the characters in the maze were little people named Hem and Haw. Two were mice named Sniff and Scurry. The characters spent every day at Cheese Station C, a huge storehouse of cheese. However, the mice and the little people differed in their attitudes about Cheese Station C. These attitudes affected their behaviors. The mice, Sniff and Scurry, woke up early each day and raced to Cheese Station C. When they got there, they took off their running shoes, tied them together, and hung them around their necks so that they would be immediately available should they need to move on from Cheese Station C. And Sniff and Scurry did something else to make sure that they were ready to move on if the need arose. Every day upon arrival at Cheese Station C, they carefully inspected the station and noted changes from the previous day.

Spencer Johnson, M.D. *Who Moved My Cheese?: An Amazing Way to Deal with Change in Your Work and in Your Life.* New York: Putman Books, 1998.

Indeed, one day Sniff and Scurry arrived at Cheese Station C and found that the cheese was gone. Sniff and Scurry were not surprised because they had been inspecting the station every day and had noticed the cheese supply dwindling. In response to the cheeselessness, Sniff and Scurry simply did as their instincts told them. *The situation had changed so they changed with it.* Rather than analyze the situation, they put on their running shoes (taken from around their necks) and ran off through the maze in search of new cheese.

The little people, Hem and Haw, were different. Long ago, when they first found Cheese Station C, they had raced to get there every morning. But, as time went on, Hem and Haw got to the station a little later each day. They became very comfortable in Cheese Station C and, unlike Sniff and Scurry, never bothered to search for changes in the station. They assumed the cheese would always be there and even came to regard the cheese as their own. Unfortunately, unlike Sniff and Scurry, they did not notice that the cheese was disappearing.

When they arrived on the fateful day and discovered the cheese had run out in Cheese Station C, Hem and Haw reacted differently than Sniff and Scurry. Instead of immediately searching for new cheese, they complained that it wasn't fair. Finding cheese was a lot of work in their maze, and they did not want to let go of the life they had built around this cheese. They wanted to know who moved their cheese.

Hem and Haw returned the next day still hoping to find the cheese. They found none and repeated the behaviors of the day before. Eventually, Haw noticed that Sniff and Scurry were gone. Haw suggested to Hem that they do as Sniff and Scurry had and go out into the maze in search of new cheese. Hem rebuffed him.

A similar scenario played out day after day in Cheese Station C. Hem and Haw returned every day hoping to find the cheese they believed they were entitled to. They became frustrated and angry and began to blame each other for their predicament.

In the meantime, Sniff and Scurry had found new cheese. It had taken a lot of work, and they dealt with much uncertainty, but finally, in a totally unfamiliar part of the maze, they found cheese in Cheese Station N.

Still, day after day, Hem and Haw returned to Cheese Station C in hopes of finding their cheese. And the same frustrations and claims of entitlement continued. Eventually, however, Haw's mind-set began to change. He imagined Sniff and Scurry in pursuit of new cheese and imagined himself taking part in such an adventure. He imagined finding fresh new cheese. The more he thought about it the more determined he became to leave. Nevertheless, his friend Hem continued to insist that things would be fine in Cheese Station C. Hem figured that if they simply *worked harder* they would find their cheese in Cheese Station C. He feared he was too old to look for cheese and that he would look foolish doing so. Hem's concerns even made Haw doubt himself until finally one day Haw realized that he was doing the same things over and over again and wondering why things didn't improve. Although Haw did not like the idea of going into the maze and the possibility of getting lost, he laughed at how his fear was preventing him from doing those things. His realization inspired him to write a message to himself (and perhaps to Hem) on the wall in front of him. "What Would You Do If You Weren't Afraid?" (p. 48), it said. Answering his own question, Haw took a deep breath and headed into the unknown.

Unfortunately, a long interlude without food from Cheese Station C had left Haw somewhat weak. He struggled while searching for new cheese and decided that if he ever got another chance he would respond to a change in his environment sooner than he had to the situation in Cheese Station C.

Haw wandered for days and found very little new cheese. He found the maze confusing, as it had changed a great deal since the last time he had looked for cheese. Still, he had to admit that it wasn't as dreadful as he had feared. And whenever he got discouraged, he reminded himself that however painful the search for new cheese was, it was better than remaining cheeseless. The difference was that *he was now in control*. Haw even began to realize, in hindsight, that the cheese in Cheese Station C had not suddenly disappeared. If he had wanted to notice he would have seen the amount of cheese decreasing every day, and that what was left at the end was old and not as tasty. Haw realized that maybe Sniff and Scurry had known what they were doing. Haw stopped to rest and wrote another message on the wall. The message read: "Smell the Cheese Often So You Know When It Is Getting Old" (p. 52).

Haw was often scared in the maze for he did not know if he would survive. He wondered if Hem had moved on yet or was still frozen by his fears. However, Haw's confidence and enjoyment grew with every day as he realized that the times he had felt best in this journey was when he was moving. He inscribed this discovery on the wall of the maze: "When You Move Beyond Your Fear, You Feel Free" (p. 56).

Soon Haw began painting a picture in his mind of himself enjoying all his favorite cheeses. This image became so vivid that he gained a very strong sense that he would find new cheese. He stopped to write on the wall: "Imagining Myself Enjoying New Cheese Even Before I Find It, Leads Me to It" (p. 58). Outside a new station, Haw noticed small bits of cheese near the entrance. He tried some, found them delicious, and excitedly entered the station. But Haw's heart sank when he found that only a small amount of cheese remained in what was once a well-stocked station. He realized that if he had set about looking for new cheese sooner he might have found more cheese here. He wrote these thoughts on the wall: "The Quicker You Let Go of Old Cheese, the Sooner You Find New Cheese" (p. 60).

As Haw left this station, he made another important self-discovery. He realized what made him happy wasn't just having cheese. What made him happy was not being controlled by fear. He did not feel as weak and helpless as when he remained in Cheese Station C. Haw realized that moving beyond his fear was giving him strength and wrote that: "It Is Safer to Search in the Maze Than Remain in a Cheeseless Situation" (p. 62). Haw also realized that the fear he had allowed to build up in his mind was worse than the reality. He had been so afraid of the maze that he had dreaded looking for new cheese. Now he found himself excited about looking for more. Later in his journey he wrote: "Old Beliefs Do Not Lead You to New Cheese" (p. 64). Haw knew that his new beliefs had encouraged new behaviors.

Finally it happened. What Haw had started his journey looking for was now in front of his eyes. Cheese Station N was flush with some of the greatest cheeses Haw had ever seen. Sure enough, his mouse friends Sniff and Scurry were sitting in the cheese, their bellies stuffed. Haw quickly said hello and dug in.

Haw was a bit envious of his mouse friends. They had kept their lives simple. When the cheese moved, rather than overanalyze things, Sniff and Scurry moved with it. As Haw reflected on his journey, he learned from his mistakes. He realized that what he had written on the walls during his journey was true and he was glad he had changed. Haw realized three important things: (1) the biggest thing blocking change is yourself; (2) things don't improve until you change yourself; and (3) there is always new cheese out there, whether you believe it or not. Indeed, he realized that running out of cheese in Cheese Station C had been a blessing in disguise. It had led him to better cheese and to discover important and positive things about himself.

Although Haw knew that he had learned a great deal, he also realized that it would be easy to fall into a comfort zone with the new store of cheese. So, every day he inspected the cheese in Cheese Station N to avoid the same surprise that had occurred in Cheese Station C. And, even though he had a great supply of cheese in Cheese Station N, every day he went out into the maze to make sure that he was always aware of his choices and that he did not have to remain in Cheese Station N. It was on one of these excursions that he heard the sound of someone moving toward him in the maze. He hoped and prayed that it was his friend Hem, and that Hem had finally learned to "Move with the Cheese and Enjoy It!" (p. 76).

BACK AT THE REUNION

After the story, the former classmates recounted situations in which they had to face changes in their work and their personal lives and they discussed which maze character they had acted most like. Most resolved to act more like Haw when dealing with changes they would face in the future. All agreed the story was very useful and that they would use the wisdom contained within to guide them.

2   Fish!

Stephen C. Lundin, Harry Paul, and John Christensen
Summary Prepared by John W. Newstrom

Mary Jane Ramirez is a manager who must create an effective team out of a set of employees who have historically been less than helpful to each other and generally unenthusiastic about teamwork. While taking a walk at lunchtime one day, she encounters a strange but compelling sight—the fishmongers of Seattle's Pike Street Fish Market. These employees have created a bustling, fun-filled, joyful work atmosphere both for themselves and for their customers. Through a series of conversations with Lonnie and some deep self-reflectiveness, she gradually uncovers some ideas that will guide her future behavior.

Using the fish market as a metaphor for other organizations, several key premises about employees are identified, and these lead logically to a short series of recommendations for personal effectiveness. The premises (underlying assumptions) include the following:

- Life is short, and our moments of life are precious. Therefore, it would be tragic for employees to just "pass through" on their way to retirement. Managers and employees both need to *make each moment count.*
- Most people prefer to work in a job environment that is *filled with fun.* When they find this fun or create it, they are much more likely to be energized and release their potential.
- People also like a work environment where they feel they can *make a difference* in the organization's outcomes. They need some capacity to assess their contribution toward those outcomes.
- Almost any job—no matter how simple or automated—has the potential to be performed with *energy and enthusiasm.*
- Employees may not always have the opportunity to choose whether to work or the work to be done itself. However, they will always have some degree of choice about the *way* in which they do their work. At the extreme, each employee can choose to be ordinary or world famous. One path is dull; the other exciting.
- Employees can legitimately act like a bunch of *adult kids* having a good time as long as they do so in a respectful manner (not offending coworkers or customers). When they do act as kids (along with choosing to love the work they do), they can find happiness, meaning, and fulfillment every day.

Stephen C. Lundin, Harry Paul, and John Christensen. *Fish!: A Remarkable Way to Boost Morale and Improve Results.* New York: Hyperion, 2000.

Based on these premises, four recommendations are offered to employees for their personal effectiveness:

1. Every morning, before you go to work, *choose your attitude* for the day (and make it a positive one).
2. Make an effort to introduce an element of **play** into your work environment; it will benefit you and all those around you.
3. Make a commitment to make someone else's day *special* for them. Do something that will create a memory, engage them in a meaningful interaction, or welcome them to your organization.
4. While you are at work, seek to be *present* with them. Focus your energy on them; listen attentively and caringly; pay attention to the needs of your customers and coworkers.

Following these simple prescriptions will make the work experience joyful for all involved, just as it has for the employees and customers of Seattle's Pike Street Fish Market.

3

The Fun Minute Manager

Bob Pike, Robert C. Ford, and John W. Newstrom
Summary Prepared by John W. Newstrom

John W. Newstrom is the Chief Funologist for Funology, Inc., where his primary task is to help managers create and sustain a fun work environment for their employees. Additional information on fun at work can be found at http://www.thefunminutemanager.com/

THE IMPORTANCE OF FUN AT WORK

A young manager, Bob Workman, is continually bombarded with problems at work that leave him and his colleagues emotionally drained at the end of each day. In sharp contrast, they find much enjoyment in activities that they engage in *away* from work (e.g., while participating in voluntary and nonprofit organizational settings, as well as truly recreational activities). Predictably, the manager embarks on a journey of discovery, in which he searches for an answer to his dilemma.

In his search for answers to his questions, Bob stumbles upon several key pieces of information. First, he discovers that most workers *want* a job that is fun (the strong interest is there). Second, he discovers a powerful fact—that "fun, play, and laughter" may actually exist at the pinnacle of the typical employee's need hierarchy as the *most sought-after environmental factor at work*. This provides a startling revelation for him: *It appears that a primary goal of any manager should be to provide opportunities for employees to have fun at work.*

After receiving an overview of the effects of fun at the physiological, psychological, and social levels, he resolves to help the people around him at work laugh more frequently. But how can he do this, he asks himself? This question challenges him to search for a set of tools by which he can create a fun work environment.

He explores what some other organizations have successfully done to implement fun at work and develops a set of initial conclusions. Fun workplaces are:

- easy to create,
- desired by most employees,
- easily identified by the presence of laughter, joy, happiness, surprise, and spontaneity, and yet
- they can mean different things to different people.

Bob Pike, Robert C. Ford, and John W. Newstrom. *The Fun Minute Manager: Create FUNomenal Results Now Through Using Fun at Work!* Minneapolis: CTT Press, 2009.

All of this makes intuitive sense to him as the reality about fun sinks in.

After reviewing the typical characteristics of many playful and recreational activities that bring out the joyful spirit within participants, Bob recognizes their applicability to the world of work. By studying the potential similarities between work settings and play, he discovers a set of criteria to apply in the creation of a fun work environment. For example, the fun activities should make people smile, be easy to prepare, be low cost, involve a low risk of physical harm to people or resources, not be time consuming, be as inclusive as possible, combine both planned and spontaneous events, and be created and administered on a participative basis.

FUN FACTORS AND A DEFINITION

Now ready to jump in with both feet, he discovers a comprehensive research study that documents a surprisingly broad set of factors that contribute to having fun in any context (e.g., recognition of personal milestones, fun social events, public celebrations of achievements, stress-release activities, friendly competitions, opportunities for community involvement, use of humor, opportunities for personal development, the use of games at work, and providing occasional entertainment at work). He experiments with several of these and concludes that they are

1. Generally easy to implement,
2. Inexpensive (often cost little or nothing), and
3. Are usually well received by his employees and colleagues.

As a consequence, he arrives at a working definition of a **fun work environment** as *one in which a variety of formal and informal activities regularly occur that are designed to uplift people's spirits, and positively and publicly remind people of their value to their managers, their organization, and to each other through the use of humor, playful games, joyful celebrations, opportunities for self development, or recognition of achievements and milestones.*

He invites his team members to create new job titles for themselves—ones that emphasize their evolving role as cocreators of fun work experiences. They enthusiastically participate (and have fun doing so). Their brainstormed list includes the titles of Corporate Cheerleader, Goddess (Empress) of Fun, Chief Energizing Officer, Funcilitator, Chief Funatic Manager, Fun 'R Us Team Leader, Joy Team Captain, Minister of Comedy, Glee Club Leader, Funologist, Funmaster (or Funmeister), Director of Fun, and Mutual Fun Manager. After a lot of laughs among the group, he chooses the title of *Fun Minute Manager* for himself, because he knows that many fun activities can be implemented in short periods of time—an important key to their success.

IMPORTANT OUTCOMES

When his proposal to formalize the fun process at work gets initially rebuffed by his boss, he carefully studies the possible impediments to a fun workplace. He discovers that a fun workplace *could* change the culture substantially, *may* lack the support of higher executives, *could* produce negative perceptions from outsiders, *may* raise some realistic fears among managers (e.g., lower productivity, dangerous behaviors, extra costs), and *might* cause managers to experience a certain degree of personal embarrassment. However, he concludes that these are not serious barriers that cannot be overcome.

Next, he searches the existing research literature on fun at work and identifies an array of work-related benefits that are reported to be likely products of a fun work environment. They include, in order of perceived importance:

Rank	Outcome
1.	Greater employee enthusiasm
2.	Higher ability to attract new employees
3.	Increased employee satisfaction
4.	Better communications among employees
5.	Improved employee creativity
6.	Richer employee friendships at work
7.	Higher group cohesiveness
8.	Increased levels of customer satisfaction
9.	Elevated level of employee commitment to the organization
10.	Stronger corporate culture (shared values and norms)

In addition, he is confident that fun at work will also reduce anxiety and stress and diminish the common complaints of boredom that he hears so often.

MAJOR FUN INSIGHTS

Finally, he prepares a set of key insights that he has gained from each step in his "journey into fun." These include the following:

INSIGHT #1: You can get a lot of people to do a lot of things if there is fun involved.

INSIGHT #2: Most people want to have fun while also doing meaningful and productive work.

INSIGHT #3: A wide range of activities exist that can provide fun at work.

INSIGHT #4: Fun at work is not traditionally viewed as an integral part of a manager's responsibilities, and consequently it will not be accepted easily by superiors without very convincing argument and solid evidence.

INSIGHT #5: Strong evidence is emerging that fun workplaces can and do produce a wide array of activities that lead to positive physiological and psychological outcomes for the individual and equally valuable benefits for work organizations.

INSIGHT #6: It is appropriate to outline—in advance—the criteria that a program for fun at work must meet, and then review them frequently.

INSIGHT #7: Using the principles of a high-involvement workplace, consultation with employees and solicitation of their ideas can provide a strong base of support and innumerable ideas for fun at work.

INSIGHT #8: The only way to conclusively determine (and demonstrate) the actual effects attributable to fun at work is to measure them on a pretest and posttest basis.

INSIGHT #9: Fun-at-work programs can be designed and implemented quickly, easily, and inexpensively by a truly committed "fun minute manager" and his or her team.

He then decides to conduct a systematic assessment of the readiness of his employees to engage in fun at work by surveying their self-reported receptivity. When the results are tabulated, they show that his employees have a strong desire to have fun and a clear sense that they aren't having much at the present time. Thus encouraged, he implements a high-involvement program that actively invites employees to design their own fun experiences. A year later, he follows up the original survey with another that assesses employee reactions to the fun-workplace initiative. The results are powerfully supportive. The ultimate outcome is that Bob enjoys *his* work as a manager much more than previously, and he also achieves a high level of satisfaction from helping *others* to have fun at work, too.

IMPLEMENTATION PRINCIPLES

Then he concludes by carefully developing and defining a set of 10 guiding principles that will help both him and other managers implement and sustain a fun work environment. The essential principles to be emphasized (and their implications) include the following:

1. *Address other employee needs first.* (Employees won't laugh at your humor if they are angry about environmental shortcomings or have jobs that are lacking in motivational content.)
2. *Make sure that "fun at work" will be a good fit with the organization's culture and with employee expectations.* (Ask yourself WHY you are trying to create a fun environment, who wants it, and whether it is needed.)
3. *Build a fun workplace on an underlying philosophical foundation, not just a set of mechanical practices.* (Make sure you aren't saying one thing [about having fun at work] and yet doing another [emphasizing work results exclusively].)
4. *Make a long-term commitment to fun as an ongoing process, not a short-term program.* (Don't be guilty of a splashy start and then a weak follow-through.)
5. *Become more playful yourself.* (Others won't follow you if you don't "walk the talk.")
6. *Involve others in creating fun experiences.* (Don't try to do it all yourself; invite others to participate.)
7. *Satisfy employee needs for recognition in new and unique ways.* (Remember that most people are hungry for appreciation and respect. Also, don't forget that "the sweetest sound in the world is the sound of our own name being called" when it is time for awards to be given out.)
8. *Use a wide variety of fun-related activities.* (Take advantage of the old adage to provide "different strokes for different folks." Keep the process new and fresh.)
9. *Capitalize on the surprise factor.* (Be unpredictable; try different things.)
10. *Assess and monitor your success at creating a fun work culture.* (Remember that nothing speaks louder than data about the results of a fun work environment, coupled with supportive personal anecdotes and endorsements from employees about their experiences of fun at work.)

Conclusion

Several valuable appendices are included at the end of the book, including sample survey instruments, illustrations of fun-at-work activities, a listing of fun workplace organizations, fun and humor websites, and a bibliography of other resources on workplace fun.

PART SIXTEEN

Contemporary Thinking About Management

In the evolution and growth of any field of science, there are usually thousands of relatively minor advances made across time, interspersed with occasional major developments (e.g., Albert Einstein's theory of relativity in physics, or Dr. Jonas Salk's development of the polio vaccine, or the creation of cloned sheep by biologists/geneticists). Sometimes, however, the greatest breakthroughs emerge when an independent thinker or critic stands back and announces that "The emperor has no clothes!" (and thus allows others to "see" for the first time what should have been apparent to them all along).

In the field of management, there has been a paucity of major breakthroughs across the past century. It could be argued that the field has edged forward in a variety of narrower domains through the persistent efforts of many but that overall progress and "big-picture" activity has been slow and fragmented. With rather rare exceptions (refer back to our references to books by Kilmann and Micklethwait/Wooldridge in Part 1), few books have provided comprehensive and critical looks at the overall field of management. Therefore, we as editors felt the need to include summaries of some key books to fill this void.

Jeffrey Pfeffer, in *What Were They Thinking?*, suggests that organizations—even when led by intelligent and dedicated executives—frequently make a variety of missteps and errors that would lead observers to wonder, "What is going on there? and Why in the world would they do that?" Pfeffer candidly points out that some business leaders fail to capitalize on simple yet powerful principles of organizational behavior, rely on naïve theories of human behavior, and neglect to consider the unintended by-products of their decisions and actions. Pfeffer proposes that managers should think before they act, use common sense, draw upon the mass of available evidence on human behavior, and get beyond "conventional management wisdom."

Jeff Pfeffer holds a Ph.D. from Stanford University and has taught there in its School of Business for over 30 years. He is now the Thomas D. Dee II Professor of Organizational Behavior. His previous books include *The Human Equation, Managing with Power, Hidden Value*, and *The Knowing-Doing Gap*. Pfeffer is the recipient of the Academy of Management's Richard I. Irwin Award for scholarly contributions to management.

Henry Mintzberg has been studying and writing about management for the past four decades. His latest book, *Managing*, is the capstone of 14 previous books and 150 articles. Mintzberg received his Ph.D. from the Sloan School of Management at MIT, and is the Cleghorn Professor of Management Studies at McGill University in Montreal, Canada. Mintzberg acknowledges that the pressures of managing are perpetual; the job requires total commitment; all managers are at least partially flawed; and a manager's job is characterized by brevity, variety, discontinuity, and a demand for action. Most significantly, managers face four types of conundrums, but can resolve these best by integrating five different mind-sets (reflective, analytic, worldly, collaborative, and proactive).

Jeff Pfeffer, along with Robert I. Sutton, wrote *Hard Facts, Dangerous Half-Truths, and Total Nonsense.* They suggest that managers often fall into the "doing-knowing" gap, wherein they take action without first learning enough about their underlying problems. They propose that executives at all levels embrace the practice of using *evidence-based management.* This perspective invites them to be cautious about "new" ideas, explore the pros and cons of new approaches, recognize the difference between anecdotal stories and research-based results, question their own assumptions, and look for data that might support the success or failure of intended actions. They conclude by offering a series of concrete suggestions for how managers might work toward evidence-based management.

Readers interested in a thorough explanation of both the principles of evidence-based management and the key factors that inhibit its use are encouraged to read Denise M. Rousseau and Sharon McCarthy's article, "Educating Managers from an Evidence-Based Perspective" (*Academy of Management Learning & Education*, 2007, Vol. 6, No. 1, pp. 84–101) as well as reviews of the Pfeffer–Sutton book on pages 137–149 of the same issue and the authors' response to those reviews on pages 153–155. More recently (2012) Denise Rousseau edited *The Oxford Handbook of Evidence-based Management*—a comprehensive overview of the topic.

Pfeffer and Sutton—coauthors of *The Knowing-Doing Gap*—were both profiled earlier (separately) in *The Manager's Bookshelf.*

Tom Friedman is the foreign affairs columnist for the *New York Times.* He has won the Pulitzer Prize three times for his outstanding and informed journalism. In addition to his regular editorials in the *New York Times*, Friedman is the author of several previous books, including *From Beirut to Jerusalem, The Lexus and Olive Tree: Understanding Globalization, Longitudes and Attitudes: Exploring the World After September 11*, and his best seller *The World Is Flat: A Brief History of the 21st Century.*

In his book *Hot, Flat, and Crowded*, Friedman contends that three powerful forces are affecting the earth in important ways: global warming, global population growth, and global flattening. These have produced disruptive climate change, energy differentials across countries, a huge transfer of wealth to oil-producing countries, an increasing demand for natural resources, and biodiversity loss. America (and its corporate executives, by implication), Friedman suggests, needs to become the leader in creating the greenest country in the world, which will result in achieving the twin goals of national security and economic prosperity.

1

What Were They Thinking?

Jeffrey Pfeffer

Summary Prepared by Adam Surma

Adam Surma is in store management with Target Corporation. Adam has held several positions with Target, overseeing store operations in Minnesota and Iowa. Primary management responsibilities include team development, providing vision and accountability, and store process execution. Adam received a B.B.A. degree from the University of Minnesota Duluth, with a major in Organizational Management.

INTRODUCTION

Today's organizations face a myriad of challenges and pressures that allow the world outside to catch a glimpse of their operations and decisions as they confront and deal with these factors. Though most organizations in every sector of the economy are undoubtedly led by some of the best and brightest the labor pool has to offer, there are countless examples of actions undertaken by these organizations that leave an outsider to pose the question: *"what were they thinking?"* All too often it seems that organizations follow the dictates of the conventional wisdom of the day, only to discover that conventional wisdom is flat-out wrong. This faulty reasoning, along with underinformed leadership and poor judgment, often finds organizations making serious errors that can be categorized into three themes—disregarding feedback, using simplistic models, and overcomplicating simple issues.

COMMON THEMES

Although there are many reasons why organizations make poor decisions that seem obvious to a great many people, *three common threads seem to unify and categorize them well*:

1. Disregarding the feedback effects of decisions
2. Believing in and using overly simplistic models of people and organizational behavior
3. Overcomplicating reasonably straightforward issues

By making these three common errors, leaders doom the outcome and execution of their vision from the start, either through stifling their workforce's productivity, creativity, and morale, or through misdirecting scarce resources away from the most value-added option for the organization.

Jeffrey Pfeffer. *What Were They Thinking? Unconventional Wisdom About Management.* Boston, MA: Harvard Business School Press, 2007.

These errors can be readily seen in the realms of people, process, leadership structure, the measuring of success, and public policy.

PEOPLE-CENTERED STRATEGIES

Much emphasis in recent years has been placed on self-led teams, the value of investing in your workforce, and removing bureaucratic barriers to promote creativity. Yet for all of the knowledge available on these subjects, many organizations still ignore the commonsense principles surrounding the motivation and retention of a great team. Businesses trying to cut costs or getting caught in the glamour of new technology invest more heavily in customer service software, computer hardware, and analysis than in the frontline workforce that sees their customers face to face every day. Management feels, especially in the United States, that lower and lower labor costs and pushing more of the work to automated or off-site systems will create a competitive edge and ultimately higher profit margins. The gap, however, between Europe and the United States in productivity has been drastically reduced over the past 30 years, with more and more of the highly skilled labor being outsourced to other nations where more resources are devoted to education and training. This "death spiral" of trying to cut costs and losing the talent and organizational knowledge of your employees poses a serious threat to the long-term competitive edge in the United States.

Another mistake that is commonly made is *the unforgiving nature that many organizations have adopted over time concerning making and admitting to mistakes.* Whether it is frontline workers admitting to production errors and thus increasing the chance of a major recall or senior executives "cooking the books" to cover up underperforming numbers from a misstep, the culture of many modern organizations does not leave much room for the inevitable mistake. This culture is counterintuitive to the very nature of what it takes to be competitive in today's world: innovation and the ability to try many new ideas to find the one that is ultimately a success.

Reluctance to admit mistakes also runs parallel to another error often found deeply seated in organizations that are not as successful as they could be, which is the fact that *people want to work and stay at organizations that treat them well.* Great pay and benefits alone will not achieve this, as much research has shown that pay is not the top motivator or reason why people join or leave an organization, but the sense of community employees feel from their employer is a vital factor. Employees are asking themselves: Does the organization care about my family? Will they take care of me when I am sick? These are the questions that often are overlooked, as senior leaders discuss why they cannot create a culture that attracts and retains top talent.

CREATING EFFECTIVE WORKPLACES

Creating effective workplaces through the reduction of benefits and imposition of human resource controls is another area in which organizations can easily fall into one of the three common theme errors. Cutting benefits and pay when times get tough is a common approach seen in today's headlines. However, this can be a very detrimental and ultimately ineffective way to cut costs. It has been found that employees, when feeling slighted by their employer, will reduce their work output to create a natural balance (sense of equity) from their own perspective. This leads to lower productivity. Many organizations in countries that are thought to have high wages or "excessive labor costs" run surpluses and profits higher than U.S. companies that compete on the low-wage strategy. This is due to the fact that many leaders forget that labor costs equal wage rate combined with productivity, and what is important is what actually is completed for the hours worked. Similarly, the long hours and weekend work that plague many organizational cultures in the United States are not a problem in many competing European companies. Research shows that a worker in the United States will work 40 percent more hours in his or her lifetime than someone from Germany, France, or Italy. However, many European countries' workforces rank higher in creativity indexes and are healthier in general according to the World Heath Organization. All of these factors show that the old dogma of if you are not "burning the midnight oil" or you are undercontributing, then the organization will suffer is simply not true.

LEADERSHIP AND INFLUENCE

Another area in which executives often find themselves making poor choices is in the basic people skills of their leadership and the culture of their organization. This deficiency allows the lack of basic influencing traits and relationship-strengthening behaviors to be rewarded or cultivated. With so many demands on the time of the leaders in charge of organizations, it is easy to see how the basics of leadership taught in college classrooms can be thrown out during stressful times. An example of this is the need for appropriate framing and repetition of key messages and strategies of the company, and how many leaders never use this simple approach. Truly effective leaders know that the following four steps will keep a large and complex organization going in the direction they want it to:

1. Define the criteria for success.
2. Project clarity and confidence.
3. Move fast to establish terms of discussion.
4. Endlessly repeat the simple message.

If more leaders took a step back in times of turmoil to keep these key points in mind, many of the decisions that find an outsider asking "what were they thinking?" could be avoided.

Clear communication and vision projection are not the only leadership behaviors that are prone to the three common errors of decision making. Problems can also occur when managers create a culture of not admitting mistakes (especially at the highest level), not accepting "it's impossible" as a valid answer to a challenge, and ensuring that leadership knows the foundations of an organization (what the business actually does on a day-by-day basis). These are all commonly seen behind the scenes of a major mistake as areas of deficit that ultimately contribute to failure. Even the use of basic psychology is often to blame in failures. The use of **psychological commitment** is a good example of this principle. This is the idea that people are interested and invested in other people's success when they have made a contribution to it and are familiar with and enjoy the company of an individual. This can be a powerful tool. More leaders need to use this to their advantage through the basics of turning on the charm, being polite, and focusing on people and family before business to ultimately gain more insight into and commitment from their workforce.

MEASURES OF SUCCESS

Two serious issues that plague many organizations today as they try to measure their success are overrewarding forecasting and budgeting (vs. actual performance) and the overreliance on shareholder return as a valid measurement for success.

In the first, it is increasingly common for organizations to celebrate and benchmark their "successes" based on their own internal profit projections and budgets. Because many leaders at the top have incentive packages that are based on meeting and beating goals and expectations, it naturally becomes an exercise on how well leadership can sell the board of directors on goals that they are confident they can hit, thus ensuring a positive outcome and the continued goodwill of all involved. The real challenge that organizations need to address is the idea of using both internal and external benchmarks and creating systems that use competitors' success and potential market share along with basic yearly comparative sales projections versus meeting or beating what can be an arbitrary budget.

Second, studies have shown that stock price is neither reliable nor valid in terms of assessing the long-term success of a company or the quality of its management. Stock price cannot be used as a valid measure, as you cannot measure a company with it time and time again and have a reliable predictor of future results. Evidence also points out that "earnings-oriented management" and the ability of a good investor relations department will have just as much sway as solid economic indicators such as earnings and sales growth on the price of the stock. When organizations focus on stock price as a major objective, they are necessarily committing scarce resources to obtain a goal that is not the most value added for the total organization (which is not only the shareholders but also the employees, community, and customers that it serves).

ORGANIZATIONS AND PUBLIC POLICY

In relation to making large mistakes in the limelight of public opinion and in the midst of the hot issues of the day, there are three areas in which organizations often find themselves struggling to make effective decisions.

Labor unions are the first issue on which organizations can often make mistakes. Although there are many complex issues when dealing with union and business interaction, one issue that organizations often forget is that increased labor costs do not necessarily mean decreased profits in every industry. On the theory of "you get what you pay for," organizations must come to terms with the fact that productivity, training, and commitment are all factored in (along with the wage rate) to determine final outcomes. This may lead some industries and businesses to avoid unions when they may not actually be harmful to the bottom line in every situation.

The second issue is executive pay. With the average pay rate going up steadily in the past decade, and public outcry over such huge bonuses, organizations must take a hard look at their compensation approach if they are to avoid overpaying, and thus may face negative media coverage and increased scrutiny, or underpaying, and may miss out on top talent who would ultimately grow the business. The "**above-average effect**" suggests that everyone views themselves as above average and demands at least the average executive pay. This along with the fact that many executives in large companies have literally become celebrities combines to make the choice of paying an organization's top people not really a decision at all when it comes to where on the sliding scale of pay they need to commit to if they are to keep top talent.

The last issue involves the many misdeeds that can be committed in organizations and how they deal with the aftermath of unethical business decisions. Our society has traditionally viewed white-collar crimes as significantly less serious than other forms of crime, and the stigmas associated with it are so reduced that even after committing serious misdeeds leaders can easily find a host of other organizations waiting to bring them aboard after being terminated or even sent to prison. Our culture has (unfortunately) made it clear—from business school to the boardroom— that the ends justify the means. Organizations must be aware of this and be extra vigilant if they are to avoid major blunders and avoid unconsciously rewarding unethical behavior.

Conclusion

Many of the mistakes and blunders that organizations make today could be avoided if they didn't overcomplicate simple business decisions, didn't ignore the feedback effects of their decisions once implemented, and viewed their workforce as a complex and dynamic group of people. If these principles were acknowledged and used as guidelines more often by today's business leaders, many of the headaches and pains they now face would be eliminated and their organizations would be better positioned to be competitive and profitable—both domestically and abroad.

2   Managing

Henry Mintzberg
Summary Prepared by Bob Stine

Bob Stine is Associate Dean for Academic Programs in the College of Continuing Education at the University of Minnesota. His program responsibilities include dual enrollment, bachelor's and master's degrees, English language for international students, and online education. Stine's academic background is in forest genetics and natural resource management and policy. His interests include leadership, organizational management, adult education, and natural resources and the environment. He earned his Ph.D. from the University of Minnesota, master's degree from Oregon State University, and bachelor's degree from Indiana University.

INTRODUCTION

Managing is complicated. It involves an unrelenting pace, brief bursts of widely divergent activities, fragmented schedules, a bias toward action, a favoring of informal verbal communication, close collaboration with peers, and covert rather than overt control of many situations. Phone calls, email, and meetings don't *distract* from the job of managing, they in large part *are* the job of managing. Writers have described managing as "calculated chaos" and "controlled disorder."

MANAGING ON THREE PLANES

There is, though, some underlying order in the chaos. *Both inside and outside their own unit, managers manage on three planes: the information plane, the people plane, and the action plane.* On the information plane, managers are continuously communicating with others outside their unit to gather information and coordinate activities, while inside their unit they are sharing information with and directing the behavior of subordinates. On the people plane, managers link with others outside the unit through networking, and lead people on the inside. This plane represents getting things done through other people. The action plane is just that—directly making deals with people outside the unit and actually doing the work inside the unit.

Effective managers become adept at knowing when and how to play these various roles, taking into account their own personal strengths and the situation in which they are managing. As a result, effective managing is better learned through experience rather than simply in a classroom.

Henry Mintzberg. *Managing.* San Francisco, CA: Berrett-Koehler, 2009.

FACTORS INFLUENCING MANAGEMENT

Even knowing the various roles they play, many factors influence how managers manage. Extensive research over the years has identified at least 12 factors that can be placed in five categories. They are:

- External context—national culture; sector (business, government, etc.); industry
- Organizational context—form of the organization (entrepreneurial, professional, etc.); the organization's age, size, and stage of development
- Job context—the level in the hierarchy; the work supervised
- Temporal context—temporary pressures; managerial fashion
- Personal context—background of the manager; time in the position; personal style

In a study that followed 29 very diverse managers through a typical day, many of these factors did not influence management activities at all, and an average of only three appeared influential per day. *By far the most prominent factor was the form of the organization* (managing in a national park was different than managing in a health-care system, which was different than managing in an arts organization, etc.).

PERSONAL STYLE

In addition to the first several factors, managers also bring their own personal style to the task of managing. The range of styles available includes *insightful* (concerned with ideas and visions; more intuitive), *engaging* (hands-on, rooted in experience), and *cerebral* (deliberate and analytical). Think of these as the three points of a triangle, with each individual having a particular blend of the three styles that fits somewhere within the triangle depending on which styles are predominant.

The various blends of styles can be categorized into nine **managerial postures** that a manager may assume for a particular situation. All managers must adopt most of these postures at some time or another, and thus must know how to blend them with one another as needed. The postures, with brief descriptions are:

1. *Maintaining the Workflow:* making sure operations proceed smoothly; fine-tuning more than major renewing.
2. *Connecting Externally:* maintaining the boundary conditions of the organization by connecting outwardly more than controlling internally.
3. *Blending All Around:* remaining close to the workflow but also connecting significantly to the outside and blending both elements into their work.
4. *Remote Controlling:* a somewhat detached, analytical approach based on information sharing, used especially by senior managers in large organizations to manage internally.
5. *Fortifying the Culture:* also used by senior managers, this posture seeks to build a strong culture through personal engagement.
6. *Intervening Strategically:* personal intervention on an ad hoc basis to drive specific changes.
7. *Managing in the Middle:* facilitating the downward flow of information and transmitting performance information back up; this is more about maintaining stability than promoting change.
8. *Managing Out of the Middle:* spearheading change by influencing people over whom the manager does not have formal authority.
9. *Advising from the Side:* serving as an adviser, specialist, or intervener, relying more on experience rather than authority.

MANAGEMENT CONUNDRUMS

With so many factors influencing managers and with so much adapting to do based on the given circumstances, it's not surprising that managers face a host of conundrums they must deal with on a regular basis. They cover four broad areas:

1. *Thinking Conundrums:* How to think, plan, and strategize when the job is hectic and there is pressure to get it done. How to find synthesis in a world decomposed by analysis.
2. *Information Conundrums:* How to keep informed when the manager is removed from what is being managed, and much of the information is personal, verbal, and privileged. How to measure what is being managed.
3. *People Conundrums:* How to bring order to the work of others when managing itself is so disorganized. How to allow some chaos when order is imposed from above. How to be confident without being arrogant.
4. *Action Conundrums:* How to act decisively in a complicated world, and how to manage change when there is a need to maintain stability.

How should a manager deal with these conundrums, which never go away? The answer lies in a nuanced, balanced, dynamic approach, with the manager anticipating and reacting to situations as they arise. This will have managers moving in one direction at certain times, then off in another as conditions change.

MANAGERIAL MIND-SETS

Given the nearly unlimited variables and multiple conundrums that managers face on a daily, if not hourly basis, how can they be effective? A useful framework includes five **managerial mindsets**, all of which must be interwoven to result in effectiveness. *The mind-sets—reflective, analytic, worldly, collaborative, and proactive—are framed within the context of a manager being personally energetic and socially integrative.*

The energy an individual brings to his or her role as a manager is largely personal. It is necessary to deal with the hectic pace of the job, the needed orientation toward action, and the varied and quick-shifting nature of the work.

In the midst of that energy, effective managers must also be *reflective*. They learn from their experiences, they explore many options, and they know when to stop one approach and try another. Reflecting means probing, analyzing, synthesizing, and connecting. In short, effective managers think for themselves.

The *analytic* mind-set includes gathering both formal and explicit knowledge along with informal and tacit knowledge. This mind-set seeks order and logic, but also applies judgment to the information that is gathered to conceptualize approaches.

The *worldly* mind-set involves being experienced in life, sophisticated, and practical. Worldly managers get outside their own realm and experience the world and thinking of others. This in turn helps them better understand their own world, partly by seeing how others see it, and partly by developing solutions based on the ideas of others.

The *collaborative* mind-set forces managers to manage their relationships with people in their unit and others outside their unit. It involves building networks, and it includes respect, trust, care, and inspiration. Done well, it allows a manager to lead from the background instead of being involved in everything.

The *proactive* mind-set requires the effective manager to not be overly reflective, and to seize the initiative rather than simply responding to what happens. Whereas reflection is mostly personal, being proactive is largely social, requiring the involvement of other people. Done well, proactive management can be experimental, incremental, and emerge from the bottom up.

Bookending the personal energy of an effective manager is the ability to be **socially integrative**. This means being able to see the whole from the miscellaneous parts. It requires integrating on the run, while working with multiple people inside and outside the unit. Integrating allows managers to navigate the dynamics of the situation moment by moment, striking the right posture for the situation at hand.

3

Hard Facts, Dangerous Half-Truths, and Total Nonsense

Jeffrey Pfeffer and Robert I. Sutton
Summary Prepared by Jannifer David

Jannifer David teaches human resource management at the University of Minnesota Duluth. She received her Ph.D. in Labor and Industrial Relations from Michigan State University. Her research projects study the use of contingent workers and how these workers affect the work relationships of others within organizations. She is also interested in international human resource management practices. Her work has been published in *Human Resource Planning, Journal of Leadership and Organizational Studies*, and other human resources–related outlets.

CAUSES OF BAD DECISIONS

Evidence-based management—decisions based upon the best research, data, and experimentation available—should lead companies to make better decisions than if companies use the prevailing approach based upon incomplete and often nonfactual hopes and fears. So why *don't* companies use evidence-based management? Three reasons stand out.

Business norms derived for decision making include many practices that hinder the use of solid evidence as the basis for decisions. First among these norms is the use of *casual benchmarking*, which happens when companies copy the visible practices of other successful companies but fail to adopt the underlying philosophy that drives these practices or fail to acknowledge that these successful companies may have different business strategies, competitive environments, and/or business models.

A second cause for not using evidence-based management is because *managers rely on (and repeat) past behaviors that seemed to be successful*, even if these behaviors are not appropriate for the current situation. Although learning from experience is important, it is equally important to recognize that the present is not always exactly like the past and that what has worked before might not work now.

Finally, managers may choose to implement a practice because *it conforms to their personal beliefs*. In these cases, it is often very difficult to convince managers that their beliefs are not supported by evidence and that these beliefs may be harmful to the organization.

Using evidence-based management requires managers to look at facts and experiment with different approaches to determine which of these approaches are the most successful rather than relying on conventional wisdom. Clearly, there are many instances when data are not available to

Jeffrey Pfeffer and Robert I. Sutton. *Hard Facts, Dangerous Half-Truths, and Total Nonsense: Profiting from Evidence-Based Management.* Boston, MA: Harvard Business School Press, 2006.

help make these decisions. When reliable data are not available, it is important find new ways of collecting data to ensure that sound decisions can be made. At a minimum, managers should ask questions about the underlying assumptions related to a practice before implementing it.

Collecting data, doing research, and examining assumptions when making decisions are the basics of evidence-based management. They seem like common sense, but many managers do not act on these ideas. Managers are often overwhelmed by the amount of information around them. The plethora of business knowledge available may make it difficult for managers to sort through this information for reliable data. However, research has shown that where the data can be found, evidence-based management has positive results for companies.

HOW TO APPLY EVIDENCE-BASED MANAGEMENT

Practicing evidence-based management can lead to better outcomes for people and companies, but problems may arise. Consider the premise of evidence-based management—that good decisions are based on data. If decisions are made based upon solid evidence and information, then any employee may possibly hold information that will guide decisions. This will change the power dynamics of the organization so that managers in higher positions may not always be the best-informed people to guide decisions. Making decisions based upon the data rather than the intuition of leaders may be threatening to these leaders. Such leaders have to be willing to accept that others know things they do not know and then both gather and act on these data. As a corollary, these leaders must encourage employees to bring up problems and not just tell leaders that they are always right. Finally, managers must exert effort to wade through the plethora of business information available to them and decide which of this information is valuable.

How can managers overcome these barriers? Relying on sound logic and analysis is the best approach. Managers should sift through and study all of the information available to them. This means looking not only at practices of successful companies but also companies that fail. Managers should develop a habit of running small experiments within their companies to determine through data analysis which approaches are the most effective. Managers can change their thought processes about the information they use in the following ways:

- Be cautious of a "new" idea, because there are very few truly new ideas.
- Recognize that information rarely is generated by individuals and most likely comes from the efforts of a group of people.
- Acknowledge the positives *and* the negatives of any idea or approach.
- Use stories from other companies' successes and failures as interesting anecdotes, but not as research-based data.
- Before supporting or rejecting any ideology or theory, look for data that could indicate the success or failure of these ideas.
- Most important, evidence-based management suggests that managers should rely on gaining wisdom to make decisions. No approach to management will answer all of your questions definitively. Wise managers will recognize what they know, but also what they don't know. Find research and people to help you understand what you do not know.

EXAMPLES OF HALF-TRUTHS IN MANAGING PEOPLE AND ORGANIZATIONS

To illustrate the dangers of not using evidence-based management, here are some common business beliefs and a review of the data and research supporting and not supporting them.

Half-Truth #1: Separation of Work and Home Life Is Necessary

Employees' work lives are different from the rest of their lives. Employers often develop policies and practices to convey the idea that once employees are on the clock, no aspects of their personal lives should ever enter into their thoughts or actions.

Companies require that employees dress in a particular manner to narrow, or eliminate (in the case of uniforms), the individuality expressed by employees. Employees are asked to follow directions without thinking about the consequences of these directions and without providing suggestions for improvements. Emotions displayed at work are sometimes expected to conform to the norms established for that company. These norms may frequently require employees to refrain from displaying their true emotions. Many companies have policies forbidding romantic relationships between coworkers and even attempting to limit friendships between employees. These policies about social interactions are reinforced by practices that encourage employees to compete against each other for promotions or other organizational benefits. Furthermore, behaviors such as bullying at work are seen as acceptable, although outside of work, such abusive behavior is clearly not socially acceptable. Last, whereas much of employees' personal lives is focused on finding personal fulfillment, work is seen as a job and nothing more.

What are the benefits of separating work life from other facets of life? By not allowing people to use work time to accomplish personal tasks, the amount of role conflict experienced by employees should diminish. Companies can focus on making objective decisions rather than decisions based on favoritism or nepotism. Defining clear boundaries between work and home life can help clarify consequences when people's home lives become impediments to their work lives.

But there may be benefits to *allowing* integration between work and home life. For example, building a strong culture of valuing employees and their personal lives can lead to lower turnover and greater employee efforts. Many companies encourage participation of family members either as a source of new employees or to help with personal responsibilities when employees are busy with company activities. Employees who hide their true emotions experience negative outcomes such as burnout and dissatisfaction. Allowing employees to express themselves (within reason, of course) can result in more creativity and better ideas being surfaced. Allowing employees to express themselves also extends to the leaders in the company. When leaders are viewed as honest and sincere, employees are more likely to believe in these leaders and be loyal to the company.

Half-Truth #2: Only Companies That Hire the Best People Will Be the Best Companies

Another common half-truth is that the best companies are that way because they hire only the best people. This argument is compelling because there is research showing that smart and skilled people perform at much higher levels than people of lesser ability. However, other assumptions about only hiring the best people make this half-truth dangerous. Many organizations claim they can spot top talent early in a person's career, but the research is inconclusive about which factors will best predict future performance. So companies engaging in this early identification are largely basing decisions on intuition. Does this early selection process create a Hawthorne effect leading to higher performance later? Another assumption is that great employees will hire other great employees and that mediocre or poor employees will hire other mediocre or poor employees. Successful organizations then need to find a few great people and let them hire others like them. A similar-to-me effect may play a role here, as research shows that conscientious people tend to hire other conscientious people, but research does not make clear whether or not poor performers will hire other poor performers.

This obsession on hiring great talent is somewhat misleading, as organizations cannot easily identify talent. Also, people's performance will vary naturally over time due to external constraints on their ability to focus and their levels of experience. Research shows that talent is not necessarily a given, but rather that talent can be developed over time through motivation, effort, and effective training. Finally, some evidence supports the conclusion that truly great people will be squashed by a truly terribly system. If an organization institutes a bureaucratic system that fails to enhance or capitalize on people's abilities, then no amount of talent will shine through.

So what approach to talent should organizations embrace to be successful? First, acknowledge that talent can be learned and demonstrated by anyone, not just the few people who walk in the door with it. Next, focus on developing good systems in which people can demonstrate their abilities. Encourage employees to ask questions and talk about what is going on at work. If employees are unable or afraid to discuss problems, nothing will ever get better.

Half-Truth #3: Financial Incentives Are a Must for Executives

Offering financial incentives to employees is so popular in the United States that the practice and the rationale behind it frequently go unquestioned. Organizations offer financial incentives as a means to make employees think like owners. Incentives are thought to motivate performance, but this assumption presumes that performance is under the control of the employees. On the positive side, incentives provide employees with useful information about what is valued by the organization and therefore where to focus their efforts. Incentives may create a self-selection effect, where employees with higher performance are attracted to companies with incentives, and employees with lower performance seek out companies that have pay structures based on seniority, but this assumption presumes that money is the primary motivator of an employee in choosing a particular place of employment. Through financial incentives, social messages will be sent about the employees who are more important to the organization than others. These messages may impact negatively the performance of employees who believe their efforts are just important, but find themselves not valued by the company.

Research shows that most people are not motivated by money when choosing a career, but rather they choose careers based upon which jobs will make them feel fulfilled. Extrinsic rewards such as financial incentives rank significantly lower in importance to people than enjoying their work. Further, financial incentives may not motivate the desired results or behaviors because they are blunt instruments. There are often unintended consequences of these incentive programs that will reflect negatively on the organization.

This is not to say that incentives should never be used, but they should be used judiciously. Relying heavily on financial incentives will limit the efforts of employees to those related to achieving the financial objectives. Using fewer financial incentives will allow employees to broaden their focus to a wider array of opportunities in the organization.

Half-Truth #4: Strategy Is Destiny

The prevailing belief in the business world is that doing the right thing, even if it is not done well, is better than doing the wrong thing well. This idea suggests that companies must have an overall plan to reach their objectives. It is based on the assumptions that each company is equipped to do some things better than other companies and that focusing on these things will result in better outcomes because of the limited time and resources available to the organization.

Again, however, the research is not always supportive of this strategic view of the world. Empirical studies show inconsistent support for the idea that strategic planning improves organizational performance. There are some external constraints on companies, such as industry structure, that will powerfully affect overall performance beyond company strategy.

Additionally, there are reasons not to engage in significant strategic planning. The time and money spent annually on strategic planning can be extraordinary. This time spent on planning and budgeting can divert people's attention away from solving fundamental problems within the organization. In addition, focusing all of people's energy on a specific strategic plan may limit the ideas that surface within a company, thereby limiting the discovery of profitable opportunities.

Nevertheless, some planning is probably better than none. A balance between focusing so much time and money on strategic planning and ignoring the planning process altogether should be achieved. First, instead of top executives developing these plans, perhaps a simpler approach such as using customer feedback would work just as well. Second, once a good strategy has been developed, be careful not to abandon it because the implementation went wrong. Fix the implementation. Third, be certain that employees understand the strategy. If a strategy is too complex, employees will not comprehend it or buy into it, thus making it virtually impossible for them to act upon it. Finally, be flexible enough to change the strategy in light of changes in the industry. Learning as you go and adapting to current conditions may be more important than blind commitment to a long-term strategic plan.

Half-Truth #5: Change Is Inevitable

Experts will tell you that if your company doesn't change it will die. But is all change good? Some change is surely valuable to organizations, but many changes are not for the best. The trick to good management is determining (ahead of time) which changes will help the company and which ones won't. Which changes are worth implementing? You might ask yourself the following questions as you decide if a particular change is right for your company:

- Will this change improve what you are already doing? And is anyone in your company already doing it?
- Are the benefits of this change really worth the costs?
- Do you need to make a real change, or would it be better to make a symbolic change?
- Is the change good for the company or just good for you?
- If you want to champion a change, do you have enough power in the organization to make it happen?
- How many changes have been implemented recently?
- Can the planned change be altered during the adoption process as people learn?
- Can this change be abandoned without significant costs or loss of face?

A review of many research studies and cases suggests that organizations can adapt quickly and easily to new realities. A few elements need to be present to make the change successful. First, people must be dissatisfied with how things are currently happening. Second, they need clear direction on where the change is headed. Third, leadership must consistently convey high levels of confidence that this change will fix the problems the organization faces. Finally, the message conveyed and enacted should be that the change will be messy and that anxiety is a normal part of change. When organizations embrace these elements, a worthwhile change can be achieved quickly and successfully.

Half-Truth #6: Leaders Are Everything

We are obsessed with leaders. We reward leaders handsomely, reflecting the organization's belief that they are in complete control of a company's fate. There is much research that leadership can affect the performance of a company and/or work group. Leaders, however, do not control everything about company outcomes. In fact, some research suggests that industry and company effects are much more influential than leaders when measuring company outcomes.

So why do we believe leaders are so important? When an organization does very well or poorly, we attribute these good or bad outcomes to the leader of the organization, because it is he or she who is the most obvious symbol of the company and we cannot see all of the individual efforts that went into making these outcomes possible. Because the complexities that make up the operations of a large company are impossible for most of us to understand completely, our attribution of the company's performance to an individual leader simplifies and clarifies our thinking.

Despite our belief that leaders are in control, we worry that they should not be in control. Complete control can lead to complete corruption. Also, by giving complete control to one person in an organization, it lessens the ability of other employees to have control over their work lives and lowers their commitment to work. This lower commitment speaks to the truth that most leaders have far less power than would be suspected by others—and most leaders admit to this fact.

Good leaders recognize the substantial limits on their abilities to direct the efforts of others. Good leaders should project confidence in the direction of the organization, but simultaneously understand the limits of their abilities. By staying unimpressed by their own authority, leaders should be able to see more clearly when to step aside and let others make decisions for the direction of the company.

Leadership cannot be learned from a book or a class. Good leaders learn their craft by experience. This is why many companies rely on internal promotions for leaders. Outside succession of leadership can complicate the job of new leaders because they do not always understand the company very well. Continually learning and practicing at being a better leader will lead to higher performance of the leader and ultimately of the organization.

HOW TO IMPLEMENT EVIDENCE-BASED MANAGEMENT

The half-truths outlined here not only highlight the potential problems of following the crowd but also illustrate the potential value of evidence-based management. Managers committed to evidence-based management can help their organizations to be more successful. A commitment to evidence-based management is not a one-time fix, but rather a permanent change in how people think about and engage with information. Here are some guidelines for working toward this method:

- Keep an attitude that things can always be improved and that continual learning about what you know and don't know will lead to improvements.
- Stick to facts and not what people want to believe.
- Learn your facts from many sources.
- See both the positives and the negatives of your organization and the practices you wish to implement.
- Check your ego at the door.
- Make evidence-based management a company-wide objective.
- Recognize that switching an organization's philosophy of management to an evidence-based approach will take some selling—and some time.
- Use evidence-based management to slow the spread of bad practices.
- Learn from failures, not only your own organization's but also those of other companies.

Conclusion

Managers are not magicians. Managers recognize the imperfections of their worlds and learn over time how to deal with problems. An attitude of wisdom bent toward continual learning is crucial to evidence-based management. Being open to creating, collecting, and analyzing data about organizational issues can lead managers to make better decisions for their companies.

4   Hot, Flat, and Crowded

Thomas Friedman

Summary Prepared by Bob Stine

Bob Stine is Associate Dean in the College of Continuing Education at the University of Minnesota, and he is responsible for academic programs. He was formerly Associate Dean in the College of Natural Resources. His interests include leadership, organizational management, adult education, and natural resources and the environment. He earned his Ph.D. in Forest Policy from the University of Minnesota, M.S. from Oregon State University, and bachelor's degree from Indiana University.

THREE CHARACTERISTICS OF THE WORLD

The world is hot, flat, and crowded. It's hot because of global warming, it's flat as a result of a growing middle class with instant connectivity around the globe, and it's crowded due to rapid population growth. The result is a planet that is dangerously unstable. Indicators include tightening energy supplies, deepening energy poverty, strong dictatorships in oil-producing countries (**petrodictatorships**), and accelerating climate change. The conditions and their symptoms are tightly intertwined, and how they are addressed will greatly determine the quality of life on earth in the future.

America will play a key role in the response to these issues, much as it has done for nearly every key global issue in the past. *America needs to become the greenest country in the world, not as a selfless act of charity, but as a core of national security and economic prosperity.* The United States cannot do this alone, but if it leads the way, others will most assuredly follow.

As of now, America (along with the rest of the world) is entering the **energy-climate era**, where energy and climate change issues will dominate. There are five key problems that define this era: growing demand for ever-scarcer energy supplies and natural resources; a massive transfer of wealth to oil-rich nations; disruptive climate change; energy poverty (large populations without access to dependable electricity); and rapidly accelerating biodiversity loss.

We arrived at this new era primarily because the parts of the world with rapidly growing populations want to mimic the lifestyle and energy consumption of Americans. Although total energy consumption is growing faster in these areas, per capita consumption in the United States

Thomas Friedman. *Hot, Flat, and Crowded: Why We Need a Green Revolution—and How It Can Renew America.* New York: Farrar, Straus, and Giroux, 2008.

is still dramatically higher (9–30 times) than in China and India. Efforts to produce the same per capita amount of energy for billions more people around the world is creating negative effects, and, in the end, is simply not sustainable.

PETRO POLITICS

U.S. dependence on foreign oil is causing negative consequences in four primary ways. First, we are helping support an intolerant, antimodern, anti-Western, anti–women's rights strain of Islam practiced in Saudi Arabia. Second, we are helping finance reversals of democratic trends in Russia, Latin America, and elsewhere. Generally, as the price of oil goes up, the pace of freedom goes down. Third, we are causing a global energy scramble, where repression, human rights, and religious freedom take a backseat to the need for oil. Finally, by purchasing foreign oil, the United States ends up funding both sides of the war on terror—our military on one hand and terrorists funded by nation-states from whom we purchase the oil on the other.

Of particular concern is the relationship between the price of oil and the pace of freedom within "petrolist" nations (defined as authoritarian states that are highly dependent on oil production for the bulk of their exports and government income). Among notable countries on that list are Angola, Nigeria, Iran, Russia, Egypt, Kuwait, Indonesia, Venezuela, Qatar, United Arab Emirates, Syria, Sudan, and Saudi Arabia. In several measures of "freedom" (e.g., open elections, invasion of other countries, nationalization of industries, coups, and independent newspapers), the price of oil and the pace of freedom or democratization are inversely related. Not one of the 23 nations that derive a clear majority of their export income from oil and gas is a democracy.

One cause of this phenomenon is the "taxation effect." Countries with high oil income need few, if any, taxes from their citizens, and therefore feel little need for their citizens to be represented in government (in a twist, the phrase becomes "no representation without taxation"). A second cause is the "spending effect," where large oil income allows patronage spending, dampening the pressure for democratization. This also tends to translate into less education and less innovation, as the government can provide everything needed for daily life. Governments can also use their oil profits to prevent the formation of groups that might challenge them in a number of ways.

ENERGY POVERTY

The World Bank estimates that one-quarter of the earth's inhabitants (many of them living in sub-Saharan Africa) do not have regular access to an electricity grid. The 47 countries in this region (excluding South Africa) only add about 1 gigawatt of electricity annually, which is about the same amount added *every two weeks* in China.

A general rule among all energy-poor countries is that they don't have functioning utilities that are able to raise the financing needed to build and operate power plants and transmission lines. This is the result of persistent misgovernance and/or civil war. The lack of reliable energy results in negative impacts on nearly every other aspect of life (e.g., access to food and clean water, quality education, manufacturing, and health care). There is little chance these countries will rise out of financial poverty and health crises without eliminating their **energy poverty**.

CLEAN ENERGY

Simply providing reliable energy to everyone who currently doesn't have it by burning more fossil fuels is not tenable. The impacts on pollution and climate would be catastrophic. Instead, *the world (with the United States preferably leading) needs to move toward the creation and deployment of "abundant, clean, reliable, and cheap electrons."* Companies that invent and deploy clean power technologies most effectively will have a dominant place in the future economy. Countries that develop integrative systems to take advantage of such clean energy will be stronger and freer in the future.

In this new system, everything must be interconnected—production, distribution, and use. Individual components of the system can be optimized to a point, but only the creation and operation of an entirely new system will make a significant difference. In order to get there, innovation needs to be stimulated. Some of that will happen naturally, but it should also be stimulated by tax and regulatory incentives, renewable energy mandates, and other market-shaping mechanisms that create durable demand for the technologies. Advancement can also be stimulated by increasing government-funded research, which leads to both steady progress on existing technologies and "eureka" breakthroughs in new technologies.

At the same time, we need to focus on efficiency to reduce the demand for energy production. Clean and inexpensive energy solutions may be years down the road, but reducing energy consumption starts lowering carbon dioxide (CO_2) emissions immediately. Using available energy more efficiently has the same effect.

MOVING FORWARD

The United States has yet to seriously embrace a "green" economy. Most efforts to date have simply been tweaking on the margins. *To keep from doubling the amount of CO_2 in the atmosphere by mid-century, the following eight actions need to occur:*

- double the fuel efficiency of two billion cars from 30 mpg to 60 mpg;
- raise efficiency at 1,600 coal-fired electric plans from 40 to 60 percent;
- replace 1,400 coal-fired electric plants with natural gas–powered plants;
- install carbon capture and sequestration capacity at 800 large coal-fired plants;
- add twice today's current global nuclear capacity to replace coal-based electricity;
- increase wind power 40-fold to displace all coal-fired power;
- halt all cutting and burning of forests;
- cut electricity use in homes, offices, and stores by 25 percent

Accomplishing one of these would be a miracle. Accomplishing eight seems nearly impossible. But this is the scale at which change in energy production and consumption must occur to slow and then start reversing the level of CO_2 in the atmosphere.

A SMART ELECTRICITY GRID

One proactive approach would be development of a "smart" energy grid. Existing electric utilities across the country grew in a haphazard manner, with little or no integration between them, and little ability to alter real-time pricing to reflect supply and demand. Imagine instead an electric grid that would include integrated large production facilities (e.g., clean coal plants, wind farms, and nuclear facilities) and many small distributed production facilities (e.g., solar panels on roofs and individual windmills). Then imagine vehicles and appliances that are able to communicate with the grid, running (or charging) and buying electricity when prices are low (middle of the night), and at times selling it back when prices are high (peak-demand times during the day). All this would happen on an **energy Internet** and be controlled by programmable chips in every vehicle and appliance.

As an example, your dishwasher would wait to run till the middle of the night, when electricity prices drop to a predetermined price. Your car would charge itself at night (using the same strategy), and sell some electricity back to the grid during the day when prices are higher, making sure to leave enough stored in the battery to get you home. Not only would your costs be reduced (by buying low and selling high), but the need to produce excess electricity to meet peak demand would also be reduced, because vehicles and other items containing batteries would serve as storage units, available for meeting peak demand. This would be a smart grid.

WHERE TO START

Homes, business, and factories would be a good place to start the smart grid. They account for 40 percent of electricity use in the country, and therefore 40 percent of CO_2 emissions. A smart grid would be more efficient, thus reducing emissions. A second key component would be to electrify most of the transportation sector. This sector accounts for 30 percent of CO_2 emissions, and making it part of the smart grid would also reduce emissions. It is estimated that 73 percent of cars, trucks, and SUVs could be replaced with plug-in hybrids without any need to build new generating capacity because they would be recharged at night with off-peak electricity.

To get to this future will require a combination of policies, regulations, standards, innovation, market incentives (and disincentives), and breakthrough technologies, all coordinated in an intelligent system that moves us rapidly from high CO_2-producing energy sources to clean energy production and efficient use of the energy that is produced. Businesses need to learn to view these policies, regulations, and incentives not as a barrier to their success but as a way to differentiate themselves from their competitors.

BARRIERS

What is in the way of moving in this direction rapidly? Primarily it is the continuing legacy of the "Dirty Fuels System": auto companies, coal companies, some unenlightened utilities, and oil and gas companies. Their influence in political decisions remains significant across the country. Second, the country as a whole really has no sense of urgency about energy conservation or clean energy research. "Green" is still viewed more as an option than a necessity.

Conclusion: Getting Started

Moving forward, we need leaders who can shape issues about energy, climate change, and global connectedness so they are viewed and understood as opportunities, not threats. We also need to be successful not only in the United States but also around the globe. Thinking globally, these changes will be successful only if China, India, and other areas with rapidly growing populations and standards of living also follow a path to clean energy production and efficient use. Is all of this possible? Yes. Do we have enough time to do it? Yes, we have exactly enough time—but only if we start doing so *now*.

GLOSSARY OF TERMS

Above-average effect The perception by many employees that they are better than most others and hence deserve additional compensation. (Pfeffer)

Achievement To take pride in one's accomplishments by doing things that matter and doing them well; to receive recognition for one's accomplishments; to take pride in the organization's accomplishments. (Sirota, Mischkind, and Meltzer)

Anchoring effect The effect on estimates when an anchor value is provided before an estimate is asked of an individual. (Kahneman)

Assortative mating The evaluative and comparative process that humans move through as they assess the qualities and features (physical attractiveness) of each other, resulting in a relative hierarchy in which many individuals are placed. (Ariely)

Authentic leadership Actions by people of high integrity who are committed to building enduring organizations by relying on morality and character. (George)

Authenticity Being true to one's word; acting sincerely and genuinely without a hidden agenda. (Bennis, Goleman, and O'Toole)

Authority Person who is an expert in a field (a niche player). (Reardon)

Availability bias Occurs when we can easily recall information. (Kahneman)

Bad bosses Managers who abuse their power, lose their temper, micromanage, and exhibit insecurity and incompetence. (Van Fleet and Van Fleet)

Bad leadership Actions—ineffective or unethical—that are a result of leaders behaving poorly because of who they are, and because of what they want, and acting in ways that do harm (either intentional or as a result of carelessness or neglect). (Kellerman)

Balanced life Leading a life that recognizes the importance of work, family, friends, faith, and community service, with none of them excluding any of the others. (George)

Battered bystanders Innocent coworkers and family who also (perhaps indirectly) suffer the effects of ugly work incidents. (Sutton)

Bayes' theorem An algorithm used to update statistical predictions to account for additional data. (Ayres)

Behaving with urgency Demonstrating (and expecting) efficiency, openness, and passion for accomplishments. (Kotter)

Behavioral economics The discipline of understanding human tendencies and determining how people can be taught to avoid temptation, increase self-control, and become more rational and efficient in reaching their long-term goals. (Ariely)

Behavioral ethics Field of study that seeks to understand why people behave the way they do when facing ethical dilemmas. (Bazerman and Tenbrunsel)

Behavioral forecasting errors Erroneous perceptions that prevent people from seeing the need to improve their ethicality. (Bazerman and Tenbrunsel)

Big losers Companies that have demonstrated a persistent lack of competitive advantage through stock market performance significantly poorer than their respective industry average over the period 1992–2002. (Marcus)

Big winners Companies that have demonstrated sustainable competitive advantage through stock market performance that significantly exceeds their respective industry average over the period 1992–2002. (Marcus)

Blind spots Ethical vulnerabilities that exist outside of our conscious awareness. (Bazerman and Tenbrunsel)

Brand The image that customers and potential customers have of a company. (Handley and Chapman)

Bringing the outside in Obtaining valuable information from customers, suppliers, and the business community, and building strong relationships with those groups. (Kotter)

Burnout The effects of a mismatch between the needs of an employee and the demands of a job, which can be manifested by an erosion of emotions, frustration, and health symptoms. (Cascio)

Camaraderie The feeling of having warm, interesting, and cooperative relations with others in the workplace. (Sirota, Mischkind, and Meltzer)

Capitulation To end all resistance; to give up; to go along with or comply; to end all resistance because of loss of hope. (Collins)

Cheese A metaphor for anything that employees are seeking (as rewards for their efforts) or elements of their environment with which they are familiar (that cause confusion if changed). (Johnson)

Choice points Natural places during a conversation where the course of action can be altered. (Reardon)

Co-opt Inducing someone to become part of your group or support your position. (Pfeffer)

Coherence The state achieved when each piece of the system integrated together is more powerful than the sum of its parts. (Collins)

Collaborative work system A form of organization that practices a disciplined system of collaboration and a set of 10 principles to achieve superior results so as to be successful in a rapidly changing environment. (Beyerlein, Freedman, McGee, and Moran)

Compassionate organization Organizations that promote a culture of and a set of practices and respectful policies that produce generative responses from their people and link the emotional health of the organization with the bottom line. (Frost)

Competitive advantage The edge a firm can gain over its competitors by providing equivalent benefits at a lower price or greater benefits that compensate for a higher price than competitors charge. (Porter)

Complacency A feeling of contentment or self-satisfaction, especially when coupled with unawareness of organizational danger, threat, or trouble. (Kotter)

Constructive confrontation Rather than attacking people, deciding when and how to fight by using evidence and logic to deal with problems. (Sutton)

Content Any writing, photos, graphs, charts, and the like produced for websites. (Handley and Chapman)

Content Creator The person who creates and approves the final content that appears on a company's website. (Handley and Chapman)

Conversational coherence Knowing when an issue is relevant to an ongoing discussion. (Reardon)

Co-opt Inducing someone to become part of your group or support your position. (Pfeffer)

Cultural paradigm A set of interrelated assumptions that form a coherent pattern regarding culture. (Schein)

Customer-focused quality A quality measurement that focuses externally on customers and uses customer feedback as the ultimate measurement of quality. (George)

Downsizing An intentional, proactive management strategy that can include reductions in the firm's financial, physical, and human assets. (Cascio)

Effective managers Managers who manage themselves and others so that both employees and the organization benefit. (Blanchard and Johnson)

Egg theory The discovery that people will feel a greater sense of pride and psychological ownership in a product if they had an opportunity to add something to it. (Ariely)

Empathy Entering the private perceptual world of another person; being sensitive moment to moment to the changing feelings that flow from the other person. (Reardon)

Employee enthusiasm A state of high employee morale that derives from satisfying the three key needs of workers, which results in significant competitive advantages for companies with the strength of leadership and commitment to manage for true long-term results. (Sirota, Mischkind, and Meltzer)

Endowment effect The effect occurring due to possession of something not regularly traded. (Kahneman)

Energy-climate era A period during which energy and climate change are the predominant social, political, biological, and economic issues. (Friedman)

Energy Internet An electricity grid that includes centralized and distributed electrical production, abundant battery storage, and computer-controlled vehicles, buildings, appliances, and so on that all communicate with one another to efficiently produce and consume electricity. (Friedman)

Energy poverty Living without regular access to an electricity grid, usually caused by misgovernance and nonfunctioning utilities. (Friedman)

Ethical fading The process of eliminating ethical dimensions from a decision. (Bazerman and Tenbrunsel)

Ethical self-awareness Recognizing our vulnerability to our unconscious biases in decision making. (Bazerman and Tenbrunsel)

Evidence-based management Decisions based upon the best research, data, and experimentation available. (Pfeffer and Sutton)

Evolved capacities Features of the brain that are a function of both genes and the learning environment, with examples including language, recognition memory, emotions, and imitation. (Gigerenzer)

False sense of urgency A sense of urgency that is filled with energy and activities that come from anxiety and anger and create behaviors that do not address the real threats or problems. (Kotter)

Feedback Information regarding results of one's efforts (how well one is performing). (Blanchard and Johnson)

Finding opportunities in crises Using potentially damaging situations to generate creative solutions. (Kotter)

Flywheel The continuous turning and momentum of effort in one direction leading to a point of breakthrough. (Collins)

Focusing illusion Allowing an event or aspect of life to take precedence over everything else and dominate our thoughts and actions. (Kahneman)

Fun minute manager Person who knows that many fun activities can be implemented in short periods of time and produce multiple payoffs. (Pike, Ford, and Newstrom)

Fun work environment One in which a variety of formal and informal activities regularly occur that are designed to uplift people's spirits and positively and publicly remind people of their value to their managers, their organization, and to each other through the use of humor, playful games, joyful celebrations, opportunities for self-development, or recognition of achievements and milestones. (Pike, Ford, and Newstrom)

Fundamental state of leadership The condition in which leaders transform themselves from their normal state to become results centered, internally directed, other focused, and externally open. (Quinn)

Groundswell The major trends in online technologies and shifting consumer behavior that are forcing companies to reexamine their traditional marketing and customer interaction models. (Li and Bernoff)

Gut feelings Also known as hunches or intuition, these are judgments that appear quickly in consciousness, whose underlying reasons are not in awareness, and are strong enough to act upon. (Gigerenzer)

Hedgehog Concept The deep understanding gained through the intersection of three circles—what you can be the best in the world at, what drives your economic engine, and what you are deeply passionate about. (Collins)

Higher-ambition business An organization that is led by a higher-ambition leader and is viewed as financially stable and successful while creating social value for its employees, customers, and community. (Beer et al.)

Higher-ambition leader A leader who is able to see the organization in its totality, its possibilities and potential, and is able to communicate to all employees so their efforts are maximized to create an organization that equally values financial and social value. (Beer et al.)

Hindsight bias The effect that occurs when we look back on experiences or situations and believe we could have anticipated an (unforeseen) event. (Kahneman)

Hope Optimistic belief that challenging goals can be successfully achieved, and if one way of getting there doesn't work, another one will be successfully applied. (Luthans, Youssef, and Avolio)

Hubris A great or foolish amount of pride, confidence, or egotism (Pfeffer). Excessive pride, pretentiousness, self-importance, ambition, or arrogance (Collins).

Humility Possessing a core belief that every employee is valuable (both as a human being and as an employee) and has vast potential. (Bennis, Goleman, and O'Toole)

Inner jerk The capacity of anyone to turn into a jerk in certain situations and become caustic and cruel. Anger, fear, and contempt are highly contagious when exhibited by others. (Sutton)

Innovation The process of transforming discoveries into products, goods, and services. (Drucker)

Institutional-building pride Intrinsic pride that is based on emotional commitment that tends to further collective rather than strictly individual sets of interest. (Katzenbach)

Integrated decision making Decision making that takes into account all business functions so the outcome is acceptable to all stakeholders. (Beer et al.)

Interactive The ability of a website to communicate back and forth with another website. (Handley and Chapman)

Interdependence Situations where two or more elements are mutually dependent on each other for success. (McGregor)

Just-in-time purchasing A supply chain management technique that minimizes inventory storage time and carrying costs while avoiding backorders. (Ayres)

Knowledge workers Employees with high levels of education, skills, and competencies. (Drucker)

Kryder's law Data storage capacity doubles roughly every two years. (Ayres)

Leadership characteristics A desired combination of heart, purpose, values, relationships, and self-discipline. (George)

Level 5 This is the top of a five-level hierarchy of executive capabilities. Level 5 leaders embody a paradoxical mix of personal humility and professional will, and exhibit ambition for the company, not themselves. (Collins)

Likeability Being easy to like; having pleasant or appealing qualities. (Pfeffer)

Logotherapy A method (developed by Viktor Frankl) by which the therapist helps the client become fully aware of his or her freedom of choice. (Pattakos)

Loss aversion The tendency of individuals to avoid losses. (Kahneman)

Major theme The basic story line or dominant message that a company uses in creating content. (Handley and Chapman)

Management by objectives (MBO) A process where employees set goals, justify them, determine resources needed to accomplish them, establish timetables for their completion, and perform accordingly. These goals reflect the overall objectives of the organization. (Drucker)

Management structure The way managers divide, share, coordinate, and evaluate the work they do in planning and organizing the firm's overall operations. (Drucker)

Managerial mind-sets Ways of thinking (reflective, analytic, worldly, collaborative, and proactive) used by effective managers. (Mintzberg)

Managerial postures Actions a manager takes in a specific situation to keep an organization running. (Mintzberg)

Mind-mapping A technique for expanding thought and encouraging insight by identifying a number of potential options and omitting ones that seem too risky. (Reardon)

Mission-driven organization An organization that utilizes its mission statement as an integral part of managing the organization, not merely as a plaque that hangs on the CEO's wall. (George)

Mojo The positive spirit that radiates to the outside and is an expression of the harmony between what we feel inside about whatever we are doing and what we show on the outside. (Goldsmith)

Mojo Scorecard Measuring tool consisting of 10 qualities, self-rated on a 10-point scale to produce a Mojo score with a maximum of 100. (Goldsmith)

Mojo Tool Kit The set of 14 specific actions that are broken down into the four building blocks of Mojo: Identity, Achievement, Reputation, and Acceptance. (Goldsmith)

Moore's law Data processing power doubles roughly every two years. (Ayres)

Motivated blindness The tendency for people to overlook unethical behavior when it is in their best interest *not* to notice the behavior. (Bazerman and Tenbrunsel)

Multiple key words The use of several appropriate words and terms to assist a viewer to access a website. (Handley and Chapman)

Neural network A system of statistical algorithms that continuously update both their predictions and the algorithms themselves to account for changes in data. (Ayres)

Nojo The negative spirit toward what someone is doing now that starts from the inside and radiates to the outside. (Goldsmith)

NoNos People who resist any form of change and undermine the efforts of others who attempt it. (Kotter)

Not-Invented-Here (NIH) bias The tendency to like our own ideas and discount or reject the ideas of others. (Ariely)

Optimism Belief that positive events will happen in the future and the reasons for those positive events are attributed to oneself, are permanent, and are likely to happen now and in the future. (Luthans, Youssef, and Avolio)

Organizational culture The pattern of basic assumptions that a given group has invented, discovered, or developed in learning to cope with its problems of external adaptation and internal integration, and that have worked well enough to be considered valid, and, therefore, to be taught to new members as the correct way to perceive, think, and feel in relation to those problems. (Schein)

Organizational restructuring Planned changes in a firm's organizational structure that affect its use of people, including the possibility of workforce reductions. (Cascio)

Outcome bias Blaming others for not anticipating negative outcomes, while withholding praise and credit for outcomes that were not previously apparent (Kahneman). Judging a past decision based on its outcomes rather than the quality of the decision when it was made (Bazerman and Tenbrunsel).

Partnership relationship A highly effective method of creating and maintaining high levels of long-term organization performance in which a bond develops among adults working collaboratively toward common, long-term goals and having a genuine concern for each other's interests and needs. (Sirota, Mischkind, and Meltzer)

Peak performance The result obtained from a group of employees whose emotional commitment enables them to deliver products or services that constitute a sustainable competitive advantage for their employers. (Katzenbach)

Personal Mojo The five benefits that a particular activity *gives back* to you. (Goldsmith)

Persuasion The ability to position ideas in an appealing manner so others will accept them. (Reardon)

Petrodictatorships Authoritarian states that are highly dependent on oil production for the bulk of their exports and government income. (Friedman)

Play The introduction of joy, fun, and enthusiasm into a work environment. (Lundin, Paul, and Christensen)

Podcasts Programs and presentations that users can play back at their convenience via audio devices. (Handley and Chapman)

Political insight The use of empathy and creativity to understand and respond to the way things work in organizations. (Reardon)

Positive organizational behavior (POB) A movement in positive psychology that focuses on the micro individual level and deals with positive attributes that are open to development and relate to an individual's work performance. (Luthans, Youssef, and Avolio)

Positive organizational scholarship (POS) Research that studies macro organizational issues and personal attributes. (Luthans, Youssef, and Avolio)

Power Possession of control, authority, or influence over others. (Pfeffer)

Power base The area or group of people that provides the main support for a particular individual. (Pfeffer)

Priming Suggesting a particular response, often subtly, before soliciting a response from a study participant. (Ayres)

Problem The difference between what is actually happening and what you want to happen. (Blanchard and Johnson)

Productivity Employee output in terms of the quantity and quality of work completed. (Blanchard and Johnson)

Professional intimacy Working in a way that honors the integrity of the position, the person, and the organization at a level of connection deeper than normal. (Frost)

Professional Mojo The five skills and attitudes we *bring* to any activity. (Goldsmith)

Psychological Capital (PsyCap) A person's positive psychological state that is characterized by the person displaying self-efficacy, optimism, hope, and resiliency. (Luthans, Youssef, and Avolio)

Psychological commitment Interest and investment in other people's success when they have made a contribution to it and are familiar with and enjoy the company of the other person. (Pfeffer)

Randomization A statistical method that controls for the effects of extraneous variables by randomly selecting subsets of participants to be exposed to variables of interest. (Ayres)

Really Simple Syndication (RSS) Feeds A technological process that allows readers to subscribe to areas of content interest, and automatically receive updates in a standardized form from a site when new content is published. (Li and Bernoff)

Recall memory The capacity to retrieve episodes, facts, or reasons from memory, based on cues or signals that help people make decisions. (Gigerenzer)

Reciprocity Doing a favor for another to induce an obligation for repayment at a future time. (Reardon)

Recognition memory The ability to tell the novel from the previously experienced or to decipher the old from the new. (Gigerenzer)

Reframing Changing your mind-set about something stressful to help you cope with the bad situation and limit the damage to yourself. (Sutton)

Regression A statistical method that results in a formula whereby future outcome predictions can be extrapolated from past observations. (Ayres)

Reprimand Negative verbal feedback provided when undesirable employee behavior and performance occur. (Blanchard and Johnson)

Resiliency Ability to bounce back and encourage/inspire others to bounce back in the face of extreme adversity or to bounce back from even positive occurrences. (Luthans, Youssef, and Avolio)

Responsible restructuring An alternative to "slash-and-burn" workforce reductions, wherein employees' ideas and efforts form the basis of sustained competitive advantage by addressing underlying competitive problems. (Cascio)

Safe zones Created spaces where toxin handlers are moved out of the stressful situations within the organization for a period of time in order to let them reenergize and rest. (Frost)

Scarcity The ability to create a high demand by controlling and providing resources that are perceived to be rare. (Reardon)

Selective adaptation Choice of a method or action that accommodates identified conditions rather than ignoring or going against those facts. (McGregor)

Self-efficacy Confidence that one will be successful even given difficult circumstances. (Luthans, Youssef, and Avolio)

Self-managed teams (SMTs) Teams of workers who, with their supervisors, are delegated various managerial functions to perform and the authority and resources needed to carry them out. (Sirota, Mischkind, and Meltzer)

Self-serving pride Individualistic pride that comes from drives for power, ego, and materialism. (Katzenbach)

Shared vision The capacity to create and hold a shared picture of the future across a set of individuals. (Senge)

Shimmer factor The glow created by a charismatic leader that can also lead to isolation and unapproachability. (Bennis, Goleman, and O'Toole)

Sisu The unwavering ability to continue pursuing a goal in the face of great adversity. (Beer et al.)

Social instinct The result of special gut feelings versus complex calculation. The two basic social instincts are family instinct and community instinct. (Gigerenzer)

Social responsibility The contribution a firm makes to its society. To some, this means making a profit, whereas others expect the firm to do more than this by ameliorating social problems. (Drucker)

Social technographics profile The product of categorizing online participants into groups based on how they participate in online technologies. This is used along with age and gender to refine classifications of customers. (Li and Bernoff)

Social values Benefits from an organization's activities that serve to aid employees, customers, communities, and the world. (Beer et al.)

Socially integrative Navigating the dynamics of the situation and selecting the correct managerial posture. (Mintzberg)

Sour spot A highly contested market position affording incumbents little opportunity to control the five classic industry forces. (Marcus)

Speaking truth to power Providing credible information to those in authority, even though it may be negative or politically incorrect. (Bennis, Goleman, and O'Toole)

Standard deviation A statistic that reports the difference between a prototypical measurement in a sample and the average of all measurements in that sample. (Ayres)

Stockdale Paradox Holding the absolute faith that you can and will prevail in the end, regardless of the difficulties, while simultaneously confronting the most brutal facts of your current reality. (Collins)

Super Crunchers People who use the best data available and a variety of statistical techniques to make better real-world decisions. (Ayres)

Sweet spot An attractive market position characterized by a lack of direct competition, and presenting incumbents with the opportunity to control the five classic industry forces. (Marcus)

Targeted approach A communication method that aims content at a distinct audience. (Handley and Chapman)

Terabyte 1,000 gigabytes. (Ayres)

The rule (Also known as the *no-asshole rule*) A combination of formal policies, rules, behavioral norms, and culture that together communicate expectations for civil human interactions and provide the tools necessary for enforcement. (Sutton)

Theory of cognitive dissonance Individuals have a strong motivation to keep their attitudes and behaviors in alignment; when they are not, tension or anxiety rises within the individual, stimulating the individual to correct this misalignment. (Ariely)

Theory X A set of assumptions that explains some human behavior and has influenced conventional principles of management. It assumes that workers want to avoid work and must be controlled and coerced to accept responsibility and exert effort toward organizational objectives. (McGregor)

Theory Y A set of assumptions offered as an alternative to Theory X. Theory Y assumes that work is a natural activity, and that given the right conditions, people will seek responsibility and apply their capacities to organizational objectives without coercion. (McGregor)

Three-factor theory of human motivation A model that asserts that there are three primary sets of goals of people at work—equity, achievement, and camaraderie. (Sirota, Mischkind, and Meltzer)

Topicality shift Knowing how and when to introduce a new concept into a conversation. (Reardon)

Tough love The leadership practice of living in the balance of being both simultaneously compassionate/concerned and assertive/bold. (Quinn)

Toxin handlers Those leaders, managers, and staff that tend to the emotional pain of the people in the organization and work to bring harmony and balance and remove stress and tension. (Frost)

Transparency Capacity to be seen through; candidness, openness, and easy accessibility. (Bennis, Goleman, and O'Toole)

Treatment effect The effect of a variable of interest after randomization has controlled for the effects of extraneous variables. (Ayres)

True sense of urgency Legitimate urgency that focuses on critical issues and problems in the organization, particularly from the external environment. (Kotter)

Unconscious intelligence The use of prior knowledge about a person, situation, or concept, combined with hidden rules of thumb that drive intuition and gut feelings. (Gigerenzer)

User-generated content Content produced by customers or other viewers that a company might use on its website. (Handley and Chapman)

Value chain The discrete value-producing activities within a firm that are potential sources of competitive advantage. (Porter)

Victims Persons who work for abusive bosses and subsequently suffer psychologically, physiologically, and in their careers. (Sutton)

Virtual organizations Companies that have groups of individuals working on shared tasks while distributed across space, time, and/or organizational boundaries. (Beyerlein, Freedman, McGee, and Moran)

Webinars Seminars in which conferences, lectures, training events, or other presentations are made to an audience connected via the Internet. (Handley and Chapman)

Whistleblowing Act of reporting behavior that is unethical and/or illegal. (Bennis, Goleman, and O'Toole)

Will to meaning The authentic commitment to meaningful values and goals (a basic human drive) that only individuals can actualize. (Pattakos)

Window and the mirror pattern Behavior of leaders who look out the window and apportion credit to factors other than themselves when things go well (i.e., other people, events, or luck). At the same time, they look in the mirror to accept responsibility, never blaming bad luck, when things go poorly. (Collins)

Workforce All of the employees across the baseline of the organization who either make the products, design the services, or deliver the value to the customer. (Katzenbach)

WYSIATI (What You See Is All There Is) The phenomenon occurring where your active mind excludes any information it cannot readily see. (Kahneman)

Yerkes-Dodson Law Performance rises only to a certain point when accompanied by incentives, and then tapers off. (Ariely)

BIBLIOGRAPHY OF INCLUSIONS

Ariely, Dan. (2008). *Predictably Irrational: The Hidden Forces That Shape Our Decisions*. New York: HarperCollins.

Ariely, Dan. (2010). *The Upside of Irrationality: The Unexpected Benefits of Defying Logic*. New York: HarperCollins.

Ayres, Ian. (2008). *Super Crunchers: Why Thinking-by-Numbers Is the New Way to Be Smart*. New York: Bantam Books.

Bazerman, Max H., and Tenbrunsel, Ann E. (2011). *Blinds Spots: Why We Fail to Do What's Right and What Do About It*. Princeton and Oxford: Princeton University Press.

Beer, Michael, Eisenstat, Russell, Foote, Nathaniel, Fredberg, Tobias, and Norrgren, Flemming. (2011). *Higher Ambition: How Great Leaders Create Economic and Social Value*. Boston, MA: Harvard Business Review Press.

Bennis, Warren, Goleman, Daniel, and O'Toole, James with Patricia Ward Biederman. (2008). *Transparency: How Leaders Create a Culture of Candor*. San Francisco, CA: Jossey-Bass.

Beyerlein, Michael M., Freedman, Sue, McGee, Craig, and Moran, Linda. (2003). *Beyond Teams: Building the Collaborative Organization*. San Francisco, CA: Jossey-Bass/Pfeiffer.

Blanchard, Kenneth, and Johnson, Spencer. (1981). *The One Minute Manager*. LaJolla, CA: Blanchard-Johnson.

Cameron, Kim. (2008). *Positive Leadership: Strategies for Extraordinary Performance*. San Francisco, CA: Berrett-Koehler.

Cascio, Wayne F. (2003). *Responsible Restructuring: Creative and Profitable Alternatives to Layoffs*. San Francisco, CA: Berrett-Koehler.

Collins, James C. (2001). *Good to Great: Why Some Companies Make the Leap... and Others Don't*. New York: Harper Business.

Collins, James C. (2009). *How the Mighty Fall—And Why Some Companies Never Give In*. New York: HarperCollins.

Covey, Stephen R. (1989). *The Seven Habits of Highly Effective People: Restoring the Character Ethic*. New York: Simon & Schuster.

Deming, W. Edwards. (1986). *Out of the Crisis*. Cambridge, MA: MIT Press.

Drucker, Peter F. (1954). *The Practice of Management*. New York: Harper & Row.

Friedman, Thomas. (2008). *Hot, Flat, and Crowded: Why We Need a Green Revolution—And How It Can Renew America*. New York: Farrar, Straus and Giroux.

Frost, Peter J. (2003). *Toxic Emotions at Work: How Compassionate Managers Handle Pain and Conflict*. Boston, MA: Harvard Business School Press.

George, Bill. (2003). *Authentic Leadership: Rediscovering the Secrets to Creating Lasting Value*. San Francisco, CA: Jossey-Bass.

Gigerenzer, Gerd. (2007). *Gut Feelings: The Intelligence of the Unconscious*. New York: Viking Press (Penguin).

Goldsmith, Marshall, with Mark Reiter. (2009). *Mojo: How to Get It, How to Keep It, How to Get It Back If You Lose It*. New York: Hyperion.

Handley, Ann, and Chapman, C. C. (2011). *Content Rules: How to Create Killer Blogs, Podcasts, Videos, Ebooks, Webinars (and More) That Engage Customers and Ignite Your Business*. New Jersey: John Wiley & Sons.

Johnson, Spencer, M. D. (1998). *Who Moved My Cheese? An Amazing Way to Deal with Change in Your Work and Your Life*. New York: Putnam Books.

Kahneman, David. (2011). *Thinking, Fast and Slow*. New York: Farrar, Straus, and Giroux.

Katzenbach, Jon R. (2003). *Why Pride Matters More Than Money: The Power of the World's Greatest Motivational Force*. New York: Crown Business.

Kellerman, Barbara. (2004). *Bad Leadership: What It Is, How It Happens, Why It Matters*. Boston, MA: Harvard Business Press.

Kotter, John. (2008). *A Sense of Urgency*. Boston, MA: Harvard Business Press.

Li, Charlene, and Bernoff, Josh. (2008). *Groundswell: Winning in a World Transformed by Social Technologies*. Boston, MA: Harvard Business Press.

Lundin, Stephen C., Paul, Harry, and Christensen, John. (2000). *Fish! A Remarkable Way to Boost Morale and Improve Results*. New York: Hyperion.

Luthans, Fred, Youssef, Carolyn M., and Avolio, Bruce J. (2007). *Psychological Capital: Developing the Human Competitive Edge*. New York: Oxford University Press.

Marcus, Alfred. (2005). *Big Winners and Big Losers: The 4 Secrets of Long-Term Business Success and Failure*. Philadelphia, PA: Wharton School Publishing.

Maslow, Abraham H. (1998). *Maslow on Management*. New York: John Wiley & Sons.

McGregor, Douglas. (1960). *The Human Side of Enterprise*. New York: McGraw-Hill.

Mintzberg, Henry. (2011). *Managing*. San Francisco, CA: Berrett-Koehler.

Pattakos, Alex. (2004). *Prisoners of Our Thoughts: Viktor Frankl's Principles at Work*. San Francisco, CA: Berrett-Koehler.

Pfeffer, Jeffrey. (2007). *What Were They Thinking? Unconventional Wisdom About Management*. Boston, MA: Harvard Business School Press.

Pfeffer, Jeffrey. (2010). *Power: Why Some People Have It—And Others Don't*. New York: Harper Business.

Pfeffer, Jeffrey, and Sutton, Robert I. (2006). *Hard Facts, Dangerous Half-Truths, and Total Nonsense: Profiting from Evidence-Based Management*. Boston, MA: Harvard Business School Press.

Pike, Bob, Ford, Robert C., and Newstrom, John W. (2009). *The Fun Minute Manager: Create FUNomenal Results Now Using Fun at Work!* Minneapolis, MN: CTT Press.

Porter, Michael E. (1985). *Competitive Advantage: Creating and Sustaining Superior Performance*. New York: Free Press.

Quinn, Robert E. (2004). *Building the Bridge As You Walk on It: A Guide for Leading Change*. San Francisco, CA: Jossey-Bass.

Reardon, Kathleen Kelley. (2005). *It's All Politics: Winning in a World Where Hard Work and Talent Aren't Enough*. New York: Currency Books.

Schein, Edgar H. (2010). *Organizational Culture and Leadership* (4th ed.). San Francisco, CA: Jossey-Bass.

Senge, Peter M. (1990). *The Fifth Discipline: The Art and Science of the Learning Organization*. New York: Doubleday.

Sirota, David, Mischkind, Louis A., and Meltzer, Michael Irwin. (2005). *The Enthusiastic Employee: How Companies Profit by Giving Employees What They Want*. Philadelphia, PA: Wharton School Publishing.

Sutton, Robert I. (2007). *The No Asshole Rule: Building a Civilized Workplace and Surviving One That Isn't*. New York: Business Plus.

Van Fleet, Ella W., and Van Fleet, David D. (2007). *Workplace Survival: Dealing with Bad Bosses, Bad Workers, and Bad Jobs*. Baltimore, MA: PublishAmerica.

INDEX